THE FALSE PROMISE OF THE JAPANESE MIRACLE

Illusions and Realities of the Japanese Management System

S. PRAKASH SETHI, Baruch College, The City University of New York

NOBUAKI NAMIKI, University of Windsor

CARL L. SWANSON, North Texas State University

Pitman

Boston · London · Melbourne · Toronto

To Our Parents

For helping us to be
What we are; and
Guiding us to be
Where we are.

Pitman Publishing Inc.
1020 Plain Street
Marshfield, Massachusetts 02050
Pitman Publishing Limited
128 Long Acre
London WC2E 9AN

Associated Companies
Pitman Publishing Pty. Ltd., Melbourne
Pitman Publishing New Zealand Ltd., Wellington
Copp Clark Pitman, Toronto

©1984 S. Prakash Sethi, Nobuaki Namiki and Carl L. Swanson

Library of Congress Cataloging in Publication Data
Sethi, S. Prakash.
    The false promise of the Japanese miracle.

    Bibliography: p.
    Includes index.
    1. Industrial management—Japan. 2. Industrial manage-
ment—United States. I. Namiki, Nobuaki. II. Swanson,
Carl L. III. Title.
HD70.J3S4635 1984 658'.00952 83-19511
ISBN 0-273-02032-3

Manufactured in the United States of America
10 9 8 7 6 5 4 3 2 1

PITMAN SERIES IN
BUSINESS AND PUBLIC POLICY

CONSULTING EDITOR
EDWIN M. EPSTEIN
University of California, Berkeley

CURRENT BOOKS IN THE SERIES:

John D. Aram, *Managing Business and Public Policy: Concepts, Issues and Cases*

R. Edward Freeman, *Strategic Management: A Stakeholder Approach*

S. Prakash Sethi, Nobuaki Namiki and Carl L. Swanson, *The False Promise of the Japanese Miracle: Illusions and Realities of the Japanese Management System*

PREFACE ▰▰▰▰▰▰▰▰▰▰▰▰▰▰▰▰▰▰▰▰▰▰▰▰▰

> Almost all absurdity of conduct arises from the
> imitation of those whom we cannot resemble.
> —Samuel Johnson

Even the most casual observer of the business scene is aware that the Japanese business and management system (JABMAS) is being routed as the panacea for all that currently ails business firms in the United States, Canada, and Western Europe. Having been badly bruised by the Japanese export juggernaut, business executives in Western industrialized countries are eagerly seeking the secret of Japan's success. Their hope is that the alchemy of that nation's management system will transform their corporations into lean and mean competitors. The drive is in full swing and shows no sign of abating. Unfortunately, like some of the management fads that have preceded JABMAS—systems management, zero-based budgeting, participative management—this one may also be doomed to failure. Unless ills are diagnosed correctly and effectiveness of proposed remedies evaluated carefully, it is a solution that is quite likely to lead to a wrong outcome.

The False Promise of the Japanese Miracle explores this current misguided attempt at a myopic imitation of the Japanese management system by businesses in the United States and other industrialized countries of the Western World.

Its objective is to understand the conditions and limitations within which Japanese management practices are indeed adaptable in the North American context, and to the extent that they are, to develop a set of guidelines that corporate managements can follow to ensure success in this adaptation process. The question is not whether there are benefits in utilizing Japanese techniques in the North American or Western European context, but given the externalities or second-order effects, whether the benefits justify the costs. To put it differently, do we want to measure success in terms similar to those used by the Japanese? Is American society prepared to become somewhat more like the Japanese in its values and norms?

The False Promise has six important elements that distinguish it from most other books dealing with the Japanese business and management system both in Japan and in other parts of the world. First, it analyzes Japanese management practices not only as a system of concepts and techniques, but

v

more important, within its unique sociopolitical context. JABMAS operational success, in large part, has been due to its favored position as the principal recipient of political and government support, often at the expense of other societal interests in Japan (Chapters 2–3).

A more significant point developed in the book, and one that is conveniently ignored by the promoters of Japanese management practices, is the limitations and drawbacks of the Japanese system. When viewed in the Western cultural and sociopolitical context, many aspects of JABMAS are socially and politically unacceptable and even illegal. The system is also limited in the extent to which some of these concepts and techniques are used in Japan. For example, the benefits of the so-called lifetime employment contract and seniority-based compensation system are available to only about a third of the Japanese working population.

The system also systematically and blatantly discriminates against large segments of the Japanese population, notably women and older people. They are deliberately paid lower salaries and benefits and denied career opportunities commensurate with their abilities and experience. Even the 35 percent of the working population that enjoys these privileges pay a cost: extreme job immobility through virtual collusion among employers, suppression of individual expression, and denial of personal fulfillment through recognition of individual performance.

Nor should we ignore the unrepresentative character of the democratic system in Japan and the dominance of a governing cabal. Entree into the upper strata of society is restricted and is acquired via passage through a narrow and predefined route of social institutions. While this governing elite provides the nation with a vision of the future, it also controls the legal, political, and economic mechanisms through which that vision will be implemented to the exclusion of any other. The interests of the masses, subservient by tradition, are further suppressed by call for loyalty to the nation.

Second, the book creates a parallel description of the American business and management system (ABMAS) and how it operates in harmony with Western notions of individualism, limited government, and voluntary association. It also examines the drawbacks and limitations of the system as it currently operates and the costs ABMAS imposes on individuals, institutions, and the nation. The book explores the sociocultural and political conditions of the Western cultural environment (particularly in the United States) within which JABMAS must operate and the flexibility of JABMAS in functioning in an alien culture and society. Specific attention is given to the ability and willingness of American executives, workers, and other stakeholders, and of the societal system operating through the judiciary, to adapt JABMAS in a manner that will provide the "best fit" within the American sociopolitical milieu.

Third, it develops a conceptual framework that enables us to analyze the dimensions of an emerging social issue, and the suitability of corporate response patterns. This analytical framework is used to undertake a systematic identification and evaluation of the types and extent of Japanese management practices as employed by Japanese controlled companies in the United States, and American owned and operated companies using such techniques in their U.S. operations.

A unique feature of this segment is a detailed analysis of the operational processes and management practices of a major Japanese trading company that used two personnel management and worker compensation systems in its U.S. operations: JABMAS for its Japanese expatriate personnel and ABMAS for its local American employees, including those of Japanese descent. The result was disharmony between the two classes of employees; extensive and costly litigation as disgruntled American employees alleged discrimination and asserted their rights under the civil rights laws of the United States; and a foreshadowing by the American courts that portions of JABMAS may be rejected as legally incompatible with American societal norms as codified into U.S. laws.

The fifth section of the book takes a look at the changes that are currently taking place in Japanese society and that are forcing the Japanese business community to modify some of its current practices. More important, we consider the intensity and direction of American societal expectations regarding its business and economic institutions in the coming decade, and analyze the gap between the prevailing and projected societal expectations and the ability of American and Japanese corporations to respond to them. Societal expectations are broadly grouped into four categories: (1) the individual-group dimension; (2) the business-government relations dimension; (3) the corporate decision-making process and style dimension and the degree to which it ranges between authoritarianism and consensualism; and (4) the system of corporate employee performance evaluation and compensation that may range from highly individualistic to largely group-based.

Our prognosis in both the cases is less than heartening. In the case of Japanese business, we do not suggest that the Japanese business and management system is so unique as to be totally inappropriate for American society or any other Western nation, and that we have nothing to learn from the Japanese. But our analysis does indicate that a healthy dose of cynicism is needed to protect us against a widespread and wholesale adoption of Japanese practices.

We also feel that a large part of the current problems of American industry is the fault of the short-term orientation of our managers; their inability to foresee changes in technology, manufacturing processes, and global competition; and their failure to prepare their organizations to cope with these changes.

This section also takes a look at an important issue pertaining to preparing American industry for a drive to regain its competitive position at home and abroad. The issue has to do with the role of government in developing an industrial policy so that specific industries would be targeted for government help as the growth industries of the future while certain declining industries would be helped toward an orderly contraction. Such an industrial policy has been used in Japan, and is given substantial credit for the phenomenal success of the Japanese in becoming a major industrial power. Having looked at all aspects of such an approach, we conclude that the benefits of an industrial policy, even in Japan, have been grossly exaggerated, and that a policy that calls for a significant expansion in the role of the U.S. government in the private sector is likely to be unproductive, unworkable, and incompatible with American cultural and sociopolitical norms.

We also contend that revisionist Japanese scholars have tended to underplay the power and influence of the Japanese bureaucracy in determining Japan's industrial policy, and at the same time to overplay the successes of such a policy. Further, the implementation of such a policy in Japan depends to a large extent on the tradition of acquiescence to the government's will by the Japanese business community—an identity of interest developed by belonging to common sociopolitical institutions and sharing common interests. More important, this bond is fortified by an incestuous relationship among government bureaucracies, top corporate positions, and the elected political leadership. None of these systems and techniques is available in America, nor are they necessarily desirable. By forcing ourselves into the Japanese mold, we would be playing on our weaknesses and discarding our strengths.

The final chapter deals with a variety of specific measures that American business must take if it is to maintain its technological leadership and regain its international competitive position as a major industrial power. The issue of decline of America's basic industries is discussed in terms of the changing nature of international competition, outmoded American plant and equipment, and new computer-based technologies that are bringing radical changes in manufacturing processes. We suggest that America needs *more* competition, not less. Evidence shows that industries facing increased competition at home and abroad have been at the forefront of plant modernization, whereas industries that are sheltered from competition have lagged behind. Furthermore, diversification away from core businesses will not necessarily solve the problems of America's smokestack industries. Instead, there must be increased emphasis on internal growth. No business by definition is either basic, mature, or declining. Instead, these designations indicate that the industry is at the end of one lifecycle and is ready to undergo a process of creative destruction, thereby offering tremendous new opportunities and challenges for rejuvenation and growth.

We outline a number of specific measures American corporations could take to harness the qualities of entrepreneurship, creativity, and aggressiveness possessed by many American managers, professionals, and workers. Conventional wisdom notwithstanding, it is not the decline of the work ethic among America's workers that is the cause of the decline in productivity. Evidence shows that the work ethic is still quite strong and may be even getting stronger. The problem lies in the inability of American managers to harness this work ethic. Plant modernization and automation is unlikely to solve this problem simply by reducing the number of workers employed. Ironically, the new technologies have had the perverse effect of increasing the degree of discretion and control new workers have over how they perform their work. Thus management is likely to be confronted with workers who are intelligent, more powerful and independent, and more determined to have a say in how they do their jobs.

What is needed is a modification of current organizational structures, decision-making processes, and performance evaluation and compensation systems away from bureaucratic and hierarchical modes to more individualistic and less adversarial modes. The answer does not lie in group-based systems that seek employee loyalty for the corporation. Managing this new kind of employee with "high discretion" would require not an autocratic style with trappings of power, but a more collegial style, where informed consent of the governed would become increasingly important. It would not be enough for management to demand performance and sacrifices while considering itself immune to such measures. Above all, American managements will have to *convince* employees that they are competent to ask what they ask, is reasonable, and that the employee stands to benefit from increased effort.

Finally, we address ourselves to another important item of public debate pertaining to America's competitive position vis-à-vis the Japanese. This has to do with the erection of both direct and indirect barriers by the Japanese to protect the less efficient segments of their economy from foreign competition, while at the same time inundating foreign markets with products where free trade prevails. We suggest the Japanese have adroitly manipulated the rules of international trade to their advantage. When called upon to make amends, they have managed, through astute diplomacy and propaganda, to deflect these charges, thereby putting the victims of the competition on the defensive. We argue that Western nations must become more aggressive in correcting the inequities in the rules by which the Japanese operate in international markets.

We contend that American and other Western nations must improve their productivity and efficiency if they are to compete successfully with the Japanese in the international arena. There is no substitute for quality products and services that meet the needs and demands of consumers at competitive prices. We also firmly believe that there must be a change in the international trading system that permanently favors certain countries and their industries through excessive government subsidies and protected national markets.

Improvement in the American business and management system will come not from imitation of the Japanese model, but from carefully developed indigenous approaches. Many of the so-called examples of successful adaptation of Japanese management practices by American companies, ballyhooed by the promoters of JABMAS, are not Japanese innovations. They are simply excellent examples of good management techniques that were developed in the United States long before the Japanese management practices became fashionable. The fact that they share some characteristics with Japanese practices is coincidental. The American management system is more flexible and therefore more easily adapted to rapidly changing economic, technological, and social conditions. There is an explosion of truly new innovations in virtually all industrial segments, propelled by advances in such areas as microelectronics, bioengineering, telecommunications, and information generation and management, to name a few. The technological future is likely to be very different from even the recent past. It will call for organizational structures, decision-making processes, and approaches to human resource management that must be innovative, flexible and adaptable if America is to meet tomorrow's challenges.

Even in Japan, there is evidence that many companies, especially those facing intense foreign competition, are moving away from the traditional Japanese system and opting for some of the techniques of decision-making and employee compensation, based on individual merit and performance, that are hallmarks of the American system. Thus, if Americans were to follow Japanese management practices or attempt to imitate that country's system of business-government collaboration, it would be the wrong thing to do, at the wrong time, and for the wrong reasons. No doubt it would make the Japanese quite happy if, for no other reason, than for Americans it would be a case of being not good enough and a bit late. If in the process we were to fail, we would have no one to blame but ourselves.

This book is the culmination of fifteen years of research. The antecedants of *The False Promise* date back to the late 1960s and early 1970s when one of the authors (Sethi) initiated research in the ways in which Japanese business was responding to societal pressures and public discontent because of public dissatisfaction with corporate performance in such areas as environmental degradation, product safety, workplace health hazards, corporate political involvement, and insensitivity to community needs. The objective was to see whether the JABMAS, which was considered to be in harmony with Japanese society and therefore more responsive to its societal needs, might offer some guidelines for American business, which was then confronted with intense social discontent and public hostility, and a new wave of laws and regulations affecting almost every aspect of business. This research resulted in a series of articles and a book, *Japanese Business and Social Conflict: A Comparative Analysis of Response Patterns with American Business* (Ballinger, 1975).

The second phase of the research occurred in 1979, when Sethi and Swanson undertook to investigate the personnel management behavior of some leading Japanese companies doing business in the United States. Their interest was aroused because of a lawsuit, soon to be followed by others, filed by American employees against a major Japanese firm and alleging discrimination based on race, color, and national origin in violation of U.S. civil rights laws forbidding employment discrimination. This case was unprecedented at that time because it raised some unusual questions of immunity from compliance with U.S. laws emanating from the U.S.-Japan Treaty rights, and the problems of establishing the fact and intent of discrimination under a system that was radically different from the American system in terms of value underpinnings, management philosophy, and operating procedures. This research also yielded a major monograph and a series of articles in various business and legal journals.

The third phase of the research occurred in 1982, when Sethi and Namiki collaborated in a research study to compare the Japanese decision-making processes with matrix decision-making system. The purpose was to evaluate the former's suitability in dealing with highly innovative and complex decisions made under conditions of extreme technological uncertainty, when organizations must bring together the skills of different kinds of scientists, engineers, and other professionals in a manner that does not fit traditional organization structures and decision-making processes. The findings of this research are incorporated in a book by David Cleland (ed.), *Matrix Systems Handbook* (Van Nostrand Reinhold, 1984).

The final phase of the research came about as a consequence of an invitation by Lethbridge University in Canada for Sethi, Swanson, and Namiki to co-author a paper entitled "Transfer and Adaptation of Culturally Unique Management Practices to other Socio-Cultural Environments: The Case of Japanese Management Practices in the U.S." (1983). This paper allowed us to bring all our previous research together and place it in proper perspective. The paper gave us the impetus that led to the publication of this book.

For us, this book represents an unusual collaboration of authors with different, but complementary academic and professional skills. Sethi has extensively taught and published in the areas of business policy/social issues and international management practices, and pioneered some of the analytical techniques employed in this book. As lead author, he was responsible for the overall structural arrangement of the book. He developed the conceptual models used in analyzing JABMAS and ABMAS and oversaw the myriad of details that must be performed to bring a book to fruition, including the final editing. Sethi was also the principle author responsible for those chapters pertaining to the future prospects of JABMAS in the United States, and the strategies that American businesses should pursue to rejuvenate their industries in meeting future challenges of growth and international competition.

Namiki was born and raised in Japan and is a scholar of Japanese business practices. He brought to the book an understanding of the Japanese mind and culture that are not generally found in most works on JABMAS and was, therefore, responsible for those sections dealing with the sociopolitical environment of Japan and Japanese business practices. Namiki also made a major contribution to the chapters dealing with the comparative analysis of introducing Japanese practices in the United States both by the Japanese controlled companies and by the U.S. owned and operated corporations.

Swanson is an attorney, with more than 25 years experience in the regulatory field, and a recent addition to the academic community teaching strategic management and regulatory law. His responsibility was for those sections relating to the socio/political environment of the United States and American management practices. Swanson made a substantial contribution to the book through his insight into the cultural values and legal system of the United States.

S. Prakash Sethi, New York, New York
Nobuaki Namiki, Windsor, Ont. Canada
Carl Swanson, Dallas, Texas
March, 1984

ACKNOWLEDGMENTS ˙˙˙˙˙˙˙˙˙˙˙˙˙˙

No scholarship is truly independent. In the best traditions of academic inquiry and research, all new research is built on the contributions of a multitude of other scholars. The process calls for a constant questioning of the status quo—a search for what could be rather than what is. It demands that established values and institutions be challenged in spite of the fact that they work, not because of it. This book is no exception. In addition to drawing from our own research, we have benefited from the research and writings of a large number of American and Japanese scholars. To the best of our ability, we have acknowledged the sources of our data and attributed to the various scholars appropriate credit for the insights they have provided us. If through oversight we have overlooked any acknowledgment, we apologize here for any errors of omission.

In the preparation of the book we have sought the advice and counsel of many colleagues. Of these, four deserve special mention and grateful acknowledgment: to Professors Chalmers Johnson and Carl Mosk, The University of California at Berkeley, we are indebted for their comments on the overall concept of the book, its contents, and the major findings; to Professor Howard Van Zandt of the University of Texas at Dallas, we owe thanks for his careful review of our treatment of the Japanese business and management system and the case of C. Itoh & Co.; and to Professor James Sagovis, we owe thanks for his assistance in reviewing the chapter dealing with organizational characteristics of the American business and management system. We, of course, must bear full responsibility for the contents and conclusions in this book.

Finally, we are grateful to Professor Edwin Epstein and Mr. William Roberts, Consulting Editor and President, respectively, of Pitman Publishing Inc., for their enthusiastic support of this endeavor.

Most of the research for this book was done during 1981-83 at the Center for Research in Business and Social Policy at the University of Texas at Dallas, where the three authors worked together as director and research associates. The revisions of various drafts, and especially the research and writing of Chapter 10 and 11, were done under the auspices of the Research Program in Business and Public Policy, Center for the Study of Business and Government, Baruch College, The City University of New York. We are grateful to the Center for providing us with logistical and secretarial support.

In Dallas, Mame Chambers, the Executive Secretary of the Center, provided prodigious support in shouldering a major part of the typing of never-ending versions of the manuscript. We are all indebted to her for the assistance she cheerfully gave when time constraints were severe. Additional typing assistance was provided in New York, by, among others, Francis G. Krull, Jean Cracchiolo and Amanda E. Larrick and is gratefully acknowledged. We would also like to thank two doctoral students, Mohamed Nabil Allam and Amr Elmonoufy at UTD-Dallas and Sateesh Bhagwat, Baruch College-CUNY, for their assistance in the library research.

CONTENTS ▪▪▪▪▪▪▪▪▪▪▪▪▪▪▪▪▪▪▪▪▪▪▪▪▪▪▪▪▪▪▪▪▪▪▪▪▪

ONE

Economic Institutions and Social Systems

THE ROLE OF CORPORATIONS AND OTHER ECONOMIC INSTITUTIONS IN a society, their justification for a claim on a society's physical and human resources, and the processes they use to mobilize these resources to achieve their institutional goals cannot be studied in isolation, divorced from the environment or other societal institutions. Business and corporate behavior must be analyzed within the framework of a social system, where all the elements of a society are intricately linked together and affected by one another's actions.[1]

A nation's management system is not just a set of tools and techniques that can be applied anywhere and at any time without regard to the sociocultural context. We demonstrate that, to the contrary, the effectiveness of any management style can be understood only within the cultural, sociopolitical, and economic framework of the people who are doing the managing or being managed.

The success or failure of the adaptability of Japanese management practices in the North American and West European contexts must therefore depend to a large extent not only on the inherent characteristics of those practices themselves, but on:

1. The sociocultural and political conditions in the environments within which the elements of the Japanese system must operate.
2. The extent to which the Japanese management techniques can be adapted to the peculiar conditions of alien environments.
3. The ability and willingness of executives, workers, and other stakeholders to adapt those techniques in a manner that will fit their own sociocultural milieu.

THE SOCIOCULTURAL AND POLITICAL CONTEXT OF CORPORATE BEHAVIOR AND MANAGEMENT PRACTICES

The legitimacy of a corporation's goals and its modus operandi can be evaluated along three dimensions:

1. The extent to which the corporate culture and value set is in harmony with the cultural ethos and values of the larger social system.
2. The degree of congruity between corporate goals and those of the sociopolitical system and other stakeholders in society.
3. The extent to which the management practices and operating philosophies of a business system are in harmony with the cultural values, social norms, and mores of the larger society, and are able to mobilize its physical and human resources with the fewest possible dysfunctional effects on the larger system.

Society as a Social System

A social system is a complex arrangement of individuals who organize themselves into various institutions—subsystems of the main system—to perform various activities and to pursue commonly accepted goals. A social system, however, is not merely the sum total of its subsystems; it is much larger in concept and practice and has a life of its own. Society is not a mere expression of the economic self-interest of individuals or of a particular subsystem. It is best conceived of as a system of mutual, though varying, delegation of interconnected and interdependent social obligations. Furthermore, this interdependence is increasing for societies that are becoming technologically oriented, and even more so for societies whose historic antecedents emphasize interdependence.

Within each social system are subsystems that differ in relative size; basic function; the satisfactions they generate for members; the influence they exercise over the lives of the individuals they touch; and the power they exert against each other and over the community. These subsystems have their own value sets, which are largely self-defined to give specific expression to those needs of their members that can be satisfied only within the narrower space, time, communal, and personnel dimensions of the subsystem. Business institutions or corporations represent one such subsystem.

The Value Set

Every society or culture contains a whole set of social norms, based on its particular history, religions, philosophies, and the nature of its people. The value set of a social system at any given time is based on a consensus of the value sets of various subsystems and reflects their relative strengths in the overall system. It is influenced by three other factors: (1) History provides a sense of continuity, physical possessions, data, and an institutional framework. History provides the raw materials from which to construct the generalizations essential to prediction. (2) Traditions and values provide a source of legitimacy for social institutions, an outlook, and a framework within which to analyze and interpret new phenomena. (3) The external environment and level of technological sophistication provide more raw material for predictions about the future.

The value set of a society is not easily definable and certainly not quantifiable. This fact makes it all the more difficult to analyze its impact on the behavior of economic institutions in a society.[2] A society's value set must represent a consensus of individual members and constituent units on their expectations, aspirations, and modes of behavior. Otherwise, it is unlikely to endure or to retain the support of all segments of society in times of crisis. A social system must provide mechanisms for voluntary change and adjustment among subsystems and constituent units. Failure to do so creates a lag in terms of the system's overall goals and the expectations of the body politic, and may cause violent internal disruption. The value set of a social system is affected not only by internal changes, but also by changes in its external environment. According to Chamberlain:

> The value set also establishes the norms which govern economic strategy. The internal distribution of power; the accepted avenues of social change; the ways in which interpersonal competition is expressed; sentiments which determine the roles and rights of the young, the elderly, women, minority groups; . . . these and other persisting guides to conduct growing out of a society's values will delimit the manner in which specific objectives are sought.[3]

However, it must be clearly understood that no single criterion—economic or otherwise—can determine a society's value set, which must be satisfactory to all its constituent units and produce an optimally integrated system. Wherever a society exists, there exists a system of obligations and rights. A social system continually creates these reciprocal relations between every person and all other persons. If the philosophy of a society is to be effective, it must be as dynamic and realistic as the forces it controls. Thus, it would be fallacious to argue that a society can produce a unique hierarchy of social choices—alternative uses of its resources—according to some criterion of economic efficiency. By doing so, the society might maximize its economic resources without necessarily maximizing all the satisfactions desired by its members.

Conflicts between and within Subsystems

A dynamic social system and its subsystems are constantly under pressure to change. The need for change results from the reaction of individuals to new circumstances and their consequent efforts to understand these circumstances, make them meaningful, and build them into new values and new systems of allegiance. As Nisbet has pointed out:

> It is thus a matter of conflict within a social system—family, or community, or church—and more significantly, a matter of frequent conflict among institutions. For, since each institution is a pattern of functions and meanings in the lives of individuals, and hence demanding of individual loyalties, the change in one institution—the loss or addition of functions and meanings that are vital—most frequently reacts upon the structure of some other institution and thus awakens conflicting responses in the mind of the individual. . . .[4]

These pressures are of three kinds. (1) They may result from an abrupt or even violent occurrence outside the system, forcing the system to change its overall objectives and setting up a chain reaction for readjustment. (2) The futuristic orientation of the system may lead it to change its current objectives, necessitating alterations in the relationships among its subsystems and the distribution of power among them. (3) All major social institutions, in their own inner logic, tend to be all-embracing—laying claim to the entire person—and showing a tendency to assume all responsibility for the governance of society.[5] Conflicts arise when there is pressure for a shift in the balance of power from one dominant institution to another. These conflicts are not confined to the struggle for power between various subsystems, but extend to similar struggles among different units within a subsystem.

The state's role in the total system is somewhat unique. First, as one of the subsystems, the state vies for its share of social power to achieve those objectives its constituent members demand. Second, as manager of the overall system, the state administers that set of rules and regulations designed to settle temporary disputes between different subsystems and smooth over temporary disruptions in the system within the existing value set of the society. The third and perhaps most important role of the state often consists in speeding up or slowing down the rate of change that would occur in existing relationships among the subsystems if change were allowed to occur "naturally." For it is the rate of change that determines whether or not the dispossessed and the deprived can successfully adjust to changed conditions and avail themselves of new opportunities.

THE JAPANESE BUSINESS AND MANAGEMENT SYSTEM (JABMAS) IN THE CONTEXT OF WESTERN CULTURE

The objectives of this book, briefly described are as follows:

1. Describe the JABMAS within its own cultural and sociopolitical milieu.
2. Provide a comparative description of the American business and management system (ABMAS) within its own cultural and sociopolitical milieu. It also examines the drawbacks and limitations of the system as it currently functions.
3. An important element of the book is the development of an analytical framework which enables us to identify the life cycle and critical path through which a new idea moves from initial introduction to wide acceptance in a society. This framework is used as a means of evaluating the strategies employed by the change agent in introducing that idea and the pattern of responses it evokes from different segments in society.
4. Evaluate the appropriateness of various response patterns in introducing the JABMAS by:
   a. The American managements in their own companies; and
   b. The Japanese controlled and managed companies in the United States.
5. Provide guidelines that can help firms develop programs for bringing about changes in their management systems. More importantly, criteria are proposed to assist firms in evaluating when certain types of changes in management practices may not be feasible and, therefore, should not be introduced. A systematic approach and concrete guideline for the American executives is offered to improve the economic and social performance of their enterprises.

Our purpose in writing this book and the major themes we wish to sound have been set forth in the Foreword and need not be repeated here. Essentially, we contend that the effectiveness of any management style, particularly one that is being considered for adoption in an alien environment, must be understood within the cultural, social, political, and economic framework of the people who are doing the managing or being managed. The problem of adoption is further compounded by the fact that opposing societal forces simultaneously slow down and speed up the acculturation process in organizations. On the one hand, cultural traits remain constant for long periods and act as regulators to ensure that changes do not occur too quickly, lest they become revolutionary instead of evolutionary. Society is essentially conservative in nature and often hostile to new values that may cause serious tears in the social fabric. The problem is aggravated when the new values represent a threat to existing institutions that have a vested interest in maintaining the status quo. At the same time, sociopolitical and economic conditions change more quickly than cultural values, particularly in today's rapidly changing world, and demand quick and flexible responses that may not always be appropriate in a given value system.

Since any management system is a product of its social environment, it is our contention that any study of a management system is deficient without an understanding of that environment. Conversely, any study of a society must take into account the manner in which it conducts its commercial affairs. Our focus, of course, is not on the latter, but on the former. It is for this reason that we have concentrated in the initial chapters of this book on describing JABMAS and ABMAS before examining the problem of importing JABMAS into the United States. Our purpose is not to suggest that JABMAS is inherently inappropriate in a Western cultural or sociopolitical context, but to urge caution in adopting individual elements of that system. Nor can one select only those aspects of JABMAS that are considered desirable, for it may not be possible to discard other aspects of the system that are considered adverse or undesirable. To some extent, the system is a unit. And ill-conceived change, imposed on unwilling and hostile recipients, is doomed to failure before it has received a fair trial.[6]

NOTES

1. The discussion in this section is largely drawn from Chapter 1 of S. Prakash Sethi, *Business Corporations and the Black Man* (New York: Harper & Row, 1970).
2. Neil W. Chamberlain, *Business and Environment: The Firm in Time and Place* (New York: McGraw-Hill, 1968), p. 131.
3. Ibid., p. 136.
4. Robert A. Nisbet, *The Quest for Community* (New York: Oxford University Press, 1953), as reproduced in Clarence Walton and Richard Eells, (eds.), *The Business System,* vol. II (New York: Macmillan, 1967), pp. 1149–1154.
5. Frank Tannenbaum, "Institutional Rivalry in Society," *Political Science Quarterly* (December 1946), pp. 481–504.
6. S. Prakash Sethi, "Drawbacks of Japanese Management," *Business Week,* November 24, 1973, pp. 12, 14.

TWO ▞▞▞

The Cultural and Sociopolitical Context of the Japanese Business and Management System

THE JAPANESE BUSINESS AND MANAGEMENT SYSTEM (JABMAS) IS strongly rooted in Japanese culture and tradition. Japan's social fabric, the relationships between institutions and the state, between individuals and institutions, and between individuals and individuals, is inextricably linked to its past. Moreover, Japan is a homogeneous society that puts a high value on maintaining the purity of the race as a prerequisite for sustaining and propagating itself. It is therefore willing to pay a high price to keep its exclusivity by denying non-Japanese entry and integration into Japanese society.[1]

This homogeneity exerts strong pressure on institutional structures and management processes to evolve in a manner that is in harmony with the society's value set. A divergence from cultural norms, under these conditions, will be counterproductive because the institution will lose its legitimacy, and its moral and intellectual support. Japanese society also has a very long history, and it is one of the few nations that have never been colonized. It has developed a set of rules by which institutions organize their relations and mediate their differences while maintaining the society's network of institutional arrangements. So it is understandable that an ancient society like Japan, with a past that extends back into antiquity, a society of more than 118 million people crowded into a chain of small islands, would emphasize collective responsibility and group loyalty.

THE CULTURAL MILIEU

The core values of Japanese culture are (1) *amae* (dependence), (2) *on* (duty), (3) *giri* (social obligation), and (4) *ninjo* (human feeling). The Japa-

7

nese concept of *amae* is so unique that it makes Japanese society distinct from both overtly similar Asian socieites and seemingly different Western societies.[2] The substance of the Japanese psyche can be summarized in the term *amae*—that is, a feeling of dependence (from *amaeru,* a verb meaning to depend and presume on another's life; to seek and bask in another's indulgence). It is not a pejorative term, but a state of mind that describes a desire to be passively loved, a desire to be protected—as in a mother-child relationship—from the world of objective "reality." Doi, a noted Japanese psychoanalyst, maintains that in the Japanese these feelings are prolonged into adulthood and shape character to a far greater extent than in the West.[3] The *amae*-based relationship between two adults assumes a degree of emotional attachment that may lead the dependee to resort to "irrational" behavior and avoid taking individual responsibility for his own actions, expecting the dependor to "indulge" him by protecting him. Since in Japan *amae* is vitally important to the individual's psyche and emotional stability, the entire social structure is set up to fulfill this need. *On* implies obligations passively incurred. One "receives an *on*"; one "wears an *on*." *On* are obligations from the point of view of the passive recipient.[4] *Giri* refers to a bond of moral obligation and debt that must be repaid "with mathematical equivalence to the favor received, and there are time limits."[5] "*Giri* obligations often are mutual and reciprocal, especially within a collectivity."[6]

Ninjo refers to "human feelings" and includes all the natural human impulses and inclinations. Doi, however, maintains that for the Japanese *ninjo* is something more specific. It is

> . . . specifically knowing how to *amaeru* properly and how to respond to the call of *amaeru* in others. Japanese think themselves especially sensitive to these feelings, and those who do not share that sensitivity are said to be wanting in *ninjo.* . . . *Giri* . . . refers to a bond of moral obligations. . . . Whereas *ninjo* primarily refers to those feelings which spontaneously occur in the relations between parent and child, husband and wife, or brother and sister, *giri* relations are relations between in-laws, neighbors, with close associates, or superiors in one's place of work.[7]

Benedict, Beardsley, and others maintain that the "circle of human feelings" and the "circle of duty" are mutually exclusive.[8] For example, Beardsley states: "*Ninjo* refers to what one would like to do as a human being and equally to what one finds distasteful or abhorrent and of personal sentiment. *Giri* pertains to what one must do or avoid doing because of status and group membership."[9] However, Doi contends that it would be erroneous to consider *giri* and *ninjo* as mutually exclusive: "They are not simply opposed but would seem to exist in a kind of organic relationship to each other. . . .

[Furthermore] *ninjo* and *giri* indicate responses that have a close bearing on *amae.*" The nature of *giri* relationships may be interpreted to mean that one is "officially permitted to experience *ninjo,*" while in relationships like parent and child, *ninjo* occurs spontaneously.[10]

Amae can also be used to describe the underlying reasons for the vertical one-to-one relationships typical of Japanese society. Although the recognition and pursuit of *amae* in Japanese society accounts for both its virtues and its faults, the suppression or diversion of *amae* in human relations in the West explains the strengths and flaws of Western traditions. Doi also argues that these traits of mutual dependence and reciprocal obligations account for the fact that the attempt by Occupation authorities to democratize Japanese society did not necessarily promote individualism, but by destroying the traditional channels of *amae,* contributed to Japan's postwar spiritual and social confusion.

Group Formation

The familiar Japanese social characteristics variously called "paternalism," "groupism," and "familyism" originated in the strong tradition of *ie,* which literally means "household" or "family." But the term has a broader meaning in Japan; it relates to any context—for example, the workplace—and is social in orientation.[11] Simply put, this is the Japanese sociopsychological tendency that emphasizes (in the sense of protecting, cherishing, finding needs for, or functioning best in) "us" against "them." In social organization, the Japanese put far more emphasis on situational frame than on personal attributes. When a Japanese faces an outside group, he establishes his point of reference not in terms of who he is, but in terms of his group. According to Chie Nakane, a distinguished cultural anthropologist:

> . . . the *ie* is a corporate residential group and, in the case of agriculture or other similar enterprises, *ie* is a managing body. The *ie* comprises household members (in most cases the family members of the household head, but others in addition to family members may be included), who thus make up the units of distinguishable social groups. In other words, the *ie* is a social group constructed on the basis of an established frame of residence and often of management organization. What is important here is that the human relationships within this household group are thought of as more important than all other human relationships.[12]

The "situational frame" in Japanese is *ba,* literally "location," but connoting a base on which something is placed for a given purpose. For a Japanese, a frame, such as a company, is of primary importance; personal attributes such as kinship, caste, and descent group are of secondary importance. This is the source of the commitment and loyalty to the frame-based group, which may have originated in the communal life of rice-growing villages, which demanded that members cooperate closely, and been fostered by Confucianism; the feudal clan, which demanded a warrior's total commitment and loyalty; and the wartime state control over business.[13]

In modern Japan, a company is conceived as an *ie;* its employees are the household members, and the employer is its head. However, a company, or any frame-based social group that includes members with commonality of residence or situation but without commonality of attributes must fulfill several requirements to satisfy its members in order to strengthen the frame and make the group element tougher. This is in contrast to the group formed by attributes such as kinship and caste, whose members may possess a strong sense of exclusiveness and cohesiveness mainly because of the commonality of their attributes.

A frame-based group must be able to provide its members with a sense of the permanence of its existence, since once joined, change of membership to another group is difficult. Conversely, a group needs to guarantee membership (the lifetime employment system). This condition can be fulfilled only by the government and large-scale, successful corporations. A frame-based group must also be able to provide its members with a feeling of "oneness"; the group as a "family" must engage them totally, and must foster emotional as well as financial well-being. Such "paternalistic" arrangements induce in the employees an emotional attachment to the *ba* and people within the organization. For example, an employer shows paternalistic (or *ninjo*) attitudes to employees, which gives them a sense of *on* to the employer. Because of such reciprocal relationships, employees have a moral obligation to work diligently and honestly for their employer.

Veneration of Authority and Interpersonal Relationships

The basic single-unit interpersonal relationship between two Japanese persons is *oyabun-kobun* (*oya,* father; *ko,* child), in a vertical system. Members in a work-related group, or in any Japanese organization, are tied together by this kind of relationship. According to Nakane:

> The extension of this kind of dydadic relationship produces a lineage-like organization. The organizational principle of the *Oya-bun-Kobun* group differs from that of the Japanese family institution in that the *Oyabun* normally has several *Kobuns* with more or less equal status, not only one as in the case of the household unit

> ... whereas the Japanese father may discriminate in the treatment of his sons . . . the essential requirement of the *Oyabun* is that he treat his *Kobuns* with equal fairness according to their status within the group, otherwise he would lose his *Kobun* because of the unfair treatment. . . .
>
> In this system, while the *Oyabun* may have several *Kobuns*, the *Kobun* can have but one *Oyabun*. This is the feature that determines the structure of the group based on the vertical system. . . .
>
> Within the *Oyabun-Kobun* group, each member is tied into the one-to-one dydadic relation according to the order of and the time of his entry into the group. These dydadic relations themselves form the system of the organization. Therefore, the relative order of individuals is not changeable. Even the *Oyabun* cannot change the order. It is a very static system in which no one can creep in between the vertically related individuals.[14]

A group in Japan is based on the accumulation of such relationships between individuals. This is also the case with the corporate group. When a class of university graduates enters a corporation, they are assigned to a section of a department for training after a short orientation period. A person will stay in a section for several years and then be transferred to another section within the corporation. Because most of the university graduates have economics or law degrees, they usually do not have any understanding of business operations. The number of Japanese universities with departments of business is very small.[15] Thus, most of the training is provided by managers who are at a level above those of the trainees. Moreover, because of the Japanese respect for seniority, *oyabun-kobun* relationships will be developed within this work-related group.

The concept of the *oyabun-kobun* or superior-subordinate relationship in corporate life has the following characteristics:

1. The senior manager is older than his junior, has worked longer for the company, and is in a position of relative power and security. This position enables the senior to assist the junior.
2. The senior is beneficially disposed toward the junior and befriends him.
3. The junior accepts the friendship and assistance of the senior.
4. These acts and related feelings are the basis of the relationship. There is no explicit agreement.
5. Ideally, the junior feels gratitude toward the senior for his beneficence, and this feeling is accompanied by a desire on the part of the senior to become a good older friend for the younger.[16]

The relationship is developed not only through social norms, but also through time-consuming group-centered activities. Members of the work-related or office group participate in many activities together in order to promote an open and harmonious atmosphere. Development of trust among members is the most important objective. These activities are usually financed by the company and include annual trips, frequent drinking parties after working hours, and monthly Saturday afternoon recreation. The activities also serve as a bridge between generations, and help reduce the sense of rank differential by intensifying the individual friendships. It should be noted that such activities, coupled with the training by rotation, help enhance trust and harmony between management and labor.

In a Japanese corporation, authority is absolute and greatly respected.[17] Authority-based power is derived not so much from legal or contractual considerations, but is based primarily on customs, traditions, leadership style, and the nature of the interpersonal relationships between senior and junior employees.

The leader must act as a leader and demonstrate leadership qualities such as magnanimity, compassion, vision, and wisdom. This ethical code of conduct is a legacy of the Confucian system that was the basis of the feudal system. Absolute loyalty and devotion to one's master (the leadership) is considered a virtue. Superiors, in turn, are expected to exemplify the virtues of sagacity, benevolence, and purity.

> Masters (leaders) who failed to demonstrate such qualities were belittled as "small men" in the eyes of observer-critics cultivated in the Confucian tradition. This moralistic standard by which the leaders were evaluated still lingers with Japanese institutions. Under this master-follower relationship, subordinates were not only expected, but obligated to help their master attain exemplary conduct; even such extreme forms of self-sacrifice as disemboweling themselves and thereby performing the "protest of death" were not unheard of. The merchant class emulated such ideologies of the ruling class of *Samurai.* [18]

In the context of senior-subordinate relationships in a corporation, the leadership must be perceived as "sympathetic, protective, and unselfish."[19] In other words, the leader is to be a guardian who looks after the best interests of his subordinates. He is a "warm leader" in contrast to a "rational leader" in the Western context. There is also the notion of apprenticeship in the senior-subordinate relationship.[20] Juniors or subordinates are expected to follow the leader's explicit as well as implicit orders in the best interests of the group. Nonetheless, the leader is also expected to be flexible (or "mature") and willing to accommodate a subordinate's opinions, thereby giving subordinates a sense of participation. By and large, a senior's authority can be limited by this set of reciprocal and mutually binding expectations.

Japanese also place great value on "purity of intent," even when such intent is misguided and results in financial or other injuries to the group or corporation. One manifestation of such "purity of intent" is found in the notion of "loyal insubordination." A Japanese employee feels impelled to disregard his superior's instructions if he believes, albeit incorrectly, that he can perform a task better. Thus a foreman may change the production schedule or construction plans if he thinks these actions are in the best interests of the company. However, if such changes turn out to be ill-advised, he is unlikely to be punished because his intentions were pure. This system encourages initiative on the part of employees by protecting them from the consequences of their mistakes. However, it also risks greater exposure to risk from disrupted plans and unforeseen dangers when overzealous employees take unwarranted actions. Japanese companies and other institutions also use the "wayward but well-intentioned" employee as an excuse to shelter the group from outside criticism and avoid group responsibility.[21] An interesting example of the approach can be seen in the recent incident involving Hitachi employees who were caught in buying stolen IBM secrets through illegal channels. The Hitachi Corporation claimed that the employees acted without prior authorization. However, citing "pure motives," the company not only retained these employees, but also praised and protected them.[22]

Faction: Its Formation and Personal Ties

The vertical system of personal relationships coupled with the Japanese need to belong are the main bases for the formation of and cliques (habatsu) within a large group. This is true of political parties, government bureaucracies, large corporations, and emerging radical and dissent movements. Factions and cliques protect the interests of their members and also provide a system of checks and balances within an organization. At the same time, surface group harmony is maintained and rigidly enforced until the group in power is challenged by another group. Membership in a faction depends on a combination of such factors as coming from the same university, ties of marriage, or assignment to the same section or department of the company.[23]

Factionalism is seen as an evil in Japan, especially for government bureaucrats. But it is tolerated because it has a positive function as well, particularly in communication within an organization. A faction promotes and sustains informal and personal relationships between juniors and seniors and facilitates a two-way flow of communication. Factions provide for one-to-one relationships between a junior employee and his superior, a relationship far more important than larger, more formal, group relationships. This is one of the reasons why bottom-up communications are inordinately slow in a Japanese bureaucracy; they must go through the entire chain, one link at a time. Factions also facilitate lateral communication and coordination.[24] The need for coordination, ease of two-way communication, and one-to-one relationships are some of the reasons why it is extremely difficult for Japanese companies to hire outside experts at a higher level of management. These people could not become part of the internal networks.

Factions and cliques provide one of the main underpinnings for faster promotions and increased individual rewards in corporate and government bureaucracies. Faster promotion is one of the major rewards for a Japanese employee under the lifetime employment, seniority-based wage and promotion system, which makes rewarding individual excellence difficult. The problem is complicated by the widespread use of official retirement at age 55 for an employee who has not been promoted to a top or senior management position.

THE SOCIOPOLITICAL CONTEXT

Industrialized societies create interdependences between various institutions that must cooperate to make the system work. Business, as an institution, must also coordinate its behavior and activities in a manner congruent with the goals of other institutions and those of the larger society. The nature of the relationship between these institutions in the Japanese society, however, is quite different and distinct from that prevailing in North America and Western Europe.

Here we examine the set of relationships that exist between business and other institutions on the one hand, and between business and political institutions on the other hand. We also analyze the process through which these relationships are formed and nurtured, and how they affect the formulation of the national agenda and influence the goals and activities of other institutions and stakeholders in Japanese society.

The Cooperative Relationship between Government and Business

Most observers of the Japanese economic and political scene would agree that there is a high degree of cooperation between Japanese business and government. Exhibit 2–1 shows the typical process for the formation of public policy and the roles played by governmental agencies, political parties, big businesses, and other groups. This close relationship has deep historical roots. From the beginning of the Meiji era, economic power has been shared between government and private business. The government deliberately set out to create industry in order to modernize Japan, often by building factories

EXHIBIT 2-1 Major Influences on International Policymaking

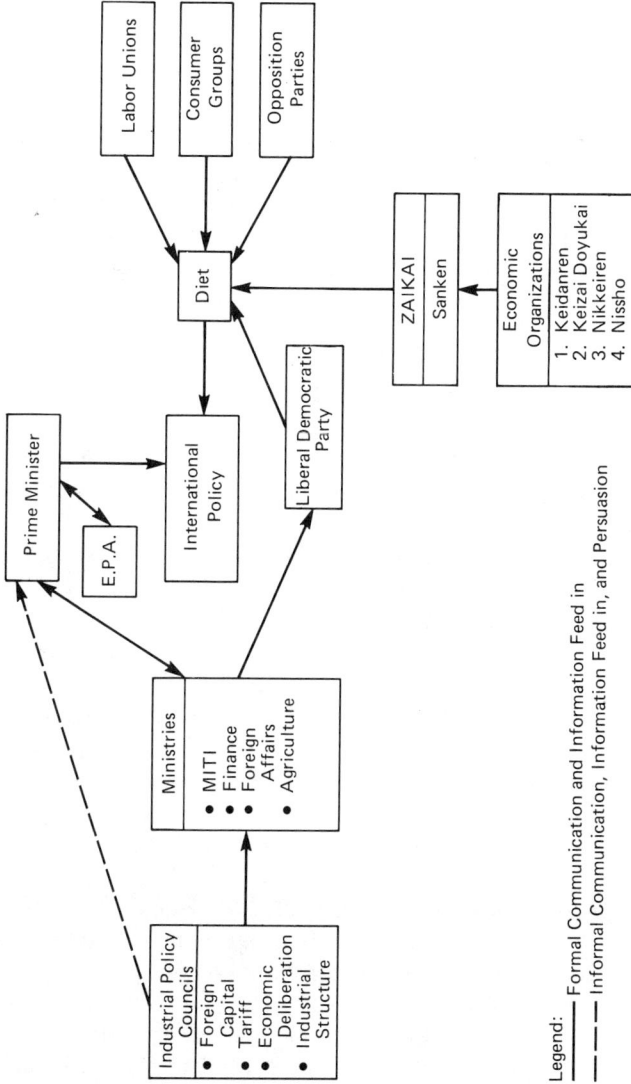

Labor Unions

Consumer Groups

Opposition Parties

Diet

ZAIKAI

Sanken

Economic Organizations
1. Keidanren
2. Keizai Doyukai
3. Nikkeiren
4. Nissho

Prime Minister

E.P.A.

International Policy

Liberal Democratic Party

Ministries
• MITI
• Finance
• Foreign Affairs
• Agriculture

Industrial Policy Councils
• Foreign Capital
• Tariff
• Economic Deliberation
• Industrial Structure

Legend: —— Formal Communication and Information Feed in
        ----- Informal Communication, Information Feed in, and Persuasion

15

and then turning them over to private business. In the process, the government retained a large degree of control over business affairs.[25] The growth of private monopolies and cartels has continued unabated, despite the passage of an antimonopoly law and the abortive efforts of the American Occupation authorities. The same identity of interests held when the Japanese political system sought to create a militarily strong Japan. This goal required close cooperation with and supervision of business.

Japanese capitalism has continued to develop under the benevolent protection of the Japanese government because of the close ties between business and the government bureaucracy on the one hand, and between business and the Liberal Democratic Party (LDP) on the other hand. According to Jun Ui, a scholar who has done much work on Japan's pollution-related problems, the Japanese economy is a classic example of "state monopolistic capital," where capital and state operate in a condition of complete mutual support.[26]

Government Bureaucracy and Business

In Japan, the government bureaucracy, the political system, and the private sector are tied together in an incestuous relationship fostered by four factors.

1. Economic controls through the availability of public funds for R&D, capital expansion, export subsidies, and even protection from failure.
2. Regulation through "administrative guidance" under which recalcitrant industries or businesses can be denied such assistance and otherwise punished through various bureacratic impediments.
3. Provision of lucrative executive positions in the private sector for senior bureaucrats upon their retirement from civil service jobs.
4. Campaign financing of political candidates, especially those belonging to the ruling Liberal Democratic Party, without which it would be almost impossible for a candidate to run for office.

Japanese government coordinates business activities in terms of planning and implementing a long-range industrial and economic policy; it also helps manage troubled industries and corporations. Within the Japanese government there are six "economic bureaucracies," of which the two most important are the Ministry of International Trade and Industry (MITI), and the Ministry of Finance.[27] These ministries wield significant influence over the economic sector under their respective jurisdictions through their ability to provide financial help. They also hold general implied administrative responsibilities well beyond those available to regulatory agencies in the United States. The Japanese Diet (parliament) enacts laws that are more akin to policy statements. The interpretation of these laws and their conversion to operational rules is left largely to senior civil servants, thereby giving them enormous power and influence.

The respect for authority and the power of bureaucracy has a long tradition in Japan. In a penetrating analysis of the Japanese bureaucracy, Chalmers Johnson observes:

> Japan has long displayed a marked separation in its political system between reigning and ruling, between the powers of the legislative branch and the executive branch, between the majority party and the mandarinate—and, in the last analysis, between authority and power. As a result, a discrepancy exists between the constitutional and the actual locus of sovereignty that is so marked the Japanese themselves have invented terms to discuss it—*omote* (outer, in plain view) and *ura* (inner, hidden from sight), or *tatemae* (principle; Edward Seidensticker once proposed the word should be translated "pretense") and *honne* (actual practice).
>
> Japanese and foreign observers are aware that the discrepancy generates a degree of hypocrisy or euphemism, and they often enjoy criticizing this hypocrisy. Kakuma Takashi, for example, argues that in the postwar world the business community likes to pretend that it is "yielding under protest" to the powers of MITI when it is actually doing nothing more than pursuing its traditional relationship with the bureaucracy. Goshi Kohei is irritated by the senior business leaders who refer their decisions for approval to government section chiefs often not much older than their own grandchildren and then speak ill of them back at the Industrial Club. Obayashi Kenji believes that the numerous "deliberation councils" (what Berger calls "policy councils," or *shingikai*), in which officials and entrepreneurs coordinate policies, are really covers for MITI's "remote control of the industrial world"; and he speaks somewhat cynically of "Japanese-style free competition." And a foreign analyst, John Campbell, shrewdly draws attention to the fact that "nearly everyone involved with Japanese budgeting finds it in his interest to magnify the role played by the majority party."[28]

Bureaucrats in modern Japan are the *samurai* of the feudal era. They inherited the legacy of their prewar predecessors, who were appointed by the emperor and were accountable to him, thereby giving them an exalted status. The modern bureaucrats also inherited from the *samurai* something akin to a code of ethical conduct and an elite consciousness. This is perpetuated through a spirit of service or "sacrifice for the public good," and keen competitive examinations that foster a sense of meritocracy. The bureaucrats are thus described as "those above" *(okami)*. So the *samurai* tradition leads most Japanese not to question the authority of the government.[29]

The Japanese government systematically selects target industries, products, or technologies as strategically important and desirable for the national interest and promotes them. The primary national interest has been exports —to build internationally competitive export industries—mainly because of Japan's poor natural resources. MITI has been a primary instrument in formulating and implementing industrial policies in Japan.[30] For example, during the 1950s and the 1960s, MITI and the Japanese government decided to promote basic industries such as shipbuilding, chemicals, and synthetic fibers, and provided a variety of financial and other incentives to targeted industries and corporations.[31] More recently, MITI has been providing financial support and administrative guidance to direct efforts toward the development of supercomputers ahead of American companies.[32]

For declining industries, the government takes an active role in helping them shift their resources from the weaker segment of the economy to the healthier segment without much pain.[33] It encourages the formation of cartels to rationalize the industrial structure, reduce excess capacity, and ensure the survival of the strongest firms. It assists in the transfer of excess labor force from declining to expanding companies, encourages the regulation of temporary and seasonal workers, and provides employment adjustment benefits to workers who are transferred with pay cuts, voluntarily retired, or fired. It also reimburses 50 percent of workers' pay while they are in retraining and education programs.[34] Systematic exchange of information between government bureaucrats and representatives of particular industries has been facilitated by an elaborate formal structure of advisory councils, *shingikai,* inherited from the American occupation. Because the ministries select the councils and serve as their secretariats, these councils are heavily influenced by the government bureaucracy. Such a close working relationship between government and business has led some Western scholars and business people to call it "Japan, Inc."[35]

Amakudari (Heavenly Descent)

The relationship between government bureaucracy and business is further reinforced by regular and frequent formal and informal contacts between the two, and by *amakudari* (heavenly descent), the movement of retired officials to jobs in business, often to companies with which their ministries have close working relations. The movement of retired government officials to industry is promoted by early retirement and low pensions for civil servants. Each ministry takes responsibility for placing its people with private industry, and significant numbers of government retirees move to private industrial organizations each year.[36] This system encourages government officials to conduct themselves in a manner that will enhance their prospects for private employment after retirement. The retirees also facilitate freer communications between government and business and reinforce their working relationships.

Business Involvement in the Political Process

A retiring bureaucrat, with ambitions to achieve a cabinet post, must first be elected to the Diet. He needs business support for running a campaign, so money is another strong link between business and politics. In Japan it is perhaps more prevalent, pervasive, and openly practiced than in most industrialized nations. The most notorious example of this phenomenon was the alleged millions of dollars of bribes channeled to the then Prime Minister Tanaka and other politicians in 1972 in the sale of Lockheed 1011 aircraft to All-Nippon Airway. The case came to light in 1976 and resulted in the ouster of Mr. Tanaka and the conviction of other leading Japanese politicians and influential "deal makers."[37]

Despite the appearances of democracy, Japan's political system is semi-feudal in character. Japan has never undergone a "people's revolution" that would have created a feeling among the Japanese that "the government is something they created themselves."[38] Although the Constitution of 1947 provided for a highly responsible democratic government, the bureaucracy has avoided public plebiscites and direct participation in politics by the people. Thus, in the eyes of the people "the Constitution of 1947, as liberal as it unquestionably is, was bestowed on the society from above just as was the Meiji Constitution of 1889."[39]

The political parties are less concerned with policies and programs than they are with the accumulation of power and privileges for special groups and factions within the parties. These factions are organized around strong leaders and vie for political plums—for example, a ministership or premiership. The Liberal Democratic Party is an unstable coalition of more than half a dozen factions. Despite the Lockheed scandal and the court trial, and his resulting resignation from the LDP, Mr. Tanaka has managed to maintain significant influence in Japanese politics. He still commands by far the largest faction in the LDP, which is made up of more than 100 LDP Diet members.[40] The current prime minister, Nakasone, has been a close associate of Tanaka. His cabinet includes so many members of Tanaka's faction that it is widely called the "Tanakasone cabinet" in Japan. Professor Yanaga says: "Wheeling and dealing, bribery, coercion, collusion, threats and violence (including assassination) are as much a part of Japanese politics as they are of Japanese life."[41]

Big business also has a close relationship with Japan's long-time ruling party, the Liberal Democratic Party.[42] About one-fourth of the LDP membership comes from former civil servants who have had a long working relationship with business groups and would be dependent on business funding for their electoral progress. The influence of former bureaucrats has also tended to strengthen and perpetuate the power of the bureaucracy. Big business has direct communication channels to the LDP leadership through clubs, the best known of which is *Itsukakai,* or Fifth-Day-of-the-Month Club. These meetings, which are usually held in expensive geisha restaurants, are traditionally used by top politicians to maintain contacts with business groups.

Industry also organizes in-plant campaigns in which all employees are urged to vote for the company's chosen candidates for various electoral offices. The process is quite similar to running for office in a company town with a single party fielding all the candidates. Pledge cards are distributed at work by foremen, and pressures to conform and vote for the preferred candidate are strong and quite successful. For example, during the 1974 election, the LDP was facing major losses in the elections to the Upper House. Big business came to the rescue. It organized corporationwide election campaigns. Industrial groups vigorously promoted LDP candidates throughout Japan by pressuring employees, subcontractors, and their family members to vote for them. But despite all the pressure, these campaigns had only limited success.[43]

Policymaking Councils

Policymaking councils composed of political leaders and other experts from various segments of Japan's professional elite are for window-dressing purposes only. Although responsible for developing long-range policies, these councils initiate no action or recommendations and instead concentrate on discussing proposals made by various officials before sending them to the ministers. Official proposals are never rejected or changed by a council. These councils have been derisively called "gimmicks" and "ornaments" even by some critics in Japan.[44] Consumers, labor unions, and other groups have little to say in economic policy formulation because of their weak position in the Diet and also because few important decisions are determined or affected by the Diet.[45]

The Zaikai

The primary influence of business on government in Japan is wielded through the *zaikai,* defined as "a politico-economic group of wealthy financial leaders who can exert tremendous influence on the government and politics."[46] The term *zaikai* is used to denote financial circles, or even more broadly, business circles—but always meaning big business. *Zaikai* leadership consists primarily of the top executives of four big business organizations, of which the most powerful is Keidanren, or the Federation of Economic Organizations, whose board of directors consists of the presidents of the key organizations and the elder statesmen of business, industry, and finance.[47]

One should not interpret the term *zaikai* to imply that big business in Japan always has a unified position on matters affecting it. Within the *zaikai* there are differences based on special interests, regional interests, attitudes toward the West, political leanings, and most important, closeness to the seat of political power—the LDP and the government. Similarly, the internal differences should not be misinterpreted to mean a lack of power and influence or inability to act on issues affecting business in Japan.

Organized business exerts a strong influence on virtually all aspects of government decision making. This influence is openly acknowledged and recognized by all concerned. No legislation strongly opposed by the *zaikai* is introduced by the government or passed by the Diet. Japanese business, therefore, does not have to resort to lobbying in the sense that it is practiced in the United States, since it holds a virtual veto over all important economic decisions.

Industrial Groups

In addition to the *zaikai,* there are also huge economic organizations, *zaibatsu* or *keiretsu,* consisting of many oligopolistic firms from a number of industries.[48] The American Occupation broke the economic monopoly of the great prewar *zaibatsu,* but the necessity for economic recovery and industrialization, coupled with the basic aversion of Japanese government and business to unfettered competition, led to the formation of new groups (usually old groups in new garb). Instead of *zaibatsu,* they are called industrial or enterprise groups or *keiretsu* and are a less tightly structured type of association. The industrial groups are (1) those organized around the former *zaibatsu* and using the old names, such as Mitsui, Mitsubishi, and Sumitomo; and (2) those clustered around large banks, such as Fuji, Daiichi, and Sanwa. Through a succession of mergers and consolidations, the two major *zaibatsu,* Mitsubishi and Mitsui, which were broken into some 200 successor companies, reemerged as single entities. Their core companies were either expanded or remained similar to the prewar ones. The postwar industrial groups, or *keiretsu,* differ from the prewar *zaibatsu* in several ways: Family control is largely missing; the firms have become more diversified, entering into many nontrading activities; and many non-*zaibatsu* firms have joined the ranks. The dominant segment of the new industrial groups is trading companies, which evolved from the old *zaibatsu,* especially those with origins in the textile and steel industries.[49]

There is considerable competition between these industrial groups. However, almost no competition exists between companies within an industrial group because each group tries not to duplicate activities among member companies. The mechanisms for coordination were restored following the Occupation in the form of presidents' clubs (with regular meetings) and interlocking directorates.

Large corporations form such industrial groups because of their substantial benefits. When a member company has excess labor, it can transfer it, either temporarily or permanently, to another member company with needs for more labor, thereby avoiding layoffs. There is a higher level of access to, and exchange of, information. Companies can have stronger financial support from the group's main bank. Member firms can also secure resources, and their prestige is enhanced by being part of a powerful and venerable business group. Except for a few companies such as Honda and Sony, most of the big companies in Japan have some relationship with one of the industrial groups.[50]

THE ADVERSE IMPACT OF CLOSE BUSINESS–GOVERNMENT LIAISON ON OTHER ASPECTS OF JAPANESE SOCIETY

The Japanese miracle of growth and prosperity has not been achieved without costs to the society and sacrifices in terms of other societal goals and objectives. Some of these sacrifices and tradeoffs are inevitable in any society when it pursues a particular set of goals as a national priority. However, some costs are incurred because the narrow pursuit of one set of objectives also causes a concentration of power in fewer hands, weakens countervailing systems, and creates circumstances for the abuse of power on the part of those exercising it. In this section, we will briefly discuss the social costs of JAB-MAS as they pertain to the close cooperation between business and government and the active involvement on the part of businessmen not as individuals, but as heads of economic institutions, in the country's political and electoral process.

During the reindustrialization period following World War II, the goals of Japanese business have matched closely with those of the national government. Concerns over the congruity of the business system's goals with those of the other interests, such as environmental protection, consumer protection, and labor, were largely ignored in the name of reindustrialization, "growth," and international competitiveness. Although interest groups exist in Japan, there is no true tradition of pluralism or political activism. Political factions represent essentially private interests, and there are very few appeals or complaints from constituents. The Diet is generally lacking in initiative and influence and acts largely at the behest of the bureaucracy.

The government's policy is generally to ignore outside criticism emanating from consumer or environmental groups, and when this not possible, to seek compromises within the LDP.[51] The system, according to Kawanaka Niko, is more akin to that of interlocking decision making as opposed to consensus building, "and acknowledges the symbiotic relationships among the bureaucrats, LDP, and the business community." The characteristics of such interlocking decisions, suggests Niko, are bureaucratic leadership, obscured responsibility, and fictive kinship ties.[52]

The disregard for societal concern is also manifested by the almost absolute notion of loyalty to one's corporation or faction above all other concerns, including those of society in general. There are extreme social pressures for overt demonstration of loyalty to one's company or employer, especially in large enterprises and trading houses. This loyalty is "demanded," and disloyalty is severely punished. Loyalty is demonstrated not only by working hard and by longer work hours, but also by unquestioned obedience to the employer.[53] In Japan, where lifetime employees in large enterprises are seen as an elite and privileged class, the loss of such jobs is an unbearable catastrophe. The employee loses not only economic, but also social status. Japanese are usually regarded by other nations as diligent and hard workers. But they are to a large extent forced to be hard workers, because the penalty for failure to conform is just too great.

The Supremacy of Private Economic Activity

An indirect consequence of the postwar industrialization effort was the considerable destruction, deterioration, and pollution of the physical environment of Japan. The most famous pollution-related incidents were Minamata disease and Itai-Itai ("ouch-ouch") disease.[54] In the early 1950s, residents of Minamata Bay, a small city on the western coast of Kyushu island, began to be afflicted by, and sometimes to die of, a strange disease. In the mid-1950s, medical researchers and scientists discovered a relationship between the disease and the chemical methyl mercury discharged into the bay by the Chisso Corporation. The corporation had continued to deny its responsibility, and moreover had tried to obstruct private as well as government investigations. Such was the pervasive influence of the corporation that employees suffering from the disease were shunned by their friends and relatives (who were also company employees) because the former had dared to blame the company, thereby giving their employer a bad name. The victims' misery was further compounded by the Japanese government's indifference to their plight.

In Japan, the Ministry of Health and Welfare traditionally acts as the mediator between a company and its employees in cases where payment of compensation for work-related injuries is involved. The ministry's attitude is generally quite sympathetic to the employers, and the recommended payments have been historically small even in the Japanese context. They would be considered grossly inadequate in the U.S. context when balanced against the loss of future earnings and the mental and physical harm inflicted on the victims. The city government as well as the national government had not been sympathetic to the plight of the victims, who were left without any help until they won their lawsuit against Chisso in 1973, about twenty years after the tragedy began. In 1974, the number of officially recognized victims was about 750. The same mercury poisoning took place in Niigata, and another pollution incident (cadmium poisoning) took place in Toyama Prefecture. All the victims received the same treatment by both the responsible corporations and the government.[55]

The cumulative effect of such pollution incidents, however, could not be ignored for long. Moreover, Japan was "losing face" in the arena of world opinion. By late 1960s, large segments of the Japanese population had come to recognize the problem of massive pollution. Fish caught around Japan was no longer edible. It was even said to be dangerous for a baby to consume its mother's breast milk for fear of pollution-related contamination. The tremendous increase in public concern over the environment led the Japanese Diet to enact strict environmental protection laws in the early 1970s, some provisions of which were very similar to those of the pollution-related laws passed in the United States. In other areas, they were even stricter than those in U.S. laws. Thus, a national consensus was made to put environmental protection and pollution control at the top of the government's priorities. Japanese business also undertook to reduce pollution problems by exporting its smokestack industries to less developed countries, notably South Korea. Companies abiding by the new environmental laws are offered substantial benefits by the government in the form of fast depreciation of pollution-control equipment and the provision of low-interest loans. The government (MITI) has also helped finance R&D programs in pollution-control technology.[56]

There has indeed been a change in the treatment of Japanese business as it relates to the problem of protecting the environment. However, the problem persists because the sociocultural and political factors that exacerbated the problem in the first place are still very strong. The most recent example of a company's violation of the environmental laws was a series of radioactive spills at a nuclear power plant of the Japan Atomic Power Company in March 1981.[57] The plant in Tsurunaga, located in north-central Japan about 200 miles west of Tokyo, leaked radioactive waste water in early March, allegedly due to human error. Management ordered its fifty-six workers to carry the waste water away by hand in plastic buckets, and did not report the accident to government authorities. The waste water seeped into a general drainage pipe and then into a nearby bay and contaminated a large area. The contamination was detected about six weeks after the accident, but by that time the company had deliberately exposed a large number of people to radiation hazard. Moreover, during the investigation, it was discovered that the plant had had another unreported accident in January 1981, which had exposed forty-five workers to excessively high levels of radiation. The following May, the government ordered the plant to shut down for six months to improve safety procedures. It was also decided not to prosecute the company criminally because, reportedly, the available legal penalties that could be imposed amounted to only a few hundred dollars in fines.[58]

Stockholders

Under the laws of Japan, stockholders are owners of the corporation and make major decisions such as selecting the board of directors and voting on mergers. The Japanese Securities and Exchange Act was enacted during the American Occupation after the World War II, and is almost identical to the U.S. Securities Act of 1933 and the Securities Exchange Act of 1934. Although one may argue about the extent of real power exercised by stockholders, especially small individual stockholders, over the affairs of a corporation in the United States, the situation is far worse in Japan.

The most glaring example of shareholder abuse is the widespread use of paid professional thugs, called *sōkaiya*, by most Japanese companies to intimidate shareholders at stockholders' meetings and deter them from asking embarrassing questions of management.[59] The *sōkaiya* system was developed after World War II, when Japanese companies were forced by the Occupation authorities to accept public ownership along with shareholders' meetings. (In prewar Japan most large businesses were privately owned, and their managements were immune from public criticism.) Because of the widespread use of *sōkaiya*, most shareholders' meetings are over within 15 to 30 minutes.

Until recently, the situation had become so bad that even Japanese companies that did not want or need *sōkaiya* were forced to employ them for the very real fear that *sōkaiya* would disrupt their meetings. The extortion sums paid could be very large indeed, and *sōkaiya* leaders lived in royal splendor. Moreover, *sōkaiya* would often force corporations to hold shorter meetings, and to schedule them sequentially with reasonable time intervals so that *sōkaiya* men could cover all the meetings conveniently and in an organized manner. Spurred by industry complaints and adverse media coverage, Japan amended its commercial code last year.[60] This amendment raised the required number of shares for a shareholder to be able to attend the annual meetings, forcing the *sōkaiya* to incur large investments in stock purchases in order to attend "unwanted" annual meetings. Of course, this change also had the "desirable" effect of excluding small shareholders with legitimate complaints. Notwithstanding, these changes, the use of *sōkaiya* is likely to continue in Japan in the foreseeable future because a significant number of corporations still want it, and stricter regulatory reforms are unlikely because the *sōkaiya* have close ties to powerful factions in the LDP.

Stockholders in Japan play only a nominal role as providers of capital, and their interests are generally ignored. Nearly 70 percent of Japanese corporate shares are institutionally held, and institutional ownership is encouraged and promoted by the government.[61] Therefore, major corporate decisions are made by managements, banks, and related institutions, often in consultation with government bodies, but without much input by and regard for the interests of individual shareholders.

The financial statements and accounting systems used by Japanese corporations excel in obtuseness. It is all but impossible for the stockholder or potential investor to judge the performance of a Japanese corporation through the perusal of that company's financial statements. The public does not often learn of the financial difficulties of a Japanese company until it is too late. One such example was the sudden bankruptcy of Nihon Netsugaku Kogyō, an Osaka-based manufacturer of air conditioners, and Aeromaster, its principal subsidiary, with debts of $220 million in May 1974. Before its collapse, there was little public indication that such an event was imminent.[62]

In spite of all the trappings of a formal legal process, neither government agencies nor the courts have shown any interest in securities law enforcement of the type practiced in the United States. Nor can the investor depend on an independent auditor, a species anything but independent in Japan. Instead, the shareholder or lender must depend on the integrity and reputation of the firm and those of its bankers, suppliers, and major customers. Government regulation takes the form of strong " 'administrative guidance,' or moral suasion, over Japan's four largest brokerage houses [and] counts on them to keep in line the corporations they service and the rest of the brokerage industry."[63] It does not necessarily amount to effective law enforcement or always work in the public interest. For example, in 1973 government prosecutors had enough evidence to indict three of the four largest brokers for alleged manipulation of the stock of Kyodo Shiryō, a leading Japanese feed producer. However, the Finance Ministry's securities department dissuaded the prosecutors from bringing any indictments "because top officials of the houses involved were 'self-reflecting' on their companies' actions and had promised to stop all manipulative practices."[64]

One of the major reasons why environmental and consumer activists have not been able to gain strong public support in Japan is that affiliation with such groups is seen as not conforming to the social norms and mores.

In Japan, where group conformity is viewed as indispensable, nonconforming groups or individuals are usually excluded from the mainstream and severely penalized. Although most societies discriminate against nonconformists, the degree and pervasiveness of the discrimination in Japan are considerably higher than elsewhere.

Business and the Consumer

Close cooperation between state and business in Japan, coupled with the national pursuit of industrialization, resulted in irresponsible behavior toward consumers and victims of consumer-related hazards in the name of profit maximization, growth, and export promotion. At first glance, this allegation would appear preposterous because of the fanatical emphasis on quality and perfection by Japanese businesses. However, like all perfections in an imperfect world, there is a large gap between illusion and reality. Consider the following examples:

The most widely publicized and the worst episode of food poisoning in the world occurred in Japan in the summer of 1955.[65] Some 12,000 bottle-fed babies were poisoned (130 of them died) with arsenic, which was contained in the powdered milk marketed by the Morinaga Milk Company. During the following year, the Ministry of Health and Welfare examined the children who had survived and concluded that all of them had been cured, despite the continued appearance of symptoms and other side effects. As a result, those who were poisoned and continued to suffer from the aftereffects faced tremendous hardships in getting proper monetary compensation and medical assistance. The compensation suit was first filed in 1973, almost twenty years after the poisoning, and charged both Morinaga and the government. The plaintiffs alleged that the government failed to prevent the additive from being used by omitting sodium phosphate from the list of restricted items, and that the government mistakenly diagnosed the patients and did not provide proper assistance and help to the victims despite continued symptoms and disease.

Japanese manufacturers have also not always been honest with their customers about the safety of their products, especially cars, machinery, and household appliances.[66] In the late 1960s, automobile manufacturers, notably Toyota and Nissan, secretly recalled and repaired defective cars sold in the United States, but withheld information about those recalls in Japan. Japanese consumers learned about the recalls through revelations by a reporter on *The New York Times* and were shocked at the realization that "their" major companies had concealed information from them about the safety of their products. Japanese consumers also blamed the government for not providing enough quality-control inspectors. (It was discovered that there were only seven inspectors in charge of checking the millions of cars produced annually at that time.)

Other areas of controversy in Japan are frequent price fixing and hoarding by big corporations. Vertical pricing has been prevalent in many industries, especially those that manufacture consumer products. The Japanese distribution system permits manufacturers to keep virtually complete control over dealers and retail stores, and therefore over pricing policies. Retail stores or distributors violating a manufacturer's orders are denied their dealership.

Japanese firms did not hesitate to exploit consumers during the energy crisis in 1972–73. On February 8, 1974, the chairman and president of General Sekiyu K.K., a major oil refiner, resigned from his post after assuming responsibility for having instructed the company's dealers to defraud the government, consumers, and the news media over the price increases of its products by taking advantage of the oil crisis. The alleged profiteering was disclosed by a Communist member of the Diet at a meeting of the House of Representatives Budget Committee. According to the allegations, the firm sent a circular to its branches and dealers dated November 14, 1973, urging them to raise prices as much as possible. Dealers were told to tell the government, consumers, and the news media that the retail prices of its products had not been raised. The circular instructed salesmen to suggest to dealers that the company would stop dealing with them if they informed the government or other sources about the price markups. The company also told its dealers how to reply if they were asked to explain the price increases. The circular, issued by the chief of the sales department, called the oil shortage a "rare chance to increase sales."[67] Moreover, although extreme, this was not isolated example. Many other companies increased prices and blamed increased costs resulting from the oil crisis.

The response of the Japanese government to a dramatic increase in consumer complaints has been marked by a high degree of vacillation and has generally been too little and too late. With few notable exceptions—such as reform-minded mayors in Tokyo and some other municipalities—this has been true at all levels of government. The response patterns have been quite similar to those in the pollution cases. There has been a large gap between rhetoric and action, and the types of actions taken have been similar—at least in form if not substance—to those taken in the United States, but they have inevitably followed after a lag of two or more years.

NOTES

1. S. Prakash Sethi, *Japanese Business and Social Conflict* (Cambridge, Mass.: Ballinger, 1975), pp. 52–53.
2. For an excellent treatment of this subject, see Takeo Doi, *The Anatomy of Dependence* (Tokyo: Kodansha International, 1973).
3. Quoted in Sethi, *Japanese Business and Social Conflict*, p. 38.
4. Ruth Benedict, *The Chrysanthemum and the Sword* (Boston: Houghton Mifflin, 1946), p. 116.
5. Chitoshi Yanaga, *Japanese People and Politics* (New York: Wiley, 1965), p. 58.
6. John Whitney Hall and Richard K. Beardsley, *Twelve Doors to Japan* (New York: McGraw-Hill, 1965), p. 95.
7. Takeo Doi, "Giri-Ninjo: An Interpretation," in Ronald P. Dore (ed.), *Aspects of Social Change in Modern Japan* (Princeton, N.J.: Princeton University Press, 1967), p. 330.
8. Benedict, *The Chrysanthemum and the Sword*, pp. 177–194; Hall and Beardsley, *Twelve Doors to Japan*, p. 95; Dore, *Aspects of Social Change in Modern Japan*, pp. 113–152.
9. Hall and Beardsley, *Twelve Doors to Japan*, p. 95.
10. Doi, *The Anatomy of Dependence*, p. 33.
11. For an excellent treatment of this subject, see Chie Nakane, *Japanese Society* (Berkeley: University of California Press, 1972); Chie Nakane, *Human Relations in Japan* (Tokyo: Director General of the Public Information Bureau, Ministry of Foreign Affairs, 1972).
12. Nakane, *Japanese Society*, pp. 4–5.
13. Takeshi Ishida, *Japanese Society* (New York: Random House, 1971), pp. 39–48.
14. Chie Nakane, "An Interpretation of Group Cohesiveness in Japanese Society." Paper presented at the regional seminar, Center for Japanese and Korean Studies, Berkeley, University of California, March 1, 1974, pp. 4–5; See also John W. Bennett and Iwao Ishino, *Paternalism in the Japanese Economy: Anthropological Studies of Oyabun-Kobun Patterns* (Westport, Conn.: Greenwood Press, 1963).
15. I. Ueno, "The Situation of Management Education in Japan," in *Management Education* (Paris: OECD, 1972), pp. 38–39. Sixteen percent (or 62/389) of colleges in Japan had departments of business administration, and only 7 percent of the total college student population was registered in those departments in 1972.
16. Thomas P. Rohlen, "The Company Work Group," in Ezra F. Vogel (ed.), *Modern Japanese Organization and Decision-Making* (Berkeley: University of California Press, 1975), p. 197.
17. Thomas P. Rohlen, *For Harmony and Strength: Japanese White-Collar Organization in Anthropological Perspective* (Berkeley: University of California Press, 1974), chap. 5.
18. Yoshi Tsurumi, *The Japanese Are Coming: A Multinational Interaction of Firms and Politics* (Cambridge, Mass.: Ballinger, 1976), pp. 220–221.
19. Rohlen, "The Company Work Group," p. 198.
20. George A. De Vos, "Apprenticeship and Paternalism," in Vogel (ed.), *Modern Japanese Organization and Decision-Making*, pp. 210–227.

21. Tsurumi, *The Japanese Are Coming*, p. 219.
22. "IBM Spying-Case Indictment of 3 Persons Thrown Out by Judge, Who Bars Refiling," *Wall Street Journal*, September 29, 1982, p. 7; "Judge Mulls Dismissal of One of Three Cases on IBM-Secrets Theft," *Wall Street Journal*, September 27, 1982, p. 20; Jim Drinkhall, "Hitachi Case's Last Defendant Has Plea of No Contest Accepted by Federal Judge," *Wall Street Journal*, May 16, 1983, p. 14; Jasuhiro Nara, "Japanese Media Coverage of the IBM Case," *Wall Street Journal*, August 2, 1982, p. 13; Conputopia, *IBM Spy Jiken no Zenbou* [All About the IBM Spy Incident], (Tokyo: Computa-Eigi, Inc., 1982).
23. Albert M. Craig, "Functional and Dysfunctional Aspects of Government Bureaucracy," in Ezra F. Vogel (ed.), *Modern Japanese Organization and Decision-Making*, pp. 11–15.
24. Ibid., p. 14.
25. Paul A. Davis, *Administrative Guidance in Japan—Legal Considerations*, Bulletin No. 41 (Tokyo: Sophia University Socio-Economic Institute, 1972), p. 7.
26. Jun Ui, "The Singularities of Japanese Pollution," *Japan Quarterly*, July–September 1972, pp. 281–291.
27. Chalmers Johnson, *MITI and the Japanese Miracle: The Growth of Industrial Policy, 1925–1975* (Stanford, Calif.: Stanford University Press, 1982).
28. Johnson, *MITI and the Japanese Miracle*, pp. 35–36.
29. Ibid., pp. 39–40.
30. Ibid.
31. Ministry of International Trade and Industry, *Tsusho Sangyo-Sho Niju-nen Shi* [Twenty-Year History of MITI], 1969, pp. 62–66.
32. Steve Lohr, "Computer Technology Pervades Life in Japan," *New York Times*, September 15, 1981, pp. 1, 27; "Where Japan Has a Research Edge," *Business Week*, March 14, 1983, p. 116; Bro Uttal, "Here Comes Computer, Inc.," *Fortune*, October 4, 1982, pp. 82–90.
33. Edward Boyer, "How Japan Manages Declining Industries," *Fortune*, January 10, 1983, pp. 58–63.
34. Masayoshi Kanabayashi, "Japan's Recession-Hit Companies Make Complex Arrangements to Avoid Layoffs," *Wall Street Journal*, February 17, 1983, p. 32.
35. Gerald L. Curtis, "Big Business and Political Influence," in Vogel (ed.), *Modern Japanese Organization and Decision-Making*, pp. 33–70.
36. "Heavenly Descent," *Japan Times*, March 29, 1974, p. 15; "Occupational Mobility—Not Yet," *Japan Times*, March 16, 1974, p. 1.
37. Urban C. Lehner, "Jail Term Requested in Tanaka Trial," *Wall Street Journal*, January 27, 1983, p. 36.
38. John C. Campbell, *Contemporary Japanese Budget Politics* (Berkeley: University of California Press, 1977), p. 128, cited in Johnson, *MITI and the Japanese Miracle*, p. 44.
39. "Shihai Taisei no Seisaku to Kiko" [The Politics and Structure of the Ruling System], in Yoshitake Oka (ed.), *Gendai Nihon no Seiji Katei* [The Political Process of Modern Japan] (Tokyo: Iwanami Shoten, 1958), pp. 53–68, cited in Johnson, *MITI and the Japanese Miracle*, p. 43.
40. Urban C. Lehner, "Tanaka, Former Japan Leader, Wields Big Power Despite Corruption Charges," *Wall Street Journal*, May 6, 1981, p. 30.

41. Yanaga, *Japanese People and Politics,* p. 9; see also Michael K. Blaker (ed.), *Japan at the Polls: The House of Councillors Election of 1974* (Washington, D.C.: American Enterprise Institute for Public Policy Research, 1976).

42. Curtis, "Big Business and Political Influence," pp. 33–70.

43. Tsurumi, *The Japanese Are Coming,* p. 295; see also Satoshi Kamata, *Japan in the Passing Lane: An Insider's Account of Life in a Japanese Auto Factory* (New York: Pantheon, 1982).

44. Johnson, *MITI and the Japanese Miracle,* p. 48.

45. Sethi, *Japanese Business and Social Conflict,* pp. 31, 34.

46. Ibid., p. 34.

47. Yanaga, *Big Business in Japanese Politics,* pp. 32–35, 38–39.

48. Richard E. Caves, "Industrial Organization," in Hugh Patrick and Henry Rosovsky (eds.), *Asia's New Giant: How the Japanese Economy Works* (Washington, D.C.: The Brookings Institution, 1976), pp. 494–502; Henry C. Wallich and Mable I. Wallich, "Banking and Finance," in Patrick and Rosovsky (eds.), *Asia's New Giant,* pp. 294–315.

49. Sethi, *Japanese Business and Social Conflict,* p. 36.

50. Naoto Sasaki, *Management and Industrial Structure in Japan* (New York: Pergamon Press, 1981), p. 89.

51. Johnson, *MITI and the Japanese Miracle,* p. 51.

52. Cited in Johnson, *MITI and the Japanese Miracle,* p. 51.

53. Arther S. Golden, "Group Think in Japan Inc.," *New York Times Magazine,* December 2, 1982, pp. 137–138.

54. Norie Huddle, Michael Reich, and Nahum Stiskin, *Island of Dreams: Environmental Crisis in Japan* (New York: Autumn Press, 1975), pp. 102–132.

55. Sethi, *Japanese Business and Social Conflict,* pp. 84–86.

56. For an exhaustive treatment of the environmental law in Japan, see Julian Greasser, Koichiro Fujikura, and Akio Morishima, *Environmental Law in Japan* (Cambridge, Mass.: MIT Press, 1981); for a citizens' environmental protection movement, see Margaret A. McKean, *Environmental Protest and Citizen Politics in Japan* (Berkeley: University of California Press, 1981).

57. "Nuclear Contamination Found in Japanese Soil," *New York Times,* April 19, 1981, p. 7; "Japan Says Nuclear Mishap Exposed 56 to Radiation," *New York Times,* April 22, 1981, p. 5; "45 Japanese Workers Are Reported Exposed to Nuclear Radiation," *New York Times,* April 26, 1981, p. 6; Henry Scott Stokes, "For the Japanese, Sudden Misgivings About Nuclear Power," *New York Times,* May 16, 1981, p. 3.

58. "Japanese Nuclear Plant Closed for Six Months for Not Reporting Spill," *Wall Street Journal,* May 20, 1981, p. 30.

59. S. Prakash Sethi, "An Analytical Framework for Making Cross-Cultural Comparisons of Business Responses to Social Pressures: The Case of the United States and Japan," in Lee E. Preston (ed.), *Research in Corporate Social Performance and Policy,* vol. 1 (Greenwich, Conn.: JAI Press, 1978), pp. 46–47; see also Norman Pearlstine, "In Japan the Sokaiya Rise to the Rescue at Firm's Meetings," *Wall Street Journal,* May 29, 1974, pp. 1, 25.

60. Amendment to the Commercial Code, promulgated June 9, 1981, effective October 1, 1982, circular at *The Securities Deals Association of Japan,* June 1982.

61. Kenichi Ohmae, *The Mind of the Strategist: The Art of Japanese Business* (New York: McGraw-Hill, 1982), p. 239.
62. Norman Pearlstine, "Tarnished Image: Global Trust in Firms in Japan Is Damaged by a Major Collapse," *Wall Street Journal,* June 19, 1974, pp. 1, 24.
63. Sethi, "Analytical Framework for Making Cross-Cultural Comparisons," p. 47.
64. Ibid..
65. Sethi, *Japanese Business and Social Conflict,* pp. 96–99.
66. Ibid., pp. 99–100.
67. Ibid., p. 101.

THREE ▰▰▰▰▰▰▰▰▰▰▰▰▰▰▰▰▰▰▰▰▰▰▰▰▰▰▰▰▰▰▰▰

Operational Elements of the Japanese Management System and Personnel Practices

THE SUCCESS OF THE JAPANESE ECONOMIC SYSTEM IS DEEPLY ROOTED IN its cultural frame, and is intricately linked to its business-government nexus. However, most observers and admirers of Japanese business associate its success primarily with its management system and employee relations practices. The most important elements in the traditional Japanese management system consist of: decision making by consensus, a highly ritualized internal communication process, the active role of top and middle management, lifetime employment, a seniority-based wage and promotion system, company training by rotation, and company-based unions.

As has been stressed before, the drive toward group harmony and overt avoidance of conflict are crucial elements of Japanese life. In Japanese companies, as in Japanese life, an immense amount of energy is spent on finding out what others are thinking and how others feel about an issue, whether personal or professional. It is simply a *sine qua non* of Japanese life to know what everyone else is thinking and feeling. It is a world in which it is hard to keep secrets, in which housewives' gossip mills and businessmen's drinking parties churn every scrap of personally related news. But this is not to say there is invasion of others' privacy or that one acts on the basis of all information so received. The Japanese executive must know how his colleagues and superiors feel about a certain issue if he is to maintain group harmony. This must be preserved at all cost, or else he will suffer a loss of face and social ostracism.

The other factor is that Japanese companies foster this conformity of viewpoint in group members by hiring mostly at entry level and training employees not only in the functional aspects of business, but also in the company's philosophy, through in-house indoctrination programs. Through rigorous preemployment testing, referral systems, and long interviews, potential employees whose ideas and outlooks may be at variance with those the company wishes to encourage are not hired.[1]

Conformity of viewpoint in group members is further strengthened by the prevailing culture and social norms. The social status of a Japanese person depends largely on the status of the group to which he or she belongs. A Japanese employed at a well-established, large-scale company carries higher status, which can be extended to family members and relatives. He belongs to a "privileged" class. Accordingly, he is obligated to live up to the expectations and standards of his employer as well as the norms and expectations of the society. At the same time, an employer must also meet his employees' expectations. In other words, there is an implied "social contract" between employee, employer, and society at large. It should be noted here that there is usually no formal employment contract between an employee and an employer in Japan. Even under the lifetime employment system, an employee can be "pushed away" if he misbehaves—acts dishonestly or misappropriates corporate funds; becomes alcoholic; marries an "inappropriate" woman (someone from a low-status group); or associates with groups such as the Communist Party, consumer organizations, environmentalists, or other groups the company may view as undesirable. Employees are expected to abide strictly by the group's mores, norms, and philosophy. Discharge from employment is an unbearable event because the employee loses his base not only for economic life, but also for social life.

DECISION MAKING BY CONSENSUS

The Japanese decision-making process is that of consensus building, which is known as *ringisei,* or decision making by consensus. Under this sytem, any changes in procedures and routines, tactics, and even strategies are originated by those who are directly concerned with those changes. The final decision is made at the top level after an elaborate examination of the proposal through successively higher levels in the management hierarchy that results in acceptance or rejection of a decision only through consensus at every echelon. The decision process is best characterized as bottom up instead of top down, which is the essential characteristic of the decision-making process in a U.S. corporation (Exhibit 3-1).

Ringiseido literally means "a system of reverential inquiry about a superior's intentions." In this context, the term means obtaining approval on a proposed matter through the vertical, and sometimes horizontal, circulation of documents to concerned members in the organization. The *ringi* process may vary from one organization to the other, but usually consists of four

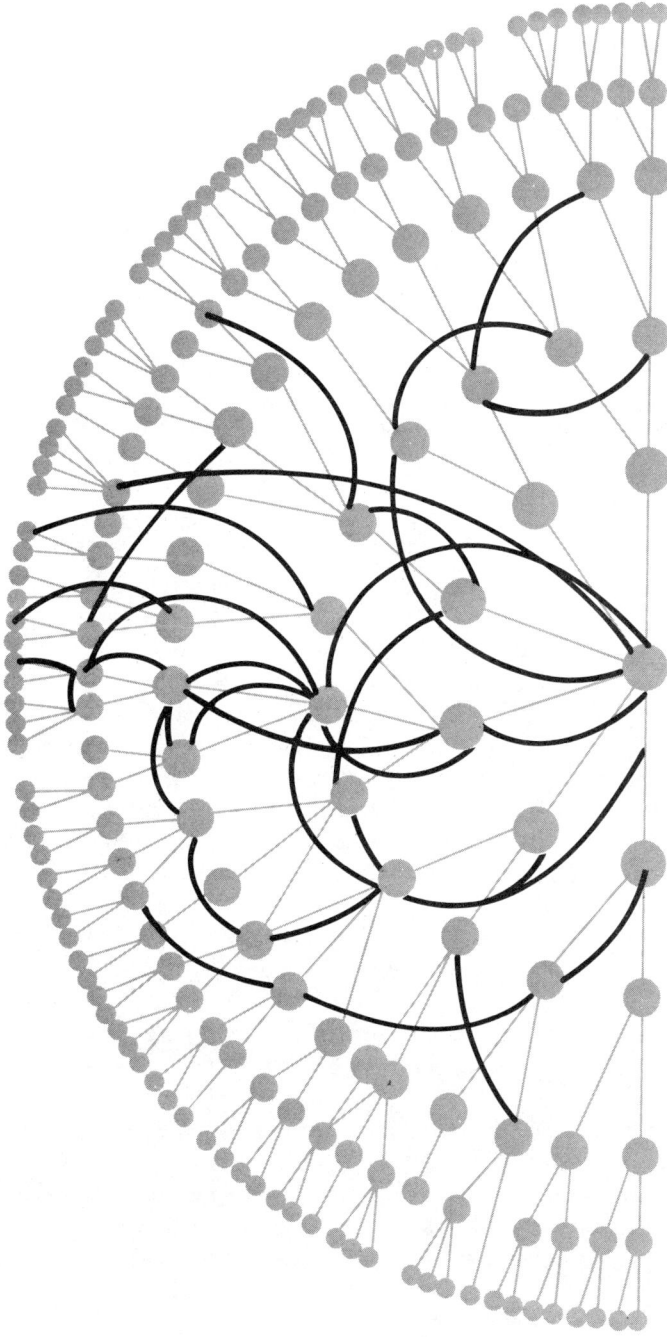

EXHIBIT 3–1 *Ringiseido:* Decision Making by Consensus

steps: proposal, circulation, approval, and record. The typical procedure, in simplified form, is described below.[2]

In case the decision to be made is of some importance, the initiator takes pains to ascertain, by informal discussion among other ways, the opinions and viewpoints of those who may be affected by it as well as of those who are in a position to influence its outcome[3]—especially the chief executive. The final document thus reflects the views of all concerned, thereby minimizing areas of potential disagreement and conflict. This point is of considerable importance and should not be overlooked.

When a lower- or middle-level manager is confronted with a problem and wishes to present a solution, a meeting is called in that particular section by the section chief (*kachō*). The members of a section may agree that the idea should be pursued, but they may also feel that it needs the overall support of the firm. The section chief reports this to his department head or department manager (*buchō*), and consults with him. If the department head expresses support for the section's proposal, the time-consuming activity of getting a general consensus starts.

First, a general consensus among the persons who will be directly and indirectly involved with implementation in a department is sought. Then an overall, but informal, consensus in the firm is sought. The department head may arrange a meeting with the other departments concerned. Each department sends one department head, one section chief, and perhaps two subsection chiefs (*kakarichō*, sometimes called supervisors). They are the ones who would be involved in the implementation stage. If there are four departments involved, 16 to 20 persons will attend the meeting. If the opinion of specialists or experts on the shop floor is needed, they will be represented. In fact, the meeting is aimed mainly at exchanging information among the involved persons in order to implement the plan. Through the discussion, other information and materials may be found to be needed. In that case, the initiator and his colleagues, under the leadership of the section chief, go about, formally and informally, from section to section and from department to department to collect the necessary information and prepare the documents to be presented at the next meeting. This prior coordination is vital for the *ringi* system.

After more meetings, the department judges it has attained an informal agreement from all other departments concerned. The procedure up to this point is called *nemawashi* (meaning informal discussion and consultation before the formal proposal is presented). This is the moment when the formal procedure starts. First, the initiator and his colleagues under the section chief's supervision write up a formal document of request, the *ringi-sho* (*sho* means "document"), which outlines the problem and details of the plan for its solution. Also enclosed are supportive information and materials. The *ringi-sho* is then circulated among various successively higher echelons of management for approval. Each responsible manager or executive concerned affixes his seal of approval. The number of seals can reach 10 or 12. The *ringi-sho* finally goes up to top management for formal authorization and the final "go-ahead."

The *ringi* process can be divided in two broad categories: *nemawashi* and *ringi.* The *nemawashi* process is that of decision making by consensus, and the *ringi* process is the formal procedure to obtain authorization.[4] Once a proposal is accepted during the *nemawashi* stage, it is seldom opposed or rejected at the *ringi* stage. Some scholars have labeled the *ringi* system a "consensual understanding,"[5] and "confirmation-authorization"[6] process of decision making. The *ringi,* in this context, is used to confirm that all elements of disagreement have been eliminated at the *nemawashi* stage. It ensures that the responsibility is assumed by all persons who have affixed their seals of approval.

Consensus Decision Making and Internal Communication[7]

The process of communication within a Japanese organization is very much akin to the mating dance of penguins. Communicators resort to both verbal and nonverbal communication. A great deal of ritualistic communication precedes and follows any substantive discussion. Participants know and understand who is going to say what, and to whom, before it actually takes place. And yet all concerned would be quite offended if the ritualistic behavior was not strictly observed. A great deal is made of forms and gestures, leaving the listener to interpret the meaning of what is being said.

The communication process, however, is quite different when it takes place *within* a group and *between* two or more groups. A group is defined here as those who work together in an office, section, or department, and have face-to-face, intimate, and less structured relationships. The size of the group varies according to the company. Note that this is the group that plays an integral role in initiating a proposal, in getting coordination from other groups to promote informal consensus among the concerned groups, and in writing up a *ringi-sho.* Employees who are in different offices or departments may not have similar relationships and personal ties and therefore their relationships are more functional, formal, and vertically structured. For ease of analysis, the former group will be referred to as the *primary* group, and the latter as the *secondary* group. According to Nakane: "Since the groups are highly institutionalized, it is easy to recognize the hierarchical order among them; and this is the only acceptable pattern among the Japanese for communication that takes place between individuals and between groups, who otherwise have weak relations or none at all."[8]

There are many differences between the behavior patterns of the two groups. When a primary group holds a meeting, the subject to be discussed is gone into at length. The atmosphere is highly informal. It engenders a feeling of camaradarie and encourages all group members to talk freely. There is an intimate and familiar feeling of participating in a democratic process that helps members of lower status feel comfortable. The first part of the meeting consists of discussing factual information pertaining to the issue. Gradually the members begin to sense the direction of the group's opinion. Exposition rather than argument is the nature of the discourse. Understanding and acceptance among members is appreciated. After this is done, the members try to adjust or arrive at a new line based on the points of disagreement.

Direct conflict is avoided. If a member wishes to present an opinion, he does so by prefacing it with "I happen to know someone who thinks that . . ." or "Let me say this, but I'm just thinking out loud." This gives him a way out if he sees that what he says is radically opposed by other members. What he wants is a situation of understanding and acceptance by the other members before he lets his own opinion be known. Occasionally a heated argument does take place. When this occurs, one of the more prestigious members tries to reconcile the two sides, or one of the middle- or lower-status members tries for some sort of comic relief. After working very hard toward acceptance by all, everyone knows that consensus is near when 70 percent of the members are in agreement. At that point the minority concedes and is willing to support the decision. Primary groups believe that there must be a basic accord, and that if they try their best, they can come to a unanimous conclusion. In this way, the decision will be implemented with a high degree of cooperation.

The secondary groups, on the other hand, are the formal, more ritualistic organs of the company. Their meetings are all ceremony and mark the final stage of reaching a decision. Although the members are also members of various primary groups, when they become members of a secondary group, they change their behavior accordingly. Each man represents a particular group, and must act in exactly the manner the group tells him to. If something unexpected arises during the course of the meeting, he may have to ask that the meeting be suspended so he can confer with his group in order to ascertain how it wants him to handle the new situation.

The real power sources at these meetings are the "men of influence," sometimes called the "black presence." They always remain behind the scenes and can be found in every field and every large or influential group in Japan. Over a period of time, they have managed to establish effective personal relations with influential members of various groups. The Japanese term for these influential men is *kuromaku* (a term from the traditional kabuki drama meaning "black curtain"). Figuratively, it is used to connote power behind the throne. Perhaps the two most influential power brokers in business and politics in Japan are Yoshio Kodama and Kenji Osano (who were involved in the Lockheed scandal in 1976.)[9]

Relations between these "men of influence" are established through common bonds of age, school, or workplace. If these contacts are lacking, a relationship can be developed through attraction during the course of various meetings attended by both. These men rarely hold meetings together. Instead, they use informal channels to relay information among themselves. Their intercommunication is even more open than that among members of a primary group because they can always say that they are stating their group's opinion. Once they have reached a decision, they go about writing the scenario for the coming meeting. By the time the meeting is convened, each participant has been well rehearsed for the drama that is to unfold. There is even a scenarist, who sits next to the chairman to make sure the meeting goes exactly as planned. If a minor figure who was not given any lines, presents a contrary opinion, it is listened to politely; the chairman thanks him for his opinion, and says it will be considered. This is a face-saving way of ignoring him. Actually, the scenarists want situations like this to arise so that the process will have the appearance of being democratic. The dissenter is well aware of his powerlessness in the hierarchy, and his purpose is expressive rather than communicative. And since he is given a chance to express himself, it is easier for him to accept the final decision. In Nakane's words, "It is thus a highly political procedure. The power and the authority of both a formal and an informal hierarchy are effectively employed."[10]

Role of Middle Management

Middle managers perform an essential role in the *ringi* system. How well a middle manager can perform this role will depend largely on his personal relationships and ties with other managers. Consensus, before a decision is taken, requires a flood of information, and much of the information that is relevant is produced at the place of implementation.[11] Thus, the demand for information functions to pull the decision process down toward the implementation level, while the need for the decision process to be exposed to corporate strategies pushes it upward. The equilibrium point of these two conflicting demands is generally found at the middle management level. The system is effective only if the middle management is competent in terms of its abilities to bridge the gap between lower and higher levels of management. Personal relationships with other people in the organization thus become critically important. In Japanese firms, middle managers acquire these attributes though the system of job rotation from one function to another and the training programs that go with them. The system also encourages personal ties that enhance the efficiency of information flows. Japanese middle

EXHIBIT 3–2 Organizational Structure and Seniority Order

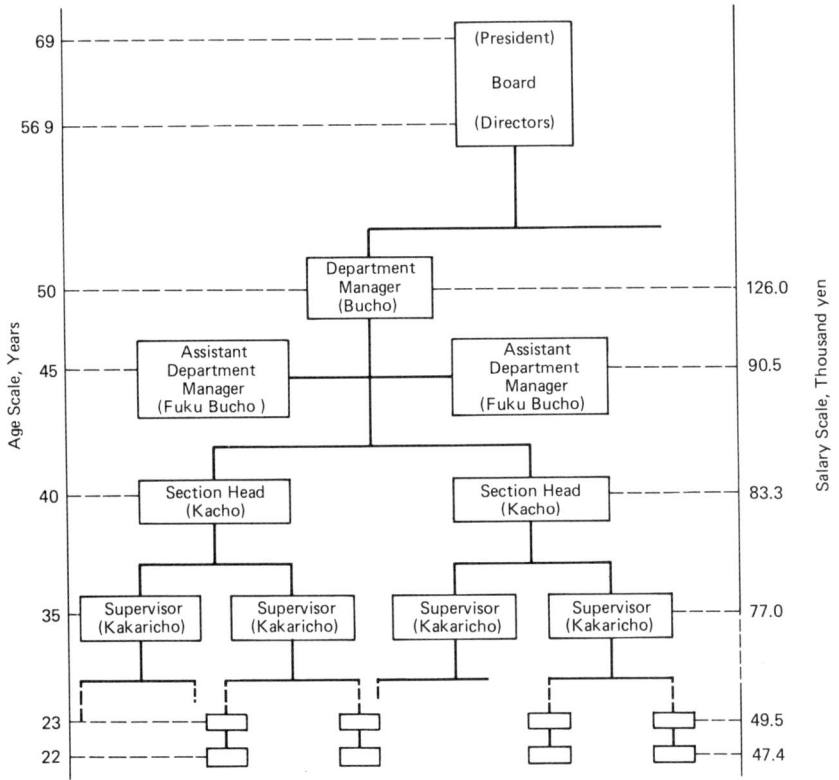

EXHIBIT 3–3 Typical Office Layout: One Department in One Room

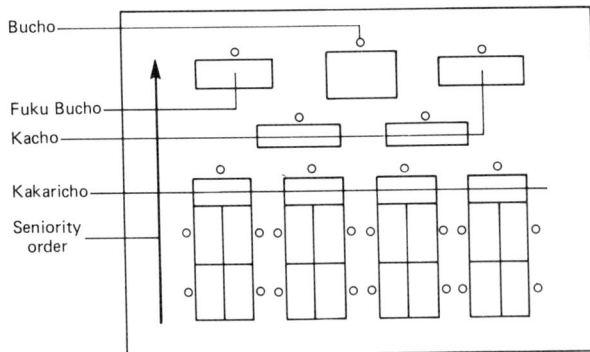

SOURCE: Naoto Sasaki, *Management and Industrial Structure in Japan* (New York: Pergamon, 1981), pp. 73–74.

managers, therefore, perform the essential role of closing the gap between decision making and its implementation in their activity domains. The closeness of the decision making to the implementation results in a high level of morale and motivation among middle and lower managers.

The ideal office, from the point of view of smooth relations and a "better" working environment, has few members and an ascending distribution of ages within its hierarchy. Under the seniority-based promotion system, older men usually occupy higher positions. Exhibit 3–2 is an example of a seniority-based system in a large bank in Japan. Note that seniority is a major source of control. Exhibit 3–3 shows a typical office layout in Japanese corporations. One department occupies a large room in which employees of all levels sit at desks arranged in much the same order as the organization chart. It takes about 13 to 15 years to get a section chief position. During this period, an employee may be transferred around in the department and in other departments in order to become a "generalist" rather than a "specialist" in the American or Western sense.[12]

The group is not static but dynamic; the members transfer in and out frequently.[13] Whenever a member is transferred to another section, he establishes a similar relationship in the new department. He may still keep personal relationships with his former senior and junior officials. These personal ties are sometimes transformed into factions, which were explained in the previous chapter.

Role of Top Management

Under the *ringi* system, presidential or top management leadership is expected to cope mainly with crisis situations or with abrupt and clear-cut changes in the direction of the firm.[14] The chief executive cannot alter the *ringi-sho,* and since he seldom disapproves of it, this could mean he has little or no real authority in the running of the organization. However, since the lower-echelon managers will take every precaution to ensure that no *ringi-sho* which will not meet his approval will reach the chief executive, such conflict is avoided. Once the general direction of the firm is communicated to the middle and lower management echelons, both operational decisions and incremental changes are entrusted to their initiatives. Most of the working hours of the top management in Japanese corporations are occupied with establishing and maintaining "private" relations with responsible men in policymaking positions in other corporations and government departments. This is accomplished through the regular and frequent, formal and informal, contacts demanded by the sociopolitical environment in Japan and evidenced in the close cooperation between the Japanese government and private industry.[15]

PERSONNEL POLICIES

Japanese business has been very successful in harnessing such elements of
Japanese culture as loyalty to superiors, group orientation, self-pride, and
hard work to its advantage and ultimately that of the nation. Most large
Japanese corporations have personnel policies quite distinct and different

EXHIBIT 3–4 Employee Composition of a Japanese Firm

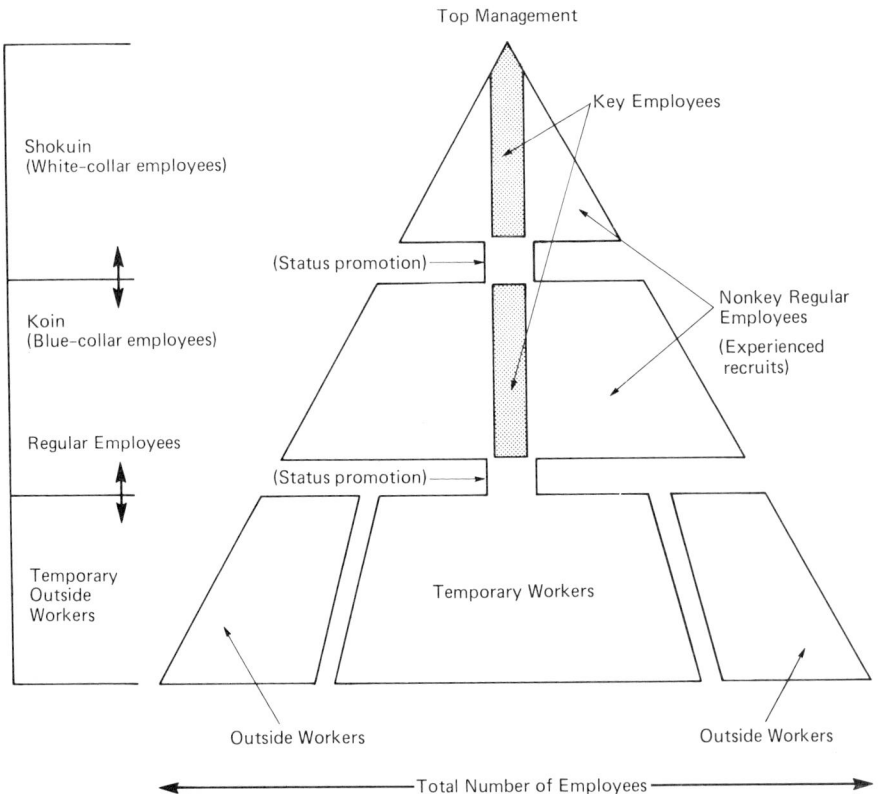

Top Management

Key Employees

Shokuin
(White-collar employees)

(Status promotion)

Nonkey Regular
Employees

(Experienced
recruits)

Koin
(Blue-collar employees)

Regular Employees

(Status promotion)

Temporary
Outside
Workers

Temporary Workers

Outside Workers   Outside Workers

Total Number of Employees

SOURCE: S. Prakash Sethi, *Japanese Business and Social Conflict* (Cambridge,
Mass.: Ballinger, 1975), p. 64.

from those of the West: lifetime employment, seniority-based wage and promotion systems, and company- rather than trade- or profession-oriented unions.[16] Employees are usually trained within the company, typically on more than one job or function. It must be noted that all these practices are found to some degree in Western countries, including the United States. However, in Japan they have been in widespread use since World War II, and their use is culturally accepted, socially encouraged, and officially sanctioned. Exhibit 3–4 shows the composition of the workforce in a typical Japanese firm.

Lifetime Employment

Lifetime employment creates a high degree of employee stability and, coupled with other management practices and personnel policies, generates tremendous employee loyalty toward the company, with all that it entails. A company can invest money in the training of an employee, confident in the belief that once he is trained, he will not be hired away by a competitor. A Japanese enters a company right after graduation from his school and stays in the company until the official retirement age of 57 to 60. His job security is virtually guaranteed unless he is accused of misconduct.

The origin of lifetime employment can be traced to the family tradition of the old *zaibatsu,* according to which a youth entered the firm as an apprentice and ended up being a trusted manager or founder of a new branch house. The bureaucratic structure of government and early state-owned enterprises provided another forum for the adaptation of the old master and vassal system. An element that added a fillip to this practice and institutionalized the arrangement in modern enterprise came into its own after World War II, when prevailing socioeconomic conditions made such an arrangement both feasible and desirable.

The present form of the lifetime employment system, which includes both blue-collar and white-collar workers, emerged after World War II when workers and unions tried to improve employment security because of the crisis atmosphere of the postwar period.[17] In the 1950s, this kind of job security became an established practice primarily in large firms, mainly because the system was found to be the most effective means to make employees identify their own interests with those of the corporation. Tsurumi holds that the job security offered by lifetime employment is "not a product of Japanese paternalism, but a necessary economy to all persons in the firm."[18]

The success of the system depends on the fulfillment of a dual set of expectations that are deeply rooted in Japanese traditions and cultural norms. For the worker, there is the expectation that he will be able to stay with his chosen firm, and that he intends to do so. This intention is conditioned by the fact that he will be within the norm of Japanese occupational life and that he has a good deal to gain financially by staying on. For the employer, there is the expectation that the worker will stay, provided he is offered "standard" wages and conditions of employment. Social conditions and cultural norms impose a sense of obligation on the employer, who is expected to provide work for his employees and take care of them. Moreover, he stands to face a tremendous loss of worker morale, not to mention union resistance, government pressure, and public ill will, if he chooses to deviate significantly from the social norm.[19]

This system provides the employee with a sense of security. He has a multitude of opportunities for training and upward mobility within the company, with the accompanying psychic satisfaction. At the same time, the performance of an employee can be evaluated over a period of years.

Seniority-Based Wage System

Under the seniority-based wage system, the remuneration of a worker is determined primarily on the basis of the number of years he has spent with the company, subject to age and level of education at the time of entry.[20] The wages neatly coincide with the peaks and valleys in expenditures over the life cycle of the worker and his family (Exhibit 3–5). The seniority-based wage system is the dominant practice in Japan and, although the difference between the incomes of younger and older workers is greater in larger enterprises, the prevalence of wage differentials according to age and length of service is found in all enterprises, regardless of size.

The seniority-based system takes away the often destructive individual competition between employees and promotes a more harmonious group relationship in which each employee works for the benefit of the entire group, secure in the belief that he will prosper with the group and that, in due time, he will acquire the benefits that accrue for long and faithful service. The seniority-based system assumes that longer experience makes an employee more valuable. Because of the *ie* (group or community) framework, a supervisor must be more than a technically superior worker. He must be able to maintain order in the group and look after its well-being. Thus, the older manager acts as the symbol of group strength and continuity. He also functions as the opinion leader and consolidates the community. He acts as the elder statesman and assists group members in all aspects of their lives, including non-job-related activities such as arranging marriages, settling family disputes, and so on. Middle managers contribute to the achievement of community purpose by educating, training, and controlling the young, and by acquainting them with the rules of the community. "These abilities correspond to a skill of seniority. . . . Seniority-based skill is not a simple manual skill, but an overall mental and physical skill originated in a community."[21]

EXHIBIT 3–5 Relationship between Seniority-Based Wage System, Family Expenditure Pattern, and Life Cycle

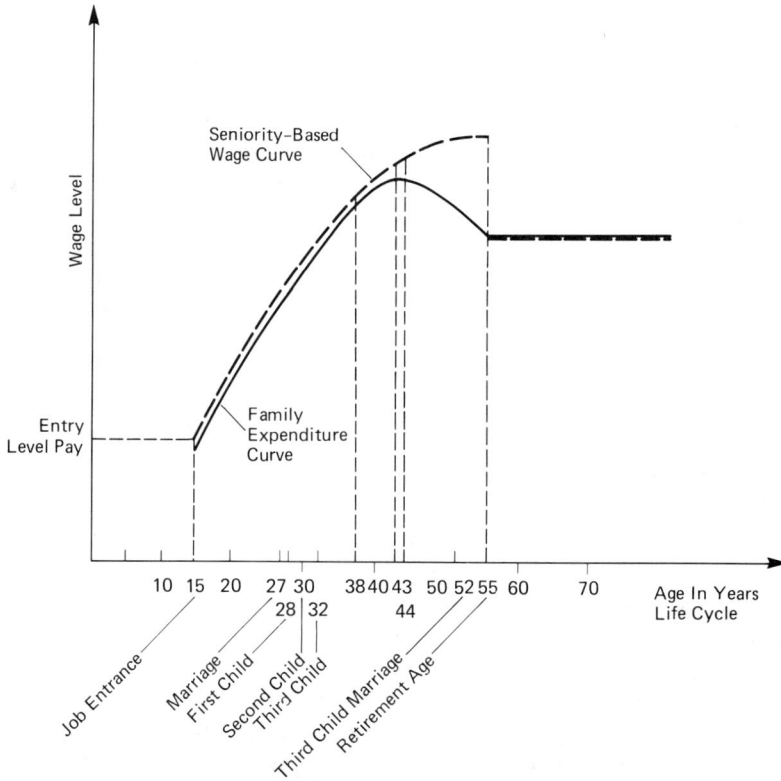

SOURCE: S. Prakash Sethi, *Japanese Business and Social Conflict* (Cambridge, Mass.: Ballinger, 1975), p. 70.

In-Company Training by Rotation

A Japanese employee keeps on training as a regular part of his job until he retires. At the same time, he is trained not only in his job, but in other jobs at his job level. The on-the-job training by rotation promotes tremendous flexibility in the workforce, and also helps develop the middle or upper managers into "generalists" with broader perspective on and experience of the company's business and with the wider human contacts and friendships that are vital for generating consensus. Due to lifetime employment, an employee seldoms gets an opportunity to work outside his corporate group. Generally speaking, mobility between firms is almost nonexistent, whereas mobility within a firm is almost unlimited.

The merits of management development by job rotation are several. (1) It enables the firm to reassign production and office workers more freely. (2) The Japanese employees, also because of their job security, are more receptive to organizational changes and introduction of new technology or machinery.[22] (3) Wider experience within the firm tends to nurture the goals of the total firm, rather than those of specific subunits. (4) It can produce high-quality general managers. The job rotation system allows an employee to build wider interpersonal relationships that may result in freer information exchange. (5) Finally, widespread use of on-the-job training in large companies tends to diminish an employee's capacity to work effectively if he moves to another corporation and thus discourages mobility between competing firms.

Management of Human Resources

The Japanese notion of family—involving not only its own employees but also it suppliers and subcontractors—has been instrumental in creating a highly efficient and fully integrated system of manufacturing, with the resultant lowering of costs and improvement of quality. The essential elements of this system are as follows.

1. An extensive effort is made to integrate human factors into the production system. Japanese companies strive to improve the quality of their products not only by automation and capital investment, but also by taking seriously their employee's suggestions for improvements, especially through employee participation in quality control circles. It should be noted here that Japanese employees tend to be receptive to automation primarily because of their job security. Japanese workers are encouraged, even required, to make suggestions as to how the production process can be improved. Middle and even top managers take them seriously because they readily acknowledge and admit that the workers are closest to a problem. The workers make suggestions primarily because of their sense of "oneness"; they see management problems as their own. The suggestions make the managers aware of shop floor problems and improve the situation.[23]

2. There is an emphasis on quality control, often referred to in terms of "do it right the first time." The quality control circles (QC) not only identify a problem, but also collectively solve it. On an average, a QC circle

has eight to ten members, with a supervisor as the leader. The circles emphasize not only technical matters, but a sense of involvement and quality consciousness on the part of the workers.[24]

3. Another important element is the low level of inventories, made possible through close location of subcontractors and finely coordinated delivery schedules. The system is nicknamed "just-in-time" or *Kanban* and is widely practiced by Japanese companies. For example, by maintaining close ties with suppliers, financially and geographically, Toyota, Toyokogyo and other auto companies are able to maintain production schedules with less than a day's worth of parts on hand. One of Toyota's suppliers was reported to deliver parts almost every hour by truck, based on the needs of Toyota.[25] This schedule is striking when compared with those of U.S. producers, who usually stock several weeks' worth of parts in inventory. The system provides significant cost advantage to the Japanese auto producers. It is estimated that the Japanese hold a cost advantage of over $2,200 per car, which is attributed to such production improvements as efficient assembly lines, automation, and low inventory levels.[26] The entire process of integrated production flows involving all elements of the system has been heralded as the "sixth stage" of the manufacturing revolution and is credited to a significant degree for the Japanese success.[27]

The small inventory level in each stage of production makes the weak links clear, because any breakdown in one stage has spillover effects on all the later stages. As a result, the weak links get much attention. The system also places considerable pressure on suppliers. Usually, suppliers have a long working relationship with the companies. If the supplier delivers defective parts, the company's production line is shut down because of the small inventory level. This system makes the suppliers constantly conscious about the quality of parts and aware of the consequences of failure.[28] The production efficiency from the integration of the labor force into production process, however, does not comes about without social costs and economic risks. For example, low inventory levels places constant pressure on managers and workers. Even a slight mistake in inventory orders or unforeseen interruptions in delivery lead to downtime and loss of production.

Company-Oriented Unionization

Japanese unions are usually organized on a company basis, as opposed to the craft or industrywide unions common in the United States. The company union gives both management and workers an identity of purpose and provides an environment in which there is greater cooperation for the achievement of common goals. The system had its origins in the pre-World War II Japan. The company-oriented unions (hereinafter referred to as *enterprise unions*) have the following distinct characteristics: The membership extends to both blue-collar and white-collar workers with regular employee status. White-collar employees up to the level of section chief are included. Union officials consist solely of the company employees. The union is regarded as an autonomous organization whose sovereignty is recognized within the nationwide union power structure.[29] An enterprise union will negotiate independently with its own employer, except for a short period of collective bargaining with the affiliated federation, the so-called Spring Labor Offensive.

The characteristics of the resolution of labor disputes are quite different from those of the West. First, there is the societal pressure toward consensus. Two, there is the tendency for industrial action to be taken in a demonstrative form—to make the public aware that the workers feel the employer has failed to do what he should to meet their needs. Three, the union, mindful of the extent to which its members' interests are bound up with those of the enterprise, is likely to refrain from any action likely to prejudice its long-term future.[30]

LIMITATIONS AND DRAWBACKS OF THE JAPANESE MANAGEMENT SYSTEM

The benefits of the Japanese management system have been well publicized. Little attention, however, has been paid to the costs the system afflicts on society in general, and workers in particular. And these costs may be substantial in terms of loss of individual freedom that may border on involuntary servitude, a rigid social structure, and sacrifice of other values individuals and groups may cherish but may be unable to exercise because of the intolerance of a system that is structurally imposed and from which escape may be all but impossible. Another fact that is little known outside academic circles is that the benevolence of the Japanese management system is not bestowed on even a majority of workers, but instead is limited to a small minority. The large majority of workers toil for substandard wages, work under unsafe conditions, and account for a greater part of the Japanese success.

Another inherent drawback of the system is that it imposes inefficiencies on the decision-making process and creates rigidity in a firm's operating costs. The system is slow to respond to changes in the external environment, lacks incentives to reward creativity and innovativeness, and has adverse second-order effects on those who are forced to bear the brunt of its costs.

Estimates vary as to how many Japanese workers actually enjoy the privileges of lifetime employment because of the ambiguous nature of the employment relationship. Various scholars put the number at approximately 35 to 40 percent of the total workforce, with large manufacturing companies and trading houses covering between 40 to 60 percent of their employees. Women are almost never granted this benefit and therefore invariably occupy the lowest-paid jobs in the industry. The secondary and tertiary sectors of the economy provide lifetime employment and seniority-based wages to a very small fraction of their workers. The remaining workforce is divided into two groups: Experienced recruits or midterm employees who did not join the company right after school graduation, and temporary workers. Temporary workers include manual workers and part-time, seasonal, or subcontracted workers.

Thus while one may marvel at the dignity conferred on the worker by guaranteeing him a job and a wage quite independent of his precisely measured performance, the reality of the system is quite different. The segregation of employees into lifetime employees and temporary workers means differential treatment for doing essentially similar work. It creates considerable financial hardship for temporary workers because they lack job security and other job-related fringe benefits, and gives rise to other social problems. Since unions in Japan do not protect their workers in the sense that American and European unions do, corporations can shift the burden of extra costs to subcontractors and temporary workers, who end up bearing the major brunt of downturns in economy. The plight of temporary workers, even in such large organizations as Toyota, has been one of Japan's best-kept secrets and has only recently begun to surface. In a recently published book, *Japan in the Passing Lane,* the author, Satoshi Kamata,[31] a freelance reporter, presents a vivid and painful picture of a Toyota assembly plant where workers are constantly subjected to assembly line speedups; where worker-related injuries are quite high; and where the best safely devices are worker exhortation to avoid accidents regardless of unsafe equipment, poor working conditions, or fatigue. Moreover, workers rarely have any privacy or individual freedom. They are closely supervised in their "bachelor" dormitories. Some critics of this book have argued that Toyota is not a typical Japanese employer, having close ties with the erstwhile Imperial Army and present Defense Forces. It is further suggested that even Toyota has made changes in its operations, and current working conditions are not so harsh.[32] Nevertheless, the case does point to another side of Japanese business that must not be ignored in balancing the costs and benefits of the Japanese miracle. Good fishing can be fun from the fisherman's viewpoint. However, the fish will have an altogether different perspective.

Another loophole in the practice of lifetime employment is the retirement age, which for most employees is 55. It should be noted that the retirement age varies according to the prosperity of the industry or company. For a prospering or healthy company and government, the retirement age is now around 58. For a declining industry it is typically below 55. The retirement benefits offered by Japanese companies are quite meager. Therefore, a retired person faces considerable financial hardship.[33] Because of the widespread development of the nuclear family, social norms have changed. The eldest son (or other children and their wives) are not as willing to take care of the retiree as they had been in the past. The practice of retirement at 55 was culturally accepted based on the old custom that the eldest son would look after the well-being of the father, or retiree. In Japan, average life expectancy now goes well beyond 70, and 55 is only late middle age. Eligibility for welfare pensions does not begin until 60. However, work does not end even at age 60. Pension payments are not large enough to afford the retiree a work-free living income. Thus, for almost a third of his productive, and most experienced, life a Japanese worker is forced to work as a "temporary" worker at wages that are only a fraction of those he is worth, and that are paid to other employees with less experience and maturity.

Another by-product of compulsory early retirement and low level of retirement benefits is that the relatively small number of executives who escape retirement at 58 and reach the exalted state of senior executives are not to prone to retire at 60 or 65. Firms are thus often burdened with highly paid senior executives who are long past their productive years. They also become barriers for younger executives waiting to move up the corporate ladder.

The 1980 census revealed that 81.6 percent of Japanese men between the ages of 60 and 64, and 45.4 percent of those age 65 and over, were still in the labor force.[34] These figures are by far the highest in the industrialized world. In short, Japanese employment is structured around young workers. Taking this into account, employment practices in the West may come closer to the ideal of "lifetime" employment than those of Japanese companies. In the West, the word "retirement" carries a sense of happiness and reward. In Japan, the word "retirement" means a cut in pay, almost no job and financial security, and substantial loss of rank. In the current state of the economy, it is hard for the retirees to find jobs; workers at 55 years of age and over have found ten applicants waiting in line for every job.[35]

There are other drawbacks to the lifetime employment system from the viewpoint of the firm. Lifetime employment turns labor costs into fixed overhead costs. Large-scale firms are not immune to recession, and are also subject to cyclical changes in the economy. Even under recessionary conditions, they are forced to operate their plants at maximum capacity and push for exports at low prices in order to keep their workers employed. So Japanese companies have developed other ways to gain flexibility in using their workers.[36] Employees who are in a depressed division may be transferred to an expanding division within the company or loaned out to other companies in a related group. Some companies put idle employees into training programs. Production employees become janitors or repairmen or gardeners and even salesmen. Another tactic is the practice of retirement at age 58. A permanent employee "retires" at 58 and may become a temporary worker at the company or at another related company with much lower salary, fewer fringe benefits, and practically no job security. Another limitation of the lifetime employment system is that corporations have difficulty in assimilating and developing new ideas and technology by hiring experts from outside. Because of the closed nature and rigidity of the system, it is rare that a company can hire outside experts on demand.

Another apparent drawback of the seniority-based wage system is the difficulty in rewarding individual creativity and excellence, thereby possibly reducing motivation among able employees. And since compensation is based primarily on seniority but not on performance, companies may be paying higher wages to those who are not capable or competent. Another problem is that the system has created a large numbers of middle managers in Japanese companies.[37] The high rate of economic growth in the 1960s caused many companies to hire more college graduates. The years 1965 to 1971 were the ones during which large numbers of the baby-boom generation (born right after World War II) graduated from universities. They will become middle managers as they age. Usually, a healthy hierarchical organization consists of a relatively larger number of lower-level managers and a smaller number of middle- to high-level managers. However, an inevitable result of the seniority-based system, coupled with the lifetime employment system, is the accumulation of employees at the middle management levels. Since upward mobility is not likely to be available to most of them, it has the potential for creating a large number of frustrated and even despondent managers, a situation that does not augur well for Japan.

The *ringi* system avoids individual assumption of responsibility for mistakes, just as it denies credit for bold decisions, mainly because of the nature of the superior-subordinate relationship. Because of subordinates' veneration of the authority of higher management, they will accept the group's decision if it is approved by higher management and commit themselves to implementing the plan. In return, higher management, especially the president, is willing to accept a decision approved by lower management, and to assume the responsibility for its outcome and consequences.[38]

The drawback of the consensus system is its excruciatingly slow pace. However, as Peter Drucker has argued, the strength of this system stems from its ability to induce the commitment of those involved in its implementation, thereby speeding up the whole process.[39] The longer period of decision making may also allow for many considerations to be taken into account, thereby increasing the probability that the decision will be a correct one. Decision making by consensus fosters group strength to cope with pressures from outside. Notwithstanding, this system may not work efficiently if a problem suddenly becomes acute and demands a decision in the middle of the process. In this case, a decision has to be made without a consensus and may result in lower morale and commitment during the implementation stage.

NOTES

1. Sethi, *Japanese Business and Social Conflict,* (Cambridge, Mass.: Ballinger, 1975), pp. 52–53.
2. Naoto Sasaki, *Management and Industrial Structure in Japan,* (New York: Pergamon, 1981), pp. 57–58.
3. Michael Yoshino, *Japan's Managerial System: Tradition and Innovation* (Cambridge, Mass.: MIT Press, 1968), p. 225.
4. "Japanese Managers Talk about How Their System Works," *Fortune* (November 1977), pp. 131–132.
5. William M. Fox, "Japanese Management: Tradition under Strain," *Business Horizons* (August 1977), p. 79.
6. Ichiro Hattori, "A Proposition on Efficient Decision-Making in the Japanese Corporation," *Columbia Journal of World Business* (Summer 1978), p. 12.
7. The discussion in this section is substantially derived from Sethi, *Japanese Business and Social Conflict,* pp. 56–59.
8. Chie Nakane, "An Interpretation of Group Cohesiveness in Japanese Society." Paper presented at the Regional Seminar, Center for Japanese and Korean Studies, Berkeley, University of California, March 1, 1974, p. 12.
9. Richard Halloran, "5 Japanese Had Key Roles in Pushing Lockheed Bids," *New York Times,* March 1, 1976, pp. 1, 8.
10. Nakane, "An Interpretation on Group Cohesiveness in Japanese Society," pp. 19–20.
11. Sasaki, *Management and Industrial Structure in Japan,* p. 77.
12. Peter F. Drucker, "What We Can Learn from Japanese Management," *Harvard Business Review* (March–April 1971), pp. 117–118.
13. Thomas P. Rohlen, "The Company Work Group," in Ezra Vogel, *Modern Japanese Organization and Decision-Making,* (Berkeley: University of California Press, 1975), pp. 200–201.
14. Yoshi Tsurumi, *The Japanese Are Coming: A Multinational Interaction of Firms and Politics* (Cambridge, Mass.: Ballinger, 1976), pp. 229–231.
15. Peter F. Drucker, "Behind Japan's Success," *Harvard Business Review* (January–February 1981), p. 87.
16. The discussion in this section is largely derived from Sethi, *Japanese Business and Social Conflict,* pp. 60–71.
17. Bradley M. Richardson and Taizo Ueda (eds.), *Business and Society in Japan: Fundamentals for Businessmen* (New York: Praeger, 1981), pp. 31–32.
18. Tsurumi, *The Japanese Are Coming,* pp. 221.
19. Ronald P. Dore, *British Factory—Japanese Factory: The Origins of National Diversity in Industrial Relations* (Berkeley: University of California Press, 1973), p. 35.
20. *The Development of Industrial Relations Systems: Some Implications of Japanese Experience* (Paris: OECD, 1977), p. 19.

21. Masumi Tsuda, "Lifetime Employment and Seniority-Based Wage System." Paper presented at the International Symposium on the Japanese Way of Management and International Business, Tokyo, November 27–28, 1973, p. 25.
22. Arthur M. Whitehill and Shin-ichi Takezawa, "Workplace Harmony: Another Japanese 'Miracle'?," *Columbia Journal of World Business* (Fall 1978), pp. 26–28.
23. For a contrary view, see Kamata, *Japan in the Passing Lane.*
24. David M. Amsden and Robert T. Amsden (eds.), *QC Circles: Applications, Tools and Theory* (Milwaukee: American Society for Quality Control, 1976). Sang M. Lee and Gary Schwendiman, *Management by Japanese Systems* (New York: Praeger, 1982), part II.
25. John Holusha, " 'Just-in-Time' System Cuts Japan's Auto Costs," *New York Times,* March 25, 1983, pp. 1, 37; see also, for a detailed discussion of Toyota's *kanban* system, Nihon Noritsu Kyokai, *Toyota No Genba Kanri* [Shopfloor Management System of Toyota] (Tokyo: Nihon Noritsu Kyokai, 1982).
26. John Holusha, "Japan's Car Makers Facing Tests Abroad as Industry's Leader," *New York Times,* April 1, 1983, pp. 1, 41.
27. William J. Abernathy, Kim B. Clark, and Alan M. Kantrow, *Industrial Renaissance: Producing a Competitive Future for America* (New York: Basic Books, 1983), p. 40; See also Steven C. Wheelwright, "Japan—Where Operations Really Are Strategic," *Harvard Business Review* (July–August 1981), pp. 67–74; Robert E. Cole, "Learning from the Japanese: Prospects and Pitfalls," *Management Review* (September 1980), pp. 22–28, 38–42.
28. Holusha, " 'Just-in-Time' System Cuts Japan's Auto Costs." See also the book by Taiichi Ohno, the retired Toyota executive credited with the development of the "just-in-time" system, Taiichi Ohno, *Toyota Seisan Hoshiki* [The Toyota Production System] (Tokyo: Diamond, 1978); Taiichi Ohno, "How the Toyota Production System Was Created," a translation of chapter I, "Needs Kara No Shuppatsu" [Needs as the Mainspring], J. T. Gallagher, *Japan Economic Studies* (Summer 1982), pp. 83–101.
29. Ernest Van Helvoort, *The Japanese Working Man: What Choice? What Reward?* (Vancouver: University of British Columbia Press, 1979), pp. 130–131; See also Tadashi Hanami, *Labor Relations in Japan Today* (Tokyo: Kodansha International, 1979); Koji Taira, *Economic Development and the Labor Market in Japan* (New York: Columbia University Press, 1970).
30. *The Development of Industrial Relations: Some Implications of Japanese Experience,* pp. 25–26; John Holusha, "Japan's Productive Car Unions," *New York Times,* March 30, 1983, pp. 27, 43.
31. Kamata, *Japan in the Passing Lane* (New York: Pantheon, 1982).
32. See the Introduction by Ronald Dore in Kamata, *Japan in the Passing Lane,* pp. ix–xi.
33. Mitsuo Tajima, "Japan's Cold Indifference toward Old People," *Wall Street Journal,* November 8, 1982, p. 23; Masayoshi Kanabayashi, "Economic Woes Spur Firms in Japan to Alter Lifetime Job Security," *Wall Street Journal,* December 21, 1977, pp. 1, 25.
34. Tajima, "Japan's Cold Indifference."
35. Ibid.

36. Masayoshi Kanabayashi, "Japan's Recession-Hit Companies Make Complex Arrangements to Avoid Layoffs," *Wall Street Journal,* February 17, 1983, p. 32.
37. For some examples of this phenomenon, see *Salary-Man: Document #2* (in Japanese) (Tokyo: Nihon Keizai Shinbun, 1981).
38. Urban C. Lehner, "Heads of Japan Airlines and Mitsukoshi Bucking a Venerable Japanese Tradition," *Wall Street Journal,* September 22, 1982, p. 31.
39. Drucker, "What We Can Learn from Japanese Management," pp. 112–113.

FOUR ▪▪

Innocents Abroad: The Case of Itoh (America), Inc.

NOTHING ILLUSTRATES SO VIVIDLY THE PROBLEMS AND PROSPECTS OF applying Japanese management techniques in an alien sociocultural environment as the case of Itoh (America), Inc., a wholly owned subsidiary of Itoh Company, one of Japan's big nine trading houses. The case is currently in pretrial before the United States District Court for the Southern District of Texas, Houston, Texas. Twice in the past eight years, Itoh has attempted to have the case dismissed on legal and procedural grounds. Twice it has failed. The case has yet to be tried on its factual merits and a verdict rendered in favor of one of the parties to the lawsuit.

This case has raised a host of major issues that lie at the core of the Japanese management system and how it is practiced by Japanese companies in the United States. Regardless of how the Itoh case is eventually settled, it will have a profound effect on the manner in which Japanese and most foreign companies operate in the United States. It will also impose severe limits on the discretion of foreign-based companies in introducing management techniques that are at variance with U.S. laws and customs.

The Itoh case demonstrates, more than anything else, the claim of the Japanese, rarely made otherwise, that their management techniques are unique, that they are best suited to the Japanese psyche, and that they cannot be successfully adapted to the needs of American employees. It also shows the unwillingness of Japanese companies to extend their employee relations policies, with all their attendant benefits, to their non-Japanese employees. The Itoh case, which is not atypical when compared with other Japanese companies operating in the United States, also illustrates how Japanese companies use their U.S. operations as training grounds for their Japan-based employees. Japanese citizens are used in the U.S. operations of Japanese companies in positions that reach quite low in the organizational hierarchy and for which equally capable, if not actually better-qualified, American citizens may be available.

And herein lies another major dilemma for Japanese companies in particular, and most foreign companies in general, in their U.S. operations. These discriminatory practices may be in violation of the U.S. civil rights and other laws that forbid discriminatory employment practices based on age, sex, race, or national origin. The legal dimensions of the conflict have yet to be precisely determined, even after eight years of litigation. Moreover, because the employment practices of Japanese companies are based on such fundamentally different premises, it is not clear how they will ultimately be accepted in an American judicial context.

The issues involved are by no means simple either as to fact or as to law. Although they are pertinent to all foreign companies operating in the United States, they are particularly relevant in the case of Japanese companies. For the Japanese, their personnel practices represent the extreme point in terms of their divergence from traditional American management and personnel relations practices. For example:

- Should a Japanese company have the right to bring its own people (foreign nationals) into the United States for specific management jobs, or must it hire local people if similar qualified people are available?
- The comparative similarity of candidate qualifications and job functions may be more apparent than real. Japanese corporations may have a different managerial philosophy and operational style that are the product of the sociocultural milieu of the home country and its people. This difference in management philosophy and operating style may make it difficult, if not impossible, for any direct comparisons of job specifications or individual qualifications as to suitability for certain jobs. What criteria can be used for comparing job performance and individual qualifications under those circumstances?
- When a Japanese firm uses its own people for certain jobs with its U.S. affiliate because it considers those jobs "highly sensitive" and important not only in terms of its U.S. operations but also in terms of its overall global operations, must it justify those actions to avoid charges of job discrimination?
- A Japanese company may have a psychological predisposition to hire its own people for certain top management jobs in its U.S. and other overseas operations. Should this be considered a prerogative of the owners, or should it be considered a job restriction based on national origin and therefore *ultra vires?*
- The civil rights laws were essentially a societal response to a dramatic change in the national climate of the United States as regards employment discrimination against blacks. Further, in many instances, expatriate per-

sonnel of foreign multinationals are members of a racial, color, or national origin minority group by statutory definition. Considering these factors, should foreign multinationals doing business in the United States be subject to the civil rights laws in their employment practices?

- Foreign multinationals are entitled to operate in the United States under treaties of friendship, commerce, and navigation that carefully define the rights each nation will render to the nationals and products of the other. Distinctions are made in many of the treaty provisions between U.S. subsidiaries of foreign firms incorporated under U.S. laws and branch offices of foreign multinationals. Essential to the successful operation of a multinational is the ability to use nationals from the home country of the parent firm for "sensitive" positions, a right recognized by treaty. Do these treaties permitting such commercial activities exempt or qualify the applicability of the civil rights laws to foreign multinationals?

- Not all discrimination is prohibited under the U.S. civil rights laws. Discrimination resulting from a *bona fide* occupational qualification (BFOQ) is permitted. Do expatriate personnel job positions constitute a *bona fide* occupational qualification? Are there other exemptions by which expatriate employment practices can be legally justified, such as the business necessity rule?

THE LAWSUIT: SPIESS et al. v. C. ITOH & COMPANY (AMERICA)

The Judicial Proceedings

On February 21, 1975, three executives of C. Itoh (America), Inc., sued Itoh as individuals and as representatives of a class. Itoh was charged with the unlawful deprivation of their civil rights and the rights of other employees similarly situated. The civil action was brought under Section 1981 of the Civil Rights Act of 1966 (hereinafter Section 1981), and Title VII of the Civil Rights Acts of 1964, (hereinafter Title VII). Compensatory damages of $8 million and punitive damages of $5 million are being sought.[1]

The plaintiffs, Michael E. Spiess, Jack K. Hardy, and Benjamin Rountree, are all American citizens and white Caucasians of non-Japanese national origin. Spiess worked for Itoh from January 10, 1972, to January 9, 1976, Hardy from September 22, 1969, 'to January 9, 1976, and Rountree from June 12, 1970, to September 30, 1973. The plaintiffs performed middle management duties. At the time their complaint was filed, all worked in Itoh's Houston office.

Rountree left Itoh's employment shortly after the civil action was filed. Spiess and Hardy were notified on December 30, 1975 (less than one year after the filing of the civil action) that Itoh was terminating their employment as of January 9, 1976. Itoh's reason was that Spiess and Hardy had surreptitiously removed certain documents from company files. These documents had been given a confidential status and could not be removed without permission from company officials. Spiess and Hardy alleged that Itoh had engaged in "retaliatory firing" in violation of their civil rights. They sought a temporary restraining order, contending that the documents in question were furnished only to plaintiffs' counsel to be used in furtherance of their Title VII suit.[2]

The District Court refused to grant the temporary restraining order. An employee, the court held, may not engage in unlawful or unethical conduct under the guise of promoting the public's interest in nondiscriminatory employment practices. Nor would the court countenance the "theft" of confidential data based on an attorney-client relationship rationale, since plaintiffs' counsel could have sought the documents in question through discovery. The court concluded: "Judicially protecting an employees' assistance and participation equitably is one thing; protecting the taking of documents unauthorizedly is another."[3]

The defendant, Itoh (America), first attempted to have the case dismissed on the grounds that Section 1981 and Title VII did not protect white citizens, but were intended to grant statutory protection to individuals who have been the subject of previous job discrimination, such as blacks. Consequently, the plaintiffs, being white, were not entitled to sue. The U.S. District Court ruled against Itoh's motion to dismiss, citing as authority the U.S. Supreme Court's decision in *McDonald* v. *Santa Fe,* handed down only a few months before.[4]

Itoh (America) then attempted to have the case dismissed, contending that Itoh (America) was immune from the jurisdiction of the U.S. civil rights laws because of the special status accorded U.S. subsidiaries of Japan-based corporations under a 1953 treaty of friendship, commerce, and navigation (FCN) between the United States and Japan. The District Court rejected Itoh's argument that the 1953 treaty allowed it to hire only Japanese for managerial and technical positions in spite of American laws prohibiting employment discrimination based on national origin.[5]

The decision was appealed by Itoh to the United States Court of Appeals, Fifth Circuit, sitting in New Orleans. That court, in a 2 to 1 decision, reversed the decision of the District Court and held that Itoh (America) could assert rights under the FCN treaty and that such rights permitted it to hire only Japanese personnel for executive and technical positions.[6] On June 21, 1982, the Supreme Court of the United States granted the plaintiffs' petition for a writ of certiorari (agreed to consider the plaintiffs' appeal). The Supreme Court, having rejected Itoh's treaty argument in the case of

Sumitomo Shoji America, Inc., v. *Avagliano,* returned the matter to the lower courts for trial on the merits.[7]

The Sumitomo Case

Itoh (America) was not the only Japanese trading company to be sued in the American courts for employment discrimination. Some former and current female secretarial employees of Sumitomo Shoji America, Inc., a wholly-owned Japanese subsidiary, had brought a class action against Sumitomo alleging that its practice of hiring only male Japanese nationals for management-level positions discriminated against them on the basis of sex and national origin, in violation of Title VII. Sumitomo defended on the same grounds as Itoh (America); it held that the 1953 FCN treaty exempted it from compliance with U.S. civil rights laws. The U.S. District Court in New York denied Sumitomo's motion to dismiss. Sumitomo appealed that decision to the U.S. Court of Appeals, Second Circuit, sitting in New York City. That court also held for the female plaintiffs.[8] Sumitomo again appealed, this time to the U.S. Supreme Court.

On June 15, 1982, the legal issue of treaty rights, raised as defenses in both the Itoh and Sumitomo cases, was finally resolved. The Supreme Court, in a unanimous decision, held that Sumitomo was a U.S. corporation, since it was constituted as such under the applicable corporation laws and regulations of New York State. As a U.S. corporation, Sumitomo could not invoke rights given only to Japanese firms by the 1953 treaty. Accordingly, Sumitomo was subject to the civil rights laws of the United States like any other U.S. corporation. The Sumitomo case was remanded back to the U.S. District Court for trial on the facts.[9]

Allegations of American Employees against Itoh[10]

Spiess, Hardy, and Rountree alleged that they performed the same type and quality of work as did certain of Itoh's nonsecretarial employees who were of Japanese national origin, except that they were unlawfully excluded from participating in the management of Itoh. In instances involving negotiations and servicing of major contracts with U.S. corporations and various agencies of the United States government, they contended that their understanding of American business and social practices enabled them to outperform their Japanese counterparts. Yet despite their accomplishments, the plaintiffs charged that Itoh discriminated against them in favor of employees of Japanese national origin with respect to compensation, terms, conditions, and privileges of employment.

This discrimination, in direct violation of Title VII, included, but was not limited to, the following practices:

- Paying monthly salaries to the Japanese that were at least 20 percent greater than the monthly salaries paid to the non-Japanese
- Paying midyear summer bonuses in excess of $4,000 to Japanese employees, but not making such payments to the non-Japanese
- Paying year-end bonuses to the Japanese substantially greater than those paid to the non-Japanese
- Providing direct reimbursement of substantially all medical and dental expenses, in excess of that provided by insurance, to Japanese employees, but not to non-Japanese employees
- Paying personal automobile insurance premiums for Japanese employees, but not for non-Japanese employees
- Providing loans to Japanese employees to enable them to purchase automobiles, homes, and speculative securities for their personal accounts, but not making any such funds available to non-Japanese employees
- Providing automatic pay increases of up to 50 percent of monthly compensation based upon marital status and size of family to Japanese employees, but not to non-Japanese employees
- Providing to each Japanese employee but not to non-Japanese employees a subsidy for the rental of personal living quarters in amounts equal to one-half of the excess of such rental payments over 20 percent of monthly net salary
- Unlawfully segregating and classifying its employees according to whether they were of Japanese or non-Japanese national origin, as demonstrated by the initials "J" (standing for "Japanese") and "A" (standing for "American") appearing after each employee's name on the monthly payroll records
- Limiting the employment opportunities of its non-Japanese employees by refusing to promote them to managerial positions
- Regularly holding evening staff meetings to discuss and plan management policies which only the Japanese employees were permitted to attend, and excluding all non-Japanese employees

The American complainants further alleged that the discriminatory employment practices described above were in existence during the entire tenure of their employment. They charged that these discriminatory employment practices remained a closely guarded secret among Itoh's Japanese employees until one such employee unintentionally indicated the existence of these practices to Hardy. At no time before plaintiffs accepted the Itoh job offers did any representative of Itoh inform them of the existence of these practices.

To the contrary, the plaintiffs, as intelligent and capable American businessmen, were induced to work for Itoh by company representations that it treated its employees with fairness and impartiality and that positions of management and responsibility could be attained by dedication and hard work, regardless of one's national origin. Plaintiffs alleged that they were thus induced to spend what could otherwise have been some of the most personally and financially rewarding years of their lives working for Itoh. They finally realized with the filing of their civil action that Itoh was a company that considered and evaluated its employees on the basis of characteristics attributed to national origin rather than on the basis of individual capacities, and refused to train its non-Japanese employees for management level positions. Itoh evaluated its employees on the basis of a double employment standard, one for the Japanese and the other for the non-Japanese staff, which effectively precluded non-Japanese employees from attaining management-level positions. Plaintiffs contended that had they known of these discriminatory employment practices, they would never have accepted jobs with Itoh.

THE MANAGEMENT AND PERSONNEL PRACTICES[11]

The "Japan Staff" and the "American Staff"

Itoh made a fundamental distinction between its "Japan staff" and "American staff." Japan staff were employees of Itoh sent by the parent company, Itoh (Japan), to work in the United States for Itoh (America). American staff were all other employees of Itoh (America) and included Orientals of Chinese and Korean origin. American staff also included individuals of Japanese origin born and raised in the United States. While they would be considered of Japanese national origin as that term is used in the civil rights laws of the United States, they were not viewed as Japan staff by Itoh. According to the testimony of Sadao Nishitomi, secretary and EEO coordinator of Itoh (America), taken during the course of depositions by plaintiffs' attorney in September 1975, this staff distinction appeared on all payroll records. The letter "J" was used to designate members of the "Japan staff." The letter "A" was used to identify members of the "American staff." The letters "JA" designated American employees of Japanese national origin, who for purposes of compensation were treated as members of the American staff. A review of Itoh (America)'s organization structure and personnel roster shows that, with a few exceptions, most of the executive and professional positions were occupied by the Japanese staff (Exhibits 4–1, 4–2, 4–3).

EXHIBIT 4–1 Organizational Chart of C. Itoh & Company (America), Inc.

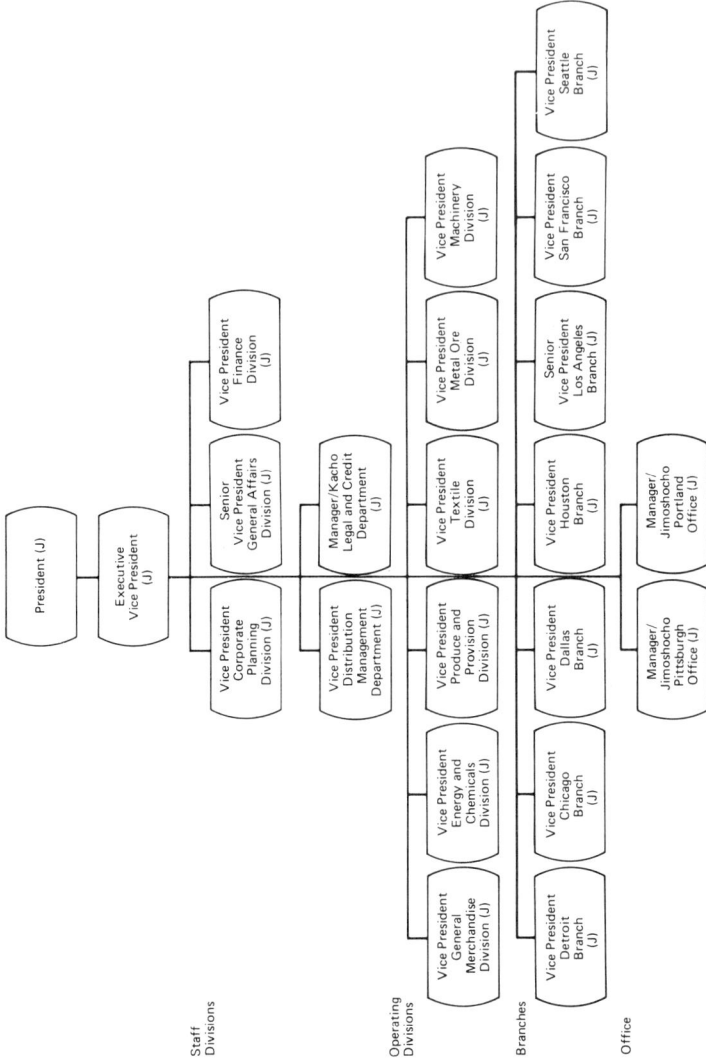

EXHIBIT 4-2 Organizational Chart of a Typical Staff Division

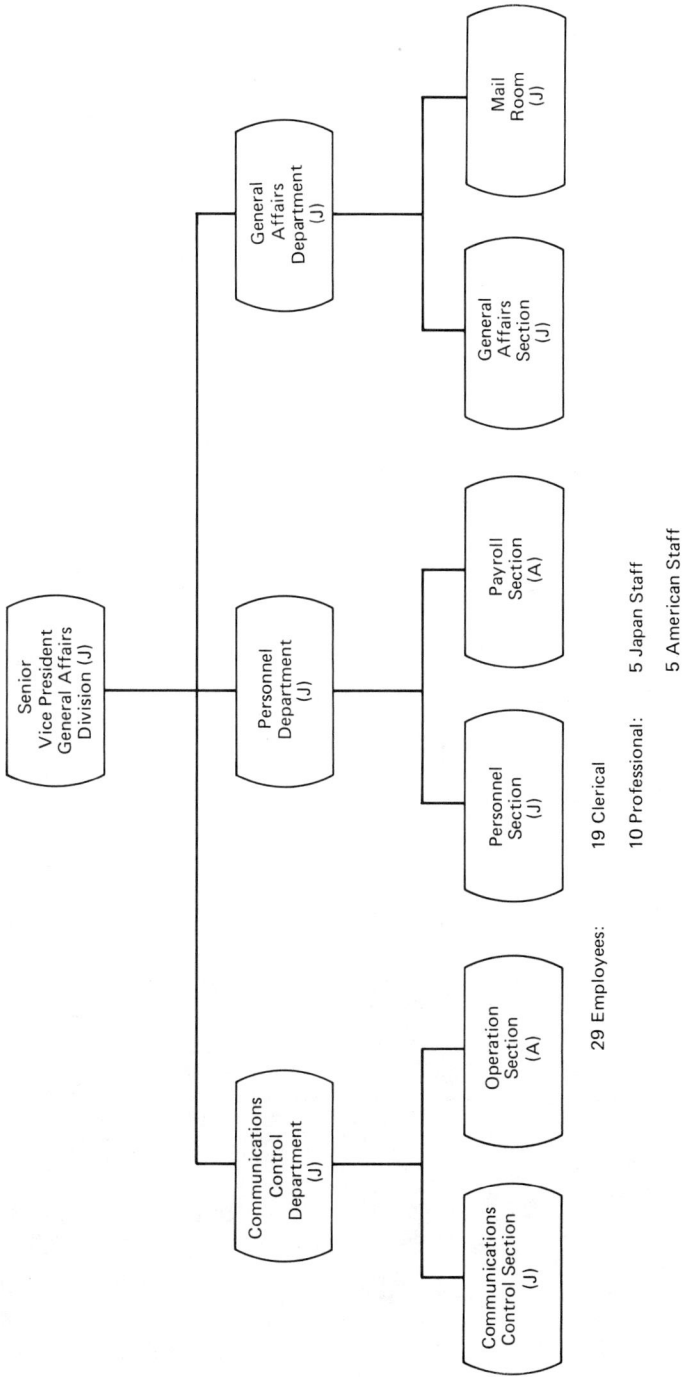

Senior
Vice President
General Affairs
Division (J)

Communications
Control
Department
(J)

Communications
Control Section
(J)

Operation
Section
(A)

Personnel
Department
(J)

Personnel
Section
(J)

Payroll
Section
(A)

General
Affairs
Department
(J)

General
Affairs
Section
(J)

Mail
Room
(J)

29 Employees:

19 Clerical

10 Professional: 5 Japan Staff

5 American Staff

EXHIBIT 4–3 Organizational Chart of a Typical Operating Division

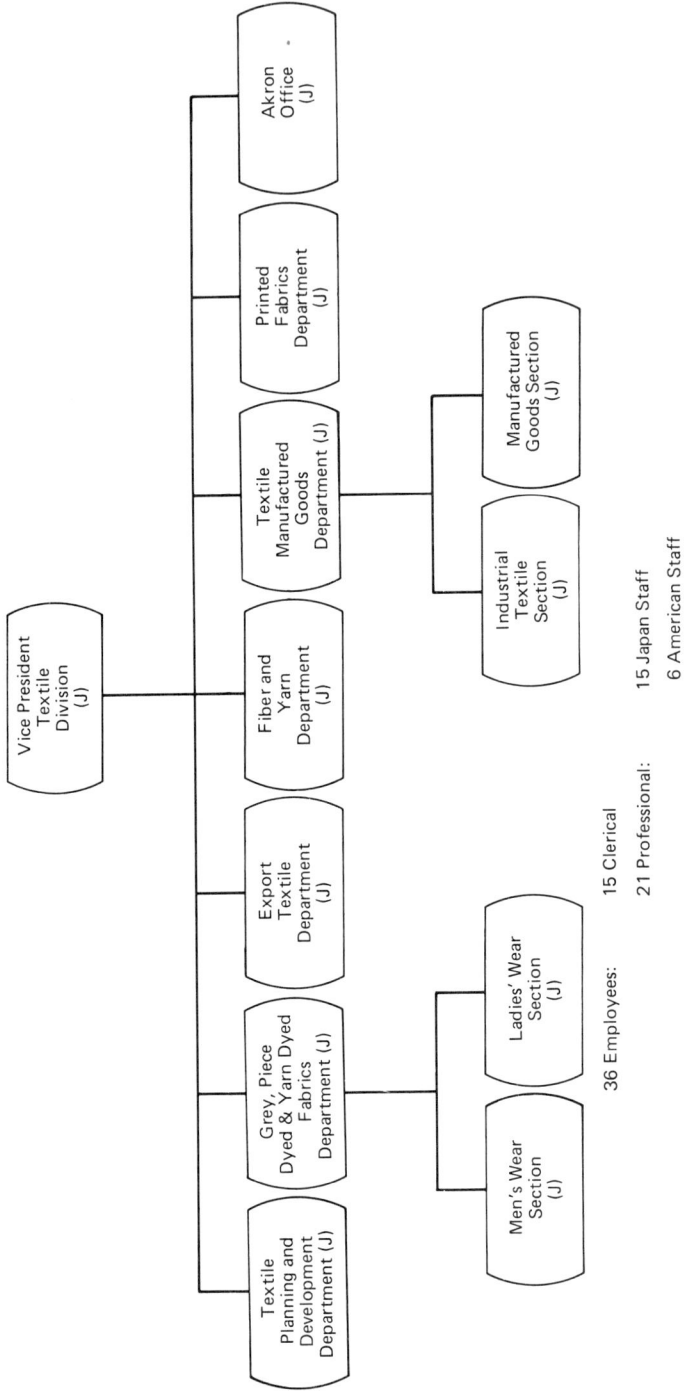

Vice President Textile Division (J)

Textile Planning and Development Department (J)

Grey, Piece Dyed & Yarn Dyed Fabrics Department (J)

Men's Wear Section (J)

Ladies' Wear Section (J)

Export Textile Department (J)

Fiber and Yarn Department (J)

Textile Manufactured Goods Department (J)

Industrial Textile Section (J)

Manufactured Goods Section (J)

Printed Fabrics Department (J)

Akron Office (J)

36 Employees:

15 Clerical

21 Professional:

15 Japan Staff

6 American Staff

Distinction between Status Levels and Functional Authority

Itoh's differing treatment of Japan and American staff can be best understood within the context of the distinction made by Itoh between "status levels" and "functional authority." Functional authority is a familiar concept for American managers. It describes the typical chain of command found in the organizational charts of American firms. Each position on the chart has certain assigned job responsibilities or functions. Distinctions are drawn between line and staff functions. Hierarchical relationships between members of the organization, the degree of authority within the organizational structure, and the nature and magnitude of compensation are all determined by the functional position of the individual within the organization.

"Status" is a Japanese concept that was practiced by Itoh at the time of the Spiess-Hardy-Rountree lawsuit. It reflected an individual's standing in the Itoh organization based on such factors as length of service (seniority) and level of achievement or accomplishment. A correlation between an individual's status and his functional position was not necessary, according to Itoh's personnel practices. Status is best described in terms of an attitudinal response that American firms may informally display toward an "old and trusted" employee who is given supervisory responsibilities, special assignments, and additional compensation because of "long and faithful service" to the company that may not be reflected in the actual functional job position occupied by the employee. The concept of status is a formalized organizational response by Itoh to its system of lifetime employment. Once an individual is employed, he remains with Itoh until retirement age is reached, unless employment is terminated for breach of company rules and regulations.

Itoh (America), like its parent, had eight status levels, ranging from *sankyū* to *sanyo* (see Appendix for a glossary of Japanese terms and explanation of the various status levels). *Sankyū* is the lowest level and is assigned to an employee who has just graduated from college and joined the Itoh (Japan) staff. His position is that of a recruit, or in the words of Sadao Nishitomi, a private in a military organization. *Sanyo* is the top level, awarded to employees who have been with Itoh (Japan) for a number of years and contributed to the firm's welfare through loyal and dedicated service. This position can best be described as that of a commissioned officer.

The distinction between "status" and function for Japan staff is demonstrated by the career of Sadao Nishitomi. Born in Japan on March 12, 1924, Mr. Nishitomi graduated at the age of 17 from a "commercial school" and attended Kansai University, from which he graduated in 1946. At the university, he was in the Division of Commerce, where he took such courses as economics and accountancy. In addition, he received training in English (reading, translating Japanese to English, grammar, and composition) for eight or nine years, while attending both the commercial school and the university.

Mr. Nishitomi began working for Sanko and Company, Ltd., in 1942, a predecessor firm to Itoh (Japan). He was employed first in the accounting department, and in 1943 was transferred to the section responsible for exports of textile products. He joined the Itoh (Japan) staff in 1945. Transferred to the United States in 1959, Mr. Nishitomi bought and exported cotton from the United States. After a year, he was promoted to the position of deputy manager of the Dallas branch office, supervising approximately 10 subordinates. After six and a half years, he returned to Japan in 1965 and continued to rise in the hierarchy of Itoh (Japan), becoming deputy manager of the administrative and coordinating department, responsible for preparing management plans and coordinating the activities of the various Itoh divisions. In 1971, Mr. Nishitomi was again transferred to Itoh (America). His present position with the firm is secretary of Itoh (America) and manager of the general affairs division. This automatically makes him a vice president of Itoh (America). Although he has no special training in communications, he also acts as manager of the communication control department. Additionally, he is designated program director for Itoh (America)'s affirmative action plan, or EEO coordinator.

At the time Mr. Nishitomi joined the Itoh staff in 1945, there were only six status levels (see appendix). He started at level 5, or *gotōshain.* While a member of the Itoh (Japan) staff from 1945 to 1959, he rose to level 4, or *yontōshain,* in 1950 and to level 3, or *santōshain,* in 1956. During his second period in Japan, he moved to level 2, or *nittōshain,* in 1966 and to level 1, or *ittōshain,* in 1969. In 1973, while in the United States as an employee of Itoh (America), he moved to the highest status level in the Itoh organization, *sanyo.*

Status was determined only by Itoh (Japan). Within the Itoh (America) staff, it applied only to Japanese employees on temporary assignment to the United States. Even though a member of Itoh (Japan) might transfer to the United States and be on the payroll of Itoh (America), he maintained the status level established by the parent firm. While employed in the United States and on the payroll of the U.S. subsidiary, the Japanese employee might be promoted from one "status level" to a higher one on the records of the parent company. His pay with the U.S. subsidiary would then rise to reflect his new status.

Status could be obtained, but only by employees of Itoh (Japan) and by satisfying certain prerequisites, such as applying for a position with the parent company in Japan after completing the necessary university level academic work in Japan, passing a very competitive examination for entrance into the lower ranks of the company's staff, and being offered lifetime employment with Itoh (Japan). No American had obtained status in this manner at the time the plaintiffs filed their lawsuit. Since Itoh (America) did not have its own status system independent of the parent, American staff, including American-born Japanese, were excluded from any participation in status levels. Accordingly, no American had status either with Itoh (America) or with Itoh (Japan).

Though it is possible that a person of higher status may report to a person of lower status because of differences in functional authority, Itoh made an effort to avoid this kind of conflict. Thus individual positions existed in Itoh (America) with no functional titles, and individuals occupying those jobs performed managerial functions. A Japan staff member will rarely be in a subordinate position reporting to an American staff member to minimize the inherent conflict in status and function.

Compensation

Itoh's dual management system resulted in a dual personnel compensation and promotion system, one for the Japan staff and one for the American staff, each with its own employee operating manual. Japanese staff were paid on the basis of their status and Americans on the basis of their functional authority. The result was a notable difference in pay and benefits.

Americans started at a salary level substantially lower than that of a Japanese at the same functional level. Americans were paid a gross salary. Japan staff were guaranteed a net salary. Itoh therefore followed a practice of "grossing up" for its Japan staff. All taxes, federal, state, and local, were estimated, and that amount was added to the Japan staff's salary so that the employee would receive the guaranteed net. In addition, midyear bonuses were paid to Japan staff, but not to American staff. The amount of the midyear bonus was determined by Itoh (Japan), but charged against the accounts of Itoh (America). Medical insurance was available for both American staff and Japan staff. However, the Japan staff was immediately eligible for benefits, whereas the American staff had to first satisfy a three-month eligibility requirement before benefits could be received.

Until March 31, 1974, Itoh sponsored a program of rental subsidies for the Japan staff only. Although that program has been discontinued, the Japan staff still had available a lease termination subsidization not open to the American staff. Automobiles and vehicle insurance were subsidized by Itoh (America) only for Japan staff.

The Japan staff also received a family allowance—30 percent of the base salary for the wife, 10 percent for each child of school age and above, and 5 percent for each child under school age, not to exceed 50 percent of the base salary. The allowance was paid, if necessary, directly to the family member who remained in Japan. Itoh (Japan) paid an allowance in yen to children of Japan staff attending college in Japan. Itoh (Japan) then charged Itoh (America) for the amount of this allowance in dollars, to be included in the salary of the employee. The allowance paid by the parent company appeared on the withholding tax statement furnished the employee by Itoh (America) for income tax purposes. This family allowance was not available to American staff, since their salaries were paid "according to what is practiced generally in the U.S. business environment," based on the assumption that the American staff employee had taken into consideration the amount needed as a family allowance.

Promotional Opportunities

Itoh had a stated policy of nondiscrimination set forth in the American staff's employee's manual:

> It is the policy of C. Itoh & Company (America), Inc., and its subsidiaries that all applicants for employment are considered only on the basis of merit, without discrimination because of race, creed, national origin, age or sex. Our employment practices ensure equal treatment to all employees without distinction in pay or opportunity because of an employee's color, religion, national origin, age or sex.

When asked how far up in the ranks of C. Itoh (America) a member of the American staff can climb, Sadao Nishitomi, the EEO coordinator for Itoh (America), responded: "As far as I understand it, any employee can climb up in rank, all the way up, excepting for the position of president."

The Notion of Shosha, or Moving Think Tank

Testimony of Sadao Nishitomi, however, indicated that Japan staff were favored over American staff in management positions because Japan staff were believed to possess *shosha*. Literally translated as "knowledge-intensive industry" or "moving think tank," *shosha* describes an individual with extensive knowledge about his industry. He possesses the ability to collect relevant information, analyze this information, and apply the result to a business transaction on a higher level. While the American staff could, "with good effort on their part," acquire this capability, Mr. Nishitomi testified that there were very few who had that capability. When asked how an American would acquire *shosha*, Mr. Nishitomi responded that the American would have to apply for a position with Itoh (Japan), after overcoming very stiff employment competition, and work up the employment ladder with Itoh (Japan). Training courses for Americans to develop *shosha* were not available at Itoh (America), and Americans were not transferred to Itoh (Japan) for experience. Although Japanese language training through the Berlitz schools was subsidized for all employees by Itoh (America), no formal notification of the availability of the program was circulated to the American staff.

Itoh (America)'s stated nondiscriminatory policy notwithstanding, there was no established procedure or criteria by which management staff was selected to head departments or fill other supervisory positions. The result, as demonstrated through Mr. Nishitomi's testimony, was a general systematic exclusion of Americans from managerial positions. Mr. Nishitomi himself had never chosen an American manager. Only one American in the Itoh (America) organization served at the level of vice president or above. This title is largely illusory, however, since the employee functioned only as *shitenchō daikō,* or assistant manager of a branch office. The employee performed the same job and exercised the same authority as he did when first employed by Itoh (America). Significantly, his position as vice president did not appear on a formal list of the executive officers of Itoh (America).

The disadvantages under which American staff operated in rising to a managerial position was demonstrated by the appointment of Mr. Ogata, formerly with Itoh (Japan), as *kachō* or department manager of the personnel department, in February 1975. The *kakarichō* of the personnel department was a member of the American staff. Since the work of the personnel department related to both Japanese and American staff, Itoh (America) felt that the position should be filled by a Japan staff member. Testimony by Mr. Nishitomi established that while Mr. Ogata lacked knowledge about American personnel matters, this deficiency was overcome by appointing a knowledgeable American staff member to assist him. Conversely, there was reluctance to appoint an American staff member as *kachō* and give him a knowledgeable Japan staff member to compensate for his lack of expertise in Japanese personnel matters. Thus, if a Japanese candidate with suitable qualifications could not be found within the Itoh (America) organization, a request would be made to the personnel department of the parent company for some Japanese candidates who might be transferred to the United States. Recruitment from outside the organization was not even considered.

It was not at all unusual for a Japanese to hold a number of unrelated functional positions within the Itoh (America) organization until a certain position could be filled by the parent company. Mr. Nishitomi's many "hats" —secretary of Itoh (America), manager of the general affairs division, manager of the communication control department, and EEO coordinator— illustrated this tendency. Nor did it appear to be essential that the Japan staff members have special training in the activity they were managing. Thus, American staff members might have better credentials than the Japan staff;

however, since the Japan staff persons were considered to be on 24-hour duty while the Americans worked designated hours, Itoh felt that the nature of the Japan staff work was different.

An essential difference between the Japan staff and the American staff resulted from special skills "not able to be acquired in the United States." Mr. Nishitomi testified that Japan staff were ". . . mostly engaged in the transaction of business within Japan which would require in-depth knowledge of customs and habits of business transactions in Japan, which would not be too easy for American staff to acquire. . . ." The converse, however, was not necessarily true. American staff were not assumed to have a "correspondingly greater knowledge of American business practices and companies than members of the Japan staff" when doing business in the United States.

The Defendant: C. Itoh & Company (America), Inc.[12]

Itoh (America), is a wholly-owned subsidiary of C. Itoh & Company, Ltd., of Japan. It is the flagship subsidiary of the parent. C. Itoh (America) does annual business of over $1 billion, of which approximately 65 percent constitutes exports from the United States to Japan and other countries. Itoh (America) and the parent company deal in some 50,000 commodities. The parent company is one of the four largest general trading firms in Japan. Started with modest beginnings in 1858, it merged with Marubeni and Kishimoto Shoten in 1941 to become Sanko. It then merged with Kureha Spinning and Daido Boeki (a trading firm) in 1944 to become Daiken Sangyo. In 1949, Daiken Sangyo was reorganized into two companies, C. Itoh & Company and Marubeni, according to the requirements of the deconcentration law promulgated by the American Occupation forces at the end of World War II. At the time of its rebirth in 1949, C. Itoh (Japan) was exclusively engaged in textiles. The growth of the heavy and chemical industries in postwar Japan led the company to move into these areas. Currently, textile transactions account for only 40 percent of the company's business. Nevertheless, C. Itoh (Japan) still considers itself the largest textile dealer in the world. It accounts for about 30 percent of the total textile transactions by Japan's nine major trading companies.

Itoh (Japan) maintains locally incorporated companies in 12 major countries in the world and also branches and representative offices in more than 100 principal cities in Japan and overseas. The total number of employees, including locally employed personnel, is approximately 9,000. Moreover, 500 to 600 employees from C. Itoh's head offices and other offices in Japan and overseas may be found at any time making on-the-spot surveys, serving as liaison between home office and branch offices, handling import and export business, and so on. The company plays a significant role in the economy of Japan.

Itoh (America) is a trading company and offers its services to others in exports and imports, transportation, brokerage, financing, warehousing, insurance, technical and engineering consultation, marketing research, and information of almost every kind. In addition, it is "steadily acquiring new 'software' in fields ranging from mining to hotel construction and management." At present, C. Itoh's American business of $1 billion annually is nearly 65 percent outward-bound from the United States to Japan and third countries.

The relationship between Itoh (America) and Itoh (Japan) is that of subordinate and superior. Decisions regarding management staff, particularly top management and Itoh (America)'s Japan staff, rest largely with Itoh (Japan). In choosing an executive vice president to serve as "the right hand or left hand" of the president of Itoh (America), the board of directors of Itoh (America) has the authority, theoretically speaking, to approve a candidate. In reality, the candidate is selected by and sent from Itoh (Japan). According to Nishitomi's deposition testimony, Itoh (Japan) sends someone suitable for the position, having taken into consideration the wishes of the American *soshihainin.* On the other hand, Nishitomi testified that if a decision is made on whether to establish a new division in America, it would be made by Itoh (America).

ITOH (AMERICA)'S DEFENSES

To date, Itoh's defenses has been procedural ones directed at challenging the plaintiffs' right to sue for damages under the civil rights laws of the United States.

Employment Discrimination does not Apply to White Citizens

Itoh's first line of defense was a motion to dismiss, filed March 6, 1975. Itoh contended that the plaintiffs, as white citizens, were not protected by Section 1981 of Title VII. Section 1981 provides that:

> All persons within the jurisdiction of the United States shall have the same rights . . . to the full and equal benefit of all laws . . . as is enjoyed by white citizens. . . .[13]

Itoh argued that since the standard set forth in Section 1981 are rights "enjoyed by white citizens," only nonwhites have standing to sue under Section 1981 and Title VII. Plaintiffs, by the clear and unequivocal terms of Section 1981, must demonstrate as whites that they have been denied the same rights given by Itoh to its other white employees. Since Itoh treats all its white employees or American staff equally, plaintiffs have failed to satisfy the statutory burden imposed under Section 1981.

The motion was denied by the District Court on January 29, 1976. The court stated that the statute eradicates "all social discrimination in the enumerated rights rather than merely elevating nonwhite citizens above white citizens to a privileged legal status because of race." The cutting edge of Section 1981, the judge held, was "protection against discrimination on the basis of race, not protection against discrimination by numerical majorities."[14]

Five months later, the Supreme Court would rule in the McDonald case that both Section 1981 and Title VII prohibit racial discrimination in private employment against white as well as against nonwhite persons:

> . . . we cannot accept the view that the terms of Section 1981 exclude its application to racial discrimination against white persons. On the contrary, the statute explicitly applies to "all persons." . . . While a mechanical reading of the phrase "as is enjoyed by white citizens" would seem to lend support to respondents' reading of the statute, we have previously described this phrase simply as emphasizing "the racial character of the rights being protected."[15]

The Immunization of Itoh's Practices by the U.S.–Japan Treaty

The second legal defense raised by Itoh (America) in a motion to dismiss filed on May 10, 1978, was that Itoh's employment practices were "immunized" under the terms of the U.S.–Japan Treaty of Friendship, Commerce, and Navigation. Itoh argued that the effect of the treaty was to create an *absolute* (Itoh's language) right on the part of American and Japanese firms to employ in each other's countries managerial and specialized personnel of their choice *to the exclusion of nationals* of the host country (Itoh's emphasis).[16]

The District Court rejected that defense as well, and Itoh (America) appealed to the United States Court of Appeals, Fifth Circuit. In a decision handed down on April 24, 1981, the court, in a 2 to 1 decision, agreed with Itoh (America)'s reasoning and remanded the case to the District Court for dismissal of plaintiffs' lawsuit.[17] Before that action could be taken, the United States Supreme Court considered the legal defense raised by Itoh (America) in a companion case involving another large Japanese trading firm, Sumtiomo Shoji America, Inc.

In that case, the Supreme Court held that the purpose of the postwar friendship, commerce, and navigation treaties was not to give foreign corporations greater rights than domestic companies, but instead to ensure them the right to conduct business on an equal basis without suffering discrimination based on their alienage. The treaties further allowed foreign individuals and companies to form locally incorporated subsidiaries. These local subsidiaries are, for purpose of the treaties, considered companies of the country in which they are incorporated. As such, they are not only entitled to the rights, but, more important, are subject to the responsibilities imposed on other domestic companies, including the obligation of complying with federal laws prohibiting employment discrimination based on national origin and sex.[18]

ANALYSIS: THE MANAGEMENT ISSUES

Are Itoh's Employment and Compensation Practices Unique?

Most multinational corporations (MNCs), regardless of their country of origin, maintain separate compensation and promotion plans for local employees and for employees transferred from the parent MNCs' home country. For the local employees, MNCs follow the laws, customs, and competitive wages in the host country. However, for the foreign employees, MNCs must provide wages and benefits comparable to those available in the expatriate's home country. In addition, companies invariably provide premium pay, commonly called overseas "hazardous duty" pay, to induce expatriates to work abroad.

Surveys and studies by The Conference Board, a business-supported, nonprofit research organization based in New York, show that special benefits granted American employees sent abroad by MNCs cover a wide range. Thus it would appear, at least on the surface, that the employment promotion and compensation policies followed by Itoh (America) for its Japanese staff were not unique; they could be found, to a greater or lesser degree, in all MNCs.[19]

Itoh Personnel Policies in the Japanese Context

On the face of it, Itoh could argue that it paid its American employees on the basis of their functional responsibility, and its Japan staff on the basis of "status" acquired through years of faithful service. Such a distinction would be in clear violation of the U.S. civil rights statutes. However, it points out the difficulty in comparing overt job descriptions and task analyses to see whether two persons are performing similar tasks. Once we get away from the essentially routinized or mechanical tasks, comparing complex and managerial jobs becomes infinitely more difficult. Itoh's wages to its Japan staff allegedly take into account the cultural determinant of the company's expectations of its employees—their willingness to take different assignments, undergo long periods of varied training, almost total loyalty to one's employer, and acceptance of wages that are based on seniority rather than job performance. American employees do not meet these expectations. What is more important, there are no social conventions and group norms that would force them to do so.

However, even if this argument were valid at a conceptual level, it falls down at the applied level on two accounts. One, Itoh must demonstrate that wage and salary differentials between Japanese and American staff are precisely commensurate with different job requirements and job skills. Two, the opportunities for acquiring status and job-related benefits must be equally accessible to both the Japanese and the American employees.

Itoh could also justify differential wages and employment conditions on the basis of a longer time dimension within which it viewed employee performance and also on the basis of a differing perception of job requirements and performance standards. Itoh might well feel justified in paying its Japanese staff on a basis different from that used for its American staff. Comparing the performance of an American employee with a Japanese employee at an arbitrarily truncated time in the employment cycle of the two employees might appear to make the practice illegal as interpreted under the U.S. statutes, but it would not make it necessarily unjustified. The difficulty lies in the inability of the Japanese to so quantify and define the differences between the two systems that they would meet the precise contractual standards of the American system.

Furthermore, even this argument is likely to fail because of an absence of "good intent" on the part of Itoh (America). Itoh (America)'s rationale appears at best to be *post facto* justification. There has been no showing on the part of the company that it made any attempt to inform, persuade, or train American employees to acquire Itoh's corporate cultural values and to become part of Itoh's corporate family. What is unique, moreover, is the extent to which Itoh (America) employed Japan staff even at the lowest levels of its management echelons, and the pernicious nature of its discrimination against American employees.

ANALYSIS: THE LEGAL ISSUES

The Itoh case illustrates some of the growing legal problems faced by foreign multinationals doing business in the United States. The unusualness of the Itoh case stems from the use of the civil rights laws of the United States to challenge the expatriate management practices of a foreign multinational doing business in the United States. Two legal threads run through the Itoh case and interface with each other. One is the international legal concepts which define the right of a nation-state to impose its laws upon the business operations of a foreign corporation doing business within its territory or employing its nationals. The other is the U.S. discrimination laws governing employment practices.

Three legal questions were initially posed by the Itoh case, the resolution of which affects the management of a multinational's foreign personnel. Two of these legal issues were answered by the U.S. Supreme Court in the Sumitomo case: The friendship, commerce, and navigation treaties do not exempt U.S. subsidiaries of foreign multinationals from compliance with U.S. domestic laws, and the employment discrimination laws are applicable to foreign multinationals doing business in the United States. The question that remains unanswered is whether expatriate personnel job positions can be justified as a bona fide occupation qualification (BFOQ), thus excluding expatriate personnel practices from the strictures of the employment discrimination laws.

International Conventions on Employment Discrimination

The prohibition against employment discrimination is not unique to the United States. International conventions have established international standards for employment. The Universal Declaration of Human Rights, often cited as an authoritative interpretation of the United Nations Charter, states: "Everyone, without any discrimination, has the right to equal pay for equal work."[20] The ILO's Convention on Employment Discrimination, entered into on June 15, 1960, by some 75 nations, requires each signatory to: "declare and pursue a national policy designed to promote, by methods appropriate to national conditions and practice, equality of opportunity and treatment in respect of employment and occupation, with a view to eliminating any discrimination in respect thereof."[21]

The policy of nondiscriminatory labor practices is also contained in the Declaration on International Investment and Multinational Enterprises adopted by the Organization for Economic Cooperation and Development (OECD) Council on June 21, 1976. The guidelines to the declaration provide that enterprises should implement employment policies to eliminate discrimination in hiring, discharge, pay, promotion, and training. Both the United States and Japan are members of the OECD, and under international law these 1976 guidelines constitute "state practices" for signatory nations.[22]

Impact of FCN Treaty Obligations

Foreign multinationals are permitted to organize and do business in the United States under the provisions of treaties of friendship, commerce and navigation. Bilateral FCN treaties, rather than international conventions, are the most familiar form by which nations bind themselves in reference to their commercial activities. These treaties define the kind of treatment each nation will render to the nationals or products of the other. Two principal standards are employed to define the kind of treatment each nation will render to the other's nationals or products: the most favored nation clause and the national treatment clause. The most favored nation treatment assures nondiscriminatory treatment as compared with other foreign nationals—in other words, all foreigners are treated equally. The national treatment clause assures nondiscriminatory treatment as compared with the citizens of the host country—in other words, all aliens are to be treated the same as the local citizens.[23]

While some FCNs provide that workmen's compensation laws and social security systems may be applied by the host country to foreign nationals (for example, see Article III of the U.S.–Japan Treaty of Friendship, Commerce and Navigation), FCNs generally do not define the extent to which other labor legislation, particularly employment discrimination laws, may be applied to foreign nationals. This is not to suggest that FCNs are devoid of any provisions dealing with the employment of foreign nationals in the host country. A customary provision in FCNs permits nationals and companies to employ their own nationals for limited purposes, such as making examinations, audits, and rendering reports in connection with the planning and operation of their enterprises.[24] FCNs also provide that a nation engaging in commercial activities through publicly owned or controlled enterprises within the territory of the host country is subject to the taxes, lawsuits, and other liabilities imposed by the host country upon privately owned and controlled enterprises.

Underpinning customary law concepts is the "fundamental right" every nation-state has by virtue of its national sovereignty to exercise jurisdiction over all persons, property, and conduct within its sovereign territory.[25] Generally speaking, while the international community requires that all treaty obligations be carried out, those obligations are not themselves the law. This is not true, however, for the United States. The Constitution of the United States declares that such treaties are the "law of the land" and therefore enjoy the same legal status as domestic legislation. If there is a conflict between treaty obligations and domestic legislative requirements, whichever is later in time prevails.[26]

The Right of Foreign Firms to Employ Their Own Nationals

Common to most FCNs is the right of foreign multinationals to employ in each other's country managerial and specialized personnel of their own choice. The U.S.–Japan Treaty signed on April 2, 1953, eleven years before the enactment of Title VII, provides in Article VIII:

Nationals and companies of either party shall be permitted to engage, within the territories of the other Party, accountants and other technical experts, executive personnel, attorneys, agents and other specialists of their choice.[27]

Testimony of the assistant secretary of state for economic affairs before the United States Senate Subcommittee of the Committee on Foreign Relations on July 13, 1953, indicates that his treaty provision was not intended to grant any absolute rights. Its aim was not to free a foreign multinational from the dictates of the U.S. employment discrimination laws. Article VIII is an example of a national treatment clause, not an exemption provision. The object was to secure for American nationals doing business abroad the right to engage in extensive fields of business activity upon as favorable terms as the nationals of the host country by granting similar rights to the other FCN party. *Americans were to be treated no differently from Japanese citizens when doing business in Japan, and Japanese nationals were to be treated no differently from U.S. citizens when doing business in the United States.* Each national remains subject to the laws of the host nation. Neither is given greater rights than those enjoyed by the nationals of the host country, and neither is exempt from the laws of the host country.[28]

This view is also shared by American and Japanese commentators. Dan F. Henderson, in a major study of Japanese law and practice on foreign enterprise, observed: "These straightforward provisions (U.S.–Japan Treaty, Article VII) establish the rights of U.S. citizens to 'national treatment' in the establishment and operation of businesses in Japan and vice versa, and the apparent purpose is to award the 'foreign enterprise' the same rights, *duties* [emphasis added], and privileges, legally, as those enjoyed by domestic business."[29] In discussing the application of the Japanese Commercial Code to foreign enterprises, a Japanese academician, Yasuhiro Fujita, contended that if a Japanese domestic law is applicable to Japanese nationals as well as foreigners, the law does not violate the national treatment clause of the U.S.–Japan FCN Treaty.[30]

The recognition that FCNs do not exempt U.S. subsidiaries of foreign multinationals from domestic laws is also supported by the recent congressional policy articulated in the Foreign Sovereign Immunities Act of 1976.[31] The current international position was expressed by Deputy Secretary of State Robert S. Ingersoll in a statement dated March 5, 1976:

In international discussions of enterprise behavior, the United States has supported two basic principles: First, all sovereign states have the right to regulate the activity of foreign investors in their territory, consistent with the minimum standards of justice called for by international law; and, second, investors must respect the laws of the nations in which they operate and conduct themselves

as good corporate citizens of these nations, refraining from improper interference in their international affairs.[32]

The Supreme Court, in handing down its decision in the Sumitomo case,
noted that:

> Both the Ministry of Foreign Affairs of Japan and the United States
> Department of State agree that a United States corporation, even
> when wholly owned by a Japanese company, is not a company of
> Japan under the Treaty . . ..[33]

Treaty Trader Status

The ability of MNCs to move foreign employees to the United States to
perform services of either a temporary or permanent nature is of considerable importance to an understanding of the legal issues in the Itoh case and
a right recognized in FCNs. Thus, the Immigration and Nationality Act of
1952 (INA) and subsequent amendments have established various nonimmigrant visa categories to facilitate the entry of foreign nationals for temporary
periods to work for U.S. firms or individuals. One visa category permits
aliens to enter the United States as nonimmigrants if they are nationals of a
country that has an FCN treaty with the United States. Visas in this category
are designated E-1 (treaty trader) and E-2 (treaty investor).[34]

The requirements for the treaty trader status are:

- The treaty trader must be a treaty alien who enters the United States for
  the sole purpose of carrying on a substantial trade, principally between
  the United States and the alien's home country.
- The alien may be self-employed. If he is not, his employer must be a
  person or organization having the same nationality as the alien. The
  employer must be engaged in substantial trade with the United States.
- The alien must be engaged in a supervisory or executive capacity; if he
  is not, he must then possess special qualifications that make his services
  essential to the efficient operation of the employer's enterprise.
- If the employer is a corporation (whether the corporation is chartered
  under U.S. laws or in a foreign country), at least 51 percent of the
  corporate stock must be owned by persons having the same nationality
  as the alien. Thus, U.S. corporations, the majority of whose stock is
  owned by foreign investors, can employ a treaty trader.[35]

The Department of State, for administrative purposes, designates corporations with a majority of stock owned by foreign investors as "foreign corpora-

tions" in determining treaty trader status. Does this designation exempt U.S. subsidiaries of foreign MNCs from the applicability of domestic civil rights laws as a foreign corporation? While the question has not been definitively resolved, the legal rationale behind the nonimmigrant visa status suggests that the treaty trader status is an individual right and not a corporate right and is designed to permit individuals to enter the United States to do business. Its purpose is not to exempt U.S. firms employing aliens from the requirements of domestic laws. The legal rationale of the Supreme Court in the Sumitomo case would also support this view.

Two U.S. District Court cases, in determining the eligibility of an alien to enter the United States as a treaty trader, held that this right, while granted under an FCN treaty, could not be exercised by a foreign corporation through its employment practices. The decision as to whether to grant treaty trader status was properly under the jurisdiction of the Immigration and Naturalization Service and the Department of State.[36]

Bona Fide Occupational Qualification (BFOQ)

As the Supreme Court held in the Sumitomo case, Title VII is applicable to the management and personnel practices of all U.S. subsidiaries of foreign firms doing business in the United States. It should be noted, however, that Section 1981 and Title VII do not forbid *per se* all employment distinctions based on race, color, religion, sex, or national origin. The law recognizes that there may be occasions where one of these "discriminatory" characteristics constitutes a "bona fide occupational qualification (BFOQ) reasonably necessary to the normal operation of that particular business or enterprise."[37] The courts and the EEOC have viewed a BFOQ exception with distaste and have imposed stringent standards on what will be recognized as a BFOQ.[38]

A leading case that established basic criteria for the BFOQ is *Diaz* v. *Pan American World Airways.*[39] Pan American argued that its airline attendants must be only female, and this was a proper BFOQ. Passengers preferred women as airline hostesses, and such a preference was based on psychological reasons. The airplane cabin represented a unique environment which demanded that airline consider the psychological needs of its passengers—a need better satisfied by female attendants. The Supreme Court's response was that the statutory term "necessity" required the courts to apply a business necessity test, not a business convenience test. Consequently, a business firm must not only show that the favored group has abilities not possessed by the group being discriminated against, but that these abilities are necessary, not merely tangential, to the essence of the business involved.

The extent to which *shosha* (the concept of a moving think tank) will be recognized as a BFOQ is therefore a matter of conjecture. Both the Court of Appeals and the Supreme Court recognized the availability of a possible BFOQ defense when considering the Sumitomo matter. As the Second Circuit noted:

> Although the "bona fide occupational qualification" exception of Title VII is to be construed narrowly in the normal context, . . . we believe that as applied to a Japanese company enjoying rights under Article VII of the Treaty it must be construed in a manner that will give due weight to the Treaty rights and unique requirements of a Japanese company doing business in the United States, including such factors as a person's (1) Japanese linguistic and cultural skills, (2) knowledge of Japanese products, markets, customs, and business practices, (3) familiarity with the personnel and workings of the principal or parent enterprise in Japan, and (4) acceptability to those persons with whom the company or branch does business.[40]

While the Supreme Court did not go as far as the lower court in stating its position on the applicability of a BFOQ to the Sumitomo facts, it did add in a footnote to its decision that:

> We express no view as to whether Japanese citizenship may be a bona fide occupational qualification for certain positions at Sumitomo. . . . There can be little doubt that some positions in a Japanese controlled company doing business in the United States call for great familiarity with not only the language, but also the culture, customs, and business practices of that country.[41]

Two earlier decisions by lower federal courts in determining treaty trader status shed some light on how subsequent courts might interpret the BFOQ decision within the context of Japanese management practices. In both cases, Japanese firms sought to employ Japanese nationals in their U.S. operations under the FCN treaties. The Japanese companies argued that the employees possessed special qualifications which made their services essential to the efficient operation of the American enterprises and were thus entitled to treaty trader status.[42] In both cases, the U.S. district judges disagreed. One employee was a TV repairman. The court held that if the firm could not obtain the services of American technicians qualified to perform TV warranty repair work, it was the responsibility of the firm to establish training programs and develop qualified American technicians. The other employee was hired as a bookkeeper-accountant. She possessed a high school diploma and had taken a few courses in accounting. Her special qualification was that she spoke Japanese. The court held that the mere fact that she spoke Japanese was not sufficient to create a treaty trader status. She was hired to keep books.

Knowledge of Japanese was not job-related; there was no showing that the ability to speak Japanese was essential to the effective performance of her job as a bookkeeper. In the words of the Diaz decision, there was an absence of business necessity, only a showing of business convenience.

APPENDIX

Glossary of Japanese Terms with English Equivalents

Japanese Terms as Used by Itoh*	English Equivalents and/or Explanations
Organizational Titles	
yakuin	Member of the board of directors
sōshihainin	President
sōshihainin daikō	Executive vice president
buchō	Division manager (vice president)
shitenchō (equivalent to *buchō*)	Branch office manager (equivalent to vice president)
buchō daikō	Assistant division or department manager (equivalent to assistant vice president)
shitenchō daikō (equivalent to *buchō daikō*)	Assistant branch office manager (equivalent to assistant vice president)
kachō	Department manager/section chief
kachō dairi	Assistant department manager/section chief
jimushochō	Manager of a sub-branch office
kakarichō	Assistant section manager or supervisor
kakarichō daikō	Assistant supervisor
SM	Section members (low-level employees within a section, excluding secretaries, clerks, and porters)
daikō (the term *dairi* was used prior to April 1, 1975)	Assistant

*Other Japanese companies may use slightly different titles.

Status Levels—Old and New Systems

Old System (before April 1, 1975):

sanyo	Head
ittōshain	Level 1
nittōshain	Level 2
santōshain	Level 3
yontōshain	Level 4
gotōshain	Level 5

New System (effective April 1, 1975):

sanyo	Head
buchō-yaku	Chief (equivalent in military hierarchy to a commissioned officer)
buchō-ho	Assistant chief (commissioned officer status)
kachō-yaku	Manager (equivalent in military hierarchy to a noncommissioned officer)
kachō-ho	Assistant manager (noncommissioned officer status)
ikkyū	First grade status (equivalent in military hierarchy to enlisted personnel—i.e., corporal)
nikyū	Second grade status (private first class)
sankyū	Third grade status (recruit right out of college)

Miscellaneous Terms

Dowa Kaijō Kasai Hoken	Marine Fire and Casualty Insurance Company in Japan
gyōmuhonbu	Administrative and coordinating division of C. Itoh Japan
hikitsugi-sho	Document verifying transfer of authority upon resignation
honbusho	A unit consisting of several divisions
jimusho	Office
ka	Departments (sections under the old status system)
kaigaisojatsu-bu	Overseas department
kaigaitenshukansha	Emergency expense approved by the manager of an overseas branch office
kanrishoku-kyū	Management positions
kanrishoku	All status levels above *kachō-ho* that allow employees to receive certain allowances
karibaraikanjō	Suspense account—an account used for purchases of items that do not bear a clear purpose

kyuyogakari	Personnel in charge of payrolls
naiki	Company regulation—policy giving guidance as to whether a loan will be extended
saigaihukyūhi	Repair expense for damages related to the employee's property
sangokukan	Third country transaction—transaction with countries other than Japan and the United States
shiten	Branch office
shosha	In Japan, the term usually refers to a "general trading company." Itoh management uses the term to designate knowledge-intensive industry—ability to look at an entire industry, absence of a narrow perspective, "moving think tank."
shōyo	Bonuses
sōgokaihatsubu	Project development department
sōmubu	General affairs division—department that pays salaries
torishimariyaku	A level of employment above *sanyo*— equivalent to members of the board of directors, or *yakuin*
ukewatashi	Delivery of general machinery
zaimubu	Finance department
zaikinkyū	Overseas base salary—base salary plus family allowances

NOTES

1. *Michael E. Spiess, Jack K. Hardy and Benjamin F. Rountree* v. *C. Itoh & Co. (America), Inc.,* Civil Action 75-h-267, First Amended Complaint filed February 21, 1975, United States District Court, Southern District of Texas, Houston Division.

2. *Memorandum and Order* by the U.S. District Court, filed January 9, 1976.

3. Ibid., p. 6.

4. *Memorandum and Order,* filed January 29, 1976, p. 22; See also *McDonald* v. *Santa Fe Transportation Company,* 427 U.S. 273, 96 S.Ct. 2574 (1976).

5. *Memorandum and Order* filed March 1, 1979.

6. *Spiess, et al.* v. *C. Itoh & Company (America),* 643 F.2d 353 (1981).

7. *Spiess, et al.* v. *C. Itoh & Company (America),* 182 S.Ct. 2951 (1982); See also *Spiess, et al.* v. *C. Itoh & Company (America),* 687 F.2d 129 (1982).

8. *Avigliano, et al.* v. *Sumitomo Shoji America,* Inc., 638 F.2d 552 (1981).

9. *Sumitomo Shoji America, Inc.* v. *Avagliano, et al.,* 102 S.Ct. 2374 (1982).

10. All data regarding the plaintiffs' allegations was taken from the First Amended Complaint filed February 21, 1975.
11. All data regarding the management and personnel practices of Itoh (America) were compiled from the deposition of Sadao Nishitomi taken at the offices of Itoh (America), New York, by the plaintiffs' attorney during the period September 10–26, 1975. Readers desiring more detailed citations of Mr. Nishitomi's testimony are referred to the following publications by S. Prakash Sethi and Carl L. Swanson: *American Subsidiaries of Foreign Multinationals and U.S. Civil Rights Laws —Can Alien Executives Be Treated Differently Than American Executives?* Working Paper No. W-79-02 (Dallas: Center for Research in Business and Social Policy, The University of Texas at Dallas, 1979). "Are Foreign Multinationals Violating U.S. Civil Rights Laws," *Employee Relations Law Journal,* (Spring 1979), pp. 485–524. "Hiring Alien Executives in Compliance with U.S. Civil Rights Laws," *Journal of International Business Studies* (Fall 1979), pp. 370–380.
12. Corporate data, history, sales figures, and so on were obtained from brochures disseminated by C. Itoh & Co., Ltd. of Japan and C. Itoh & Co. (America), Inc., or from the deposition of Sadao Nishitomi.
13. 42 U.S.C.A. Section 1981.
14. Court's *Memorandum and Order* filed January 29, 1976, p. 22.
15. Ibid.
16. Motion to dismiss filed May 10, 1978, pp. 1–7.
17. See note 6.
18. See note 9.
19. *Extra Pay for Service Abroad,* Conference Board Report No. 665 (New York: The Conference Board, 1975); *Compensating Key Personnel Overseas,* Conference Board Report No. 574 (New York: The Conference Board, 1972). See also, Susan S. Holland, "Exchange of People among International Companies: Problems and Benefits," *ANNALS, AAPSS,* 424 (March 1976), pp. 52–66; and Dan S. Moore, "New Expatriate Policies Announced by Exxon," in *Innovations in International Compensation* (New York: Organization Resources Counselors, Inc., March 1978), pp. 3–5, 8.
20. Article 23 of the UN Charter; see also W. Joseph Dehner, Jr., "Multinational Enterprise and Racial Nondiscrimination: United States Enforcement of an International Human Right," *Harvard International Law Journal,* 15 (1974), pp. 71–125. The Universal Declaration of Human Rights was passed unanimously by the UN General Assembly on December 10, 1948.
21. Article 2 of the U.N. Charter; see also Dehner, "Multinational Enterprise," p. 88.
22. *1976 Digest of United States Practice in International Law,* pp. 518–527.
23. Gary Z. Nothstein and Jeffrey P. Ayres, "The Multinational Corporation and the Extraterritorial Application of the Labor Management Relations Act," *Cornell International Law Journal,* (December 1976), pp. 1–58, 16–17.
24. Ibid.; see Article VIII of the U.S.–Japan Treaty of Friendship, Commerce and Navigation, 4 U.S.T. 2070.
25. *Restatement (Second) of the Foreign Relations Law of the United States,* Section 17 (1965); Nothstein and Ayres, "The Multinational Corporation, pp. 11–16.
26. U.S. Constitution, Article VI, Section 2; Nothstein and Ayres, p. 16.

27. 4 U.S.T. 2070.
28. *Hearings before the Subcommittee of the Committee on Foreign Relations, United States Senate,* Eighty-Third Congress, First Session, July 13, 1953, pp. 2–3.
29. Dan F. Henderson, *Foreign Enterprise in Japan* (Chapel Hill: University of North Carolina Press, 1973), p. 274.
30. Yashiro Fujita, "Does Japan's Restriction on Foreign Capital Entries Violate Her Treaties?" *Law in Japan,* (1969), note 29.
31. 28 U.S.C. section 1602.
32. *1976 Digest of United States Practice,* pp. 505–506.
33. See note 9, p. 2379.
34. 8 U.S.C.A. 1101 (E).
35. 22 C.F.R. 41.40; see also 22 C.F.R. 41.41.
36. See *Nippon Express U.S.A., Inc.* v. *Esperdy,* 261 F.Supp. 561 (S.D.N.Y. 1966) and *Tokyo Sansei* v. *Esperdy,* 298 F.Supp. 945 (S.D.N.Y. 1969).
37. 42 U.S.C. 2000e-2(e); see also Harold Levy, "Civil Rights in Employment and the Multinational Corporations," *Cornell International Law Journal,* 10 (December 1976), pp. 89–90.
38. For example, the Supreme Court, New York County, in *American Jewish Congress* v. *Carter,* 190 N.Y. Supp. 2d Series 218 (1959), refused to permit an oil company doing business in Saudi Arabia to inquire into the religion of job applicants as a BFOQ because the king of Saudi Arabia prohibited the employment of Jews in Arabia.
39. 442 F.2d 385 (5th Cir, 1971), *cert. denied* 404 U.S. 950 (1951).
40. See note 8, p. 559.
41. See note 9, footnote 19, p. 2382.
42. See note 36.

FIVE ▚▚▚▚▚▚▚▚▚▚▚▚▚▚▚▚▚▚▚▚▚▚▚▚▚▚▚▚▚▚▚▚▚▚▚▚▚▚▚

The Cultural and Sociopolitical Context of the American Business and Management System

THE AMERICAN BUSINESS AND MANAGEMENT SYSTEM (ABMAS) HAS certain dominant and clearly identifiable traits that can be used to compare it with the Japanese system (JABMAS). It does not, however, enjoy the same degree of internal cohesiveness and continuity. A major factor is the absence of a stable, homogeneous society with a common value set. The United States is largely populated by descendants of immigrants from other countries, many of whom fled religious or political tyranny and still others who sought economic prosperity in a new land. As colonists, they brought their own customs and traditions and created a new society that is only three centuries old. Another major factor is the sheer geographic immensity of America. America is still a "frontier" society in its orientation, despite the sociopolitical dominance of its urban, high-technology population centers.

THE CULTURAL MILIEU

Lacking communal traditions and a long cultural history, ABMAS is much more oriented toward the individual and concerned with the immediate present and the short-term future. It operates in an environment where adversarial relationships, rather than partnerships, are the order of the day. The American business and management system operates against a backdrop of a distinct American ideology that has evolved over the past three centuries. This ideology defines for Americans a vision of what their society should be like. It provides a dynamic system of objectives, priorities, and criteria that affect all facets of American society.

86

Many distinctive core values in the American cultural milieu characterize how Americans approach human relationships and participate in informal groups and societal institutions. In examining the feasibility, as well as the viability, of transferring or adapting Japanese management practices to the United States, we must carefully consider some major conceptual components. Human relationships in the United States are established in terms of an ideology based on the supremacy of the individual, the notion of rights or entitlements, and the institution of private property. The outcome is a system of social ordering and conflict resolution expressed in terms of written contracts to define and delineate human relationships, the use of litigation to reconcile differences, and the use of competition for allocating societal rewards and creating social hierarchies. The supremacy of individualism also affects the American attitude toward group membership and societal institutions. There is a strong emphasis on voluntarism and satisfaction of self-interest, a belief in constitutional pluralism as a basic condition for political governance, and the acceptance of laws and due process as a societal norm.

Cultural Values Relating to Human Relationships

The Supremacy of Individualism. Americans place a high premium on the concept of individualism—the atomistic notion that their society is no more than the sum of the individuals who comprise it. This focus arises from the Judeo-Christian heritage, which speaks of individuals in relation to a personal God, in contrast to the Japanese-Confucian ethic of relationships that does not require the acceptance of a Divine Being. The American ideology is a product of Western thought and tradition, which emphasizes the uniqueness and independence of each human being.

This belief received further impetus in the Protestant theology of Martin Luther and John Calvin that emerged in the sixteenth and seventeenth centuries, at a time when America was being colonized as a new community for God's people. Protestant reformers in those centuries rediscovered the theology of St. Paul who, in his letters to the young Christian churches in the first century A.D., interpreted the Gospel message of Christ as an individual, not a collective act of faith.[1]

Individualism was harnessed in the seventeenth through nineteenth centuries for the benefit of American capitalism through a secular-theological concept called "the Protestant work ethic." It was the product of a marriage between John Calvin's theology of redemption and Adam Smith's advocacy of competition as a means of allocating economic resources in a society. It drew its major strength from the notion that labor is not merely an economic activity, but a spiritual end that is pleasing to God. Each human being should pursue work in the sense of religious mission designed to hasten the establishment of God's kingdom on earth.[2]

As the United States became more secularized in the twentieth century, some segments of American society rejected the idea of a personal creator and, in doing so, the transcendental aspects of the Protestant work ethic. Hard work was no longer considered to be its own reward, but a necessary and unpleasant means of satisfying an individual's desire for a greater share of society's finite resources. Self-reliance and self-discipline gave way to a sense of self-fulfillment and self-entitlement, but the emphasis remained on self. It was a trend that had been foreseen one hundred and fifty years before by Alexis de Tocqueville, who predicted that the enlightened self-interest of Americans would ultimately lead to selfishness.[3]

This new individualism dominates American thinking. Current societal institutions and cultural values are highly oriented to the self-fulfillment of the individual. The concept of self dominates philosophy and psychology. It permeates language and literature. Americans see themselves as distinct entities and their world as separate categories of individuals. Furthermore, since the individual does not wish to be subjugated by the institutions of society, self-fulfillment can be achieved only under confrontational conditions that demand aggressive assertion of one's own interests to the exclusion of externally determined notions of public interest.

The Ideology of Rights, Not Duties. Closely tied to the concept of individualism is the idea of rights. Since each human being is equal in the eyes of God, he or she is equal in the eyes of the law. It is a notion that led to the establishment of the American republic in 1776 and was best articulated by Thomas Jefferson in the Declaration of Independence: "We hold these truths to be self-evident, that *all men are created equal,* that they are endowed by their Creator with certain *inalienable rights,* that among these are life, liberty and the pursuit of happiness . . ." [emphasis added].

Initially, rights were thought of in terms of equality before the law and equality of opportunity. Rights are now translated, particularly by disadvantaged groups, in terms of equality of results or entitlements. This notion assumes that discrimination or injustice of long standing may not be rectifiable solely through equality of opportunity. It must be reinforced, at least in the interim, through equality of outcome. The concept finds support in the egalitarian notion that a just society requires that individuals are not only politically or legally equal, but equal in all respects—in income, influence, and quality of life.[4]

The Institution of Private Property. The institution of private property is based on the fundamental notion that since each individual owns himself, he owns his labor and the product of his labor. Part of the American creed is the right of each individual to hold and use property as the primary means of ensuring political and economic independence from the oppressive demands of the community acting through an all-pervasive state. The ownership of property has been described as "the handmaiden to individualism."[5]

The principal contributor to this component of the American ideology was John Locke, a seventeenth-century philosopher whose treatises influenced American political thinking at the time of the Declaration of Independence and the adoption of the U.S. Constitution. Locke advocated individual property rights against community interests by placing extreme emphasis on the doctrine of natural rights. The concept found fertile soil in a new country where unlimited quantities of resources were available for individual exploitation.

The concept of private property is not limited to private ownership of tangible objects like land or an automobile. Property is better understood as a relationship between individuals and groups, where the owner of property has the power to exclude others from its use—for example, the power to deny access to land on the legal grounds of trespass. As more and more of the nation's wealth assumed intangible forms, modern American legal thought expanded the private property concept to include new forms of ownership primarily concerned with earning capacity, such as an individual's right to practice a profession such as attorney or physician. Another major development was the emergence of the American government as a major source of intangible properties or entitlements. Initially, entitlements were granted in the "public interest." However, the right to grant an entitlement also carried with it the authority to withdraw it, thereby creating the potential for abuse of bureaucratic authority. Such entitlements soon became a property right that could not be granted or withdrawn by the state arbitrarily or without due process.[6]

The Private Law of Contract. The emphasis on rights in American society has also engendered the greater use of written and legally enforceable contractual processes to define rights and resolve intergroup relations than is found in Japan and other traditional societies.[7] The specificity of a written document also facilitates judicial determination of rights when parties to the contract are in conflict. For Americans, the contractual relationships represent a faith in a closely defined set of values; that is, the belief that a society can not function, particularly in trade and commerce, if its members cannot enter into and honor agreements freely made.

The private law of contract had its roots in English common law, which presupposed only two individuals, reasonably equal in bargaining power, making mutually binding commitments. Traditionally, the government was interested in enforcing such contracts only to avoid the private use of force in the event of default. The growing societal emphasis on rights and the emergence of a more complex and interrelated society has transformed contract from a single exchange of promises into a series of prescribed norms of conduct governing a continuous relationship. It has also expanded the number of parties to the contract, with the government asserting a third interest—that of the general public. A prime example is a management-union agreement. Nor are contracts limited to private parties. The laws of Congress, the implementing rules of the executive branch, and the orders of the judiciary are more specialized contractual arrangements designed to encompass new types of relationships between individuals and groups.

The Role of Litigation and Due Process. The American social process encourages individuals to seek a judicial determination regarding their rights and obligations—to define their relations with others through the filing of a lawsuit. Consequently, no society anywhere in the world is more litigious than the United States. No subject is "taboo" for judicial resolution. The basic assumption is that all members of society are entitled to their "day in court," to have the benefit of the law in protecting their rights and redressing their grievances.

Two assumptions underlie the use of litigation in the United States. First, societal relationships are generated and sustained in an adversary and bargaining environment. There is a continuous process of adjustment of social power among all members and subsystems in the social system. Legislation becomes a compromise, execution of laws an accommodation, and judicial determinations a vindication of conflicting goals among competing groups. Second, if this confrontation cannot be resolved through negotiation, it must be contained and controlled for the sake of societal harmony. This is accomplished through litigation, a formalized and socially approved adversary process in which each side presents its selected version of the facts by maximizing the strengths and minimizing the weaknesses of its relative position. Each seeks a verdict in its favor. The judicial emphasis is on due process, the fair and impartial administration of the judicial process in a nondiscriminatory manner.[8]

Competition as a Social Control Mechanism. Competition as a societal control mechanism draws its roots from the right of an individual to hold and use private property. Even if every individual uses his property for his own self-interest, the entire community will benefit through the operation of the "invisible hand of competition." It was a notion proposed to the world in the same year as the Declaration of Independence by Adam Smith in *The Wealth of Nations*.[9] His main thesis that economic decisions are best made by individual sellers and buyers competing in an open market came to serve as the intellectual linchpin in the American economic system.

Only in the United States has competition become the main force in establishing and defining societal relationships and a pragmatic tool for resolving conflicts in a highly pluralistic society. Public policy issues are thought to be best resolved through public advocacy and confrontation between groups competing for support from other individuals and institutions. Judicial support for the First Amendment right of free speech is based, in large part, on the constitutional belief that a free society benefits from competition in the marketplace of ideas, just as better economic decisions result from competition in the marketplace of products and services.[10]

Cultural Values Relating to Groups and Institutions

American Collectivism. A corollary of individualism, in what may first appear to be a contradiction, is the tremendous thrust toward group formation in American society. Americans are joiners. They belong to a staggering array of organizations where voluntary cooperation and teamwork are important. For Americans, the right to associate represents a philosophical paradox: There is the emphasis on the inviolability of the individual even as that person asserts his dependence on others for the fulfillment of his individual potential.[11]

There are two critical distinctions, however. First, Western society has evolved separate institutions with separate functions. For example, satisfaction of an individual's economic needs is provided by the nation's commercial institutions, while matters of faith and spiritual well-being are the responsibility of the church. Second, individual participation in groups is not required because of societal norms. Membership is entirely voluntary. An American joins a group generally because he or she wants to. Joining is viewed as a normal extension of individualism and, more important, as a right that is guaranteed in the Bill of Rights of the American Constitution.[12]

The American collective experience is essentially an associational one. Life is given to an American's individual need for self-realization through participation in many diverse groups, rather than through an all-inclusive attachment to the state or a single organization such as the corporation. These associations operate as units within the social system, but not as units thereof, since each is narrowly focused on the commonality of interests that personifies its membership. Each demands only a fraction of an individual's loyalty and each receives only a portion of the individual's time, effort, and support. A person may join a multitude of associations with conflicting purposes, causing him or her to vacillate in loyalties to competing groups. Thus, a worker may feel a sense of loyalty to an employer to increase production, but not hesitate to strike that same employer in support of the union's demands that production quotas be modified.[13]

The Limited Role of the Work Group in American Society. This attitude toward group formation and participation is particularly significant for the American corporation, both from the standpoint of the employer and the employee. Neither views the work group as the primary societal entity that demands their first or only loyalty. American executives tend to treat their membership in the corporate group as a limited one. Their focus is on commercial matters, with minimal concern for the social, psychological, or spiritual needs of subordinates. Employees also have a limited view of the work group. They look to the employer as the primary source for the income that will satisfy their economic needs, including support of other groups. The corporate group phenomenon is viewed in terms of one's role and function vis-à-vis other group members, and not as an emotional attachment to the group or its output.

It is not surprising that Americans tend to be insensitive to and unconcerned about interactions and relationships in the work group. There is often an unwillingness to put forth the necessary effort to sustain or increase group productivity. After-work fraternization among members of the work group is not a norm. The emphasis is on getting the job done so that an individual can go home and participate in other groups. An individual's work "friends" are not necessarily and even ordinarily his or her social friends. Employers who encourage after-hours socialization among employees with company picnics or other activities are often viewed as "paternalistic" and therefore old-fashioned in their management values.

A Belief in a Limited and Pluralistic State. Individualism also defines the role Americans desire for government in societal affairs. One of the fundamental political precepts for most Americans is the notion that the least government is the best government. Notwithstanding the current size of American government and the greater public demand for government intervention in such areas as environmental protection, most Americans are reluctant to grant too much authority to government lest individual rights be trampled. Americans view politics as a government Goliath versus an individual David. This approach supports the Lockean thesis that the primary function of government is to protect the individual's person and property. Any other role would constitute a serious interference with a citizen's independence.

The Constitution of the United States functions as a symbol of the rights reserved to the people and constitutes a limitation on the powers of government. It provides for a separation of powers among units of the national government and creates a structure of built-in checks and balances against the inherent abuse of government authority that might endanger individual rights.

Pluralism is the other major component in the American system of government. It exemplifies a nation characterized by a multiplicity of interests that are in a perpetual state of conflict and interaction. For the individual, access to a multiplicity of groups enables him or her to reach alternative power centers when one or more subsystems are constraining. Pluralism encourages individuals to form new groups when existing groups are unable or unwilling to serve their emerging needs. Society benefits, since a system of multiple-group pressures provides reasonable assurance that the most important problems will be channeled to the public arena for debate and resolution.[14]

A Government of Laws, Not Men. The notion of "the rule of law" has been the cornerstone of American society since its inception. It imposes constraints on group behavior and ensures that individual relationships are determined objectively by universal standards that are not subject to individual idiosyncrasies. In the words of one of the most distinguished justices of the U.S. Supreme Court, Felix Frankfurter: "The historic phrase 'a government of laws and not of men' epitomizes the distinguishing character of our political society. When John Adams put that phrase into the Massachusetts Declaration of Rights he was not indulging in a rhetorical flourish. He was expressing the aim of those who, with him, framed the Declaration of Independence and founded the Republic."[15]

This concept had its origin in England prior to the Magna Carta, which used the term *per legem terrae*—the law of the land. It drew its political strength from the belief that individuals should not be subject to the whims of other individuals, even kings. Since a major reason for the American Declaration of Independence was to free the American colonists from the tyranny of the Crown, it is understandable that "rule of law" would become the political religion of the United States.

Law serves as a stabilizing force for the American economic system and as a framework in which all societal affairs are conducted in the United States. It embodies the notions of objectivity and fairness in making economic decisions and regulating business conduct. Finally, the law provides a climate and a framework not only for improving society, but for curing social ills. Thus, law has become the principal tool employed by individuals and societal subsystems to correct perceived wrongs, to gain political power, and to influence the public policy process in the United States.

THE SOCIOPOLITICAL CONTEXT

The American political system, like those of most stable democratic societies of the Western world, operates through a network of governmental bodies consisting of public officials who are subject to public accountability through the electoral process. However, unlike those of most other democracies, the American system is much more oriented toward local and regional constituencies rather than broad national groupings. This orientation is encouraged by the American belief in the separation of powers between various governmental bodies. A more recent political phenomenon has been the creation of a new branch of federal government not directly provided for in the Constitution—the independent regulatory agency.

The two American political parties are quite pragmatic in developing a broad political base that will appeal to diverse and competing constituencies. However, they do not represent strong ideological philosophies that can be implemented through centralized party discipline. Thus, people of equally liberal or conservative orientation can be found in two different political parties. More important, the "umbrella" approach to American political party organization facilitates the participation of special or single issue groups in the electoral and political processes. All these factors contribute to an adversarial relationship between government and business that differs dramatically from the working partnership that characterizes the rest of the Western world.

The Federal Separation of Power

The political mood of the late eighteenth century and the motivation of the framers of the American Constitution was to divide and limit the power of the state and thus make it difficult for a strong national executive, king, or dictator to emerge. American government thus differs from other nations of the Western world in that it provides for competitive centers of power within the structure of government itself.

First, power is divided between the national government and the fifty states, the latter including thousands of local communities. All power not granted to the national government is expressly reserved to the states. Despite the growth of the national government, state and local governments oversee a tremendous range of public needs—education, crime prevention and control, and the regulation of local utility services. Second, power is divided among the three branches of the national government: Congress, the presidency, and the Supreme Court. Power in Congress is further divided between a House of Representatives and a Senate. Representatives are elected every two years from various geographic districts with roughly equal numbers of voters. Senators, on the other hand, are elected for six-year terms, with each state having only two senators regardless of its geographic size or population.

The president is chosen by the entire national electorate every four years and is charged with administering the laws passed by the Congress, with the assistance of a federal bureaucracy. He serves as the chief of state. He is generally viewed as the head of his political party, although a large measure of power may rest in the hands of other party members. Since the United States does not have a parliamentary system, as does Japan and other countries in the Western world, the president is not a leader in the legislative process but an administrator, albeit with a public mandate. He is not always of the same political party as a majority of the elected representatives in Congress. In order to influence the legislative process, the president must therefore rely on persuasion and political compromise.

The Supreme Court and the subordinate federal judiciary are appointed by the president with the advice and consent of the Senate. They serve for life and can be removed from office only for malfeasance in the performance of their duties, in order to free them from the influence of the electoral process. This ensures their independence from political pressures in rendering decisions. In the past two decades, the judicial branch has assumed a new role in the process of government. Recent social and economic legislation has compelled judges to render decisions on complex social matters formerly considered the prerogative of the legislative and executive branches of government, such as school segregation and environmental protection. In many instances, the U.S. Congress has encouraged this development. In an effort to placate diverse and competing special interest groups, Congress has found it expedient simply to establish social norms through legislation and then allow the litigation process to allocate entitlements among competing groups.

The Independent Regulatory Agencies

A major political phenomenon has been the establishment of independent regulatory agencies under the executive branch to perform some of the functions of Congress. These agencies are granted limited power to promulgate rules (a legislative activity), to administer the basic laws establishing the agency and the rules issued by it (an administrative activity), and to act as a court of first resort for lawsuits brought by agency staff for violations of the organic law or rules (a judicial activity). Thus, there currently exists within the framework of American government a governmental body generally associated with the parliamentary process in other democratic nations.

Members of regulatory agencies are appointed by the president and their budget is authorized by him, thereby giving him some control over the executive functions of the agency. Agency membership, however, must reflect a previously determined ratio of the two U.S. political parties. Appointment of agency members must be with the advice and consent of the Senate. Agency budgets and operations are also subject to congressional approval and oversight, thereby creating a dual command and control system over agency affairs. All agency judicial decisions can be challenged in the federal courts. Thus, the constitutional separation of powers is satisfied, since each constitutional branch of the federal government exercises some control over the activities of the regulatory agencies.

In reality, Congress dominates the regulatory agencies. The president's power is limited so that the regulatory agencies operate independent of the politics of the White House. The judiciary cannot act unless it is presented with a case or controversy, and then its role is limited to the factual and legal questions presented by the lawsuit. Thus, until some American employees challenged the U.S.–Japan Treaty of Friendship, Commerce, and Navigation, it was not possible for the U.S. Supreme Court to decide whether the right of Japanese firms to establish U.S. subsidiaries and to employ their own nationals in managerial positions isolated them from the requirements of the U.S. job discrimination laws.

A key control mechanism employed by Congress has been the legislative veto. Congress, under a broad grant of legislative authority, authorizes an agency to issue statutelike regulations having the full force of law. To ensure that this grant is not abused, Congress reserves the right to review any proposed regulation before it becomes final and to veto it. It is a concept that arose during World War II, when the president needed authority to make fast, unilateral decisions in order to prosecute the war by exercising what were considered to be the constitutional responsibilities of Congress. As public concern has grown in the past two decades over the growth of government bureaucracy and the electoral unaccountability of regulatory officials, the legislative veto has become a common provision in enabling statutes.

The legal rationale was appealing. Since Congress granted a portion of its power to legislate to an executive branch entity, it surely had the right to veto the results of the exercise of that legislative power. Not so, said the U.S. Supreme Court in June 1983. The objective of the Constitution was to divide the delegated powers of the federal government into three defined categories and to assure, as nearly as possible, that each of the three branches confined itself to its assigned responsibilities. A majority of the Court would view the legislative veto as an attempt by Congress to overstep its boundaries and improperly intervene in the functions of the executive branch. Thus, the concept of the federal separation of powers was reasserted.[16]

This decision is likely to cause two changes in the current system of regulation. It will lead Congress to enact laws that are more precise in intent and application. Regulatory agencies will have less discretion to interpret and administer the laws in a manner that responds to changing societal needs and expectations. This problem characterizes the regulatory environment associated with the Environmental Protection Agency (EPA) and the Food and Drug Administration (FDA), which are compelled to issue regulations despite their harshness and questionable cost-benefit ratio because Congress has mandated a desirable outcome regardless of societal costs. It presents an even sharper contrast to the Japanese system, in which government regulation is largely practiced through administrative guidance. On the other hand, once a law has been enacted, the regulatory agencies will have a freer hand to administer it, since congressional intervention on an ad hoc basis has been made more difficult.

While the regulatory decision-making structure and process in the United States are highly complex and, to the untutored eye, confusing, some common threads are present. It is adversary. The agency staff views its role as that of a "watchdog" protecting the "public interest" in contrast to the self-interest of the firms being regulated. It is essentially a legal process that operates in a judicial arena and is dominated by lawyers. It functions in the open and is subject to public and particularly news media scrutiny. This process of checks and balances again manifests the basic American fear of concentration of too much power in the hands of either bureaucrats or political entities.[17]

The Revolving Door Syndrome

Government administrators, especially at policymaking levels, are paid lower salaries compared to those paid in the private sector. Public servants are not supposed to "get rich" serving the public. At the same time, they wield considerable influence over the outcome of certain government actions that can greatly benefit affected parties. These factors encourage a "revolving door" syndrome in which talented and experienced young executives sacrifice short-run earnings in order to gain government experience that can be used to earn higher salaries in the private sector at a later date. The process allows each new administration to appoint its own people and discourages the creation of a permanent bureaucracy with its own vested interests. The high turnover also results in a paucity of experienced administrators and an inefficient system of management. Although the system has strong built-in incentives for crossover between private and public sectors, such a movement is not viewed as beneficial to the public interest. Instead, there is a strong presumption of conflict of interest. An elaborate system of rules and regulations has been enacted to minimize such conflict and severely limit its potential benefit to the individuals involved.

The Growth and Influence of Special Interest
Groups in American Politics

Politics in the United States has become a competition between special interest groups, each attempting to make the political process responsive to its needs and reflective of its institutional values. In the past, groups were generally consensual in their orientation, pragmatic in their attempts to achieve political results, and prepared to function under the umbrella of a larger and more comprehensive political organization, such as the Democratic or the Republican party.[18] In the past two decades, there has been a marked shift from broadly based political parties to a conglomeration of more narrowly based "interest groups" within these parties, with mixed results for American business. Corporations have a new political role and further access to the political system, particularly through corporate political action committees, increased lobbying, and more widespread advocacy advertising. But there have also emerged groups diametrically opposed to the goals propounded by American business. Contributing to this shift have been a number of major changes in the American political scene.

1. The cost of political campaigns has increased phenomenally due to the lengthening campaign periods and the use of electronic media for paid political messages. Individual candidates, especially incumbents, conduct their own fundraising functions, raising sizable amounts of money from their own constituencies. While this frees them from the financial domination of the party apparatus, it also makes them more susceptible to local and regional interests.
2. There has been a relative decline in the power of political parties to forge a cohesive set of national priorities or policies. Primaries have become the principal means of nominating candidates, thereby ensuring more equitable representation and the participation of groups formerly excluded in the electoral process. Gifted candidates can ignore party discipline, since they are not beholden to the party convention for their candidacy or election.[19]
3. This period also has been marked by the growth of highly militant interest groups, often concentrating on a single or a limited number of issues to the exclusion of all other political and social needs. Invariably, these groups have been unwilling to compromise their views in order to achieve consensus support for their positions and often view the corporation as a perpetual adversary of the public interest. They challenge any attempt by government officials to form coalitions with business and to develop and implement a national response to external forces in the international marketplace, similar to Japan's MITI and business coalition, as a betrayal of the public interest.[20]

4. There has been a progressive decentralization of power in Congress. Responding to the Watergate political excesses, reformers have succeeded in reducing the importance of seniority in Congress, opening up committee proceedings to public scrutiny, and providing for the "popular" election of committee chairs. This dispersal of power has meant that more representatives now have more influence over the outcome of legislation, while they are less wedded to the major parties for financial support and political nuturing.[21]

Business Participation in the Political Process

Corporate participation in elections is severely constrained in the interest of protecting the electoral process from too much money. Corporations are forbidden to contribute directly to candidates for federal office. They are, however, permitted to form political action committees (PACs). PAC membership is limited to corporate executives and shareholders. Severe restrictions are imposed on employee membership, since employees are supposed to join their labor union PACs. Membership is voluntary. Potential members must be informed of the political purpose of the fund and their right not to participate without fear of reprisal. PAC funds must be separate and segregated from the corporation's general treasury. Severe restrictions are placed on the amounts contributed: no more than $5,000 per candidate per election, with a maximum of $15,000 per election cycle.[22]

Lobbying is protected, since the essence of a constitutional democracy is the right of the electors to influence the formulation and implementation of public policy. Corporate lobbying activities are open to disclosure so that the public may know who is attempting to influence the policy process. However, lobbying is perceived by large segments of American society as an attempt by special interest groups to frustrate the will of the people. Consequently, proposals for tough lobbying laws designed to identify individual contributors with greater specificity and provide more extensive disclosure on grassroots lobbying enjoy wide support among the American people.

A more recent political phenomenon has been the growth of corporate advocacy-issue advertising or grassroots lobbying. It represents an effort by the business community to argue and defend its viewpoint on controversial issues of social importance. There has been some concern that corporate advocacy advertising distorts complex public policy issues through oversimplified marketing approaches better employed to sell goods and services. Some critics have argued that corporations, with their vast financial resources, may dominate the public policy agenda to the exclusion of alternative viewpoints competing for public attention in the marketplace of ideas.[23]

The Adversarial Relationship between Government and Business

Most observers of the American sociopolitical scene, particularly foreigners, cannot avoid noting the often hostile environment that confronts business in many agencies of American government today. The antagonism and sometimes open hostility between business and government can be seen in candidates who run for federal office against "big business," national news media exposés that focus on "corporate profiteers," and special interest group studies that advocate little, if any, role for business in the public policy process. While some tension between business and government is generally considered beneficial to a capitalistic economy and the natural outcome of a pluralistic democracy, the degree of the current hostility reflects a decline in mutual trust that would be needed if the United States were to establish the type of partnership characterized by Japanese business and MITI.

For most of the life of the American republic, business entities have operated subject to a series of federal and state laws that constrained their discretionary acts. Organic restraints were imposed on the creation, structure, and management of the business corporation. Corporate decision making was directly restrained through taxation and regulation of corporate affairs.[24] The free enterprise market system was carefully policed through antitrust legislation designed to protect American society against monoplies, unreasonable restraints of trade, and other acts that might interfere with the effective operation of the competitive system.[25] The basic premise underlying these governmental constraints has been the fear that corporations would abuse their economic power unless constrained in the interests of other subsystems. Government has been placed in the role of a "police officer" enforcing the economic "rules of the game." It has discouraged cooperative efforts between business and government and fostered a hands off attitude by government officials in developing a partnership between government and business.

Until recently, regulation of business affairs was largely limited to economic regulation that was industry-oriented and focused on rate structures and service performance. It was the type generally associated with the Civil Aeronautics Board regulation of air transportation or the Federal Communications Commission regulation of telephone, radio, and television. Effective economic regulation demanded a close working relationship between regulator and regulated. This form of partnership, conceptually similar to Japan's MITI and the Ministry of Finance, has been the subject of constant attack by various segments of society arguing that the "public interest" is best served by an adversarial relationship between government and business.[26]

The result has been a move toward "social regulation" that cuts across industry groupings. The new social regulation is concerned with the conditions under which goods and services are produced or the physical characteristics of products being produced for resale to the public—for example, the Consumer Product Safety Commission (CPSC), the Equal Employment Opportunity Commission (EEOC), the Environmental Protection Agency (EPA), and the Occupational Safety and Health Administration (OSHA). The purpose of these agencies is not to regulate certain industries with problems, but to eliminate problems common to all industries. The agency's enforcement approach is to mandate precise engineering controls rather than performance standards, thus allowing management discretion in achieving societal goals. The "social" regulatory agency is therefore more involved in the details of the management process that its predecessor "economic" agency.

This approach, in part, has been encouraged by Congress. The agencies are often mandated to pursue their appointed statutory goals more or less singlemindedly, with little or no concern for the compliance costs or economic consequences of their actions. The universe being policed by the government agency becomes so vast that opportunities for friendly relationships between the governing and the governed are diminished, if not eliminated. This approach enhances the adversary relationship, since the differences in the objectives of public sector bureaucrats and private sector managers become more pronounced. It encourages private sector management to focus on profitability and leave social values, the general public interest, and the needs of specially targeted interest groups to the public sector administrators.[27]

Lack of a National Industrial Policy

The United States is one of the few nations in the free world that does not have a central economic planning process and a national industrial policy. This is partly due to the free enterprise ideology that resource allocation decisions are best made in the marketplace. Another factor is an apparent lack of national consensus, even within the business community, as to the components of such a policy and the manner in which it might be implemented. Further, the idea of centralized national economic planning runs counter to the heterogeneous nature of a nation with diverse political groups and economic interests that fear concentration of power in the hands of government bureaucrats.[28] As Franklin Lindsay of Itel Corporation noted: "We in America profoundly distrust any central group picking the losers and winners."[29] This attitude can be seen in the fragmented manner in which U.S. trade and investment policies are currently formulated and implemented, as shown in Exhibit 5–1.

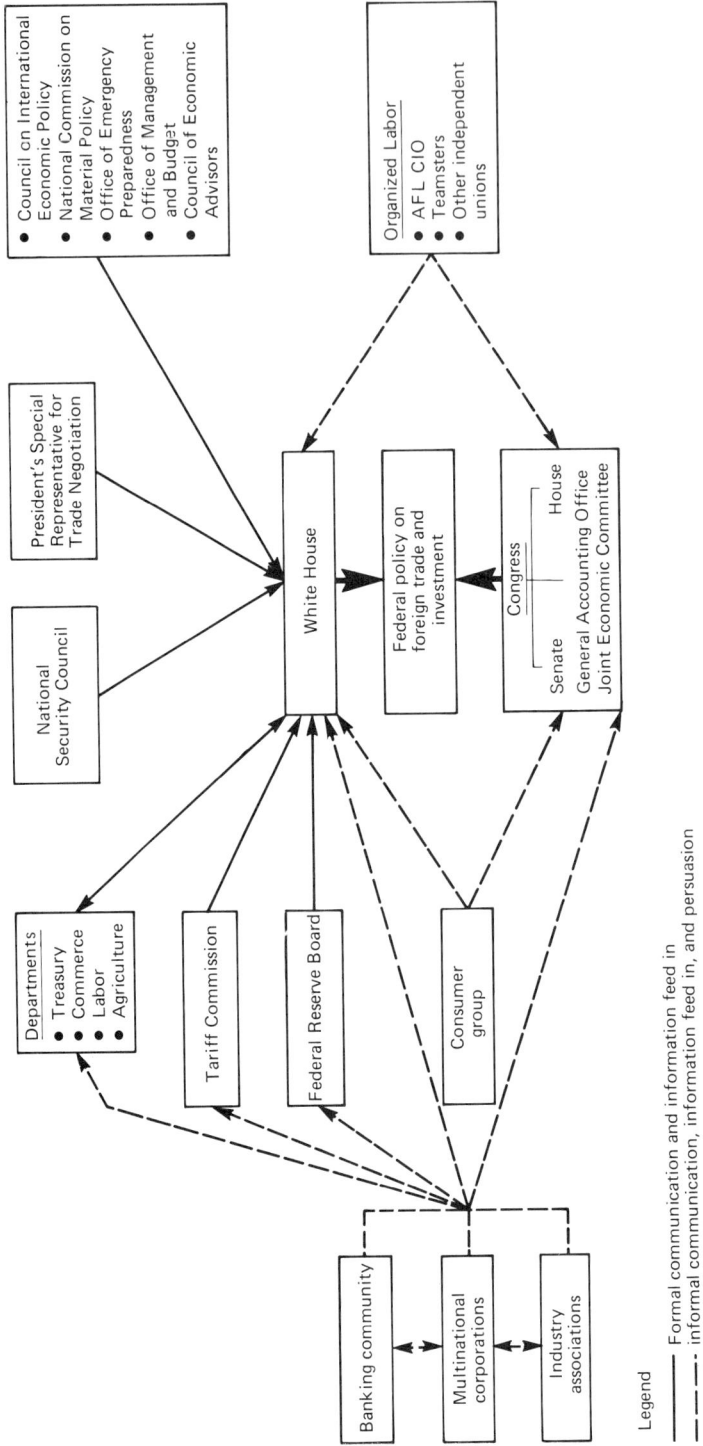

EXHIBIT 5–1 Major Influences on Foreign Trade and Investment Policymaking (USA)

Legend

——— Formal communication and information feed in
— — — informal communication, information feed in, and persuasion

SOURCE: S. Prakash Sethi, *Japanese Business and Social Conflict* (Cambridge, Mass.: Ballinger, 1975), p. 32.

Currently, there is considerable discussion as to the need for a national industrial policy, largely because of the declining competitive position of major U.S. industries, both in the domestic U.S. market and in overseas markets. Prior to the 1960s, foreign trade, either exports or imports, was not a significant factor in the American economy, and the need for a national trade policy seemed academic. In the ten-year period from 1970 to 1980, exports of American goods jumped from 9.3 to 19 percent. Conversely, by 1980 more than 70 percent of all goods produced in the United States faced direct competition from foreign imports. The world has fast become a single marketplace where goods are produced wherever the costs are lowest, without regard for national boundaries. America's former competitive advantage of being able to operate a high-volume, standardized, assembly-line production economy to produce quality goods at low cost has been lost to the Third World. The less developed nations (LDCs) now have a lower wage structure and employ the production concepts and machinery formerly associated with American industrial technology. The current automation of the factory has accelerated this trend by encouraging the industrialized nations to farm out the production of standardized parts to developing nations.[30] Thus, it is not surprising that sales of U.S. merchandise abroad—counting farm goods as well as military hardware—were down 9.1 percent to $233 billion in 1982.[31]

Europe and Japan have responded to this challenge by shifting their national industrial bases toward products and processes that require technical skills not possessed by the workforce in the developing nations. More important, business firms in these nations are being aided by government policies and programs that call for a restructuring of the commercial life of the nation and the direction of the nation's economic institutions in this new, single international market—that is, a national industrial policy. Americans are being urged to adopt a similar approach, particularly by Japanese officials who contend that "if the United States had such a (trade) policy, we feel that we could avoid unnecessary restrictions on trade."[32]

The cultural history of the American people and their institutions constitute a formidable barrier to the idea of an effective centrally planned, or at least directed, economy that is the natural outcome of a national industrial policy. The focus of constitutional federalism is to fragment the power of the sovereign state among many governmental units. The problem is further complicated by the complexity and fragmentation of the American economic system, which often represents individualism at its extreme. Examples of almost every conceivable type of economic organization can be found in the United States. The American belief that "big is bad" enjoys wide acceptance as a societal creed. When this is coupled with a populist disdain for and mistrust of government officials, it is not surprising that American experiments with central planning during World Wars I and II were dismantled as rapidly as possible once the national emergency ended.

LIMITATIONS AND DRAWBACKS OF THE AMERICAN
SOCIOPOLITICAL ENVIRONMENT

The ideological underpinnings of American society, its social organization
and system of government, have been instrumental in providing the nation
with an environment that has been conducive to the economic growth and
well-being of its people. However, like all other systems, it has also created
circumstances that are inimical to the growth of business and economic
institutions. To some extent, these disadvantages are in the nature of tradeoffs and the price paid for the positive virtues of a given value set. To a
large extent, they also reflect the manner in which the basic values and
processes of government have been operationalized and manipulated by
various groups, thereby diminishing the positive benefits for the entire system.

The American Ideology

The notion of individualism, as expressed in terms of the Protestant work
ethic, has undergone a profound change in the United States. What has
remained are the hedonistic features in which self-fulfillment, not self-discipline, is the benchmark for all judgments. Equality is also viewed in a different context. It is no longer equality of opportunity, but equality of outcome; each individual must receive some sort of fair share of society's
resources. It is no longer an interim step in society's efforts to achieve
individual liberty, but the end product itself. Justice is defined as fairness
and considered the highest social value. As equality in social and economic
conditions came to enjoy the same status as political equality, government
was used more and more to reduce or shift certain societal risks formerly
borne by individuals. Reliance by citizens on government for limited solutions to certain economic, social, and cultural problems grew to include
demands for mitigation of almost every risk an individual might be asked
to bear.[33]

More important, individualism has created tremendous societal problems for Americans, particularly in associational activities. Our cultural
preoccupation with "doing one's own thing" has often meant narcissistic
isolation from the benefits of group life or dysfunctional rivalry when involved in group activities.[34] Yet the growing complexity of an interrelated
world has generated greater interdependence among individuals, a reliance
on others and a sharing of efforts in achieving common goals. This interdependence can be seen in the member satisfaction and outcome results
experienced by members of a highly cohesive group working together and
identified as having "team spirit," such as a professional football team. Or-

ganizational memberships have become more important in a relationship sense, although Americans try to deny it in their preoccupation with self.

Constitutional Pluralism

Constitutional pluralism also has not been without its disadvantages. It has often meant fragmentation in the political life of the nation. Politics becomes a game in which adversary groups compete fully and freely to promote their interest vis-à-vis other interests. The system of checks and balances affords opportunities for political gameplayers to leverage one branch against the other. Lobbying, campaign support through PACs, and judicial challenges of governmental action become the preferred means of advancing special interest concerns. Government operates essentially as a process for balancing conflicting interests, relegating the development of a national policy consensus to a secondary position.[35]

While populism has been part of the American political scene since the founding of the nation, it has assumed a new characteristic—namely, the widespread distrust of societal institutions and their leaders by various segments of the American public. This is largely due to a perception that American institutions and their leaders too often act for their own interest rather than that of the people. This distrust is often expressed in the political arena as a negative reaction against the Establishment by emerging groups. The criteria is often a single issue, such as abortion, environmentalism, and nuclear power.

The Structure and Processes of Government

A major factor affecting American business today is the slowing of the legislative process and the apparent inability of Congress to function effectively when confronted with complex and divisive public policy questions. Although the power of Congress was strengthened vis-à-vis the presidency as an outgrowth of the Watergate reforms, it was also weakened so far as the processes of Congress were concerned. By diffusing decision-making power and increasing the number of power points, these reforms encouraged political gameplaying by those groups able to marshal sufficient forces to oppose some legislation but unable to develop a sufficient consensus to pass legislation. It has resulted in government by subcommittee,[36] a tremendous growth of congressional staff not subject to the ballot box discipline, an overreliance by elected officials on their staffs, and the enhanced role of lobbying in the public policy process.

Events of the past two decades have had a profound influence in reducing the power of the presidency to provide executive direction to the nation. A number of factors have contributed to this state of affairs: the fear of some groups of an "imperial" presidency; the decline in the support of presidential policies by the president's own party; the fragmentation of Congress, which more often than not is governed by the opposing political party; the hostility of the media and its desire to publicize all government decisions in the name of free speech; and the intransigence of the federal bureaucracy.[37]

Nor has the independent judiciary been free from public criticism of its new role. Judges have issued orders opposing public policy decisions by elected officials amid cries by many segments of society that the federal government is intruding into purely local matters. Conversely, special interest groups, dissatisfied with the response of elected officials to their concerns, have increasingly resorted to lawsuits, even though the judicial forum is often the least desirable place to resolve social issues. The outcome has been a phenomenal increase in the court docket that has seriously interfered with judicial performance and a growing credibility gap for the judiciary.[38]

Independent regulatory agencies entered the political scene before the turn of the century as a means of isolating government's decision-making processes from the ebb and flow of politics and to provide a stable and continuous public policy process that would operate in the public interest. Recently, the fear has grown that the agencies have been captured by the interests being regulated to the detriment of this public interest and are being controlled by an intransigent bureaucracy that does not have ballot box accountability.

The constitutional separation of powers was designed to ensure that a dictatorship did not emerge and to protect the interests of diverse societal constituents. Instead, it has often degenerated into a bureaucratic morass of technical due process where the government's response to a public policy issue is tedious and time-consuming. The operating efficiency of a central national government is further hampered by the fact that federal officials are elected for different and overlapping periods of time and do not have to be of the same political persuasion.

The New Social Constituencies

As the large corporation administered by salaried managers replaced the small family-owned firm as the primary instrument for managing the production and distribution systems of society, it also altered the substance of the market mechanism in coordinating the nation's economy and its resources.[39] It gave rise to new corporate constituencies that were not content to impose limitations on corporate behavior through the legal machinery of government, but demanded a greater voice in the decision-making processes of the corporation itself.

Traditionally, the corporation's constituency was the shareholders of the firm and corporate productivity was measured in terms of financial performance. Federal securities laws and proxy rules expanded shareholder rights to give shareholders a greater voice in corporate governance on the assumption that they will better represent the public interest. New York Stock Exchange rules mandated the establishment of committees for the board of directors, the election of nonmanagement representatives to the board, and the dominance of independent outside members on key board committees such as the audit committee to weaken management's control of the corporate governance process. These changes have created sociopolitical conditions that have encouraged nonprofit institutions and groups (churches, universities, social activists and other public interest groups) to become shareholders and thereby gain access to the internal communication processes of the corporation. These new groups have extended the financial criteria traditionally employed to measure corporate performance to include an evaluation of a firm's social policies and practices—for example, the social merits of investing in South Africa and thereby supporting that country's policy of Apartheid.[40]

A more significant development has been the expansion of corporate constituencies to include other subsystems of American society that are not owners of the corporate assets. Mandated disclosure of corporate activities has inserted public opinion into the corporate decision-making processes and compelled managers to account publicly for their actions. It has established a moral environment that affects management's view of its public responsibility, generated different shareholder expectations of the corporation's performance, and defined the public will in a manner that encourages greater government regulation of business activities. It has also created a new investigatory role for the news media in providing the public with almost instant exposure of business activities that might otherwise remain unknown.

Even customers are prepared to intervene in corporate affairs. Thus, when Harris Corporation lost a bid on AT&T's Northeast Corridor Lightwave Project to Fujisu, Ltd., it mounted a campaign to convince the Federal Communications Commission, the Defense Department, and Congress that buying high-tech transmission equipment from the Japanese was not in the national interest. It was an American version of the Japan, Inc., approach that has so concerned American business.[41] A more amorphous constituency is the "intellectual community" that provides an intellectual foundation for more stringent government intervention into ABMAS by advocating the transfer of power from the managerial class to the "new class" of public managers and from private and quasi-private institutions to fully public ones, in what some commentators have described as the "second managerial revolution".[42]

NOTES

1. See chapters 2, 6, 8, and 9 of Roland H. Bainton, *The Reformation of the Sixteenth Century* (Boston: Beacon Press, 1952); chapter II of John Dillenberger and Claude Welch, *Protestant Christianity* (New York: Scribner's, 1954); and chapter 10 of Martin E. Marty, *A Short History of Christianity* (Cleveland: William Collins and World, 1975).

2. Max Weber, *The Protestant Ethic and the Spirit of Capitalism* (New York: Scribner's, 1958); and Anthony Giddens, *Capitalism and Modern Social Theory—An Analysis of the Writings of Marx, Durkheim and Max Weber* (Cambridge, Eng.: Cambridge University Press, 1971).

3. Alexis de Tocqueville, *Democracy in America,* tr. Henry Reeve (New York: Knopf, 1946).

4. Dow Votaw, "The New Entitlements and the Response of Business," in S. Prakash Sethi and Carl L. Swanson (eds.), *Private Enterprise and Public Purpose* (New York: Wiley, 1981), pp. 37–52; and Neil W. Chamberlain, *Remaking American Values—Challenge to a Business Society* (New York: Basic Books, 1977).

5. George C. Lodge, *The New American Ideology* (New York: Knopf, 1976), p. 114.

6. Charles A. Reich, "The New Property," *Yale Law Journal,* 73 (April 1964), p. 733; Bruce A. Ackerman, *Private Property and The Constitution* (New Haven, Conn.: Yale University Press, 1977). See also Richard Eells and Clarence Walton, *Conceptual Foundations of Business* (Homewood, Ill.: Irwin, 1974), chap. 8.

7. Akio Morita, "Japanese Viewpoints: "Do Companies Need Lawyers? Sony's Experiences in the United States,"*Japan Quarterly,* 30, 1 (January–March 1983), pp. 2–8.

8. The right to due process is guaranteed in Section 1 of the Fourteenth Amendment to the United States Constitution and cannot be denied.

9. Adam Smith, *An Inquiry into the Nature and Causes of the Wealth of Nations* (New York: Modern Library, 1937).

10. *First National Bank of Boston* v. *Bellotti,* 435 U.S. 765, 98 S.Ct. 1407 (1978), citing *Virginia State Board of Pharmacy* v. *Virginia Citizens Council,* 425 U.S. 748, 96 S.Ct. 1817 (1976).

11. Eells and Walton, *Conceptual Foundations of Business,* p. 81.

12. First Amendment to the United States Constitution.

13. R. M. MacIver, "Bases and Types of Association," in Clarence Walton and Richard Eells (eds.), *The Business System* (New York: Macmillan, 1967), p. 1148; Michael Novak, "Mediating Institutions: The Communitarian Individual in America," *The Public Interest,* 68 (Summer 1982), pp. 3–20.

14. Robert A. Dahl, *Pluralistic Democracy in the United States* (Chicago: Rand McNally, 1967).

15. *United States* v. *United Mine Workers of America,* 30 U.S. 258, 307–8, 67 S.Ct. 677, 703 (1947).

16. *Immigration and Naturalization Service* v. *Jagdish Rai Chadha,* et al., decided June 23, 1983 and reported in *U.S. Law Week,* vol. 51, no. 49, extra edition no. 2. The appendix to this decision contains a complete listing of all U.S. statutes with a legislative veto provision.

17. A. Lee Fritschler and Bernard H. Ross, *Business Regulation and Government Decision-Making* (Cambridge, Mass.: Winthrop, 1980), chap. 5–7.
18. Jeffry M. Berry, *Lobbying for the People, The Political Behavior of Public Interest Groups* (Princeton, N.J.: Princeton University Press, 1977); Seymour Martin Lipset, *Emerging Coalitions in American Politics* (San Francisco: Institute for Contemporary Studies, 1978), p. 3. See also Harmon Zeigler, *Interest Groups in American Society* (Englewood Cliffs, N.J.: Prentice-Hall, 1964); and Peter Willetts (ed.), *Pressure Groups in the Global System* (New York: St. Martin's Press, 1982).
19. Lipset, *Emerging Coalitions,* pp. 8–10; Robert A. Goldwin, *Political Parties in the Eighties* (Washington, D.C.: American Enterprise Institute for Public Policy Research, 1980); and Gerald M. Pomper, "The Decline of the Party in American Elections," *Political Science Quarterly,* 92, 1 (Spring 1977), pp. 21–41.
20. Daniel Seligman, "The Politics and Economics of 'Public Interest' Lobbying," *Fortune,* November 5, 1979, p. 75; "Splintered America, Peril or Promise?", *U.S. News and World Report,* July 7, 1980, pp. 33–37; John L. Holcomb, "Citizen Groups and Business," in Sethi and Swanson, *Private Enterprise and Public Purpose,* pp. 304–322; and William Symonds, "Washington in the Grip of the Green Giant," *Fortune,* October 4, 1982, p. 136.
21. James G. Dalton, "Political Action Committees: Reshaping the U.S. Electoral/ Legislative Scene," *Professional Engineer,* September 1980, p. 11.
22. Carl L. Swanson, "Corporations and Electoral Activities: The Legal, Political and Managerial Implications of PACs," in Sethi and Swanson, *Private Enterprise and Public Purpose,* pp. 355–372.
23. S. Prakash Sethi, Testimony before the Commerce, Consumer, and Monetary Affairs Subcommittee of the Government Operations Committee, House of Representatives, Ninety-Fifth Congress, Second Session, July 18, 1978, pp. 381–455; and *Advocacy Advertising and the Large Corporation* (Lexington, Mass.: D. C. Heath, 1977).
24. See Ira M. Millstein and Salem M. Katsh, *The Limits of Corporate Power* (New York: Macmillan, 1981) for an excellent overview of societal constraints on corporate processes.
25. Earl W. Kintner, *An Antitrust Primer—A Guide to Antitrust and Trade Regulation Laws For Businessmen,* 2nd ed. (New York: Macmillan, 1973), chap. 1; and Dominick T. Armentano, *Antitrust and Monopoly, Anatomy of a Policy Failure* (New York: Wiley, 1982).
26. For example, see Ralph Nader and Mark J. Green (eds.), *Corporate Power in America* (New York: Grossman, 1973) and Mark J. Green, ed., *The Monopoly Makers: Ralph Nader's Study Group Report on Regulatory Competition* (New York: Grossman, 1974), to name only two books out of more than twenty that have been published under the auspices of Ralph Nader's Study Groups. A more recent publication is Mark J. Green and Norman Waitzman, *Business War on the Law* (Washington, D.C.: The Corporate Accountability Research Group, 1981).
27. Carl L. Swanson, "The Federal Regulatory Process—Public Sector Intervention in Private Sector Affairs," in Raymond Lutz (ed.), *Finance, Economics, and Accounting: Handbook for Managers and Engineers* (New York: Wiley, in press).
28. Herbert Stein, "Economic Planning and the Improvement of Economic Policy," and B. Bruce Briggs, "Prospect of a Planned America," in Lawrence A. Chicker-

ing, ed. *The Politics of Planning: A Review and Critique of Centralized Economic Planning* (San Francisco: Institute for Contemporary Studies, 1976).

29. Sandra Salmans, "American Managers Hear Japan's View," *New York Times,* November 22, 1982, Sec. D, pp. 1, 3.

30. Robert R. Reich, "The Next American Frontier," *The Atlantic Monthly,* March 1983, pp. 43–58.

31. "The 50 Leading Exporters," *Fortune,* August 8, 1983, p. 88.

32. Salmans, "American Managers." See also William Diebold, *Industrial Policy as an International Issue* (New York: McGraw-Hill, 1980); Michael L. Wachter and Susan M. Wachter (eds.), *Toward a New Industrial Policy?* (Philadelphia: University of Pennsylvania Press, 1981); R. Bolling and J. Bowles, *America's Competitive Edge: How to Get Our Country Moving Again* (New York: McGraw-Hill, 1982); Ira Magaziner and Robert R. Reich, *Minding America's Business: The Decline and Rise of the American Economy* (New York: Harcourt Brace Jovanovich, 1982); Frank A. Weil, "U.S. Industrial Policy: A Process in Need of a Federal Industrial Coordination Board," *Law and Policy in International Business,* 14, 4 (1983), pp. 981–1040; and "An Industry Plea for the Freedom to Compete, *Business Week,* June 6, 1983, p. 59.

33. John Rawls, *A Theory of Justice* (Cambridge, Mass.: Belknap Press of Harvard University Press, 1971); Robert Nozick, *Anarchy, State, and Utopia* (New York: Basic Books, 1974); and Yair Aharoni, *The No Risk Society* (Chatham, N.J.: Chatham House Publishers, 1981).

34. Christopher Lasch, *The Culture of Narcissism* (New York: Norton, 1978).

35. William E. Connelly, *The Bias of Pluralism* (New York: Norton, 1978).

36. Clifford M. Hardin, Kenneth A. Shepsle, and Barry R. Weingast, "Government by Subcommittee," *Wall Street Journal,* June 24, 1983, p. 20.

37. H. Monroe Browne, in the preface to Arnold J. Melstner (ed.), *Politics and the Oval Office* (San Francisco: Institute for Contemporary Studies, 1981), p. ix.

38. Donald L. Horowitz, *The Courts and Social Policy* (Washington, D.C.: The Brookings Institution, 1977).

39. Alfred D. Chandler, Jr., *The Visible Hand: The Managerial Revolution in American Business* (Cambridge, Mass.: Belknap Press of Harvard University Press, 1977).

40. S. Prakash Sethi, "Interfaith Council On Corporate Responsibility," in S. Prakash Sethi, *Up Against the Corporate Wall,* 4th ed. (Englewood Cliffs, N.J.: Prentice-Hall, 1982), pp. 450–480. See also Interfaith Center on Corporate Responsibility, *Church Proxy Resolutions* (New York, January 1983).

41. Edward Meadows, "Japan Runs into America, Inc.," *Fortune,* March 22, 1982, p. 56.

42. Irving Kristol, "When Virtue Loses All Her Loveliness—Some Reflections on Capitalism and the Free Society," *The Public Interest,* Fall 1970; and Paul H. Weaver, "Regulation, Social Policy and Class Conflict," *The Public Interest* Winter 1978.

SIX ▰▰▰▰▰▰▰▰▰▰▰▰▰▰▰▰▰▰▰▰▰▰▰▰▰▰▰▰▰▰▰

Operational Elements of the American Management System and Personnel Practices

THE DOMINANT FEATURES OF THE AMERICAN BUSINESS SCENE ARE A reverence for the entrepreneurial spirit, along with domination of most firms by professional managers; quantifiable profit as the prime criterion for determining business success; a relatively short-term horizon in strategic planning and implementation; and a very large measure of diversity among firms. The heterogeneous nature of American society and the openness of its economic system allow American business enterprises to follow a variety of paths to growth and expansion and to employ a diversity of styles in managing the business.

Although American business organizations, especially large corporations, do share certain common characteristics, the degree of homogeneity is not as great as it is in Japan. Therefore, the best way to describe the American business and management system is to identify certain *generalized* patterns of behavior that manifest themselves in the corporate culture of America and strongly influence its management style. There are, however, two important caveats:

1. Notwithstanding the sharing of common values, operational processes vary greatly among different corporations. Although certain stereotypes of management style will be helpful in understanding various facets of ABMAS, they are painted with a broader brush than in the JABMAS chapter. Absent is the lack of precise definition and harmony of description associated with the Japanese business and management system.
2. Entrepreneur-founder-controlled corporations appear to display patterns of behavior which, in many ways, are at variance with those of more established and mature corporations.

Our discussion in this section, therefore, will focus primarily on the relatively big corporations that account for an overwhelmingly large portion of the nation's gross national product and reflect both the best and the worst of what would be considered the typical American management style. In these publicly owned firms, the thrust is toward a technical-functional systems approach to solving problems. The professional manager is at the core of both the organizational structure and decision-making processes. These firms are characterized by a preponderance of top-down decision-making, the use of explicit communications, and the importance of advocacy in group processes, although some firms are making greater use of participative management techniques. Furthermore, the large, professionally managed firm also makes a good ABMAS sample for comparison with the Japanese management system, since the latter is largely dominated by big corporations.

This chapter will further discuss the key characteristics of ABMAS in terms and concepts that may, at first, seem too black and white and therefore not fully representative of the heterogeneity of the styles and activities that characterize the American business scene. This approach is a deliberate one and is designed to provide a more meaningful contrast with JABMAS, discussed in Chapter 3. In point of fact, many American firms are employing human relations concepts that may at first seem "Japanese," but in reality are very American in their compatibility with U.S. cultural values and the sociopolitical and business environment. One of the major problems with some of the current leading American proponents of Japanese management techniques is that they use these indigenous and distinctly American practices as successful demonstrations of the adaptability of the Japanese system.[1] Such a conclusion, however, is totally unwarranted and misleading. If pursued uncritically, it could be counterproductive. It confuses style and symbol with substance. It applies faulty logic by implying that given the similarity of outcomes, the causality and processes leading to those outcomes must also be the same.

We begin with the realization that the American business scene is a curious amalgam of high-roller, entrepreneurial risk takers and empire builders on the one hand, and conservative, bureaucratic risk avoiders on the other hand. Two important factors in the American sociocultural system give rise to this phenomenon. First is the ideology of individualism, coupled with a culture of private enterprise, and a belief in unfettered competition and private property. These have fostered a class of entrepreneurs that has become a part of American folklore—the "rags to riches" or "Horatio Alger" syndrome. The United States is still a land of opportunity for the entrepreneur—for the person with the idea, for the risk taker. Companies like Apple Computer, Genetech, Data General, and Intergraph are the latest examples of a long list of firms that have become very large, indeed, in a relatively short period of time, and have made their entrepreneur-founders millionaires many times over. This spirit of entrepreneurship thrives alongside the already established corporate behemoths of the Western World like Exxon, IBM, General Motors, and AT&T.

Second, entry to top corporate positions and therefore to power, wealth, and prestige is, for the most part, not limited to a chosen few because of inheritance or membership in a narrowly defined social elite. It is true that graduates from such elite schools like Harvard, Yale, and Princeton are to be found in large numbers on the boards of the major blue chip corporations. Nevertheless, a university education is available to all regardless of social position. Egalitarianism is a dominant American trait, so that the United States is a relatively open society, with only some vestiges of race and nationality-based discrimination still remaining.[2]

THE ENTREPRENEURIAL EMPIRE BUILDER

Three characteristics distinguish American entrepreneurs from their counterparts in large business corporations in America and also from enterprising businesspeople in other industrial countries of the Western world and Japan.

First, entrepreneurial empire builders do not reach the top because they follow a well-trodden path, but because they reject it. They do not become important by working for big companies, but by making their small companies into big ones. They rely on creative insights in formulating strategies rather than on systematic plans or incremental opportunistic responses in dealing with problems.[3] There is a strong cultural acceptance of entrepreneurship in the United States, particularly in the willingness of other American groups to permit deviations from expected behavior and their willingness to reward innovation and risk taking more than efficient management.

The successful entrepreneur is essentially a "maverick" willing to rely on self as against group dependence, to cooperate temporarily with relative strangers rather than establish long-term group relationships, to tolerate and adjust to changing conditions, since they represent challenges not problems, and to innovate in making such adjustments even though such innovations entail high risk.[4] Furthermore, entrepreneurial success breeds greater social tolerance and acceptability. Joseph Schumpeter, a distinguished American economist, recognized this quality by calling the entrepreneur the "social deviant."[5]

Intergraph, headquartered in Huntsville, Alabama, illustrates the American entrepreneurial success story. The firm designs and manufacturers CAD (computer-aided design) systems, competing with such firms as IBM and Digital. With CAD, an engineer or architect can design, draft, and analyze projects with computer graphics displayed on a screen. James Meadlock, described as a toothpick-chomping good old boy from North Carolina, started Intergraph in 1969 with $39,000, four engineering friends from IBM, and his secretary, now his wife and vice president of administration and finance. In 1981, Intergraph went public at $18 per share. Today, these shares trade at around $40, or 71 times 1982 earnings, after a 2-for-1 split. The firm has a market value of about $1 billion, sales rose by 70 percent last year, and profits have increased at a compounded annual rate of 97 percent over the last five years. Meadlock's share of his company is now worth about $80 million, and Intergraph is the principal supplier of CAD systems to the architectural and engineering markets.[6]

Second, the entrepreneurial manager is a breed apart. This can be seen from the fact that even top managers in large corporations, with well-defined career paths, will often sacrifice an assured and stable future in search of challenge, risk, or an opportunity to build a financial fortune. The more innovative and young an industry is, the greater the likelihood that it will produce entrepreneurs and empire builders. Or to put differently, it is the entrepreneurs rather than the large corporations that have been at the cutting edge of spawning new industries. The Silicon Valley of California, the home of the electronics and semiconductor industry, is full of companies launched by young upstarts, like Apple Computers, or scientist-executives from such well-known companies as IBM, Fairchild Camera, and Motorola. Thus, it is not surprising when three executives leave Polaroid to join NIMSLO Corporation, a struggling maker of a new 3-D camera, because it offers a new and more exciting challenge.[7]

There appears to be a recognition that large American corporations are not well suited to nurture truly innovative growth and risk taking. In the American sociocultural milieu, this is the forte of the individual entrepreneur. For this reason, even large corporations have started setting up separate venture capital units for investing in enterprising individuals—"intrapreneurs"—both from within and without the company.[8]

But conversely, as entrepreneur-founder organizations mature and grow beyond a certain size, they take on many of the characteristics of the larger, more bureaucratic and conventionally operated organizations. Two assumptions underlie this trend: Individual control and direction is not sustainable when an organization reaches a certain size in terms of assets and employees. The State of Israel, for example, has recognized this fact of organizational life by discouraging large business entities in order to keep its societal values of participation.[9] The need for new capital cannot always be met from the entrepreneur's own resources, and outside capital may insist on more professional control. As an organization becomes more complex, it calls for executives having different skills. Such talented people are reluctant to work under a highly personalized system of control that may be inimical to their professional advancement and personal satisfaction.

THE LARGE BUSINESS CORPORATION

The primary focus of this chapter on ABMAS, however, is the large business corporation. Like most American institutions, it is a combination of many contradictory attributes that defy easy explanation. These anomalies are reflected in the way the corporation is owned; publicly regulated; controlled and governed; organized, structured, and managed; and the manner in which it relates to its internal constituencies and external stakeholders. Some of the commonly shared attributes of the corporation are a certain degree of continuity and stability; relatively large size in terms of assets, sales, profits, and employees; bureaucratic organizational and decision-making processes; an emphasis on scientific and rational criteria for goal setting and performance evaluation; the separation of ownership and control; a highly diversified pattern of ownership combined with tight control by professional inside managers; and the public trading of equity or stock on the national stock exchanges.

The Role of Equity Capital

Equity capital from individual investors plays a comparatively larger role in the capital structure of American corporations than in Western Europe or Japan. American corporations are free-standing economic institutions and must continuously raise funds in the capital markets, often in competition with the U.S. government itself. Unlike in Japan, they are not part of a group of companies that includes banks to bail them out in difficult times. To the contrary, banks are not allowed to buy stock in American companies to avoid any possible conflict of interest. Stock markets are extremely active and sensitive to any changes in a firm's competitive situation or other factors that may affect the fortunes of a company (the exception being the trust departments of banks that invest clients' funds). One has only to reflect on the dramatic drop in the price of Texas Instruments common stock—a decline of 21 points in less than one week (July 26–29, 1983)—when it appeared to investors that TI would show a big loss in its second-quarter earnings and might not be able to maintain its learning curve competitiveness in the emerging microprocessor market.[10] Favorable or unfavorable information is immediately reflected in the trading price of a firm's stock and affects the ability of that firm to acquire resources and raise investment funds in the market.

U.S. corporations must also maintain a reasonable proportion between debt and equity in their capital structure. A highly leveraged company is more risk prone and must pay a higher cost for funds unless its growth prospects are phenomenal and investors are willing to assume above-average risks. Thus, the management of a U.S. corporation must temper its long-term plans with a higher degree of sensitivity to short-term fluctuations in current earnings. This places tremendous pressure on management to measure costs and benefits, to maintain continuous earnings growth, and to balance both the long-term and the short-term interests of its stockholders. Since management's performance is measured almost continuously, there is little opportunity to justify poor strategies by postponing evaluation to some future date under the guise of a "longer term" perspective. At the same time, the great pressure to maintain continuous growth in current (quarterly) earnings often causes managers to sacrifice long-term growth in favor of short-term earnings. This condition is changing, however, as corporate strategists become more sensitive to the competitive need for American firms to engage in long-range planning. There is a growing trend among U.S. corporations to use more long-term criteria in determining executive compensation.[11]

Corporate Governance

In theory and in law, the corporation is governed by a board of directors whose members are elected by the stockholders. Management is responsible to the board for its performance. The real world, however, is markedly different. At the risk of oversimplifying, certain observations can be made about how corporations are governed in the United States.

Shareholders, by and large, do not act as owners but as investors in a corporation. They continuously move their funds between different investment options to satisfy their personal criteria of balancing risks and rewards. They rarely have a long-term stake in the corporation and are not interested in its management. Their individual investment stakes are generally so minuscule as to give them little power to affect the corporation's affairs. To wrest power from the incumbent board and entrenched management, they must actively organize themselves—an expensive effort not to be undertaken lightly. Even in corporations where institutional investors hold large blocks of shares, both the conventional wisdom and fiduciary responsibilities dictate that institutional managers vote their stock either with the management, or if they do not agree with the management's policies, to sell their holdings. Given their primary responsibility to their clients, institutional managers consider it more prudent to invest in companies in whose management they have confidence, rather than attempt to change or improve the management of a company—an area in which they do not have any specific competence. This is still largely true, although more recently some institutional managers have begun to oppose entrenched managements when the latter have sought to increase their power to frustrate potential mergers and takeovers beneficial to the shareholders through such "shark repellent" techniques as staggered elections for board members or expensive termination contracts ("golden parachutes") for members of top management.[12]

The modern corporation has become so large and complex that its management must be left to professional managers. Therefore, even if the stockholders wanted to manage the day-to-day affairs of the corporation, it would not be feasible and efficient for them to do so. In the short run, professional managers are not concerned with excessive trading or lower prices of the company's stock because they do not affect the value of assets invested in the corporation. However, the movement in and out of different stocks by successive groups of shareholders in order to lower their risk, increase their earnings, or benefit from capital gains reduces the short-term value of the firm's stockholdings. In the long run, a lower stock price when compared to other similarly situated companies impairs a company's ability to raise equity capital in the markets. It also adversely affects top management's total compensation, which is very often tied to the market performance of a company's stock.

Conversely, through its control of the election process and proxy machinery, top management has almost total discretion over who is elected to the board. The management-nominated slate is routinely approved by the stockholders, who willingly leave the affairs of the corporation to its management. The chief executive officer (CEO) is also invariably the chairman of the board. Where he is not, the chairman's position is more honorific than substantive and is generally filled by the retiring CEO. At one extreme, the board may be dominated by insiders, thereby obliterating the distinction between management and control. Even where outside directors are a majority, they are seldom in control. It is the CEO who sets the tone not only for the management, but also for the board. It is not unheard of for a CEO to refer to his company's board as "my board." Deviations from this model occur only when large blocks of stock are concentrated among a small group of investors, or when the company has been badly mismanaged for a long time and outside directors are forced to take corrective action for fear they may be held liable for gross negligence. So the discrepancy between the legal myth of corporate governance and its reality is so large that it makes the legal model totally irrelevant, if not actually misleading.

Managements do not always, if ever, work to maximize profits or stockholder wealth. They work to find satisfactory acceptable levels for their different stakeholders.[13] Competition notwithstanding, all corporate managers have, as one of their primary goals, retention of control of the corporation and an increase in their financial rewards. Therefore they become, to use Galbraith's expression, part of the technostructure that controls the nation's industrial and financial resources.[14] Stockholders are not paid the maximum rate of dividends possible, but the going or "acceptable" rate that will keep them at bay and not invite hostile takeover attempts.

Constraints on Corporate Management

This discussion should not lead anyone to conclude that modern American corporations are run by managers unbridled by any meaningful external or internal limitations. Notwithstanding the large gap between the "received legal model"[15] and the actual practice of corporate governance, a broad array of social, legal, and economic forces have combined to impose certain constraints on management conduct. These constraints on corporate management originate from five sources: financial markets, legal constraints, peer group pressure, organizational constraints, and pressure from the news media.

Financial Markets. Managers must submit to the discipline of the financial markets by providing enough information to convince the public that they are conducting the business efficiently, prudently, and responsibly. Lack of faith in a company's management is often signalled by an unwillingness on the part of financial analysts and institutional investors to support the company's stock. This results in a declining value placed on the company's stock and restricts its management's ability to raise additional funds for investment. A low stock price—relative to book value, earning potential, or the price of other similarly placed corporations—portends trouble for management in terms of shareholder restlessness and takeover threats.

This is one of the paradoxes of the American legal system as it applies to corporations. Although top management in American corporations exercises far greater control over the affairs of the corporation when compared to managers in Japan or Western Europe, it is also subjected to greater public scrutiny and therefore must abide by the discipline of the market. Corporations in Japan, West Germany, and other Western European countries draw a large part of their equity and investment funds from banks, other financial institutions, and even government agencies. They may also have greater supervisory control through board representation of important stakeholders such as financial institutions, labor unions, and government agencies. At the same time, these corporations are not required to disclose large amounts of information about their operations.

Conversely, U.S. corporate boards represent solely the stockholders of the company. However, the law also requires that corporations must disclose all information that is likely materially to affect not only present investors, but also potential investors—which includes practically everyone. The law provides in elaborate detail the content, the timing, and the process by which such information must be disclosed. Thus, American corporations operate in a fishbowl to an extent unheard of in any other part of the world.

Legal Constraints. The gap between the "received legal model" and the working reality of corporate governance has been successively closed through changes in the rules and regulations of the Securities and Exchange Commission and judicial decisions. The legal liabilities of outside directors also have been made more stringent, thereby requiring them to exercise greater vigilance in their monitoring role.

This is the second paradox of the American legal system. The law goes to elaborate lengths to preserve the sanctity of ownership. Trading on inside information is severely penalized. Managers are more likely to face criminal penalties, including prison sentences, for securities law violations or fraud (crimes against stockholders) than for violations of environmental protection, worker health and safety, employment discrimination based on race, sex or national origin, or consumer protection laws (crimes against society).

Although there are tremendous legal and economic barriers for stockholders who desire to exercise effective rights of ownership, the law goes a long way to maintain the ritualistic rights of ownership. Annual meetings are conducted in the spirit of the "town hall," and managers are questioned by stockholders. The law even protects the right of individual stockholders to question managements on their behavior not only in the economic, but also in the social arena. Thus, with relatively little effort, dissident groups can initiate proxy resolutions and force stockholder vote on such issues as investments in South Africa and production of nuclear arms. It is irrelevant that not one dissident-sponsored proxy resolution has ever won a majority vote when opposed by management. Such resolutions provide management with a sense of prevailing social currents and exert indirect public pressure. Over time, they enable corporations to adapt to changing societal expectations about the role of corporations.

It should be noted here that this process is only rarely present in other nations and is even more rarely exercised. Moreover, as we saw in Chapter 2, in the case of Japan recent changes in the law have actually made the already negligible role of the individual stockholder even more insignificant.

Peer Group Pressures. Corporate managers, like most professionals, seek peer group approval. Executive success stories written up in the leading business publications or election to *Fortune*'s Business Hall of Fame are intangible rewards of professional success. A significant deviation from the prevailing norms of acceptable conduct, especially on the downside, exposes the CEO to peer group contempt, injures his self-esteem, and risks his financial well-being by restricting job mobility.

Herein lies another anomaly of the American sociopolitical system. Unlike in many other societies, most American corporate leaders do not come from established social elites.[16] Nor do they have recognized symbols of social class such as titles. Instead, power and prestige are measured very largely in direct proportion to status in the corporate community acquired during a career. Conspicuous consumption and overt signs of wealth are used as class symbols in the fashion of Veblen's "leisure class."[17] This is a very different kind of individuality than, for example, that expressed by a measure of aceticism among the British upper classes.

Organizational Constraints. No CEO, no matter how brilliant or determined, can subdue the entire corporation to his will in the long term. He must seek the cooperation of a large number of other managers within the organization to put his ideas and plans into action. These managers are not likely to submit to a CEO's autocratic rule if it turns out to be irrational, contrary to their own or corporate best interests, professionally demeaning, or personally repugnant. Although a revolt may not take place in the short run, plans may be sabotaged and decisions countermanded, thereby rendering dubious his authority and control, and leading ultimately to his ouster or "retirement" into a nonpower position.

Outside directors, who in a large number of cases are chief executives or senior managers in other corporations, are also not likely to condone arbitrary or unprofessional behavior. Faced with such a situation, they are likely to resign from a given board, thereby expressing their dissatisfaction and signaling to the market that all is not well with that corporation. This form of dissatisfaction can be seen in the takeover battle between Bendix, Allied, and Martin Marietta. Five prestigious directors of Bendix—Mobil Corporation's president and G. D. Searle's president among them—resigned in protest over the planned merger, which they perceived to be hostile, poorly executed, and not in the best interests of the Bendix stockholders.[18]

The conduct of top management displays all the inconsistencies and contradictions of the American cultural and sociopolitical system. On the one hand, the CEO conducts the affairs of the corporation as though he were an absolute monarch whose every wish is taken as command by staff and other executives. He also fancies himself as an entrepreneur with a flair for risk taking, moving his corporate empire according to his vision, shaking the destinies of hundreds of thousands of people, and leaving his indelible mark on corporate and industrial history. At the same time, he behaves as a professional manager and a compleat bureaucrat who works through committees and staff reports, prides himself on leaving the company running so smoothly that he will not be missed, and follows the rules of corporate succession by retiring at the customary age of 65, even though he could easily change the rules. Thus, the human elements of the management structure of the large American corporation are at once a combination of authoritarianism and pluralism, centralized and decentralized sharing of power, and a highly autocratic and participative-structured decision-making system.

Pressure from the News Media. The power of the news media to expose a corporation to public scrutiny cannot be minimized. There is no management strong enough that it can forever bar public disclosure of information it considers inimical to its interests. In an environment characterized by low public approval of large corporations, constant confrontation with the increasing fervor of corporate critics, and the growing zeal of investigative journalism, any hint of corporate impropriety, real or imagined, is likely to bring unbearable pressure on management for greater information disclosure and public accountability.

It is very difficult for non-Americans to comprehend the power of the news media in the United States. The press is truly free, with its freedom guaranteed by the Constitution, and not even the U.S. Congress or the president can abridge its power. It is also adversary in character and quite proud of that fact. This is in keeping with the cherished American tradition of checks and balances among society's powerful institutions. The news media play a key role in being the watchdogs of the public interest. Thus, while the financial press may identify with the corporate world in upholding the values of free enterprise system and minimum government intervention in the private sector, it is not part of that system. It is quite vigorous in reporting stories of corporate errors of omission and commission. Although the general news media pay more attention to political exposés than to business problems, business generally considers them as having an antibusiness bias.[19] In the United States, investigative reporting is considered the highest form of journalism, and there are no sacred cows. Unlike in Japan, and to some extent in other countries where traditions of free press prevail, reporters and leaders do not belong to the same "club."

The Functioning of a Contemporary Corporate Board

A corporate board in the American business and management system performs three broad and somewhat overlapping functions: monitoring, supervising, and advising. The monitoring function is oriented toward evaluating and rewarding management for overall corporate performance. It is also concerned with those aspects of the corporate structure and control system that affect vital ownership interests. The supervisory function comprises overseeing and approving plans and strategies that involve substantial elements of a corporation's business. The advisory function aims at providing expert and dispassionate counsel to top management on major corporate decisions.

The monitoring function implies a clear-cut separation between management and control, where evaluation is an after-the-fact phenomenon. The supervisory function requires a large measure of active examination and aggressive participation in corporate decision making. In the advisory role, however, board participation is passive in nature. It rests on the inclination of the CEO rather than on the predilections of the board. Unlike monitoring, both the supervisory and advisory functions are participative in character.

The legal model of corporate governance emphasizes the board's supervisory and monitoring roles. In the real world, though, the monitoring role, while organizationally feasible, has all but vanished. Except in the gravest of circumstances, it is rarely requested or employed. A predominantly supervisory role calls for the board to generate independent information with which to evaluate management proposals. In the real world, this is highly impractical. At one extreme, it would call for a dual decision-making structure. Such a process is likely to be slow, expensive, redundant, and only marginally productive. It would require the outside directors to devote a great deal more time to the corporation's business than they would be able or willing to do. It also assumes that inside directors would be inclined to look at management's decisions differently than they did earlier as part of the management team.

A heavy involvement in the supervisory function must ultimately undermine the board's monitoring role. Having previously played an active role in management's decisions, the board cannot later turn out or chastise management when those decisions turn sour. The element of post facto wisdom in the monitoring function would cause outside directors to run afoul of the CEO, who would be loath to have "troublemakers" on the board. A "fighting" board is conducive neither to good governance nor to effective management. In this situation, management would be put into a position of hiding information for face-saving purposes or spending considerable time planning strategies against board members rather the competition. Therefore, directors dedicated to a purely monitoring role are rarely found on boards.

In the best of all possible worlds, supervisory and advisory roles work in tandem. The CEO, the inside members, and the outside directors operate in an environment of mutual trust and close partnership. There is the assumption that management provides all information to the board to ensure that it receives good advice. The informed consent of the outside directors also serves as a protective shield from external criticism, legal or otherwise, when major strategic decisions turn out to be inappropriate or wrong. It is also assumed that in times of real crisis, the outside directors would have the stature and integrity to step outside their supervisory and advisory roles, undertake their monitoring function, evaluate management performance, and take the necessary remedial action.

During the last twenty years, American corporations have been developing boards that generally provide a good balance among these three roles. This has come about through a combination of external pressures and internal organizational needs. Major changes in contemporary corporate boards have involved three elements: structure, composition, and decision style and substance. For example, recent research studies on corporate boards undertaken by the Center for Research in Business and Social Policy, the University of Texas at Dallas,[20] and by other public and private organizations show that most boards, especially in large corporations, have been increasing in absolute size and contain a majority of independent outside directors.[21] They have been developing a more formal committee structure, and include directors with greater diversity in backgrounds than was previously thought possible. Changes in law have also made outside directors more willing to probe deeply into corporate affairs and to assert their independence when the need arises. Boards have also been obligated to make public their findings when they discover improper or potentially illegal management actions. Moreover, not only the general public, but also enlightened and informed business opinion, has been largely supportive of such changes.

KEY ABMAS MANAGEMENT VALUES

The large corporation has become the primary agent for the management of private resources in the United States. As it has taken over the economic functions of production and distribution formerly determined by competitive forces in the market, it has been compelled to play a larger role in implementing American social policy. Corporate managers, who envisioned themselves largely as managers of limited economic resources, are now faced with moral dilemmas that seem far removed from their executive offices or the plant assembly line, but that have a dramatic influence on public policy processes. Even within the narrow range of corporate activities, business goals and objectives, strategies and tactics, organizational structures and decision-making processes, interpersonal relations within the corporation, and communications and relations with external constituencies are influenced as much by the values and beliefs held by the firm's decision makers as by technical analyses of the internal and external environment.

The ethos of American corporations is as heterogeneous as American society itself. American corporations that are successful have learned the value of developing a corporate culture that is in harmony with their mission and strategies and compatible with society itself. In such firms, individuals are selected, trained, socialized, and rewarded in a manner that fits with and reinforces the corporate culture.[22] Although ideologies and beliefs may be internally consistent within a given corporation, they do differ greatly among different corporations. Nevertheless, certain traits are shared. These include certain ethical beliefs commonly referred to as the Business Creed, the importance of profit, professionalization of management, the value of segmenting decision-making, and rewards based on individual performance.

The American Business Creed and the Ethical Content of ABMAS

The American business creed, for most businesspeople, is a simple, clear-cut, tradition-based belief in "rationalized self-interest" as a guiding principle of what the corporation may or may not ethically do as a societal institution. All available information is carefully weighed, alternatives and goals are selected, and possible reactions identified before a decision is made. This approach finds its way into case law as the concept of the "reasonable man." It is positive and forward looking in orientation, emphasizes the value of the Protestant work ethic and the right of individuals to hold and use property for private use, and stresses progress and materialism as key outcomes. In picturing their role in society, businesspeople frequently resort to the symbolic values of individualism and assume that maximum satisfaction and distributive justice will result from individual egotism.[23]

Since material prosperity is the outcome of a free market economy, competition is a sine qua non in allocating resources—a notion codified into the antitrust laws of the United States. This creates a paradox for businesspeople. On one hand, they believe in competition, but their management skills are most often employed to free a corporation from the competitive discipline of the marketplace. Thus, they are constantly faced with the temptation of engaging in such heretical practices as price fixing and market allocation. Even when a societal consensus exists in a given ethical situation, the reality of the commercial world tends to treat the consensus as being of little value unless it has been codified into law. Then the question is no longer one of ethics, but of compliance with the law, with resultant penalties for violations. It is not surprising, therefore, that ethics and law are viewed as synonymous terms and that law enforcement has become the primary means of ensuring that corporations and managements act in accordance with societal notions of "right" and "wrong." This ethical fact of life can be seen in the extensive array of antitrust legislation designed to ensure that competition remains alive in the free market economy of the United States.

The problem of business ethics is further compounded by the fact that corporations are artificial legal entities and, by definition, cannot have a value system of their own. Since the modern American corporation was unknown when the Judeo-Christian tradition began, its philosophers did not anticipate the emergence of an artificial economic institution for which a code of ethics would be needed. Thus, organizational ethics is treated in the United States as a synergistic blend of the personal values of the individuals who constitute the corporation, particularly top management. The individuality of value standards has created its own special problem: whether business ethics can or should be taught in business schools or whether the subject is one better left to other societal institutions, such as the church, particularly when the message of the preacher in the pulpit on Sunday seems so far removed from the realities of the business world on Monday morning.[24]

Corporate executives tend to approach ethical issues in a radically different manner than most other groups in American society. Ethics, to them, is not an intangible, intellectual pursuit to be expressed in a special language of categorical imperatives and deontological viewpoints, but a means by which to measure a wide range of competing claims on corporate time and resources in a marketplace environment that is objective, competitive, and unrelenting in determining winners and losers.[25] Although American businesspeople recognize the need for ethical standards, they are often uncertain about the nature of their ethics.[26] Furthermore, the competitive atmosphere in which they operate seems to require suspension of ethical considerations. It is not surprising, therefore, that a large portion of business ethics arises from the operation of the marketplace and is expressed in such simplistic concepts as these: the contractual obligation must be honored; the function of the free enterprise system is to provide quality goods and services at competitive prices; the customer's needs are first and foremost; and the holding and use of property is a right subject only to an overriding public need.[27]

The Role of Profit

Business is in the business of making money, of earning a profit. The manufacture and sale of products and services is simply a means to that end. This objective, even when it is not pursued zealously, permeates all aspects of corporate rhetoric and behavior. Further, the thrust is on profit now, not later.[28] There are various justifications for this theme, including the one that profit is the prime incentive for business enterprises to provide quality products at reasonable prices. This assertion accords with a large part of American society's cultural, legal, and sociopolitical conventions. The dominant pursuit of profit justifies the rationale for a corporation being an economic institution in which managers manage stockholders' property solely for the latter's benefit. All other relationships are contractual in character; parties enter into voluntary contracts in a manner that best maximizes their self-interest. Just as a corporation does not have to sell products at unprofitable prices, consumers will buy only those products they want and at prices they are willing to pay. Thus, other things being equal, the level of profit becomes a true indicator of a firm's usefulness to society. So American executives tend to approach their businesses largely in terms of economic opportunities that must be exploited to the maximum. Relationships within and without the business firm, or with other segments of society, are important only to the extent necessary to secure and exploit a firm's profit opportunities.

The tendency toward profits is accentuated, and in many cases distorted, by an emphasis on quantification and scientific management, as discussed in the next section. Since current profits are more tangible and measurable, they receive greater attention and energy than future and long-term concerns. Moreover, since individual performance is the basis of individual compensation, profits that are directly affected by an individual tend to be emphasized over long-term performance that may be influenced by a multitude of different individuals or a variety of factors because these are difficult to measure and hard to assign in terms of individual contributions. So although long-term profits may be in the best interest of the corporation and society, their achievement is generally at odds with the goals of *current* stockholders, managers, and employees.

The Professionalization of Management

The emphasis on "scientific" management has long been the hallmark of American business. The professionalization of management resulted from the studies of Frederick W. Taylor, who reasoned that it would be easier to use human resources more efficiently if the activities of managing a task were separated from its execution.[29] Early efforts at specialization and professionalization were concentrated at the plant floor level. Later efforts encompassed the whole of the organization to meet the needs of businesses that became increasingly larger in size. Large corporations could not be managed without a large cadre of professional managers, the specialization of various managerial skills, and the development of organizational structures to direct the work of large bureaucracies.[30] The global success of American business and the large U.S. multinational corporations was not due only to the enterprising, "can do" attitude of American workers and managers and the abundant resource base of the American economy, but also to the organizing skill of the professional manager.

This attitude encompassed a whole new outlook on the practice of management, as witnessed by the enormous growth and popularity of business schools. Professional managers have become synonymous with MBAs (Master in Business Administration). To a large extent, and despite the apparent decline in the quality of American managers and U.S. corporations, this attitude still holds sway. For example, it is estimated that more than 55,000 MBAs will graduate in 1983.[31]

The professionalization of management, by American standards, implies that management skills are akin to a chest of tools and techniques that can be acquired through classroom training, studied and improved through research and analysis, and applied in all managerial and administrative situations. On-the-job or hands-on training, the hallmark of a trade, it is argued, is needed only to adapt the skill usage to specific situations and to reconstruct and redefine situations to make them amenable to the use of management tools. Thus, even human elements can be scientifically defined and measured in quantifiable terms and manipulated by scientific means. Managers differ from operating employees in that employees do the work, while managers make decisions about how employees will perform the assigned tasks. Persons are thus hired or specifically trained to occupy key decision-making positions within the corporate organization.

The Performance-Based Reward System

Given that one goal of American business is to maximize return on stockholders' investment, great emphasis is placed on improving the efficiency and productivity of employees—both workers and managers. Since American culture is based on individualism and personal achievement, the most important means for motivating employees is through a wage structure that rewards superior performance. Thus enormous energies are spent in defining jobs, measuring performance, and developing various financial systems that will match reward to performance.[32] One consequence of this approach is that managers may emphasize the development of qualities that are narrowly specialized and have a high degree of relevance to corporate functions, but at the expense of attributes that are broader and more related to personal growth. This approach also creates an apparent conflict between the corporation and trade unions, for the latter emphasize the concept of job complexity rather than individual differences in job performance. (This notion is discussed in greater detail in a subsequent section dealing with employee relations and trade unionism in America.)

The manner in which American corporations determine rewards represents yet another paradox of ABMAS. While management pays homage to the concept of performance-based reward, it does not always determine compensation in this manner. Outside factors influence the process—wage and hour legislation with its minimum wage requirement and, more important, supply and demand factors in the labor market. The latter, particularly in poor economic times when unemployment is high, may become the prime determinant of employee compensation instead of performance. Budgetary considerations and the rising cost of living as it affects fringe benefits keyed to this economic barometer become an incentive to dismiss an older and more expensive employee and to hire a younger one at a lower wage, even though the older employee may be more productive in a unit sense.[33]

The narrow specialization at the corporate level is supported by the narrow training of business managers, which in turn is reinforced by a corporate preference for narrowly specialized graduates. The vast majority of young managers entering the corporate executive ranks are the product of a professional school and are steeped in the technical skills of their profession. The young manager is at home with cash flow analysis, return on investment, sales forecasting, and management by objectives. Eager to demonstrate his or her technical skills, this manager carefully chooses projects that lend themselves to a deterministic and quantitative analysis. In this approach, the manager is amply assisted by a corporate environment that calls for systematic and sequential goal setting and program implementation. The result is an inevitable overemphasis on what is precise, immediate, and identifiable.[34]

Viewing the Environment in Fragments

American executives, in spite of their attempt to build extensive information networks, tend to view their internal and external environment within a narrow focus that permits only fragmentary perspectives. This allows them to apply their functional expertise to preconceived problems and to seek immediate solutions quickly. This can be characterized as "solutions looking for problems."[35] The young manager tends to assume that problems that cannot be quantified are not immediate, need not be solved, or perhaps do not even exist. Or he or she becomes a captive of concreteness by forcing qualitative variables into quantitative forms, thereby producing solutions that are elegant and precise but may be meaningless and even wrong.[36]

The corporate environment, as noted above, encourages this fragmented approach. The absence of a corporate culture further impedes the utilization of a holistic or global view and the resulting development of collective values. It deprives the corporation of those leadership qualities needed in its future top managers, and on which the survival and growth of the company must ultimately depend. It encourages organizational deviants or entrepreneurs to leave the organizations and seek job satisfaction in a new working environment. It enhances job mobility and weakens loyalty to existing entities. The few excellent companies that are exceptions to this approach prove the rule.

It is not surprising, therefore, that personnel control within the organization is generally considered in terms of a narrowly defined relationship between labor and management handled by a staff department rather than by all managers in the context of the whole organization, with its multiplicity of interdependent human needs. The situation has created a chasm between manager and worker that has stymied cooperation and, in union settings, become a battleground between labor and management over contractual rights.

ORGANIZATIONAL STRUCTURES AND DECISION-MAKING PROCESSES IN AMERICAN CORPORATIONS

A corporation's goals are reasonably well defined both from the perspective of the corporation's traditional external constituencies, current and potential investors, and its internal constituencies, management and employees, although they may not always be well defined from the viewpoint of some of the emerging constituencies. One of the most important characteristics of these goals is that they are embodied in the institution of the corporation itself. While there may be marginal differences between various corporate constituencies and stakeholders as to the magnitude and rate of goal achievement, the overall identity with the institution's goals, for the most part, remains unchallenged. Thus the intensity of goal achievement demanded by the corporation of its employees and the employees' own desire for approval, rewards, and achievement provides the corporation's dominant group with power to shape the outlook and character of those who serve it to their own ends.[37] Further, the legal system has given considerable support to the dominance of the corporate leaders' vision even when it has not served the best interest of the corporation's constituencies under the "prudent business judgment" rule.[38]

Organizational and Management Structure

The American corporation has gone through different stages of organizational structure in its evolution. In the early stages, when corporations dealt with a limited number of products, growth was accomplished primarily through the creation of staff departments such as marketing, finance, and accounting. When corporations began to deal with a variety of unrelated products and to sell in larger domestic or international markets, they developed a divisional form of organization, with each division controlling a related group of activities and/or geographic territories. As corporations grew even larger in size and complexity, firms like General Motors, General Electric, and Johnson and Johnson began to function as a holding company that managed autonomous subsidiaries as an asset portfolio.

Structure follows strategy. This was the conclusion drawn by Alfred Chandler, the distinguished American business historian, through exhaustive studies of the evolution and growth of American business.[39] Strategy, however, is not precisely defined and contains a large measure of vision, which the CEO utilizes in imbuing the organization with its purpose. At the same time, in order for this vision to be implemented, the CEO must have a large measure of control and influence over the organization so that a strategy can emerge and be translated into workable programs through an interactive and incremental process.[40] These trinitarian attributes—strategy, control, and rewards—lie at the core of the organizational structure and decision-making processes of large American corporations.

That organizational structure is essentially hierarchical, with divisions into line and staff functions. Increased authority for action runs parallel to an ever-enlarging responsibility for performance and rests in successively fewer hands. Although entry by individual employees into the system is voluntary, high exit barriers are created through a system of rewards and penalties that increase with length of tenure and dissuade an employee from leaving the corporation or acting counter to its interest.[41] Thus, within broad limits, top management, and especially the chief executive, sets not only the rhythm and work style for the organization, but its moral tone and how it relates to its external constituencies and responds to changing societal expectations.[42]

A somewhat more recent organizational concept that has found favor with large American corporations is the profit center or strategic business unit (SBU), with its notion of decentralized management. Profit centers are viewed as independent operations within the corporation, each responsible for optimizing its own profit and largely accountable to the parent firm in terms of its contribution to profits, return on investment, or some other financial performance measure. Its organizational value is to be found in its ability to free the more entrepreneurial management types in the company who want operating independence from the bureaucracy of the large corporation. The underlying rationale is that responsibility in a complex organization must be delegated to the lowest possible echelon to reduce costs, that authority should flow with responsibility if there is to be proper accountability, and that people who are given more responsibility and authority will perform better.

The paradox is that the independence of the profit center is a misnomer, for by definition SBUs are neither independent nor profit centers. Profit is not always a measure of management's current performance, but a reflection of a variety of factors, such as previous management decisions made over the long term or a conscious choice between long- and short-term options that may reflect a compromise between competing corporate constituencies. Nor can any specific division be viewed as truly independent, for the synergism of the organization, with its mutual support among units, may create a windfall for one division that may not have been earned. Finally, division managers are constantly faced with the choice of improving their division's profits at the expense of the other divisions or improving the organization's profits at their expense—a crucial decision, particularly if the manager's individual performance is based on the division's performance and there are circumstances, in which, for the overall performance of the organization, divisional performance should be depressed.[43]

The top management in most American corporations consists of a small group of executives, usually the chief executive (CEO) and chief operating officer (president), chief financial officer, corporate counsel, and a group of vice presidents in charge of various operating decisions and staff support departments. They are responsible for developing the corporate mission, for interpreting the environment in which the corporation operates, and for translating that assessment into operating strategies. Their principal function is planning and directing. The chief executive officer assumes the ultimate authority and final responsibility for all corporate decisions.

Middle-level managers engage in more limited planning activities by translating broad organizational objectives into specific product or service plans. Managers at this level are expected to be well versed in the technological aspects of the organization. Their leadership role is limited to furnishing guidance to subordinates and clarifying policies and decisions made by top management. Lower management is concerned largely with control and supervision of operating employees, and their planning is limited to routine functions such as scheduling. Both middle and lower management are largely viewed as "enforcers" of top management decisions. In turn, they tend to treat operating employees as individual, interchangeable units of production, rather than as teams or groups of people working together toward common goals and sharing common values.

One's level in the organization is measured in terms of one's authority, shown as a job position on the organizational chart. Salary, fringe benefits, and corporate perquisites are based on job position. Executive compensation is tied to individual performance, not to age or number of years on the job or, more important, to group performance.[44] While communications between the managerial levels do take place and are encouraged, they are invariably in the form of advice to or staff work for one's superior.

Top-Down Decision Making

American corporations generally bear the strong imprint of their top management—the founding entrepreneur or the CEO who takes his place after the company has reached maturity. It inevitably follows that decision making is essentially a top-down phenomenon in American corporate life. Explicit in the manager's power to lead is the authority to make decisions. This belief in managerial superiority rests on a basic assumption about power: ". . . an executive needs to get all the power he can, needs to use it openly, even blatantly, to keep it, and should not act in any way that reduces his capacity to impact others directly."[45] American business schools perpetuate this view with their academic emphasis on decision execution rather than decision formulation and on professional leadership instead of consultative processes.

The top-down approach to decision making is also greatly influenced by the American view of how to respond to the element of uncertainty in the decision-making process. Uncertainty is not considered a desirable state of affairs, but a problem to be reduced efficiently or eliminated through the use of analytical rationality, aggressive decisiveness, and a thrust toward predetermined outcomes.[46]

The system of rewarding and promoting employees on individual merit also strengthens this tendency toward top-down decision making. Since a manager has reached that position through individual achievement, he or she is considered superior to subordinates. This creates disincentives for the manager to listen to workers, since his or her accomplishments demonstrate that he or she is more competent than they are. The worker has less incentive to become involved because of the tacit acceptance that management is smarter and more able than the worker. Therefore, the right to make decisions becomes the exclusive province of the manager, one earned both by position and by training. Corporate managers are trained to think in terms of specific problems and specific solutions, neatly partitioned to measure success in the short run. This is an important attribute and helps management to make efficient use of scarce resources by providing a sharper focus on the problems at hand and the means to solve them.

On the face of it, concentrated authority and control would appear to be an impediment to the management of large, diversified organizations. When coupled with top-down decision making, it would seem inconsistent with promoting individual initiative and a reward system based on individual performance. ABMAS has overcome these problems through the development of complex organizational structures, the creation of profit centers, an elaborate system of rules and procedures, and a highly formalized communication system.

Assignment of Authority and Managerial Discretion

How does top management ensure that its plans and decisions will be carried out exactly as envisaged, particularly when a major strategic decision must be translated into hundreds of small tactical decisions by a multitude of lower-level employees and when it is subject to misinterpretation at every level and may actually be distorted by those who may perceive it as ill-advised for the corporation or even contrary to their own self-interest? One of the ways large American corporations accomplish this goal is by converting a large body of otherwise discretionary decisions into a set of rules and procedures that everyone at lower levels is expected to follow. The success of a large corporation often depends on the extent to which top management can routinize decision making, thereby assuring that, in a given situation, lower-level employees will follow a particular course of action predetermined by top management.

Management decisions are basically of two types: routine and innovative. (A major exception to this generalization would be the case of overseas marketing, where the decision maker is confronted with a quite different set of external variables.) Routine decisions are those aimed at solving recurrent problems. The outcome of those decisions is predictable, in the sense that an elaborate set of "rules" and "procedures" can be devised to cope with a fairly large but still finite number of situations. These situations have several important characteristics: Sufficient information is available and a tested mechanism exists to collect such information, the decision maker is trained to scan the available information and determine its relevance to the situations under examination, and the dimensions of the decision can be defined beforehand.[47]

Innovative decisions, on the other hand, deal with situations that are one of a kind, whose occurrence is largely irregular, and whose scope and effect cannot be determined or predicted beforehand.[48] Innovative decisions require discretion on the part of the manager and thereby expose the corporation to an element of risk. Therefore, the higher the degree of discretion allowed a manager, the greater will be that manager's authority to commit the corporation to a binding contract or risk exposure, and the higher up that manager will be in the corporate hierarchy. However, to ensure that a manager's discretion to exercise maximum control in the use of corporate resources is restricted to specified areas, activity levels and functional areas are often divided into small, cohesive units called strategic business units. Further, these activity levels and functional areas are often viewed as "profit centers," thereby enabling the corporation to measure the manager's performance and contribution to the corporate welfare and reward his or her efforts accordingly.

American managers are therefore reluctant to allow employees to share in management prerogatives. They have expended time and effort to gain managerial expertise. With this knowledge has come power, job position, and appropriate compensation in the form of bonuses and stock options. They are evaluated on their individual performance and not on the performance of their team.[49] To suggest that untrained employees can play a role in the management of the firm is counter to their perception of management as a profession, and also represents a threat to their job security. Finally, managers perceive that participation contributes to organizational conflict when trying to achieve results, since high interaction among the various levels of staff often acts to solidify differences rather than facilitate coordination and cooperation."[50]

Both the organizational structure and the assignment of discretionary authority are based on the assumption that employees will do their best for the corporation *only* when by doing so they also best serve their own interest. Thus, one of the fundamental axioms of organization development is to assign tasks in such a manner that successful performance enhances an employee's own rewards.[51] Otherwise, the employee is likely to tailor performance in order to reduce any conflict between personal goals and those of the organization and to minimize any loss to his or her own reward.[52]

The emphasis on personal goals by top management often manifests itself in ways that set a bad example for other employees and are often inimical to the institution's best interests. For example, top executives may give themselves hefty compensation packages that bear little relationship to a firm's performance or return to stockholders. Firms whose financial performance is average or less may be found among the top firms in executive compensation, with generous bonuses, stock options, special insurance programs, and early retirement plans.[53] A more recent compensation phenomenon has been the "golden parachute," a special employment agreement that includes a generous severance package to protect key executives if control of the company changes hands. Recently William Agee, formerly CEO of Bendix, ensured that he had a severance package that meant five years of guaranteed pay, not counting the value of his Bendix stock options. This was done shortly before the most notorious of all corporate takeover battles in American business history, involving such big names as Martin Marietta, United Technologies, and the Allied Corporation. It was estimated that Agee's 19,722 shares of Bendix had a value of $1.6 million after Bendix was purchased.[54] Supposedly stockholders benefit, since such contracts enable firms to hire and retain good executives, particularly if the firm's stock is underpriced and hence open to raiding. In reality, top management has often given greater weight to protecting its short-term financial interests in the event of a takeover than to the long-term protection of corporate assets and the financial interests of the shareholders.[55]

American management is not only problem-oriented, it is solution-oriented. Managers take pride in being pragmatic and look derogatively at abstract or conceptual notions. When confronted with a new set of circumstances, they are willing to experiment with new solutions. Thus, we find corporations constantly in pursuit of new approaches to improve performance. They have experimented with such notions as the systems approach, zero-based budgeting, job enrichment, participative management, and matrix decision making. However, it also makes them easy prey to every new fad: Unwary and insecure managers rush out to try new miracle drugs lest their competitors steal a march on them or their superiors consider them old-fashioned and lacking in initiative and drive.[56]

This approach to managerial discretion is in keeping with some of the more important attributes of the American cultural and sociopolitical system. The drive toward specialization emanates from a strong tradition in Western thought that has led us to believe we can subdivide a system into functional elements; study each one sequentially, more or less in isolation from the rest; and establish criteria for the improvement of each with little, if any, reference to the remainder of the system.[57]

The Internal Communication Process

Americans favor explicitness over indirection. The thrust is on communicating the facts, even when it may be negative feedback. The cultural preference is for clarity in communication, since it conveys sincerity and directness. Language usage favors action verbs that are hard-hitting. Communication problems in an organization are largely resolved by establishing formal networks whose effectiveness is measured in terms of speed and, more important, accuracy of information.[58] Individual satisfaction with the social aspects of the communication process is of secondary importance. There is minimal organizational effort to utilize the informal and interpersonal communication processes that exist in any firm. Thus, it is the rare American firm that deliberately creates informal communication networks through such devices as company parties and recreational activities designed to generate friendships among all levels of management and thereby enhance their understanding of one another's thinking, attitudes, and personal values.

The Formal Group Process in the American Corporation

Group activities or collective meetings are an important element in American corporate life and a major mechanism for the achievement of organizational goals despite the cultural predilection toward individualism. Although informal interest or friendship groups exist in all corporate organizations to a greater or lesser extent, the primary groups are functional-command groups specified by the organizational structure or task-project groups specifically established by top management to solve a designated problem. The terms "committees" and "meetings" are often viewed in a pejorative sense, indicating that participants consider them necessary evils that are quite often not needed and a waste of time.

Group members are expected to interact to the extent necessary to accomplish the assigned task. They operate subject to a specific agenda that contains management-established parameters for group discussion. Their interaction often consists of individual members advocating their solution to the problem and defending it before the group. The group discussion centers around which option to adopt. Group solutions are arrived at by selecting among the many alternatives or developing an interactive option that satisfies a majority of the group. Group performance is measured in terms of efficiency—the duration of meeting and the speed at which a decision is made. Any problems arising consequent to the decision are expected to be resolved during the implementation stage.

A prominent feature of the American group process is an emphasis on the advocacy presentation of an idea: one supports and defends a predetermined position that one feels is best. Participants are expected to be well prepared prior to the meeting and to contribute to an efficient meeting by quickly and vigorously presenting their ideas. This preparation may be the result of informal conversations outside the more formalized and structured group process and often represents an effort to line up support for one's position. It is expected that the participants may have to defend their ideas under adverse and hostile conditions. Different persons in the group may have also been given the same assignment to ensure that differing approaches emerge during the meeting.

One factor that may account for the high incidence of advocacy in the formal group process is the emphasis on task rather than maintenance functions. The short-term and results orientation of American executives facilitates this focus. Solving the problem is the true purpose of the group process. Thus, American business values demand that the group confront its differences and work through its disagreements in order to arrive at a genuine integrative solution. Maintenance functions, such as harmonizing and compromising, are considered to be of limited value, since they are useful only in reducing destructive types of disagreement among group members.[59]

Although group decision making has important benefits, a real concern for American managers is the emergence of "groupthink." This phenomenon occurs in highly cohesive groups where the need to conform to group norms pressures members toward a consensus that may not represent the "best" solution to the problem assigned to the group. Groupthink is an undesirable consequence of the group function by American standards, since the primary function of the group is not to achieve commitment by group members to the group solution, but to afford each member an opportunity to be heard in the group process and to arrive at a solution that will satisfy management.[60]

HUMAN RESOURCE MANAGEMENT IN THE AMERICAN CORPORATION

Job Enrichment and Participative Management

Two behavioral management themes that have gained new adherents among American business firms in recent years are subordinate participation in managerial decisions and openness in communication that enables this participation to be effective. Employee participation, expressed in such concepts as theory Y, self-actualization, job enrichment, and management by objectives, has been proposed as a means of improving organizational productivity and staff morale. Europe has formalized this participative process by placing employee representatives on boards of directors to engage in top-level policymaking under the rubric of industrial democracy. In the United States, the emphasis has been more on increased subordinate involvement in specified on-the-job decisions at the operating levels of the corporation or participative management with little commitment to these programs beyond seeking increased productivity.[61] American firms are not seeking social change and meaningful workplace democracy as it is understood in Europe.[62]

Consensual decision making or participative management is not an American societal norm. Where practiced by an American business firm, it represents a deliberate management decision to delegate leadership authority to lower-echelon staff but only on a limited basis, as illustrated by the case of General Foods' Total Quality System. Its objective was to better motivate blue collar workers by providing them with a more satisfactory working environment. Touted as a new approach to quality control and an answer to the competitive threat of the Japanese, the system places responsibility for quality control on the production worker rather than on quality checks after the fact by a quality control department. The motivation, according to corporate executives, comes from giving the low-echelon employee more responsibility and more pay.[63]

Organizations engaged in repetitive work in a highly stable environment that place a premium on results are generally task-oriented. They tend toward managerial autocracy, with little involvement of employees in the planning and organizing of work. If participative management is employed, it is limited in scope and is oriented toward production line operations. Corporations that compete in a technological environment, which is volatile and dependent on skilled and highly educated personnel engaged in more creative activities, are more likely to be employee-oriented and encourage greater subordinate involvement in a wider array of corporate affairs.[64]

For most American managers, employee participation has definite drawbacks. If immediate decisions are required, time cannot be spared for group participation, as group decision making is perceived to be less efficient.[65] American managers also rationalize that not all employees are equally desirous of being involved in what is perceived as management's job.[66] This perception is further reinforced by the ABMAS emphasis on job specialization, which tends to recruit and retain employees with a narrowly focused expertise who are not prepared to employ a holistic approach to organizational challenges. Even the current Quality of Worklife (QWL) movement has been largely sold as a way to help corporations gain in productivity and, at the same time, have more fulfilled (less belligerent) workers. It has not been presented as a means of involving the worker in organizational decision making. As a consequence, a brief review of these experimental projects reveals mixed results. For example, the famous Bulova Watch Company QWL project realized great gains in efficiency (14 percent) and in quality (16 percent), and a dramatic decrease in customer returns (50 percent). The workers achieved this with a one-third workforce layoff and slim salary raises. Workers did get improved working conditions, day care, and earned idletime. Overall, though, the QWL projects have produced questionable results due to management's focus on keeping profits high and stressing efficiency over worker participation. This theme pervades the QWL programs in the Topeka plant of General Foods, at the Rushton Mining Company, the Vermont Asbestos Group, at South Bend Lathe, and at Mohawk Valley Community Corporation.[67]

Employee Relations Practices

Nowhere is the difference between Japanese and American management more stark than in personnel policies and practices. Even the current popularization and promotion of "human resource management" tends to treat people as a resource to be exploited by management in pursuit of corporate goals, like financial or capital resources. Absence of a social contract requiring the employee to stay on the job makes an investment in the employee very risky compared to an investment in plant and equipment. Moreover, employee-based investment may restrict an employee's mobility—an outcome that may not be socially desirable or individually preferred. Employees respond to this environment by focusing on their individual careers, prepared to pursue those careers at any business firm that meets their needs.[68]

Job-Oriented Personnel Management

The thrust of American personnel management is on the job and not on the person. American corporations hire persons to fulfill specific jobs. The emphasis is on job analysis and design to ensure that the person hired has the necessary qualifications for the job. Compensation packages are designed to match the value of the job to the corporation and the price it will have to pay to entice a qualified person to take the work. Such a system also facilitates performance appraisal by comparing job requirements with employee performance. A satisfactory level of performance is rewarded. However, when performance falls below the clearly defined requirements, an employee can be terminated with a minimum of difficulty.

Such a system places a greater emphasis on utilizing the available talent pool rather than expanding it. It also discards people when they are not needed by the firm. In a free and competitive economy, the system makes good sense because it allows both individuals and firms to maximize their gains through efficient resource utilization while the second-order effects of their decisions are handled at the societal level. The limitation of the system lies in the fact that unequal bargaining power between individuals or groups and corporations may allow the latter to force wage and job solutions on the former in a manner that may be societally unacceptable—for example, hiring women for traditionally lower-paying jobs or paying them lower wages for similar jobs compared to their male counterparts. Moreover, when certain groups, such as blacks, are prevented from acquiring necessary job skills for historical and cultural reasons, they are deprived of the opportunity to compete in the marketplace on an equitable basis.

To overcome the undesirable effects of market- and performance-based recruitment and compensation systems, laws have evolved in the United States that have curtailed an employer's discretion to discriminate on such criteria as sex, age, color, or national origin.[69] While these laws were designed to solve societal problems within the American context, they also apply equally to foreign corporations and to management systems that have engaged in similar discriminatory practices, although for a totally different reasons. This aspect of the problem will be explored in greater detail in Chapter 10. However, as we have seen in Chapter 4 in the case of C. Itoh and Company, foreign managements use discriminatory practices that are illegal and socially repugnant in the United States because they are condoned in their own countries and because they perceived a foreign treaty right to use their unique cultural approaches in managing U.S. subsidiaries.

Recruitment Is Superior to Retraining

The job-oriented approach also favors the recruitment of younger executives with newly granted MBAs, particularly from select schools, to fill specified job positions.[70] Since employees are viewed as a variable cost, it is cheaper in the short run to hire new personnel fresh out of business school with the latest functional training to fill a given specialized position at a lower wage cost, rather than retrain an older employee in new skills when seniority has already placed that employee in the upper income brackets of the organization's compensation system. Thus, American business firms maintain an elaborate recruiting connection with universities that are sources of potential employees—especially professional and managerial employees. Long-term relations are built, supported, and reinforced by such corporate philanthropic activities as matching grants, scholarships, and funding for program development and curriculum enrichment.

The Mobile, Self-Centered Employee

The consequence for ABMAS is a highly mobile and self-centered employee, particularly at the management level. Loyalty is to self, not to the organization. American individualism and the desire to pursue personal and family-centered activities have tended to dampen feelings of emotional involvement in the corporate enterprise. American business firms have developed a highly rationalistic workforce with low recognition of the need for loyalty or the importance of maintaining the enterprise. The emphasis is on satisfaction of personal, not corporate, goals. Employees are prepared to move from company to company during their professional careers, depending on which firm will offer the maximum compensation in the form of bonuses, stock options, "golden umbrellas," and so on. Corporate raiding of skilled professional or key managerial personnel is quite common. Executive "headhunters" are employed even by conservative firms noted for their stable workforces.

For the top executive, what is important is a carefully drafted individual agreement providing for protection of executive "perks" regardless of corporate performance and the long-term stability of the organization. For the lower-echelon employee, it is a master contract negotiated by the employee's union representatives that guarantees minimum compensation based on job position. A late 1970s longitudinal study by American Telephone & Telegraph comparing its management force in 23 operating companies with a similar group evaluated in 1956 indicated that AT&T's current crop of managers was less motivated to achieve success and less committed to the corporate objectives than their counterparts of 20 years before.[71]

Scientific Production Management

The Industrial Revolution in American business history can best be characterized as a strict rationalization of the manufacturing system in terms of machinery and physical layout. In the drive to increase production efficiency, manufacturing processes were broken down into many separate lines to reduce production bottlenecks; machinery was modeled and used in one specialized function; and laborers were assigned to do a specialized job. The thrust in controlling the production process was on scientific rationalization. The overall objective was to achieve a smooth production process without any breakdown due to lack of inventory or raw materials. The breakdown of production flow was regarded as very expensive in terms of underutilized labor and machinery startup costs. Simple, specialized jobs required less time for training and thus led to less downtime. Workers were to be treated essentially as one replaceable component of production process, performing a simple mechanical function. Decision making as well as problem solving for every facet of the production process was performed by management and engineers operating under the belief that they, and only they, were best equipped to do so.

The apparent superiority of American firms in manufacturing capability and techniques from World War II until the late 1970s led to the conviction that these manufacturing techniques were perfect. As Abernathy and others have stated, American industry therefore redirected managerial effort and attention away from production and toward marketing and finance.[72] When rising costs of labor in the United States threatened the industrial base in the 1960s, it was natural that many American manufacturing companies transferred their plants to Third World countries, where an abundant and cheap workforce was still available.

Employee Assertion and Litigation of Rights to Define Employer-Employee Relations

The job-oriented personnel practices of many American business firms continue to be aggravated by the managerial dominance in capitalistic organizations of individuals who view workers as production units interchangeable with machines—what MacGregor calls theory X managers.[73] It is a modern version of the master-servant concept that characterized labor-management relationships at the beginning of the Industrial Revolution and has left its imprint on labor-management practices today. In spite of efforts to promote humanistic and participative approaches to personnel management, the master-servant concept still prevails in most American firms today.[74] The outcome is organizational disharmony that results in efforts by employees to assert rights and to establish entitlements in a working environment they consider hostile to their aspirations. In a 1980 address, William J. Spencer, president of Citibank, summarized the position as follows:

> The modern trend is to view employment . . . as one of many life interests—all serving the common purpose of *self-fulfillment. . . .* Thus, workers are more determined than ever to bring into the workplace the same values they cherish outside the workplace.
>
> This includes such intangible values as self-respect, dignity, and *individuality.* It also includes the particular values enumerated in the Constitution. Workers no longer consider the Bill of Rights something to be stashed out of sight, like a wet umbrella, when they arrive at work. They expect such guarantees as *"due process,"* "privacy," and "free speech" to follow them to their desks and work-stations. After all, a *right* that doesn't apply through much of your waking day and which you can be fired for exercising, isn't much of a right [emphasis added].[75]

MANAGEMENT AND THE UNION: INSTITUTIONALIZED CONFLICT

The Industrial Revolution, as it developed in United States, was highly labor-intensive and exploitative, and ultimately led to an adversary management-labor relationship and the establishment of the labor unions. In the name of production efficiency and cost reduction, the working environment was sometimes dangerous and unhealthy, and wages were low. Labor unions, formed to protect the workers, gradually gained sufficient strength to bargain successfully with management. With their unified power, they demanded higher wages and better working conditions. More important for the development of the manufacturing system, labor unions were instrumental in advancing the cause of job specialization and separation in their efforts to protect the worker's job security.

Workers individually have little, if any, bargaining power vis-à-vis management to obtain a meaningful role in corporate affairs. The assumption, because of the history of the Industrial Revolution in America, is that employer and employee are in an adversarial position and that the employee is at a disadvantage unless permitted to bargain collectively—that is, form a union. This notion was best articulated by one of the founding leaders of the labor movement, Samuel Gompers: "The primary essential in our mission has been the protection of the wage earner; to improve the safety and the sanitary conditions of the workshop; and *to free him from the tyrannies, petty or otherwise, which serve to make his existence slavery.* These in the nature of things, I repeat, were and are the objectives of trade unions" [emphasis added].[76]

This management-union antagonism is further heightened by the conflict within the labor movement itself, expressed in terms of craft versus industrial unions, each attempting to organize at the expense of the other. When American business entities were largely family-owned and single-product-oriented, workers formed craft unions based on their trade in the fashion of the guilds of the Middle Ages. Management negotiated labor agreements with a number of unions, each representing a portion of the total company workforce. As business firms grew into multiproduct corporations, unions enhanced their bargaining power by organizing as industry unions; all employees of the company and the industry belonged to the same union and were covered under a single master contract.

Although American management and labor are mutually dependent on one another for their continued existence, an inherent state of conflict exists between them. Management's main objective is to keep costs at a minimum (cheap labor), while labor naturally seeks the highest wages and fringe benefits possible (high costs). Management believes that the ownership of capital carries with it the sole right and responsibility to decide how that capital is to be used—a by-product of the Lockean theory of property. For the employee, the job represents the only source of income to gain property and, ultimately, status, security, and fulfillment.[77] Although overt anti-unionism has declined considerably in the United States, the underlying antagonism persists. In part it is due to changing public attitudes, because most Americans now make their living as wage earners and not as property owners. Professional managers of large corporations have realized that labor peace is essential to a firm's profitability, especially when higher costs can be passed on to the consumer. Finally, the right of workers to organize and bargain collectively, free of restraint or coercion, is not only authorized but encouraged by federal laws.

The prime goal of American unionism has been to better the worker's economic position and obtain for him or her economic security—a role assumed by the corporation in other cultures. Unions have exerted continuous pressure on management to reduce working hours and increase wages so that employees can obtain a larger share of the fruits of their labor and have more leisure time to enjoy the increased benefits. Other union goals have included improved working conditions and minimum compensation in periods of recession or depression—a weak form of lifetime employment. The "Wisconsin school" of management-labor relations contends that the key to understanding the role of unions in American society is an appreciation of American workers' consciousness of limited job opportunities and their desire for improved property rights in the job itself.[78] Consequently, American unions differ greatly from their counterparts in Europe. They have little interest in forming a separate political party and governing the body politic. Instead, they prefer to operate as an interest group that influences the public policy process through lobbying and political contributions.

Labor-management relations are extensively regulated by the federal government acting through the National Labor Relations Board. Employees are given the right to form unions and bargain collectively with management regarding terms and conditions of their employment. A Bill of Rights has been established for union members to protect them from misconduct by union officials.[79] But absent from all this vast body of law and implementing regulations is the notion that management and labor are part of a team working together toward common goals that will benefit the organization and the society.

NOTES

1. William Ouchi, *Theory Z: How American Business Can Meet the Japanese Challenge* (Reading, Mass.: Addison-Wesley, 1981).
2. W. L. Warner and J. C. Abeggen, *Occupational Mobility in American Business and Industry* (St. Paul: University of Minnesota Press, 1955); G. Bowman, "What Helps or Harms Promotability," *Harvard Business Review,* 42 (May–June 1964), pp. 184–196; A. R. Negandhi, "Profile of the American Overseas Executive," *California Management Review,* 1966, pp. 59–63; and D. L. Helmich and W. B. Brown, "Successor Type and Organizational Change in the Corporate Enterprise," *Administrative Science Quarterly,* 17, 3 (1972), pp. 371–388.
3. Frederick Gluck, Stephen Kaufman, and A. Steven Walleck, "The Four Phases of Strategic Management," *The Journal of Business Strategy,* 2, 3 (Winter 1982), p. 12.

4. Richard Eells and Clarence Walton, *Conceptual Foundations of Business* (Homewood, Ill.: Irwin, 1969), p. 551.

5. Joseph A. Schumpeter, *The Theory of Economic Development: An Inquiry into Profits, Capital, Credit, Interest and the Business Cycle* (Cambridge, Mass.: Harvard University Press, 1968).

6. Brian Dumaine, "Intergraph: A Good Old Boy Scores Big," *Fortune*, July 11, 1983, p. 126.

7. "Can the 3-D Camera Click This Time Around," *Business Week*, June 27, 1983, pp. 72–76.

8. "Here Comes the 'Intrapreneur'," *Business Week*, July 18, 1983, pp. 188, 190.

9. A. S. Tannebaum, B. Kavcic, M. Rosner, M. Vianello, and J. G. Wieser, *Hierarchy in Organizations: An International Comparison* (San Francisco: Jossey-Bass, 1974).

10. Karen Blumenthal, "Texas Instruments Loses $119.2 million," *Dallas Morning News*, July 23, 1983, p. 1; Scott Ticer, "TI's Loss Exceeds Estimate, Quarterly Deficit Tops $119 Million," *Dallas Times Herald*, July 23, 1983, p. 1; stock market summaries reported in *Wall Street Journal*, July 26, 1983, p. 52, and July 29, 1983, p. 32.

11. "Executive Compensation: Looking to the Long Term Again," *Business Week*, May 9, 1983, p. 80.

12. "Stockholders on the Attack," *Business Week*, June 13, 1983, pp. 32–35.

13. J. G. March and H. A. Simon, *Organizations* (New York: Wiley, 1958); and J. G. March, "Bounded Rationality, Ambiguity, and the Engineering of Choice," *The Bell Journal of Economics*, 1 (1978), pp. 587–608.

14. John Kenneth Galbraith, *The New Industrial State* (Boston: Houghton Mifflin, 1978).

15. Melvin Aron Eisenberg, *The Structure of the Corporation—A Legal Analysis* (Boston: Little, Brown, 1976); and Christopher D. Stone, *Where the Law Ends—The Social Control of Corporate Behavior* (New York: Harper & Row, 1975).

16. See note 2.

17. Thorstein Veblen, *The Theory of the Leisure Class: An Economic Study of Institutions* (New York: Macmillan, 1912).

18. Roy Rowan and Thomas Moore, "Behind the Lines in the Bendix War," *Fortune*, October 18, 1983, pp. 156–168; and H. Anderson and H. Lampert, "Bendix Bites the Dust," *Newsweek*, October 4, 1982, pp. 67–68, 70.

19. S. Prakash Sethi, *Advocacy Advertising and Large Corporations: Social Conflict, Big Business Image, News Media, and Public Policy* (Lexington, Mass.: Heath, 1977).

20. S. Prakash Sethi, Bernard J. Cunningham, and Patricia M. Miller, *Corporate Governance: Public Policy-Social Responsibility Committee of Corporate Boards: Growth and Accomplishment*, Special Report No. SR-79-01 (1979); S. Prakash Sethi, *Corporate Governance: Composition and Committee Structure of Corporate Boards—Volumes I & II*, Special Report No. SR-80-02 (1980); and S. Prakash Sethi, Carl L. Swanson, and Kathryn Rudie Harrigan, *Women Directors on Corporate Boards*, Special Report No. WP-81-01 (1981), all published by The Center for Research in Business and Social Policy, The University of Texas at Dallas. See also *Corporate Directorship Practices: The Public Policy Committee*, Research Report No. 774 (1980); and *Corporate Directorship Practices: The Planning Committee*, Research Report No. 810 (1981) issued by The Conference Board, New York.

21. Korn/Ferry International, Board of Directors Annual Study (New York, 1978); and, Board of Directors Annual Study (New York, 1980).

22. J. Van Maanen, "Breaking In: Socialization to Work," in R. Dubin (ed.), *Handbook of Work, Organization and Society* (Chicago: Rand-McNally, 1976); E. H. Schien, *Career Dynamics* (Reading, Mass: Addison-Wesley, 1978); and Thomas J. Peters and Robert H. Waterman, Jr., *In Search of Excellence: Lessons from America's Best Run Companies* (New York: Harper & Row, 1982).

23. Robert Chatov, "The Role of Ideology in the American Corporation," in Dow Votaw and S. Prakash Sethi (eds.), *The Corporate Dilemma: Traditional Values versus Contemporary Problems* (Englewood Cliffs, N.J.: Prentice-Hall, 1973).

24. Peter F. Drucker, "What Is 'Business Ethics'?" *The Public Interest,* 63 (Spring 1981), p. 18; Oscar F. Williams, "Business Ethics: A Trojan Horse?" *California Management Review,* 24, 4 (Summer 1982), p. 14; and Thomas Moore, "Industrial Espionage of the Harvard B-School," *Fortune,* September 6, 1982, pp. 70–76.

25. Laura L. Nash, "Ethics without the Sermon," *Harvard Business Review,* 59, 6 (November–December 1981), pp. 78–90.

26. Steven N. Brenner and Earl A. Molander, "Is the Ethics of Business Changing?" *Harvard Business Review,* 55 (January–February 1977), pp. 57–71.

27. George C. S. Benson, *Business Ethics in America* (Lexington, Mass.: Lexington Books, 1982).

28. Francis W. Steckmest, *Corporate Performance, The Key to Public Trust* (New York: McGraw-Hill, 1982), chap. 4; and Neil W. Chamberlain, *Remaking American Values* (New York: Basic Books, 1977), chap. 5.

29. Frederick W. Taylor, *Scientific Management* (New York: Harper & Row, 1947).

30. Eells and Walton, *Conceptual Foundations,* p. 529.

31. Elizabeth M. Fowler, "Getting Ahead: MBA vs. Law Degree," *New York Times/ National Employment Report,* October 16, 1983, p. 41.

32. L. L. Cummings and D. Schwartz, *Performance in Organizations: Determinants and Appraisals* (Glenview, Ill.: Scott, Foresman, 1973); and G. P. Latham and K. N. Wexley, *Increasing Productivity through Performance Appraisal* (Reading, Mass.: Addison-Wesley, 1982).

33. L. Dyer, D. D. Schwartz, and R. D. Therault, "Managerial Perceptions Regarding Salary Increase Criteria," *Personnel Psychology,* 290 (1976), pp. 233–242.

34. S. Prakash Sethi, "A Strategic Framework for Dealing with the Schism between Business and Academe," *Public Affairs Review,* (1983), pp. 44–59. The narrow training of business school graduates has recently become the subject of considerable soul searching by the universities and the corporate community. See, for example, Gene Maeroff, "Harvard: A Real-Life Case Study—Derek Bok Asks Review of the Business School," *New York Times,* May 6, 1979, Sec. 3, p. 11; Edward B. Fiske, "Education: Values Taught More Widely," *New York Times,* March 4, 1980, C1; "What Are They Teaching in the B-Schools," *Business Week,* November 10, 1980, pp. 61–69; and John Henderson, "Change on Campus: More Colleges to Require a Variety of Courses to Broaden Students," *Wall Street Journal,* March 9, 1981, pp. 1, 15.

35. R. M. Cyert and J. G. March, *A Behaviorial Theory of the Firm* (Englewood Cliffs, N.J.: Prentice-Hall, 1963); George C. Lodge, *The New American Ideology* (New York: Knopf, 1976), chap. 10; W. H. Starbuck, "Organizations As Action Gen-

erators," *American Sociological Review,* 48 (1983), pp. 91–102; and Morita Akio, "Do Companies Need Lawyers?" *Japan Quarterly,* 30, 1 (January–March 1983), pp. 5–6.

36. Sethi, "A Strategic Framework."

37. M. Maccoby, *The Gamesman* (New York: Bantam Books, 1976).

38. D. W. Ewing, *Do It My Way or You're Fired: Employee Rights and the Changing Role of Management* (New York: Wiley, 1983).

39. Alfred D. Chandler, *The Visible Hand: The Managerial Revolution in American Business* (Cambridge, Mass.: Belknap Press, 1977).

40. J. B. Quinn, *Strategies for Change: Logical Incrementalism* (Homewood, Ill.: Irwin, 1980).

41. R. V. Presthus, *The Organizational Society* (New York: Vintage, 1965), p. 202.

42. Sethi, "A Strategic Framework."

43. Bruce D. Henderson, *Henderson on Corporate Strategy* (Cambridge, Mass.: Abt Books, 1979).

44. Presthus, *The Organizational Society.*

45. Richard Tanner Pascale and Anthony G. Athos, *The Art of Japanese Management: Applications for American Executives* (New York: Simon and Schuster, 1981), p. 153.

46. J. R. P. French and B. Raven, "The Bases of Social Power," in D. Cartwright and A. F. Zander (eds.), *Group Dynamics,* 2nd ed. (Evanston, Ill.: Row, Peterson, 1960), pp. 607–623; J. D. Thompson, *Organizations in Action* (New York: McGraw-Hill, 1967); and C. Perrow, *Complex Organizations: A Critical Essay,* 2nd ed. (Dallas: Scott, Freeman, 1979).

47. S. Prakash Sethi and Dow Votaw, "How Should We Develop a New Corporate Response to a Changing Social Environment," *The Corporate Dilemma.*

48. Henderson, *Henderson on Corporate Strategy.*

49. David Jenkins, *Job Power, Blue and White Collar Democracy* (New York: Penguin Books, 1973).

50. Stephen P. Robbins, *Management Organizational Conflict—A Nontraditional Approach* (Englewood Cliffs, N.J.: Prentice-Hall, 1974), pp. 12–13, 46.

51. E. Huse, *Organization Development and Change,* 2nd ed. (St. Paul, Minn.: West, 1975).

52. Phillip Selznick, *TVA and the Grass Roots* (Berkeley: University of California Press, 1949); J. G. March and H. A. Simon, *Organizations* (New York: Wiley, 1958); and R. Merton, *Social Theory and Social Structure* (New York: Free Press, 1968).

53. Carol J. Loomis, "The Madness of Executive Compensation," *Fortune,* July 12, 1982. p. 42; and "How America's Top Moneymakers Fared in the Recession," *Business Week,* May 9, 1983, p. 84.

54. Rowan and Moore, "Behind the Lines in the Bendix War"; and Anderson and Lampert, "Bendix Bites the Dust."

55. Ann M. Morrison, "Those Executive Bailout Deals," *Fortune,* December 13, 1982, p. 82.

56. N. Foy and H. Gadon, "Worker Participation: Contrasts in Three Countries," *Harvard Business Review,* 54 (May–June 1976), pp. 71–83.

57. Sethi and Votaw, "How Should We Develop a New Corporate Response."

58. H. Mintzberg, *The Nature of Managerial Work* (New York: Harper & Row, 1973); and J. P. Kotter, "What Effective General Managers Really Do," *Harvard Business Review,* 60 (November–December 1982), pp. 156–167.

59. Edgar H. Schein, *Process Consultation: Its Role in Organization Development* (Reading, Mass.: Addison-Wesley, 1969), chap. 7.

60. I. L. Janis, *Victims of Groupthink* (Boston: Houghton Mifflin, 1972).

61. Henry Mintzberg, "Why American Needs, But Cannot Have, Corporate Democracy," *Organizational Dynamics,* Spring 1983, p. 5; and G. Strauss, "Worker Participation in Management: An International Perspective," in B. M. Stau and L. L. Cummings, *Research in Organizations,* Vol. 4 (Greenwich, Conn.: Jai Press, 1983).

62. D. Zwerdling, *Workplace Democracy: A Guide to Workplace Ownership, Participation, and Self Management Experiments in the United States and Europe* (New York: Harper & Row, 1980).

63. Louis Rukeyser, "Motivation Is Key, Executive Says," *The Dallas Morning News,* June 26, 1983, p. 2H.

64. Myron Magnet, "Managing by Mystique at Tandem Computers," *Fortune,* June 28, 1982, p. 84.

65. H. P. Dachler and B. Wilpert, "Conceptual Dimensions and Boundaries of Participation in Organizations: A Critical Evaluation," *Administrative Science Quarterly,* 23 (1978), pp. 1–39.

66. J. Miller, "Decision-Making and Organizational Effectiveness: Participation and Perceptions," *Sociology of Work and Occupations,* 7 (1980), pp. 55–79.

67. P. S. Goodman, *Assessing Organizational Change: The Rushton Quality of Work Experiment* (New York: Wiley, 1979); B. A. Macy, G. E. Ledford and E. E. Lawler III, *An Assessment of the Bulova Quality of Work Life Experiment* (New York: Wiley Interscience, in press); and Zwerdling, *Workplace Democracy.*

68. W. Ouchi and A. Jaeger, "Type Z Organization: Stability in the Midst of Immobility," *Academy of Management Review,* April 1978, pp. 305–314.

69. Principal federal legislation in the employment area includes: The Civil Rights Act of 1964, as amended by the Equal Employment Act of 1972; the Age Discrimination in Employment Act of 1967; the Occupational Safety and Health Act of 1970; and the Equal Pay Act of 1963. Key employment discrimination decisions by the U.S. Supreme Court are *Griggs* v. *Duke Power Company,* 401 U.S. 424, 91 S.Ct. 849 (1971); *Albermarle Paper Company* v. *Moody,* 422 U.S. 403, 95 S.Ct. 2362 (1975); *Regents of the University of California* v. *Bakke,* 438 U.S. 265, 98 S.Ct. 2733 (1978); and *United States Steelworkers of America* v. *Weber* and *Kaiser Aluminum and Chemical Corporation,* 443 U.S. 193, 99 S.Ct. 2721 (1979).

70. Roy Rowan, "How Harvard's Women MBAs Are Managing," *Fortune,* July 11, 1983, p. 58.

71. Ann Howard and James A. Wilson, "Leadership in a Declining Work Ethic," *California Management Review,* 24, 4 (Summer 1982), pp. 33–40.

72. Robert H. Hayes and William J. Abernathy, "Managing Our Way to Economic Decline," *Harvard Business Review,* 58, 4 (July–August 1980), pp. 67–77.

73. Douglas McGregor, *The Human Side of Enterprise* (New York: McGraw-Hill, 1960).

74. David W. Ewing, *Freedom Inside the Organization* (New York: Dutton, 1977). See also Ralph Nader, Peter Petkas, and Kate Blackwell, *Whistle Blowing* (New York: Grossman, 1972).

75. William I. Spencer, "Recognizing Individual Rights Is Good Business," address delivered at the Third National Seminar on Individual Rights in the Corporation, Washington, D.C., June 12, 1980.

76. Samuel Gompers, "The Philosophy of Trade Unions," in E. W. Baake, Clark Kerr, and Charles Anrod (eds.), *Unions, Management and the Public* (New York: Harcourt Brace Jovanovich, 1967), p. 42.

77. Peter F. Drucker, "The Job As Property Right," *Wall Street Journal,* March 4, 1980, editorial page.

78. Arthur A. Sloane and Fred Whitney, *Labor Relations,* 2nd ed. (Englewood Cliffs, N.J.: Prentice-Hall, 1972), p. 88.

79. The principal federal legislation pertaining to labor-management relations includes the Norris-La Guardia Act of 1932; the Wagner Act of 1933; the Taft-Hartley Act of 1947; and the Landrum-Griffin Act of 1959.

SEVEN ▪▪

A Conceptual Framework Relating the External Environment to an Institution's Response Patterns

THE NEXT STAGE IN OUR ANALYSIS REQUIRES AN UNDERSTANDING OF the impact of cultural and sociopolitical conditions on the introduction of a new phenomenon into the social system and the strategies pursued by the change agent. It is important, therefore, to have a conceptual framework that brings into focus the dynamics of the interaction between the elements of the external social environment, given society's perception of the issues involved, and its expectations of institutional behavior in dealing with that issue.

The effectiveness of an institution's policies and operations and their impact on the external environment must depend, to a large extent, on the nature of the issue under contention and review. The first point to consider is that any evaluation of the effectiveness of a particular corporate strategy or the strategies of other social institutions must be culturally and temporally determined. A specific action is more or less acceptable by society only within the framework of the time, the environment, and the nature of the parties involved. The same activity that may be considered socially responsible at one time, under one set of circumstances, and in one culture may be socially irresponsible at another time, in another place, and under different circumstances. No system for evaluating corporate behavior can therefore ignore the cultural and sociopolitical environment. A strategic plan for bringing about changes in a social system, to be relevant, must be developed within the context of a specific time horizon and relate to a particular social phenomenon that is of concern to society and its various constituency groups.

The framework briefly developed here suggests a rationale by which the activities of Japanese or American firms can be analyzed in terms of their effectiveness in introducing Japanese management practices and in gaining their acceptance by other groups.[1] It has three components. The first component deals with the definition of the external environment or the context within which the institutional strategy is introduced and evaluated. The emphasis is on the generalized external conditions created by a multitude of actions by various social actors that are essentially similar within a given contextual and temporal frame. The second deals with the categorization of the types of institutional strategies or responses. These are defined not in terms of specific activities, but in terms of the type of underlying rationale applied in responding to external conditions. The third deals with the nature of the institution itself in terms of its value set, mission, and goals; leadership style; and organizational structure and dynamics. The characteristics of an institution set the limits within which it will act; define its perception of the external environment and the relevant stage of an issue's life cycle; and determine its response modes toward other groups' actions.

In this chapter, we deal with the first two elements of the framework. First, we analyze the external environmental conditions that determine the various stages of an issue's life cycle. The focus is on how an issue or a problem reaches successive stages of severity because of its cumulative effect, real or perceived, on the public's consciousness. Second, we examine the different types of response patterns that a change agent, in this case the corporation, may pursue during different stages of the issue's life cycle and the impact these strategies may have in determining a corporation's power to manage its affairs without undue outside influence. The third element of the framework is concerned with the characteristics of the change agent. These comprise its value set, its physical and human resources, its vision of the future, and how these characteristics will shape the specific strategies selected by a particular corporation. These will be dealt with in Chapters 8 and 9.

THE EXTERNAL ENVIRONMENT

The impact of the external environment on a problem and the effectiveness of an institution's response can best be evaluated in terms of the life cycle of the problem. This can be accomplished by dividing the elapsed time between the emergence of a problem and its solution and ultimate elimination into four categories or stages: (a) preproblem, (b) identification, (c) remedy and relief, and (d) prevention. There is some overlap among these categories because social problems do not fall neatly into discrete groups, nor can they always be solved in distinct successive steps. However, the arrangement facilitates the analysis of the environmental conditions and the adequacy of the various corporate strategies.

The Preproblem Stage

Every action taken by an institution, in this case the corporation, to exploit its environment creates certain counterreactions. For example, in the process of recruiting managerial personnel, business firms are constantly engaged in a series of transactions with individuals and social groups. In these transactions, business responds to two kinds of forces: market and nonmarket. In the case of market forces, a firm adapts by varying its recruitment criteria, compensation, or fringe benefits to meet changing employee needs and expectations. Adequacy of response can be measured in terms of hiring success and turnover of personnel. All market actions have some nonmarket or indirect consequences for the society. These second-order effects are generally called externalities and have traditionally been borne by society as a whole. Taken individually, each action or incident is not significant in terms of its impact on the corporation or the affected parties. However, when similar acts are performed by a large number of companies and continued over a long period, their cumulative effect is substantial. When that happens, a problem is born—for example, minority discrimination.

   The preproblem stage has both cultural and sociopolitical dimensions. The capacity or willingness of a nation to accept and tolerate a level of societal degradation may keep a situation from accelerating to the problem identification stage. First, the time lag between the creation of a problem and the emergence of its negative side effects may be quite long. Second, the problem may be centered in isolated population pockets or geographic areas with insufficient means of communication or dissemination of news. Third, some influential groups may be able to prevent information from being disseminated or prevent its recognition by governmental agencies and political organs. Conversely, an open communication system, the availability of mass media, and the existence of politically active groups with technological sophistication may elevate a situation to the level of a crisis before all the necessary evidence is in.

   The elapsed time at the preproblem stage is probably the longest of all the four stages, although there is a tendency for the time span to become shorter with increasing industrialization. Most individuals and institutions respond to the problem passively. Their efforts are aimed at adaptation, and the problem is treated as given. Elevation to the problem identification stage varies with different cultures and is based on the relative sociopolitical strength of the affecting and affected groups, the availability of necessary expertise to various groups, the size of the affected area relative to the total area and population, the existence of mass communication systems in the society, and the media access of various groups.

The Identification Stage

Once the intensity of an issue is sufficiently heightened or the impact of a problem becomes significant enough, there is a drive among the affected groups to define it, identify its causes, and relate it to the source. This is one of the most difficult stages in the whole process. First, individual business entities may not be aware of the problem because they view it only from their own perspective. Second, a given adverse effect may have been caused by a variety of factors, and direct linkages may be impossible to establish. For example, differential treatment of Japanese and American employees in a U.S.-based Japanese firm may be caused by a variety of factors including national origin bias, lack of proper education, insufficient motivation and ambition, and the particular needs of the firm. A third difficulty arises when no definitive proof is possible because symptoms appear years later. A fourth difficulty deals with situations in which irreparable damage has been done by the time proof is available, and no corrective or preventive measures are possible.

The definition of the problem may also involve the vested interest or value orientation of a particular group. Corporations may view the establishment of quality circles as a means of involving their workers in the production process. Employees may view them as a management device to fasten blame on them for inferior work when the real problem is inadequate investment in plant modernization and bad management practices. American firms may seek wage cuts in unionized plants to lower costs so they can stay in business and compete with the Japanese, while the workers argue that the purpose is to make more profit for the shareholders and pay greater bonuses to the managers at the expense of the employees. What is an opportunity to one group may appear as a problem to another group.

This period is characterized by intense social conflict between contending groups to affix blame and identify both the culprits and the victims. Public perception of an institution's behavior during the preproblem and problem identification stages determines the extent of the flexibility available to corporations in later stages.

The Remedy and Relief Stage

Once a causal linkage has been established, the question of compensatory and/or punitive damages to the affected parties must be considered. This stage is often marked by conflict and cooperation between opposing groups as they seek to maximize the return to injured parties while passing the burden for payment to those who can most afford to pay—usually governments. The injured parties may not be the persons who were directly injured, but their families and dependents. Another question has to do with the assumption of responsibility for the payment of claims. An equally important issue is the role played by courts, legislatures, and executive and administrative agencies of the government.

There are certain interrelated issues that must be considered. For example, is it socially desirable to make companies pay all the costs for corporate actions that were not intentionally taken? If a particular business or industry is forced to pay the total cost, how would that affect the workers, stockholders, and lenders whose livelihood and life savings may be dependent on the profitability of that business or industry? The effect of the health of a particular industry on the total economy is also important in considering who should pay for the damages. Government may sometimes be called upon to subsidize payments regardless of which party is at fault.

The Prevention Stage

The prevention stage is not sequential, but generally overlaps with the problem identification and remedy and relief stages. At this point, the problem has achieved a level of maturity. The sources are either well established or easily identifiable. The attempt now is to develop long-range programs to prevent recurrence. These include the restructuring of organizations and decision-making processes, the development of new processes, and the emergence of new special interest groups to bring about necessary changes in the sociopolitical and legal environment.

This stage is marked by uncertainty and difficulty in making an accurate appraisal of potential costs and benefits. The strategies to be pursued by society will, of necessity, involve unfamiliar sociopolitical arrangements. Thus, it is not uncommon to find a high degree of self-righteousness in the pronouncements of various groups, which may be long on rhetoric but short on substance. Groups tend to advocate solutions that favor their particular viewpoint while understating the potential costs to those groups having opposing viewpoints. The conflict is also heightened by the fact that while most of the costs are likely to be borne by present members of society, most of the benefits are likely to accrue to future generations. Therefore, in order to bolster their claims and positions, different groups vie for the right to speak for posterity. The ideological antibusiness bias of certain groups at this stage can be as harmful to the development of socially equitable and feasible long-term solutions as the tendency among some businesspeople to resist every demand for change.

INSTITUTIONAL STRATEGIES

As noted earlier, the primary activities of a firm are inextricably linked with their second-order effects on society. These second-order effects, called externalities, increase almost in direct proportion to the expansion of a firm's activities in a specific area. They have been traditionally borne by society as a whole. Industrialization and economic growth have been accompanied by a tremendous increase in such costs as deterioration of human relationships within and without the organization, loss of individual freedom, and business influence on government and the political process. This has led to a greater awareness on the part of the public that there is a social limit to the capacity of various individuals and groups in a society to conform to narrowly based corporate goals, just as there is a physical limit to the environment's capacity to absorb industrial pollution. Thus, intensification of a firm's efforts to undertake activities that necessitate a change in the behavior, expectations, and rewards of affected groups brings about disharmony in the system. This disharmony generates pressures within the overall system to create a new equilibrium.

In industrialized and democratic societies, various groups are becoming more aware of their rights and how they might be adversely affected by business institutions. Their combined efforts are directed toward making business institutions minimize potential social or community harm and assume responsibility for correcting it when such harm does occur. It is business's strategy for introducing change and its response to nonmarket forces, and the negative impact of second-order effects, that have increasingly become the focus of public scrutiny.

Increased urbanization, advanced technology, and the interdependent nature of industries, locations, and services have made the operations of even a single plant so significant that externalities can no longer be ignored. Tsurumi points out that in Japan, the social character of the production process has become so important that the freedom of private enterprise can no longer remain unqualified. Conflict has arisen "between the traditional arrangement of the Japanese economy and the consequences of vastly developed productive forces, thereby creating . . . tensions and problems."[2] There have been increasing societal pressures in every industrialized nation for business to minimize the second-order effects of its activities and also to take a more active part and assume greater responsibility for correcting the social ills that inevitably do occur. It is the nature of the business response to these nonmarket forces, one compatible with a particular sociopolitical context, that is the focus of our inquiry.

Corporations, like all other institutions, are an integral part of a society and must depend on it for their existence, continuity, and growth. They therefore constantly strive to pattern their activities so that they are in congruence with the goals of the overall social system. The quest for legitimacy by the corporation and doubts by critics as to that legitimacy are the crucial issues in the concept of socially acceptable corporate behavior. One way to evaluate the effectiveness of business responses to societal pressures is to use the yardstick of legitimacy. Given that both a business institution and its adversaries seek to narrow the gap between corporate behavior and societal expectations, the social relevance and validity of any corporate action depends on one's concept of legitimacy. Viewed in this way, corporate response patterns can be described as a three-stage phenomenon based on a changing notion of legitimacy. The three patterns can be defined as social obligation, social responsibility, and social responsiveness.

Corporate Behavior as Social Obligation

When a corporation responds to market and social forces in a manner that meets only the minimally imposed legal constraints, or that is almost totally required by economic necessity, the response mode is called social obligation. The criteria for legitimacy are economic and legal only. A corporation is considered a special purpose institution, and it leaves this arena at its own risk. The legitimacy criteria are met by the corporation through its ability to compete for resources in the marketplace and through conducting its operations within the legal constraints imposed by the social system.

Competition for resources is not always an adequate criterion, however. Market conditions may force other groups to yield to the corporation's will, but they do so unwillingly and under duress. The affected groups will also use other measures—political and social—to bring about changes in the market forces themselves, thereby increasing their bargaining power. Furthermore, business institutions are not necessarily the most willing players in the competitive arena. Firms constantly strive to free themselves from the discipline of the market through increase in size, diversification, and generation of public support through advocacy advertising and other means of persuasion. Even in an ideal situation, the ethics of the marketplace provide only one kind of legitimacy, which nations have been known to modify in times of national crisis or for activities deemed vital to a nation's well-being.

Nor can the legality of an act be used as the sole criterion. Norms in a social system are developed from a voluntary consensus among various groups. Under these conditions, laws tend to codify socially accepted behavior and seldom lead to social change. There are three reasons why the legal criterion alone may not be sufficient: One, social norms are dynamic in nature and change over time, whereas legal change, which is much more formal, is delayed and must await the enactment of a law or statute. Two, specific social values may contradict each other, whereas there is a presumption of consistency in the legal code. Three, the formal nature of the law confers a degree of social acceptance on the legal code that a social system may not be willing to accord certain activities during a transitional period, although it may tolerate such activities informally and on a small scale.

And, finally, the law has left unresolved the adjustment process between utility and responsibility as legitimating factors. A democratic society must have standards concerning the use of power and the process by which wielders of power are selected, evaluated, and removed from their positions. Although the power exercised by corporate managers has vastly increased, legal criteria have not come to grips with it. Therefore, the traditional economic and legal criteria are necessary but not sufficient conditions of corporate legitimacy. The corporation that flouts them will not survive, and even the mere satisfaction of these criteria does not ensure its continued existence.

Corporate response to the external environment, in the social obligation mode, is essentially defensive in character. Under this mode, the business entity fights hard to maintain the status quo in the social system and to preserve its decision-making autonomy in areas affecting its behavior.

Corporate Behavior as Social Responsibility

Corporations may be special purpose organizations, but the nature and extent of that special purpose may change over time. Society may realize the magnitude of the negative side effects of a certain economic activity and find it unacceptable. The need for services provided by other institutions may increase and assume a higher priority than the services of business institutions. Or the society may find unacceptable the manner in which business institutions perform their economic functions.

A corporate response mode is termed social responsibility when it calls for changes in corporate behavior that bring the firm's performance to a level that is congruent with currently prevailing social norms, values, and performance expectations. Most of the conflicts between large corporations and various social institutions during the last two decades or so in the United States, Japan, and other industrial nations fall into the category of social responsibility; few corporations during these years have been accused of violating the laws of their nations.

Social responsibility does not require a radical departure from the usual corporate activities or the normal pattern of corporate behavior. The corporation is simply a step ahead, making changes before new social expectations are codified into legal requirements. By adapting before it is legally forced to, a corporation can be more flexible in its response pattern and achieve greater congruence with social norms, and therefore legitimacy, at a lower social and institutional cost. While the concept of social obligation is proscriptive in nature, the concept of social responsibility is prescriptive.

Corporate Behavior as Social Responsiveness

The third mode of adaptation to societal needs is social responsiveness. The corporation here is expected to anticipate the changes that may result from the corporation's current activities, or from the emergence of social problems in which corporations must play an important role. The issue in terms of social responsiveness is not how firms should respond to social pressures, but what their long-run role in a dynamic social system should be. Business institutions are expected to initiate policies and programs that will minimize the adverse side effects of their present or future activities before these side effects assume crisis proportions and become catalysts for another wave of protest against business. They should also prepare to accept the challenges the system may come to consider appropriate for corporations to tackle. These activities are characterized as social responsiveness. Social responsibility activities are prescriptive in nature; activities related to social responsiveness are proactive—that is, anticipatory and preventive.

Exhibit 7–1 presents a grid pattern showing the relationship between the intensity of an issue and corporate response patterns through the stages or life cycle of issue evolution. It is important to note that the speed with which an issue moves from an emerging to a critical stage, from the corporation's viewpoint, is largely determined by an interaction between external environmental forces and patterns of corporate response.

Selection of Appropriate Response Patterns

The appropriateness of a response pattern will depend, to a large extent, on the stage of an issue's life cycle; the response patterns adopted by other corporations and industry groups similarly placed; the nature of the constituency groups and the intensity of their advocacy; and prior public expectations based on a corporation's behavior in similar situations in the past.

One of the main objectives of developing corporate strategies that are appropriate to an external environment and external constituency groups is to prevent any erosion in management's discretion to manage corporate affairs in a manner it considers best for the corporation, its dependencies, and society at large. In general, the opportunity for maintaining maximum discretionary decision-making authority is greatest in the preproblem stage and lowest in the prevention stage. The public's perception of use of manage-

EXHIBIT 7–1 Stages of Conflict Evolution

Dimensions of Corporate Behavior		Preproblem Stage	Problem Identification Stage	Remedy and Relief Stage	Prevention Stage
Response Mode	**Character of Response**				
Social Obligation	Do what is required by law and economic necessity. Response is defensive and proscriptive.				
Social Responsibility	Mitigate negative side effects of corporate activities on society. Response is prescriptive and interactive.				
Social Responsiveness	Promote positive social change. Response is proactive, anticipatory, and preventive.				

ment's discretionary power during the preproblem and problem identification stages determines the extent of available flexibility in the remedy and relief and prevention stages. In case constituency groups succeed in the problem identification stage in bringing an issue to the judicial and political arena and score gains, management's discretion is likely to be minimal in subsequent stages. In the remedy and relief and prevention stages, management's discretion is also affected to a greater extent by what other corporations are doing than in the two earlier stages.

A social obligation mode of response is likely to yield maximum discretion in the early stages of issue life cycle. However, if this response pattern fails, the rate of decline in management's discretionary authority is likely to be very steep in subsequent stages. A call for using the social responsibility mode in the early stages of the issue life cycle is difficult to sell to the corporation. It may give rise to external constituencies that otherwise may not have become viable, and could be counterproductive, at least in the short run. Where a social responsibility mode is developed on the basis of accurate environmental scanning and constituency group analysis, especially in the issue identification stage, it could yield a consistently higher degree of discretionary authority for management in subsequent stages.

A social responsiveness mode is most conducive to maintaining management discretion in the preproblem stage when it becomes the core of strategic planning. In other stages of the issue life cycle, it must follow the social responsibility mode to establish credibility. It is unlikely to be acceptable to other groups in the remedy and relief stage, especially if the company had followed a social obligation mode in the problem identification stage.

JABMAS AND THE AMERICAN SOCIOPOLITICAL SYSTEM

The Japanese companies have not attempted to apply in the United States those aspects of their business system that relate to the external environment —business-government relations, involvement in the political process, and an active role in the formulation of the national agenda and public policy. These elements are, however, an integral part of JABMAS and must eventually come into play with regard to the Japanese business operations in the United States. Their potential impact is likely to be significant, although their direction is as yet unpredictable. Some possible indications of the types of strategies Japanese companies might pursue can be gleaned through an analysis of the behavior of Japanese companies in responding to societal pressures within their own sociopolitical environment. We may also draw some lessons through an analysis of the behavior of Japanese companies in their dealings with other countries, especially in Southeast Asia, where they have sizable investments and manufacturing operations.

It is interesting to note, however, that Japanese companies have moved quite rapidly to form lobbying groups, engage in advocacy, and in other ways take advantage of the American political and legal processes to further the interests in the United States of Japanese businesses in general and those of specific industries and companies in particular. For example, the Japanese electronics industry has organized a political action committee to further the interests of that industry in the United States. However, the organization is structured in such a manner that only Japanese companies are eligible to become members. Although declared legal by the Federal Election Commission, the objectives of this organization are so narrowly construed that they could be contrary to the U.S. national interest—a situation that would never be tolerated in Japan.[3]

This topic will be discussed in greater detail in the concluding chapter, where we analyze the changes in the Japanese management practices that are currently underway in Japan in response to changing societal expectations. Simultaneously, we will consider the structural and operational changes that are coming to the foreground in American corporations in dealing with the external environment and in meeting the Japanese challenge.

The primary areas of societal concern involving large corporations are those of environmental pollution, consumer protection, worker health and safety, and business influence in governmental policymaking and regulatory processes. The incidents of major involvement of the business community in Japan in all these areas were detailed in Chapter 2. Our discussion in this section will therefore be confined to an analysis of the response patterns of Japanese business in terms of issue life cycle and the impact of these responses on affected stakeholders and society at large.

The Preproblem Stage

An analysis of the activities of Japanese companies show that their response mode during the preproblem stage was that of social obligation. An analysis of Japanese and American business practices showed no discernible difference in their behavior or in their responses to social pressures. The business stance was social obligation, and responsibility was interpreted in the strictest legal sense. The companies denied they were doing anything illegal, and strongly resisted furnishing any information on the ground that it was confidential or that it had no bearing on the issue. Another measure used by individual firms was to compare their behavior with that of competitors. When there was no difference, the firms would plead inability to undertake corrective measures that would place them at a competitive disadvantage.

Japanese companies also made considerable effort to isolate and alienate the victims of their actions by castigating them as disloyal, disgruntled, and troublemakers. In this they were helped by Japan's sociopolitical environment, which is extremely hostile to dissent against an employer or senior; a dissenter ordinarily finds little support among peers at work, in the union, or in the community. Their approach was to downplay the impact of the damage to the environment, or to groups adversely affected, by dismissing them as exaggerations by vocal minorities. When some negative effects became too visible or significant to be dismissed, two approaches were used to explain them. One was to point out to the public that some adverse effects or unforeseen social consequences were unavoidable and must be borne as the necessary costs of social and economic progress. The benefits, in any case, far outweighed the social costs. Second, public and government wrath was avoided by resorting to the "rotten apple" theory—the implication that it was only a few firms that were negligent and cut corners, that the industry as a whole had an excellent record and that no public investigation, accountability, or controls were necessary.

The interesting point to note here is that the behavior of Japanese companies in the Japanese sociocultural milieu is not very different from the one observed in the case of American companies in their own sociocultural milieu, the United States. It is conceivable that the nature of private enterprise or the modern industrial sector generates similar response patterns that emphasize giving priority to corporate self-interest over community interest when the probability of being called to account is quite low and most likely avoidable. Furthermore, although we do not have systematic evidence, we sense a greater amount of violation of actual laws in the preproblem stage by corporations in Japan than in the United States. Perhaps the reason lies in closer business-government relations in Japan. Japanese traditionally resort more to informal arrangements and accommodations than to legal recourse. Japanese business may have less to fear in terms of government reprisals and penalties than American business.

The Identification Stage

During the identification stage, the practices of Japanese and American businesses were also essentially similar. There are, however, some notable differences.

As a first step, both Japanese and American firms ordinarily deny the existence of the problem and its alleged severity. Where this is not possible, they attempt to show that no direct causal linkages exist. An important difference between American and Japanese firms lies in the area of research to determine cause-effect linkages. U.S. firms engage in heavy in-house research. They support outside research efforts either alone or jointly with industry. The former is undertaken to protect the firm from competitive pressures, product liability and civil damages suits by private individuals, and civil and criminal suits by government agencies. The latter approach is undertaken to provide evidence of good faith, gain public trust and confidence, spur joint industry efforts to share the costs and develop a united front, and diffuse demand for governmental action and control. Although no hard evidence is available, our research indicated isolated cases in which U.S. firms may have deliberately refrained from carrying out any research for fear that unfavorable findings would make the firm liable for damages in the future.

In the case of Japanese companies, more aggressive behavior was evident. In many cases, Japanese firms actually impeded investigation or research by private and university-related organizations to isolate the causes of the problem. In this they seemed to have the tacit support of important governmental agencies, such as the Ministry of International Trade and Industry (MITI). When not actually impeding investigations, they refused to provide any assistance, financing, data, or technical services to encourage such research. The authors know of no cases where Japanese companies have actively cooperated in research activities leading to the identification of a problem or its cause in pollution or market-behavior incidents. This was true in the Minamata, Itai-Itai, Yokkaichi asthma, and Morinaga milk poisoning cases, and in a host of others.

This behavior is not hard to understand when we consider the nature of the Japanese social system. Big firms have always been held in awe by the masses. Loyalty toward company and government is such that complainants have a hard time securing sympathy, expert advice, or support from other social institutions. For example, in the Itai-Itai case, the company involved, Mitsui Mining, was so big and highly respected that the local community and company workers refused to believe until quite late in the dispute that such a large company could be guilty of pollution-related crimes. Indeed, there was active hostility toward the victims and their families. Furthermore, because of the one-to-one loyalty relationships and groupism of Japanese society, the companies, government, and academic elites form one Establishment. Dissidents were always a minority and could not get endorsement or assistance from university experts, most of whom, with a few significant exceptions, had sided with the companies.

Here again, the close cooperation between business and government works to the detriment of the public at large. At the national level, government sees the companies as essential tools for furthering its goal, the elevation of Japan to the stature of an economically strong, industrialized nation. Such a policy requires continuous expansion of production, high economic growth, and maintenance of a high level of exports. This goal fitted admirably with those of the private enterprises, which were only too willing to cooperate. If, in the process, shortcuts hurt some communities and people, they were written off as necessary sacrifices.

Another important distinction between Japanese and American business practices pertains to the role of protest groups. In Japan, protest groups are unable to enlist nationally known leaders from other social groups to assist them. This is because in Japan, an individual belongs exclusively to one particular group and interacts only with other individuals in that group. The likelihood of a Ralph Nader emerging as a popular hero is minimal in Japan. Thus, objective third parties with impeccable credentials are unavailable to the protesting groups, either as leaders or mediators.

The Remedy and Relief Stage

Litigation. Most of the cases studied for this analysis have been marked by long and bitter litigation. For example, in all the major pollution cases, as well as in the Morinaga milk poisoning case, the companies involved tried every means possible to harrass the litigants for continuing with their claims. In this effort, they were supported by the government as well as an archaic court system. Furthermore, as mentioned earlier, the plaintiffs were restricted in their efforts by the lack of community support and the nonavailability of expert opinion. However, the situation took a major turn between 1970 and 1973. First came the passage of two laws in 1970: the Law for the Punishment of Environmental Pollution Crimes Relating to Human Health, and the Law Concerning Entrepreneurs' Bearing of the Cost of Public Pollution Control Works. Second, after 1970, the courts also became more sensitive to the hazards of pollution. Instead of insisting on the establishment of a definite causal linkage, they began to accept "probable cause" as sufficient grounds for deciding pollution-related cases in favor of the plaintiffs. The result was that in 1972–73, all the major pollution cases we have mentioned were decided in the plaintiffs' favor, thereby giving business a warning as to what to expect in the future. However, the actual damages awarded were only a small fraction of the amounts asked for.

Solatium. The practice of solatium is unique to Japanese business. Once a linkage, no matter how tenuous, is established identifying a firm as the culprit, an initial attempt is made to settle the case informally—often with some government official as mediator—by paying a token amount for mental solace called a solatium to the injured parties. This is a quite common practice and is used as symbolic compensation for physical and mental suffering. In the pollution cases, both business and government approached the problem by offering solatium. To date, the punitive damages aspect of blame is generally absent, and there is little recognition of the potential victim's right not to be exposed to health hazards.

It should be mentioned here that Japanese corporations make a sharp distinction between Japanese and non-Japanese sufferers. For example, in 1973, Japan Airlines paid a solatium to the Japanese families of victims of a JAL airplane crash, but refused to do the same for the non-Japanese families, although many of them were in Japan. The resultant public resentment and adverse publicity was so intense that JAL finally yielded and made payments to the families of all the victims involved in that crash. Our studies of the operations of Japanese corporations in other countries (South Korea, Taiwan, and Thailand) also show that the solatium is paid to Japanese employees only and creates a source of friction between the companies and their local employees.[4]

Ritual and Ceremony. Ritual and ceremony play an important part in the settlement of disputes in Japan. The company may make a public admission of guilt and offer a public apology to the victims. This was done, for example, in the pollution cases and in the Morinaga milk poisoning case and was an integral part of the court settlement. In other cases, the heads of C. Itoh and Nissho-Iwai, two of Japan's leading trading companies, publicly admitted violating Japanese laws by hoarding raw materials and hiding excessive profits. During the recent energy crisis, the head of an oil industry group admitted making false statements in public denying the existence of an oil industry cartel. Public apology satisfies the emotional content of Japanese interpersonal relations. The victim feels a sense of betrayal when a superior, company, or government is found to have behaved in an undesirable manner. Consequently, no amount of monetary compensation can substitute for a personal admission of guilt.

Another form of ritual is for an executive in the firm publicly to admit "sole" responsibility for the alleged crime and resign from the company. This was done in the case of General Sekiyu K.K., a major oil company. The head of the firm resigned when it was found that the marketing department of the company had circulated a memorandum to its salesmen outlining how they could pressure retailers into charging higher prices for gasoline in violation of government regulations.[5] In another case, Yasutaka Konishi, president of Toho Zinc Company, "resigned in atonement" from the company presidency. The company was under investigation for covering up contamination of rivers near its zinc mining plant on Tsushima Island off northern Kyushu. Konishi stated that it was his responsibility that "our company failed to regard the pollution problem seriously."[6] This symbolic form of sacrifice or acceptance of guilt, however, should not be confused with actual punishment. To give the sacrifice a high public profile, the person chosen is invariably a senior statesman who may be nearing retirement. Even when this is not the case, the person making the sacrifice is considered a hero because he accepted the blame "for the good of the company." The corporation ensures that the chosen executive is amply rewarded for the sacrifice.

An interesting example of the Japanese insistence on formal apology involved the victims of the Turkish airlines crash of a McDonnell-Douglas DC-10. The settlement of the Japanese claim was delayed because the Japanese insisted on an apology by McDonnell-Douglas and General Dynamics and payment of punitive damages to show admission of wrongdoing.[7]

There is a reverse twist to ritual and ceremony in the case of Japanese business that should also be kept in mind. This has to do with symbolic conformity to public standards along with substantive violation of them. Consider, for example, the widespread use of paid professional thugs, called *sokaiya,* by most Japanese companies to intimidate shareholders at stockholders' meetings and deter them from asking embarrassing questions of management. According to an article by Pearlstine in *The Wall Street Journal,* the *sokaiya* system

> exemplifies the Japanese facility for embracing Western forms without compromising traditional practice. . . . Japanese executives dutifully accepted the new form (imposed by the American authorities), but in practice they rejected the idea that small shareholders should be allowed to criticize them.[8]

In analyzing the behavior of the Japanese firms, Kobayashi suggests that there is a great discrepancy between the principles Japanese businessmen proclaim and their true intentions. In order to avoid criticism from stockholders, consumers, or other social groups, they take refuge behind rhetoric by declaring their social responsibility, promising to refrain from raising prices, and so on. However, they are unable to carry out their promises because of the uncertainty of their rivals' actions in the marketplace and their belief that regardless of their actions, people are not likely to believe them anyway.[9]

The Prevention Stage

Rhetoric notwithstanding, their actual behavior in the first three stages of the issue life cycle, Japanese business employs highly positive rhetoric of corporate social responsibility to society. This conciliatory posture helps Japanese companies in dealing with their critics in the prevention stage.

Japanese business and trade associations specifically recognize and publicly state that a corporation's responsibility to its stockholders or employees transcends its responsibility to society. Criticizing the behavior of Japanese corporations, Professor Nobuo Noda, a noted Japanese management scholar, states that the "three conditions required of the corporation were to produce a profit, provide for the welfare of the employees, and be responsible to the society. This third condition has not, until the present time, been given ample consideration by Japanese enterprises." Noda advocates the establishment of "civil minimum" and "civil maximum" standards for the social impact of corporate activities and indicates that if "private enterprises do not turn in this direction, then, they will lose their very basis for existence."[10] In a similar vein, Norishige Hasegawa, president of Sumitomo Chemical, accuses Japanese companies of "social dumping" by neglecting their responsibility to prevent pollution and to pay for environmental protection.[11] He lays down three rules that a private enterprise should follow:

1. It must strive to continue to exist.
2. Business is a part of society, and therefore it must be responsible for the protection of the environment.
3. If its activities cause environmental damage, it should not survive.

In an editorial, *Management Japan,* one of the leading Japanese management journals, exhorted business managers to "work only for the true meaning of external existence of human society" and notes that "such an attitude could fully function only on the basis that the business's social responsibility never be a part of corporate strategy and tactics but ought to be a part of the corpus itself."[12] In another statement, Kenichiro Komai, president of Hitachi, declares:

> The development and growth of a firm is inextricably intertwined in the sound and stable progress of society (and therefore) lasting prosperity, in the present industrial society, will be hard to attain by merely pursuing profit. An enterprise must seriously commit itself toward solving the problems of society and lend a helping hand to mitigate the hardships of the public.[13]

Japanese trade associations have added their voice to self-criticism in the area of social responsibility. For example, Mr. Nagano, chairman of the Japanese Chamber of Commerce, recently stated that the final objective of the firms was to increase social welfare. Mr. Sakurada, chairman of the Japanese Federation of Employers' Associations, stated that top executives should first meet their own social responsibility ideals before blaming others for criticizing corporations. Mr. Kikawada, representative director of the Japan Committee for Economic Development, declared that businessmen should not look at society from the firm's viewpoint, but should look at the firm from society's viewpoint.[14]

In Japan, both trade associations and individual corporations are developing codes of corporate conduct. The notion of public accountability for corporate actions has also gained wider currency. Similarly, both at the government and the corporate level, the principle of "polluter pays" has been accepted as the basis for work on environment-related problems. In addition to developing standards of behavior, corporations are taking specific steps to forestall public complaints and avoid future problems. Many companies have donated large tracts of land to local communities for parks, recreational facilities, and community-related uses. This land was originally acquired for expansion or new construction of plants and manufacturing facilities. Firms are also paying increasing attention to community feelings before erecting new plants and, despite legal approval, abandoning many projects where strong community support does not exist.

These are very slow and hesitant steps in the proactive mode. And because they are in their infancy, it is hard to separate style from substance. There is a great deal of uncertainty as to how Japanese companies will cope with societal demands for change, especially if both domestic and international conditions cause them to lose their competitive advantage and related prosperity. There is also insufficient evidence to suggest that Japanese companies, in their overseas operations, will necessarily rise above the minimally acceptable or legally required standard of behavior and use a more enlightened attitude similar to the one exhibited in their home country.

NOTES

1. S. Prakash Sethi, "An Analytical Framework for Making Cross-Cultural Comparisons of Business Responses to Societal Pressures: The Case of the United States and Japan," in Lee E. Preston (ed.), *Research in Corporate Social Performance and Policy* (Greenwich, Conn.: Jai Press, 1978), vol. 1, pp. 27–54. See also S. Prakash Sethi, "A Conceptual Framework for Environmental Analysis of Social Issues and Evaluation of Business Response Patterns," *Academy of Management Review,* January 1979, pp. 63–74.
2. S. Tsuru, "KOGAI—Environmental Disruption in Japan—The Story of Three Cities," *Unesco Courier,* July 1971, pp. 6–13.
3. The case in point is that of the Japan Business Association of Southern California (JBA). JBA is a trade association whose membership is comprised of U.S. affiliates or subsidiaries of Japan-based corporations. The Federal Election Commission held that JBA, as a domestic corporation, could create a political action committee (JBAPAC) and contribute JBA's general corporate funds to JBAPAC. However, foreign nationals could not control the decision-making structure of JBAPAC. *Federal Election Campaign Financing Guide, Opinions,* pp. S632–33, dated January 21, 1983, Federal Election Commission, Washington, D.C.
4. Sethi, *Japanese Business and Social Conflict,* p. 116.
5. "General Sekiyu President Resigns," *Mainichi Daily News,* February 9, 1974, p. 6.

6. "Toho Zinc Head Quits in Expiation," *Mainichi Daily News,* April 11, 1974, p. 4.

7. "Japanese Settle with McDonnell-Douglas, Others in Suit Tied to '74 Crash of DC10?" *Wall Street Journal,* April 14, 1977, p. 5.

8. Norman Pearlstine, "In Japan the Sokaiya Rise to the Rescue at Firm's Meetings," *Wall Street Journal,* May 29, 1974, p. 1.

9. S. Kobayashi, "Change to Other People Oriented Management" [*Tanin-kankei Keiei e Tenkanseyo*], *Chuo Choron,* Spring 1974, pp. 103–112.

10. Noda, "The Social Responsibility of Japanese Corporations," *Management Japan,* 6 (Autumn 1972), pp. 6–8.

11. N. Hasegawa, "Environment Problems and Management," *Management Japan,* 6 (Autumn 1972), pp. 14–16.

12. Editorial, *Management Japan,* 6, (1973), p. 4.

13. Kenichiro Komei, "Working Toward a New Business Philosophy," *Management Japan,* 5, 2 (1971), p. 6.

14. "Keidanren to Take Initiative in Carrying Out Social Responsibility" [*Shakai-teki Sekinin Kodo de Shimesu Keidanren ga Undo Suishin*], *Asahi Shinbun,* June 24, 1973.

EIGHT ▚▚

Introduction of Japanese Management Techniques into the United States: The Case of the Japanese Companies

WE ARE NOW READY TO APPLY OUR FRAMEWORK TO EVALUATING THE application of Japanese management techniques in the United States. As was indicated earlier, the success of a particular strategy of social change, or the diffusion of a new idea in a social system, depends not only on the severity of an issue and the conditions in the external environment, but also on the characteristics of the change agent. This introduces the third component of our framework—the nature of the institution, its value set, mission, and goals, leadership style, and organizational structure and dynamics.

It should be clear that both the perception and the reality of the problems associated with the introduction of Japanese management practices in the United States will be different for the Japanese and the American companies. The two types of change agents would use different strategies to introduce these techniques and would evoke different types of responses in the external environment. Consequently, the problems associated with the introduction of Japanese management techniques in the U.S. sociocultural, political, and regulatory environment have been analyzed from two perspectives: that of the Japanese companies operating in the United States, and that of the American companies applying these techniques in their U.S. operations. In this chapter, the discussion is limited to the Japanese companies' operations in the United States. The issues associated with American companies will be treated in the next chapter.

The JABMAS elements that have received the most scrutiny for their application to Japanese operations in the United States pertain to internal aspects: decision making within the corporation, relationships between various levels of management, and employee relations, including terms and conditions of employment for Japanese and American workers. Moreover, these applications have been concentrated at the lower level of occupational categories, notably blue collar workers and clerical and secretarial staff. They have, by and large, not yet penetrated the middle-upper management or technical and professional cadres.

GROWTH OF JAPANESE BUSINESS AND INVESTMENT IN THE UNITED STATES

There has been a tremendous increase in Japanese investment in the United States during the last ten years, and a significant number of companies have set up not only sales, but even manufacturing operations.

Japanese direct investment in the United States increased from a low of $152 million in 1973 to a high of $4.2 billion in 1980—an almost 28-fold increase. Although the total investment is still small, representing 6.4 percent out of a total of $65.5 billion of direct foreign investment in 1980 in the United States, nevertheless its growth rate is significant: from 0.7 percent in 1973 to 6.4 percent in 1980.[1]

Two other characteristics of Japanese investments in the United States are also worth noting. One, compared with West European countries, Japanese investments are concentrated in commerce, which accounted for 50 percent of all investments in 1979. When investments in other services, such as finance, insurance, and others are added, this figure rises to over 70 percent. Manufacturing accounts for only 21 percent of Japanese direct foreign investment. In contrast, manufacturing accounted for 65.8 percent of investments in the case of Switzerland, 48.8 percent for West Germany, 48.2 percent for France, and 36.9 percent for Great Britain.[2]

Two, a large number of companies are small and medium-sized. According to a 1980 survey of Japanese manufacturing companies in the United States conducted by the Japan External Trade Organization (the JETRO survey), of the 175 companies reporting, only 33 had 300 or more employees, whereas 99 employed less than 100 workers per company. Furthermore, large factories employing over 500 workers were concentrated in California and in the Southeast—in Arkansas, Alabama, and Tennessee. Some of the largest Japanese-controlled companies included in the survey were Amdahl, California (3,500 employees); Sanyo, Arkansas (2,300 employees); Sony, California (2,000 employees); Matsushita, Illinois (1,850 employees); Sanyo, Alabama (1,500); Whitney Fidalgo Seafoods, Alaska (1,300); and Kyocera International, California (1,300 employees). In addition, Alumax, Inc., was the largest reporting Japanese-controlled manufacturing company in the United States, with plants in 51 locations throughout the country employing over 7,000 workers.[3] Notably absent were the operations of such auto giants as Honda in Ohio and Nissan in Tennessee. The survey examined a total of 238 Japanese manufacturing operations in the United States employing a total of 45,000 individuals.[4] Although it is the most comprehensive survey of its kind, its findings cannot be considered conclusive or necessarily representative of all Japanese companies in the United States. It was noted earlier that over 70 percent of Japanese investments in the United States are concentrated in commerce and service-related industries that were excluded for this study.

From all indications, it appears that the pace of Japanese investment and manufacturing operations in the United States will continue to accelerate in the future. The movement seems to have occurred—in many cases, and especially in those involving the establishment of manufacturing facilities— not because of an initiative on the part of the Japanese business, but because of U.S. pressure on Japan to invest, which arose from the continuing increase in trade deficits and U.S. domestic unemployment. Some Japanese companies continue to resist opening plants in the United States. The best-known example is that of the Japanese auto companies, perhaps with the exception of Honda. The strong protectionist sentiments in the United States about auto imports from Japan have resulted in the Japanese accepting "voluntary" export quotas. Nevertheless, Japanese auto companies remain reluctant to establish manufacturing facilities in the United States and continue to study the problem.

JAPANESE MANAGEMENT PRACTICES IN THE UNITED STATES

Two aspects of Japanese management practices deserve attention. The first has to do with the extent to which Japanese operational strategies and management practices are similar to those of most other multinational corporations (MNCs) and to those followed by most foreign-owned enterprises in the United States and even by overseas subsidiaries of U.S.-owned corporations. These practices are a phenomenon of the multinational character of a corporation and are country-neutral. The second aspect has to do with the application, by the Japanese companies, of their unique management style in their U.S.-based operations.

Similarities and Differences between the Japanese and other Foreign-Owned Companies in Their U.S. Operations

Some operating practices of Japanese companies are not atypical of those followed by other foreign-owned companies in a number of important ways. These include, among others, bringing home-country and third-country nationals into the U.S. operations for top-level and technical positions, with terms of employment and benefits not available to American employees of these companies. It should be noted here that the numbers of these employees is generally quite small in proportion to the total U.S. employment of foreign-owned enterprises and rarely exceed the strict criteria laid out in the treaties of friendship, commerce, and navigation (FCN) and the Bona Fide Occupational Qualification (BFOQ) stipulation in Title VII of the Civil Rights Act of 1964.[5]

The Japanese companies, however, differ in one major respect: The intensity of their use of these MNC country-neutral practices, and the differentials in terms of employment and compensation between home-country and host-country employees, are far greater than for other foreign-owned companies operating in the United States. The Japanese companies in the United States tend to transfer larger number of Japanese employees from the parent companies to their overseas subsidiaries. Although strictly comparable data are not available, some conclusions can be drawn from the Benchmark Survey of the U.S. Department of Commerce. According to the survey, foreign citizens employed in the U.S. affiliates of foreign multinationals represented 6.3 percent of all production workers and 11.8 percent of nonproduction workers (Table 8–1). Since most production workers are likely to be U.S. citizens, the relevant figure is nonproduction workers. Even here, at the management level the actual impact of foreign citizens may be somewhat understated because this category also includes clerical staff, which is most likely to be composed of American citizens. As Table 8–1 shows, the comparable figures for production and nonproduction workers for all *developed* countries are 5.7 and 9.8 percent; Canada, 3.4 and 6.4 percent; European Economic Community, 3.5 and 6.0 percent; France, 7.5 and 13.9 percent; West Germany, 10.1 and 13.3 percent; Italy, 27.2 and 23.2 percent; United Kingdom, 2.1 and 3.8 percent; and *Japan, 33.1 and 39.4 percent.*

A study of the economic impact of the Japanese business community in New York shows that in the Japanese companies located in New York, Japanese employees represented 47.3 percent of local employees, or a ratio of 1 Japanese employee for every 2.1 local employees. In the case of trading companies, these figures were even higher. Japanese employees were 67.3 percent of American employees, or a ratio of 1 Japanese employee for every 1.5 American employees.[6] The survey by MITI in 1975 found that the average number of Japanese nationals stationed per venture was highest in North America.[7]

In terms of top managerial positions, the JETRO survey (1981) found that of the 161 companies for which data were available, 55 percent of all directorships were held by the Japanese. It should be noted here that almost 75 percent of the companies were either owned by individual Japanese companies or partnerships of Japanese companies. Of the Japanese manufac-

TABLE 8–1: EMPLOYMENT OF U.S. AFFILIATES, TYPE OF EMPLOYEE BY COUNTRY OF FOREIGN PARENT

	Total	Production Workers	Nonproduction Workers	U.S. Citizens	Foreign Citizens	Percentage *	Percentage †
All countries	1,083,431	678,685	404,746	1,040,732	42,699	6.3	11.8
Developed countries	981,883	620,764	361,119	946,367	35,516	5.7	9.8
Canada	175,971	114,840	61,133	172,084	3,889	3.4	6.4
Europe	731,091	464,903	266,188	712,389	18,702	4.0	7.0
European Economic Community	604,243	382,216	222,027	590,855	13,388	3.5	6.0
Belgium	9,622	6,349	3,273	9,517	105	1.7	3.2
France	57,750	37,603	20,147	54,945	2,805	7.5	13.9
Germany	58,982	33,413	25,569	55,592	3,390	10.1	13.3
Italy	3,575	1,646	1,929	3,127	448	27.2	23.2
Luxembourg	12,261	8,904	3,357	11,934	327	3.7	9.2
Netherlands	172,171	109,909	62,262	170,117	2,054	1.9	3.3

TABLE 8–1: (Continued)

	Total	Production Workers	Nonproduction Workers	U.S. Citizens	Foreign Citizens	Percentage *	†
United Kingdom	284,252	181,566	102,686	280,374	3,878	2.1	3.8
Denmark and Ireland	5,630	2,826	2,804	5,249	381	13.5	13.6
Other Europe	126,848	82,687	44,161	121,534	5,314	6.4	12.0
Japan	70,886	38,504	32,382	58,126	12,760	33.1	39.4
Australia, N. Zealand, S. Africa	3,933	2,517	1,416	3,768	165	6.6	6.6
Developing countries	101,548	57,921	43,627	94,365	7,183	7.0	12.4

*Foreign citizens to production workers
†Foreign citizens to nonproduction workers

SOURCE: Adapted from Table L-2, U.S. Department of Commerce, *Report to the Congress: Foreign Direct Investment in the United States*, vol. 2, April 1976, p. 60.

turing companies, 70 percent had a Japanese person occupying the top position. Japanese also tended to occupy positions in finance, accounting, technology, and liaison with the home office in Japan. Americans, on the other hand, were more often found in marketing, labor relations (dealing with local people), and other ancillary services.[8]

Nor are the Japanese companies quite so generous in paying compensation and fringe benefits to their American employees. As can be seen from Table 8–2, U.S. affiliates of foreign multinations from developed countries distributed their total compensation this way: 86.1 percent for wages and salaries, 5.6 percent for legally required supplementary benefits, and 8.3 percent for voluntary benefits. It is the voluntary supplementary benefits that should be of interest, since it is assumed that companies would have to pay no more than the competitive wage in the area to get the best qualified people they need. Comparable figures for MNC voluntary supplementary benefits according to the country of the foreign parent were these: Canada, 7.4 percent; France, 7.3 percent; West Germany, 5.9 percent; Italy, 4.5 percent; United Kingdom, 8.9 percent; and *Japan, 5.9 percent.* Since these figures include compensation paid to foreign citizens, it is logical to assume that the greater the proportion of foreign employees to U.S. employees on a company's payroll, the lower will be the percentage applied exclusively to the U.S. employees. This is somewhat surprising, since Japanese management philosophy and style is considered to be more paternalistic and humanistic —that is, oriented toward employee welfare.

A high degree of Japan staff presence in the management cadre of the overseas subsidiaries of Japanese companies is not confined to the United States. It is one of the dominant characteristics of Japanese direct foreign investments around the world. Studies by Yoshi Tsurumi of Japanese overseas operations in Asia showed that Japanese affiliates had three to four times as many managers and engineers from the home country than comparable American or European enterprises.[9] Compared with their Occidental counterparts, expatriates in Japanese affiliates were placed very low in the organizational hierarchy. Furthermore, while American and European companies hired expatriates with nationalities different from their own, Japanese affiliates brought in expatriates exclusively from the employee rolls of the parent company in Japan. Studies by the Japanese Ministry of International Trade and Industry (MITI) also show that the presence of Japanese managers in overseas affiliates is directly related to the degree of equity ownership in the overseas subsidiary by the Japanese parent.[10] MITI, aware of the problem of overstaffing subsidiaries with Japanese nationals, issued a guidance that the Japanese-local employee ratio should be at least 1:30.[11]

Japanese companies also tend to be export-oriented, and where they are required to invest abroad, they prefer to have wholly-owned subsidiaries rather than joint ventures. JETRO's 1981 study on the Japanese manufactur-

TABLE 8–2: EMPLOYEE COMPENSATION OF U.S. AFFILIATES, TYPE OF EMPLOYEE, AND TYPE OF REMUNERATION BY COUNTRY OF FOREIGN PARENT
(Millions of dollars)

	Payroll Costs			Wages and Salaries*				Supplementary Benefits†				
	Total	Production Workers	Non-production Workers	Total	%	Prod. Workers	Non-prod. Workers	Total	Legally Required	%	Voluntary	%
All countries	$13,299	$7,086	$6,213	$11,442	86.0%	$6,058	$5,383	$1,858	751	5.6%	$1,107	8.3%
Developed countries	12,090	6,490	5,600	10,409	86.1	5,556	4,854	1,681	677	5.6	1,004	8.3
Canada	2,282	1,349	933	1,955	85.7	1,146	809	327	158	6.9	169	7.4
Europe	8,934	4,781	4,153	7,674	85.9	4,093	3,581	1,260	478	5.4	781	8.7
European Economic Community	7,406	4,025	3,381	6,348	85.7	3,443	2,905	1,058	401	5.4	657	8.9
Belgium	120	71	49	105	87.5	63	42	15	5	4.2	10	8.3
France	696	389	308	603	86.6	337	266	93	38	5.5	55	7.9
Germany	723	341	381	640	88.5	300	340	83	40	5.5	43	5.9
Italy	44	17	27	40	90.9	15	25	4	2	4.5	2	4.5
Luxembourg	154	99	55	134	87.0	86	49	19	10	6.5	9	5.8
Netherlands	2,261	1,154	1,107	1,908	84.4	981	927	353	117	5.2	236	10.4

TABLE 8–2: (Continued)

	Payroll Costs			Wages and Salaries*				Supplementary Benefits†				
	Total	Production Workers	Non-production Workers	Total	%	Prod. Workers	Non-prod. Workers	Total	Legally Required	%	Voluntary	%
United Kingdom	3,339	1,926	1,413	2,857	85.6	1,637	1,220	482	184	5.5	298	8.9
Denmark and Ireland	70	29	41	61	87.1	25	36	9	5	7.1	4	5.7
Other Europe	1,528	755	772	1,326	86.8	650	676	202	77	5.0	125	8.2
Japan	825	330	495	737	89.3	289	448	88	39	4.7	49	5.9
Australia, N. Zealand, S. Africa	50	31	19	44	88.0	27	17	6	3	6.0	4	8.0
Developing countries	1,209	596	613	1,032	85.4	503	529	177	73	6.0	103	8.5

*Percentage total payroll costs.
†Percentages total payroll costs.

SOURCE: Adapted from Table L-9, U.S. Department of Commerce, *Report to the Congress: Foreign Direct Investment in the United States*, vol. 2, April 1976, p. 60.

ing companies reported that less than 20 percent were capitalized under partnerships with American firms.[12] The experience of many Third World countries, notably Indonesia, has not been very rewarding in forcing the Japanese into joint ventures. What starts out as a joint venture often ends up by becoming a wholly-owned subsidiary. The joint ventures are often tied to exclusive supply contracts at inflated prices, high production runs, and exclusive sales contracts at preferential prices, with the result that these subsidiaries often show losses and thus squeeze out the local partners.

Three factors account for this tendency. Japanese overseas operations are considered merely an extension of domestic operations and are often manipulated in terms of accounting practices, inventory levels, and transfer pricing to serve the financial needs of the Japan-based operations. Japanese companies also consider their overseas operations training grounds for their executives to prepare them to conquer foreign markets. Since this training has to take place at all levels of management, Japanese nationals occupy more lower-level positions in their overseas operations and have greater turnover among their Japanese employees in the overseas operations. Since both practices are anathema to the host nation governments, especially in Third World countries, friction can be avoided or at least minimized if the overseas subsidiaries are wholly owned.

A third factor has to do with the Japanese self-image. Because of the sociocultural conditions prevailing in Japan, the Japanese companies have been able to achieve a high degree of productivity from their workers in Japan. Japanese companies have come to believe that their workers are indeed superior and are therefore reluctant to expand their overseas operations for fear of losing their competitive edge. An added element is the prevailing industrial structure in Japan. For example, the large Japanese automobile companies have a large network of close, exploitable, and dispensable contractors and suppliers. Their equity structure is highly leveraged, providing low-cost overall financing. Japanese companies also tend to import materials from Japan, though such processing industries as foodstuffs, lumber and lumber products, paper, pulp, chemicals, and textiles largely procure their major raw materials locally. Most other companies to a varying degree depend on Japanese suppliers for their reliability and quality despite the disadvantage of the long distance. Some large companies even bring their suppliers to the United States.

Application of Japanese Management Practices in the United States

It would be unrealistic to expect that every Japanese company will apply the JABMAS system to its fullest extent in its U.S. operations. However, our extensive analysis of Japanese businesses in the United States shows that almost every Japanese company has retained some elements of its home-based management practices. In many cases, these practices have been restricted to Japanese employees. This is especially true in the case of people in higher paid job categories, and is most prevalent in the trading companies. In other cases, different companies have chosen to apply only certain Japanese techniques to their American workforce and have limited the application of these techniques to certain classes of American workers.

Some scholars, notably Japanese scholars, have suggested that Japanese management practices are culture-unique and therefore not easily transferable.[13] The fact that most Japanese companies do make such efforts is attributed to the Japanese managers' alleged lack of familiarity with foreign cultures and management styles. It is argued that Japanese managers are insular and that there is strong resistance to, and discrimination against, those who learn from other cultures and incorporate foreign practices and attitudes, because in doing so they deviate from the "norms" of Japanese culture and management values. The corporate culture of a Japanese company tends to exclude "outsiders" and even "insiders" who become "different" in their views from others in the company.

The Japanese manager who is sent abroad fully realizes that his fortunes are not tied to his performance in the overseas territory; they depend on remaining familiar with the nuances of conditions in the home office. Thus he insulates himself from the local culture and cares little to learn anything about it. (Of course, the language barrier does not help things either.) He is always looking toward the home office for even routine decisions and avoids all possible opportunities for independent decision making. In fact, the home office management encourages these attitudes by requiring their managers to stay no more than three years in any foreign location. Japanese managers who become too identified with foreign cultures or attitudes are derisively called New York *boke* (meaning "fool") or Brazilian *boke,* implying that they have acquired the bad habits of a particular foreign culture. To the extent that Japanese managers do acquire different viewpoints in their overseas assignments, they become problems for the home office managements in terms of their integration.[14]

This is one of the reasons why "Little Tokyos" sprout up in every foreign town where a significant number of Japanese companies are located. Moreover, many Japanese companies place their expatriate managers in positions that often isolate them from local employees. This is partially due to their lack of command of the language of the host country and unfamiliarity with the ways of doing business in that country. Another element is a probable concern and doubt about the efficiency of Western management techniques. Some Japanese companies in the United States, for example, have openly expressed their distrust, and even contempt, for the quality and dedication of American workers. For example, Nissan's president, Takashi Ishihara, stated in 1981 that the reason Nissan decided to build trucks rather than passenger cars in Tennessee was that there were fewer parts to a truck and therefore fewer chances for the American workers to bungle the production.[15] Japanese have also made derogatory comments about American management.[16] Nevertheless, some companies have had a measure of success in transplanting JABMAS to their U.S. operations. Companies like Sony, Matsushita's Quasar, and Honda are often praised for their success in their use of Japanese management practices in their American operations and the resultant improvements in worker productivity and product quality.

The 1981 JETRO survey of Japanese manufacturing companies identified certain generic patterns in the application of Japanese management techniques by Japanese-controlled firms in the United States.[17] Of the 238 companies surveyed, a clear majority reported having the intention to adapt JABMAS because of their belief that such practices would increase the productivity of their American workers and managers. The survey, however, elicited mixed responses when it queried companies about the extent to which they were actually using various Japanese management practices and their reactions as to the success of these practices. A majority of the companies reported using both the American-style top-down decision making and the Japanese-style consensus decision making. The most common communication vehicle between management and workers was a meeting with employees where the emphasis was on building mutual understanding and group identification. Soliciting suggestions from the workers was found to be difficult to apply in the United States. Suggestion systems yielded very few concrete results. One of the most surprising findings of the survey was the fact that less than 10 percent of the responding companies used Quality Control circles. Many companies reported that American workers were indifferent to management matters. The JETRO survey did not find a single company using "spiritual" slogans to motivate American workers to improve product quality or to build company loyalty. Additionally, a majority of the firms reported strong resistance on the part of workers to job rotation.

Nevertheless, a "no layoff" policy was viewed as of vital importance by nearly all Japanese companies. There was general approval by the employees of such a policy. Some companies suggested that such a policy helped create a more favorable image of the Japanese companies in the United States, one that would could attract American workers. Very few firms had adopted a seniority-based wage system. Nor did the companies adopt the Japanese bonus system—ordinarily granted twice a year—which constitutes a significant portion of a Japanese employee's salary. Although most companies had organized some recreational activities, they were not as extensive as the ones in the home offices in Japan.

At the management level, some companies placed managers in large, undivided rooms, a custom prevalent in Japan. This was done largely to facilitate open, freer communication among managers.

The cumulative effect of all these companies' introduction of Japanese techniques has built up over time so that their impact, on significant segments of the U.S. population and opinion leadership, has become noticeable. Their effects, both positive and negative, have been felt by various groups who have begun to take all possible measures to protect their interests.

Exhibit 8–1 shows the evolution of the issue of Japanese management practices from the preproblem to prevention stages. The preproblem stage is shown as ending in 1975. By this time, the Japanese companies had achieved a significant measure of penetration in selected U.S. industries, where their efforts at applying Japanese management technique were beginning to have some impact. The year 1975 is also shown as the beginning of the problem identification stage. Around this time, certain Japanese companies were hit by lawsuits charging discrimination against U.S. employees. There was also increased coverage in the news media not only of the Japanese business success stories, but also of Japan, Inc., with all its attendant connotations, and the legal problems confronted by the Japanese companies in antidiscrimination and related lawsuits.

By 1980, the legal process had advanced to a stage that a number of Japanese companies had suffered major defeats in their court battles. Although appeals are still pending in almost every case, the magnitude of potential compensatory awards has become clearer.[18]

We are still in the remedy and relief stage, because as yet no consensus has appeared either from the Japanese companies or the affected U.S. groups as to the ground rules within which future negotiations for agreements will take place.

STRATEGIES AND TACTICS

Our analysis of Japanese companies in the United States suggests that these companies can be divided into four distinct groups based on their strategies and tactics in applying JABMAS to their U.S. operations. These are

- Type A companies: The imperialist approach
- Type B companies: The enclave approach
- Type C companies: The domestication approach
- Type D companies: The acculturation approach

EXHIBIT 8–1 Issue Life Cycle of the Application of JABMAS by Japanese-Controlled Companies in the United States: Stages of Conflict Evolution

Dimensions of Corporate Behavior		Preproblem Stage	Problem Identification Stage	Remedy and Relief Stage	Prevention Stage
Response Mode	Character of Response	Pre 1975	1975–1980	1980+	
Social Obligation	Do what is required by law and economic necessity. Response is defensive and proscriptive.	Type A companies Type B companies Type D companies	Type A companies	Type A companies Type B companies Type D companies	
Social Responsibility	Mitigate negative side effects of corporate activities on society. Response is prescriptive and interactive.	Type C companies	Type B companies Type C companies	Type C companies	
Social Responsiveness	Promote positive social change. Response is proactive, anticipatory, and preventive.		Type D companies		

Type A companies: The imperialist approach
Type B companies: The enclave approach

Type C companies: The domestication approach
Type D companies: The acculturation approach

The Imperialist Approach: Type A Companies

The imperialist approach implies that the companies in this group have generally introduced JABMAS "intact" from their home bases in Japan. The system of organization structure and the decision-making process is akin to a body cell or clone that is an exact duplicate of the parent cell. This approach is quite reminiscent of the way colonies were managed by the Western imperialist powers, notably Great Britain. The success of such a system depends in maintaining the internal integrity and cohesiveness of the organism on the one hand, and a separate entity that is clearly identified and is perceived as superior and powerful by the external environment on the other.

The assumptions of the system are those of working in a hostile and often dangerous environment that nevertheless must be exploited. The survival of the satellite organism depends on keeping in close touch with the parent body and, above all, maintaining the values of the corporate culture, which are considered superior to those of the external environment and are at the core of the survival of the system. The cell or clone is thoroughly and completely imbued with the values and thought processes of the parent organism, thereby ensuring that the cell will react in entirely predictable ways—and in exactly the manner that the parent would—given a specified set of circumstances. The purity of the cell is vital lest any impurities clog the highly sensitive communication channels and distort distant messages between and among the parent and the outer cells. This could be fatal for the autonomously working cells, which must depend on continuous and unambiguous signals from the parent and other cells.

The integrity of the system is also heightened by creating a clear differentiation between the internal components of the cell and alien agents the cell absorbs from the external environment. Thus Japanese managers and technical personnel are likely to keep to themselves and exclude local employees from intimate contact both at the professional-organizational and social levels. It is not unusual to see "little Japans" in foreign cities where Japanese expatriates congregate and socialize among themselves. These companies also tend to have a relatively large complement of Japanese expatriates to make the operating unit almost self-contained in terms of its internal working. This insularity tends to make the Japanese expatriates insensitive to local culture and mores and heightens a sense of "differentness" among the American employees.

For these reasons, Japanese companies using this approach are among the most tradition-bound in Japan. They have vast networks of international operations but are *primarily* focused in Japan; they view their interests as identical to those of Japan as a nation. They view their overseas operations as an integral part of Japan's foreign economic policy. This is not always an unreasonable or a totally altruistic assumption, given that these companies tend to be large economic behemoths whose welfare is inevitably tied to that of Japan.

In their overseas operations, type A companies display the attitudes of the imperialistic power in a foreign colony where home-country citizens are accorded the preferred status of master race, while the "natives" are treated according to the customs of the local society. The companies maintain two classes of employees. These companies provide differential, and more generous, benefits to Japanese employees. American employees are denied similar benefits and are treated like "temporary workers" in Japan. The application of Japanese practices to local employees is highly selective and is unilaterally determined by the company without regard to local employees' needs, preferences, or even equity with Japanese employees within the business unit. It should also be noted here that Japanese companies in general, and trading companies in particular, do not follow benevolent labor practices in their overseas operations, especially as they relate to host-country citizens.

When confronted with employee discontent, expressed in lawsuits or adverse public opinion, type A companies have responded in the social obligation mode; their response has been defensive and proscriptive. They have argued that the two groups of employees are different and perform uniquely different services; that the companies have different expectations of them, and therefore the two groups cannot be compared. Furthermore, the companies have resorted to other legal defenses disputing the rights of U.S. employees and those of U.S. government agencies to initiate legal action. It is no wonder that the groups opposing these companies have responded in kind and that there has been little spirit of natural accommodation.

Companies using the type A approach consist mostly of large trading houses or *keiretsu* such as Sumitomo, Mitsui, and C. Itoh. The practice of the imperialist approach was best illustrated in Chapter 4 in the description of the employment policies and management practices of C. Itoh and Company. It is also not surprising to note that the second most important case of job discrimination against Japanese companies in the United States was filed against another trading company, Sumitomo, where the alleged discrimination was with reference to sex and national origin. An informal survey by the authors of various Japanese companies and their employees, including management-level employees, in the United States and Canada showed that type A companies, and notably the trading houses, were extremely reluctant to alter their traditional practices except when forced to do so by adverse economic conditions and overt government pressure, such as in Canada. However, even here there was a strong tendency to resist change and revert to old practices as soon as circumstances changed or external pressures were somewhat eased.

In a sense, the reluctance of these companies to include American employees in the Japanese system is understandable. These companies are among the most tradition-bound even in Japan, and are the oldest and most ardent users of JABMAS. Japanese companies have maintained that, in order to successfully install their technological processes, they must export their "institutional atmosphere" to the environment of the host countries. To operate successfully, the U.S. affiliate needs constant home office inputs in terms of information and decisions. Moreover, U.S.-based Japanese employees must keep in constant touch with their counterparts in the home office, and must have a continuous "feel" for what is happening in Japan because it is toward the home office that they look for their own promotions and career advancement. In the organic milieu of the Japanese corporation, personnel at the home office process information and make decisions largely on the basis of the factions and groups that have sponsored a manager in a foreign affiliate. This is done to ensure that their protégé does not stub any toes and that all persons who must be consulted prior to making a decision have indeed been consulted. For this reason, middle managers in foreign affiliates constantly send "personal" reports to "their men" at home as proxies for intimate face-to-face conversations. Japanese employees spend tremendous amounts of energy, effort, and time to develop and nurture interpersonal relationships within and between groups that lubricate the flow of vertical and horizontal communications. The corporation, by and large, builds a unique internal network from which outsiders are excluded. Even the Japanese employees who do not belong to the group or do not know about the group's network would have considerable difficulty in getting anything done by the group. Therefore, it becomes critical for an overseas manager to know the right communication channel and to get a commitment by the parent company's key personnel to bring about a consensus among those involved. This knowledge and contacts can be obtained only by Japanese managers who have cultivated and nurtured the interpersonal relationships in the parent company throughout their working careers.[19]

There is also the fear that if foreigners were allowed in the system, they would somehow weaken its integrity. It is argued that most foreigners do not share the same set of cultural values that makes JABMAS so unique and effective. Furthermore, if exceptions are made in one country they will spill over into other parts of their worldwide operations, with disastrous results on their cost structure and a flexible workforce. Under these conditions, Japanese companies are extremely reluctant to integrate even the most able local employees into the communication networks.

The Enclave Approach: Type B Companies

The enclave approach involves setting up operations in fairly small and isolated parts of the country, generally in rural areas. The population mix in these communities is quite homogeneous and stable; people are hostile to''-big city'' ways and take pride in their community. Unions are almost nonexistent. Although the local population may be somewhat suspicious of outsiders, it is also willing to leave people alone if they do not intrude on their way of life.

The company using the enclave approach aims at strategic exploitation of the environment. This calls for no change in the internal workings of the organism, but instead aims at finding a niche in the external environment that minimizes conflict between the organism and the environment. Thus the sociopolitical environment is quite benign and somewhat isolated. A number of Japanese companies have established operations in such locations, where they have set up little enclaves of Japanese-style business with the Japanese philosophy and modus operandi. The most notable of these companies is Kikkoman, which established a plant in Walworth, Wisconsin, in 1973.

The Japanese companies using the enclave approach are primarily small to medium in size, and both the number of total employees and the ratio of Japanese to American employees is relatively small. These companies also use the Japanese system "intact." There is, however, one major difference between type A and type B companies. The type A companies using the imperialist approach largely exclude local employees from the system, or at best operate parallel but some what different systems for the Japanese and the American employees. The type B companies using the enclave approach make a greater effort to integrate local employees in the system. This is easier in the case of companies using the enclave approach because the local employees occupy mostly lower-level positions; do not see the company as a ladder for upward mobility and a long-term career; and are inclined to mind their own business as long as they are paid the going wages and are left alone.

Companies using the enclave approach generally tend to be involved in manufacturing and assembly operations and place heavy emphasis on employee involvement and a sense of belonging on the part of their employees. This is considered highly desirable because it lies at the root of Japanese concern for quality of production and worker efficiency. Therefore, these companies devote considerable attention to employee selection, indoctrination in corporate culture and philosophy, and training. In this sense, companies using the enclave approach are quite similar to those using the acculturation approach, type D companies, although in the case of type B companies, both the degree and intensity of involvement may not be as great as those of type D companies. For this reason, the specifics of these practices will be discussed in detail in the acculturation approach section.

The JETRO survey (1981) showed that most early Japanese entrants in U.S. markets were small to medium-sized companies. This is typical of the overseas expansion of Japanese investments.[20] These companies not only choose locations that are at a distance from big industrial metropolises, but also choose cities that are essentially agrarian in character, that do not have even small or medium-sized firms specializing in one or other type of technology or products. It is assumed that even local craftsmen would have developed work habits that would be inimical to the instillation of Japanese methods, which are institution-related and must be cultivated in virgin soil.

Kikkoman, the maker of soy sauce and other products, established its plant relatively early compared to other Japanese companies. The company's decision to invest in the United States was made primarily because of the threat of an embargo on soybean exports, its basic raw material, during the Nixon administration.[21] The choice of location for the plant was based on the availability of a labor force whose work ethics were considered similar to those of the Kikkoman in Japan. Kikkoman is a family-owned company and is quite traditional. It has brewed soy sauce in its own way for three centuries. The traditional fermentation process requires a great deal of workmanship or craftsmanship. Therefore, the attitude of the labor force toward the work is important to the company. According to Yuzaburo Mogi, executive vice president of Kikkoman's Walworth plant:

> I believe work ethic is closely related to environment. Walworth is an agricultural community. Farmers look at their crops from beginning to end; translated to the factory, it's following the product from the input of raw materials to the finished goods. People close to agriculture know they must work hard in order to gain a good crop or profit. Our Japanese plants also happen to be situated in farming areas, and our workers there bring the same attitude to their work.[22]

The Japanese companies using the enclave approach also try to facilitate local community's acceptance of their operations. For example, Kikkoman, at the time of constructing the plant in 1973, met with strong local resistance. This experience sensitized the officials to local feelings. To defuse local resentment, possibly borne out of fear of strangers, the company spread its Japanese employees and their families among many neighboring communities, thereby avoiding the formation of a "little Tokyo".[23]

Type B companies are likely to lag behind the type A companies in terms of the issue life cycle. Thus while the issue of JABMAS may reach the problem identification stage at the national level, it may still be in the pre-problem stage for type B companies. Because of their size and location, these companies are not likely to be the initiators of changes, nor are they likely to be subjected to major confrontations by outside groups. However, once the conditions in the external environment force changes in the response mode of Japanese companies, type B companies will have to follow suit because the local population is unlikely to be submissive and willing to accept wages and working conditions different from the then prevailing norms.

The Domestication Approach: Type C Companies

The domestication approach calls for the use of a modified form of Japanese management practices where the type of practice and the intensity of its use are both moderated to meet external and internal environmental conditions. This approach has been used by Japanese companies under one or both of the following conditions:

1. The Japanese companies entered into joint ventures or took over already established U.S. companies. There is the existence of a corporate culture that cannot be easily dislodged, and workers are allied with strong industry unions. The case of Matsushita's takeover of Motorola's color television operations (Quasar Electric), or the recently proposed joint venture between GM and Toyota are illustrative of this phenomenon.
2. The Japanese company is well known, large in size and highly visible, and has established operations in geographic locations with a tradition of strong trade unionism and therefore an antipaternalism bias.
3. The Japanese company operates in markets where the demand structure is quite competitive. The company's market edge may be marginal or vulnerable to factors outside its control. It would not risk instituting management or operational systems that may expose it to partial dysfunctioning of its organization or cause disharmony among its workers.
4. The Japanese company is engaged in the production of high-technology products where skilled workers and scientists may be in short supply. Given the American sociopolitical environment, these American workers are likely to be self-motivated, highly mobile, and may prefer higher current wages and performance-based compensation.

The rationale for the domestication approach is that of strategic adaptation. It aims at altering the linkages between the firm and its environment. The adaptation process would include such variables as the product-service mix offered to the markets, the type of factor inputs—labor, raw materials secured from the environment, organizational structure and internal decision-making processes, and relations with other corporate constituencies and stakeholders. In the strategic exploitation mode, the firm attempts to overcome environmental dissonance through its market, financial, or political power. It also attempts to devise new linkages to interact with the environment—including competitive, sociopolitical, and legal—in a manner that minimizes dissonance between it and the outside world.

The response mode of type C companies is that of social responsibility in the first three stages of the issue life cycle. In sharp contrast to type A and type B companies, they adopt a highly interactive and open system of communications with other groups both inside and outside the corporation, and are quite adroit in adapting to their external environment.

The application of Japanese techniques under this approach is likely to be ad hoc and low key. Moreover, a specific technique is likely to be Americanized and given a local flavor before it is introduced. Accordingly, the companies tend to operate on a case by case basis. It is not surprising that companies following this approach are generally in the high-technology area, operate in tight labor markets, need highly skilled people, and in any case are not strict adherents of JABMAS even in their Japan-based operations.

It is interesting to note that all the four major electronics companies operating in the United States, Matsushita, Sanyo, Sharp, and Sony, fall into this category. Sony was the first to set up its plant in 1972 in San Diego, California. Following the Sony move, Matsushita took over Motorola's plant in Franklin, Illinois, in 1974. Early in 1977, Sanyo acquired Warwick Electronics in Arkansas with its distributor, Sears, Roebuck (25 percent equity interest). Then Sharp bought the RCA plant in Memphis, Tennessee, in 1979.[24] Of the four, Sony built its plant from scratch; the other three took the acquisition route. This was done for competitive reasons, as the companies involved wanted speed of entry.

It seems that the Japanese electronics industry had a substantial incentive to manufacture in the United States. The U.S. market provided not only new ideas and accessibility to new technologies, but also a testing ground for introducing new products. Their moves were also encouraged because of a highly automated manufacturing process, which made labor cost differentials less important.[25] Both Matsushita and Sanyo acquired plants that had considerable manufacturing and product quality problems.[26] Matsushita had to undertake significant changes in equipment and remodeling to improve work flow on the assembly floor, and redesign Quasar's TV sets to facilitate greater automation. When Sanyo took over the Warwick plant, the plant was already unionized and Sanyo retained most of the labor force. Sanyo was even struck by the union, a strike that lasted several months in 1979.

As to the extent of the application of Japanese management techniques, the companies following the domestication approach showed considerable variation because of the differences in both their internal and their external environments. However, the companies that had less interference from the external environment were instrumental in introducing Japanese management techniques to a greater extent than the companies faced with unionized workers or other unfavorable conditions.

Where a company has started anew, it has taken pains to screen employees who were likely to be more adaptable to the company's philosophy. It was also presumed that the new workers would be less inclined toward unionization. In this sense the behavior of type C companies is quite similar to that of type D companies that follow the acculturation approach. Furthermore, companies make every effort not to lay off employees for economic reasons, because to do so would invite unionization. These companies also provide employees with extensive training for other jobs in the plant. In the case of Sony, promotions are indeed based on seniority. However, to create better understanding of its rationale, Sony has appointed a "morale officer" who promotes vertical communication in the company and even does marriage counseling. Sony has also introduced a modified version of the Japanese-style consensus technique for making decisions and professes satisfaction with this approach.[27] To date, the company has been successful in keeping labor unions out of the plant.

Other companies have followed a mixed strategy of adaptation based on circumstances. As one Japanese executive stated:

> We combine YKK and host-country management style.
> . . . We practice neither the seniority system nor the life time employment. Instead, we rate our workers once or twice a year, and rather than lifetime employment, we call it "stable employment."[28]

YKK endeavors not to lay off employees except as a last resort. The first step is a proportional wage reduction involving all employees, Japanese and non-Japanese, in the company's U.S. workforce. Sanyo has been least successful among the four electronics companies in the use of Japanese techniques. Faced with worker unrest and strikes, the company tried to maintain and enhance communication between management and labor by providing information on such company news as profits, production, and personnel matters. Nakai Hajime, executive managing director, stated:

> [As a consequence of the strike] we learned some lessons . . . and are now trying to improve the situation. In Japan, the union lives with the company and never pulls the trigger unless it finds itself in an extremely serious situation. It tries as much as possible to work with us on the same ground, because its members' future and prosperity are directly linked to ours. The important question for us right now is how to instill this concept in our American workers.[29]

Matsushita offers another example of the domestication approach. It acquired the Motorola Quasar brand and production facilities.[30] Matsushita Electric Industrial Company bought three TV assembly plants with about 6,000 workers in 1974. At the time of the purchase, the plants had considerable manufacturing and production problems, such as high rate of defects and rejection, obsolete equipment, and low worker morale. Matsushita had to invest heavily to upgrade the in-plant operations, including replacing conveyor belts, remodeling work flow on the shop floor, and redesigning the TV sets to facilitate greater automation. The company, according to *Television Digest Magazine,* paid $108 million for the plants and spent at least $25 million on automation and manufacturing redesign.

The company also took certain actions that were not typical of Japanese companies. It virtually replaced most of the former top management personnel because they would not adjust to or accept the Japanese approach. It recruited new executives from other U.S. consumer-electronics firms. Due to the operating losses in the early years, coupled with the recession, it had to trim the size of both the management and the workforce. The company closed plants in Pontiac, Illinois, and in Toronto, Canada, reducing the workforce from 6,000 to 2,000. Such dramatic changes during the early years caused significant tensions among workers over job security. An added element was that Matsushita, in order to transplant its process technology at Quasar by remodeling the plant and redesigning the engineering, brought many task forces from Japan that included both managerial personnel and engineers. The number of the Japanese expatriates, however, was reduced after the initial startups.

Matsushita brought some elements of JABMAS. In addition to improved working conditions on the shop floor, American workers were given brooms to clean up the work areas at the ends of their shifts. Though such a practice is rare in the United States, the workers did not resist and kept the areas clean by themselves. The company also assigned individual daily production quotas—called "quality bogeys"—instead of an overall production goal for the plant. And the workers hold meetings like Japan's Quality Circle once a week to discuss various company issues.[31] Matsushita also keeps its workers informed about the financial health of the company, and encourages more open communications between management and labor. According to the company, productivity went up significantly with improved quality and worker morale.

Matsushita also introduced decision making by consensus, which reportedly took a long time before it was accepted by the managers. American managers were sent to Japan and exposed to the Japanese company's management approach, in-plant production culture, and overall corporate culture. In addition, Matsushita restructured its financial arrangements with its distributors through a consensus decision-making process between the managers and the independent distributors. The process took about three years. Quasar, however, purchases most of its parts from Japan. This has resulted in the loss of local demand for the parts. Sylvania used to supply the Motorola television tubes.

Many management scholars and news media regard the Quasar plant as a "shrine exhibiting the workers of Japanese management methods." However, some analysts, including the Motorola's chairman and chief executive, Robert W. Galvin, contend that the turnaround of production quality and worker morale was not surprising. Motorola had decided to sell these plants a long time ago and had maintained its investment at a minimal level. Instead of investing in television production, Motorola opted to invest heavily in the new technology areas, such as two-way radios and semiconductors. Motorola's semiconductor plant is said to be as efficient or even more efficient than the Quasar or other comparable Japanese companies' plants.

Sharp, which was the last one to start operations, seems to have taken advantage of the experience and knowledge gained by the other companies.[32] Even though it acquired the plant from RCA, it recruited new employees with careful screening. The employees were required to take an 18-hour course in Sharp's philosophy and management approach and to be willing to be retrained for other jobs in the plant. The company introduced the Quality Circle, at first as a human relations program, the practice of no layoffs, and provided generous fringe benefits to its employees. Conflicts between Japanese and American employees were mitigated after the number of the Japanese personnel, initially quite large, was reduced. It was reported that productivity, quality, and worker morale were significantly improved, even though the plant utilized almost the same equipment and machinery as those of the other American companies. Notwithstanding all these efforts, Sharp's American workers recently voted to unionize and have the International Brotherhood of Electrical Workers, AFC-CIO represent them.[33] Another important feature of Sharp's operations is that about 70 percent of the parts used by the company are supplied locally. Sharp puts considerable effort and energy into maintaining the same relationship with its American suppliers as it does with its suppliers in Japan. Some of Sharp's Japanese suppliers have built plants in Memphis to supply the parts.

The Acculturation Approach: Type D Companies

The underlying rationale for the acculteration approach is that of cultural transformation. Under this approach, the firm attempts to transfer its "culture" more or less "intact" into an alien environment, with the objective of absorbing its local workers into the transferred culture. There are two major differences between the imperialist approach of type A companies and the acculturation approach of type D companies. Companies following the imperialist approach maintain the purity of their culture by limiting its application only to those people who belong to that culture but are now working in an alien environment. The acculturation approach attempts to do exactly the opposite; it aims to purify the alien workers by absorbing them into its culture. Two, in the case of the imperialist approach, the application of Japanese management techniques to local employees is indifferent, incidental, and forced. The acculturation approach calls for creating a new corporate culture where both Japanese and American workers will share a common set of values and outlook toward work, organization, and the corporation. It requires a slow and painstaking indoctrination of the American workforce in order to imbue it with the thought processes and habits of Japanese workers, which are considered a necessary precondition for the successful introduction of Japanese management practices.

The acculturation approach is quite bold and demonstrates a conviction on the part of Japanese management that their system and style of management is transferable, and can be transplanted to a foreign culture and operate with foreign workers, provided careful attention is paid during the incubation and early growth period. However, it also carries with it a sizable risk, the magnitude of which is uncertain at present.

Companies using the acculturation approach undertake a number of similar activities that are briefly described here:

1. Employees are carefully selected and screened to ensure that workers hired will have a positive attitude toward the Japanese management system, including an aversion to outside unionism, a willingness to learn, a capacity for obedience and discipline, and loyalty to the company, flexibility in accepting different job assignments, and acceptance of the philosophy of placing group welfare over individual welfare in the belief that what serves the group best serves the individual.
2. To the extent possible, workers who have had no prior experience are preferred. This is done to avoid the hiring of workers who may have developed unhealthy work habits, have belonged to unions, and may be antagonistic toward the new employer. This tactic also has the effect of discriminating against workers for union membership, and also against workers who are older and more experienced.
3. Workers are given extensive training not only in job-related skills, but also in corporate history, folklore, culture, and traditions.
4. Any manufacturing operation is preceded by a long period of careful planning and painstaking attention to every detail of the human and technological aspects of the operation.
5. A selected number of workers is sent to the parent company in Japan, where they live and work in the parent company's plants side-by-side with the Japanese workers. On their return, the "instructor workers" are expected to train other workers in the Japanese way of doing things. These workers are accorded a higher status in the plant hierarchy through the use of different color uniforms or identifications caps and badges.

6. Not only do the Japanese companies bring in their management philosophy, they also bring in "intact" their manufacturing processes.

Unlike American companies that buy standard machines and build their manufacturing operations around these machines, Japanese companies modify machines to blend them into an organic whole which, in many ways, is company-specific and quite unique.[34] Little, if any, changes are made in transferring technology from the parent plant to the overseas plants. These include the types of machines used, the plant layout and machine setup, and the system of work flows. The combined effect of employee relations and management practices on the one hand, and manufacturing practices on the other, is to create the "right atmosphere conducive to employees' dedication to their production work."[35]

Arguing that culture-bound technologies, such as production processes, can be successfully transferred and sustained within "different cultures" only by persons familiar with the specific corporate culture and production process, Japanese firms insist on having their own managers assume overall responsibility for production operations abroad.[36] Therefore, in companies using both the acculturation and enclave approaches in particular, and other approaches in general, the number of Japanese technician-managers seems to remain disproportionately large in their overseas operations compared with non-Japanese multinationals. The Japanese ignorance of local language and culture, fear of antagonizing local employees (disharmony), and reluctance to entrust quality control to local employees when products are intended for internal markets also contribute to this tendency.

The acculturation approach, like the imperialist approach, greatly depends on intimate relationships between executives from the foreign affiliate and their home office counterparts and superiors. This condition appears to be endemic to all large Japanese companies, where groups and factions are an integral part of bureaucratic functioning and reciprocal obligations and mutual IOUs are way of life.

Examples of the Acculturation Approach

The Nissan truck plant in Tennessee and Honda's motorcycle and auto plants in Ohio offer two examples of the overt similarities and differences in transplanting Japanese management techniques to the United States. Honda has operated and manufactured its motorcycles in the United States since 1979, and started the manufacture of passenger cars in 1982, while Nissan, after a long preparation, started manufacture of pickup trucks in the fall of 1983.[37] Honda has had some experience with the American workers, although the motorcycle plant employs fewer than 400 workers.

Encouraged by its experience with American workers at the motorcycle plant, Honda was the first Japanese auto company to establish an auto plant in the United States. However, the Honda approach to transplanting Japanese management techniques seems to be more moderate than that of Nissan. Nissan is currently building a pickup truck plant in Smyrna, Tennessee. One feature of the plant is the high degree of automation (over 200 robots). The company is planning to run this plant under Japanese-style management with very little modification.

It is not surprising that these two companies would use the acculturation approach. The auto companies are at the forefront of the Japanese companies that have developed highly automated and integrated manufacturing systems, which have enabled them to produce high-quality cars under conditions of mass production, including the "just-in-time" form of inventory controls. These systems have been called the sixth stage of the Industrial Revolution.[38] They would be quite difficult to operate if modified to a significant degree to suit local conditions because the tradeoff costs between suitability to local conditions and maintaining the integrity of the system may be too high. Since the concepts and practices of the Japanese manufacturing system are significantly different from those of the USA, substantial changes are needed, esepcially on the part of production workers, to adjust to the new system. Therefore, the Japanese companies expend a tremendous amount of effort, time, and energy to instill Japanese concepts and ideas of production into American workers and managers.

For those companies, selection of the "right" employees is imperative. Marvin T. Runyon, Nissan's president, stated:

> Human resource selection and use is critical in a participative management system. . . . We're looking for people who are capable of a high degree of cooperation and teamwork. We're looking for workers who are motivated by group achievement as well as their own personal achievement. And we're looking for workers who share the company's commitment to building the best quality trucks on the market.[39]

Employees are hired only after long and careful interviews. The trend is to select those who are likely to be "predisposed" to the Japanese style of management, and to exclude diversity that could lead to disharmony or disunity. The two companies prefers employees with no prior experience in American auto plants (and thus with the UAW or other unions). Mr. Hayano, vice president of Honda, U.S.A., said that Honda wanted "very fresh people, like blotting papers," who would readily absorb Honda's way of management and its emphasis on quality.[40] The companies also prefer to select employees who are willing to move from job to job in the plant at the management's discretion. This is considered necessary to gain flexibility in the workforce for minimizing layoffs during business downturns. Providing a sense of job security through a no layoff policy is considered important to enhance the employees' loyalty to the company. Also employees' willingness to move to different jobs within the plant allows for the looser job specifications that are necessary for promoting cooperation among employees.

Both auto companies, Nissan more so than Honda, have used almost all the techniques of the acculturation approach discussed earlier. For example, Nissan's American workers typically spend three months in Japan, compared with three weeks for Honda's. A typical training program at Nissan for a supervisor lasts more than 4 months.[41] He gets an orientation program in Tennessee for 12 days, including such sessions as Nissan's philosophy, Japanese language, and the working of Quality Circles. His training in Japan includes such programs as performing each operation in his department, drafting job instruction sheets, observation of Japanese supervisors' work, and participation in Quality Circle sessions. Honda's employees go through a similar training, but on a smaller scale.

One of the important features of the Japanese manufacturing system is the close working relationship between managers and production workers. In the ideal situation, both consistently strive for improvement of the production system, cost reduction, quality, and productivity. Production workers with extensive hands-on experience are urged to make suggestions for possible improvements and to bring management's attention to problem areas. The supervisors, middle managers, and even top managers pay careful attention to workers' suggestions and ideas. This atmosphere of cooperation is vigorously promoted through the various settings and arrangements in the plants.[42] For example, status distinctions are played down by minimizing the number of ranks between top management and assembly line workers, and by lowering the differences between salaried and hourly workers. Honda's employees are called "associates"; Nissan's, "production technicians."

Therefore, it is understandable that companies using the acculturation approach resist unionization of the workforce. The resistance against unionization is common among most of the Japanese companies operating in the United States. But the effects of unionization are more serious and could impede the very purpose of the acculturation approach. Both Honda and Nissan have resisted unionization of their workforces. Honda has already faced some problem with the UAW, which tried to unionize its motorcycle plant. The company has since reportedly changed to a "neutral" stance. Nissan still openly opposes the union.[43]

The practice of training workers on many jobs in a Japanese plant provides for flexibility in the use of the workforce and may provide greater job satisfaction to the workers. However, it may also discourage the workers from leaving the company. In the Quality of Work Life (QWL) program, a worker is trained for every job in a section so that he can have wider experience in his work, leading to improved work performance and great job satisfaction. At the same time, as he is trained in many lines of work, his pay is increased because his job skills have expanded. However, if he chooses to leave the company, his wages may not be sustained because not many companies expect workers to be capable of handling many other jobs but one. This may also cause possible conflict with the labor union. The same may be true for American workers who are trained on many jobs in a Japanese plant. Moreover, as we explained in Chapter 3, many Japanese manufacturing companies' equipment is tailored to their specifications. Therefore, the skills obtained in one company may not be easily transferable to other companies.

The acculturation process involves not only the workers, but also the managers. Both Honda and Nissan managements plan to institute, with few modifications, most of the Japanese management practices, such as decision making by consensus, a wage system primarily based on seniority, on-the-job training and rotation, and a no layoff policy (though no written guarantees).

Response Patterns of the Acculturating Japanese Companies

During the preproblem stage, type D companies use the social obligation mode; while they do things differently, they do them for their own reasons and not because the environment has dictated them. Type D companies, however, exhibit a radical departure in their response mode from those followed by most other Japanese companies. By anticipating problems, these companies take steps long before they are required to do so. They make changes in the internal corporate environment congruent with the internalized values of the *external environment,* thereby defusing some of the hostility in the external environment. The important point to note, however, is that these changes are being made by the Japanese companies on their own terms, in anticipation of environmental pressures, but not as an immediate response to them. The acculturation process puts the type D companies in the social responsiveness mode during the problem indentification stage.

It is ironic that we find type D companeis back again in the social obligation mode during the remedy and relief stage. And therein lies the dilemma and a serious risk for the Japanese companies. When pressures in the external environment call for changes in corporate practices by the Japanese companies, type D companies resist these pressures because:

1. They feel they have gone a long way in creating a better work environment for their U.S. workers; some discrepancy in the wages, working conditions, and decision-making processes between the Japanese and American workers is inevitable but is based more on the "needs" of the

company, however defined, rather than a result of racial or other biases. Therefore, they should not be lumped together with other nonconforming Japanese companies and meted out similar punishment.

2. There is tremendous pressure for all Japanese companies to stick together in the face of a common external threat. Type D companies feel obliged to join type A and B companies in resisting externally imposed demands for change. Moreover, like the companies using the imperialist and the enclave approaches, type D companies also subscribe to the notion that JABMAS is culturally unique, and would lose its effectiveness if forced to modify along lines that are externally dictated.

3. By using a social responsiveness mode in the problem identification stage, type D companies raise societal expectations as to their future behavior. Other groups in the external environment view these companies as enlightened, and count on them to be leaders in bringing about changes in their behavior that are in greater harmony with societal expectations. However, when these companies revert to the social obligation mode, they evoke a very bitter response from the environment. Once a company has moved to the social responsibility or social responsiveness mode, it is very difficult for it to revert to a more restrictive response mode, because the environment reacts very negatively to such a tactic. The company loses considerable public goodwill and flexibility in choosing a response mode in subsequent stages of the issue life cycle.

NOTES

1. *Japanese Manufacturing Operations in the United States* (New York: Japanese External Trade Organization [JETRO], September 1981), pp. 7–8; hereinafter referred to as JETRO survey; see also the more detailed Japanese version, Japan External Trade Organization, *Zaibei Nikkei Shinshyutsu Kigyo no Keiei no Zittai* (Tokyo, September 1981).
2. U.S. Department of Commerce, *Survey of Current Business,* August 1980, cited in JETRO survey, pp. 9–10.
3. JETRO survey, pp. 12, 15–16.
4. JETRO survey, pp. 12, 17.
5. 42 U.S.C. 2000e-2(e).
6. Japan Society, *The Economic Impact of the Japanese Business Community in New York, 1978* (New York: Japan Society, Inc., with the cooperation of Conservation of Human Resources, Columbia University, April 1978), pp. 18–19.
7. Ministry of International Trade and Industry, *Wagakuni Kigyo no Kaigai Jigyo Katsudo* [Overseas Business Activities of Our National Enterprises], Tokyo, 1975, p. 91, cited in Terutomo Ozawa, *Multinationalism, Japanese Style: The Political Economy of Outward Dependency* (Princeton, N.J.: Princeton University Press, 1979), p. 215.

8. JETRO Survey, pp. 34, 35.

9. Tsurumi, *The Japanese Are Coming:* A Multinational Interaction of Firms and Politics (Cambridge, Mass.: Basic Books, 1976), pp. 190–193, 260–261.

10. Ministry of International Trade and Industry, *Wagakuni Kigyo no Kaigai Jigyo Katsudo,* Tokyo, October 1973, pp. 81–82, cited in Tsurumi, *The Japanese Are Coming,* pp. 189–190.

11. Cited in Ozawa, *Multinationalism, Japanese Style,* p. 212.

12. JETRO Survey, p. 34.

13. See, for example, Hideo Ishida, "Human Resoruces Management in Overseas Japanese Firms," translated by William Testa, *Japanese Economic Studies,* 9 (Fall 1981), pp. 53–81; Mitsuhiko Yamada, "Japanese-Style Management in America: Merits and Difficulties," translated by Dennis M. Spackman, *Japanese Economic Studies,* 9 (Fall 1981), pp. 1–30; Toyohiro Kono, "Japanese Management Philosophy: Can It Be Exported?" *Long Range Planning,* 15, 3 (June 1982), pp. 90–102; Seiichi Kikuchi, *Nigai America: Shinshutsu Nihon Kigyo No Zittai to Taiyo* [Bitter America: Realities and Countermeasures of Japanese Companies in the United States], (Tokyo: Nihon Noritsu Kyokai, 1982).

14. S. Prakash Sethi, "Drawbacks of Japanese Management," *Business Week,* November 24, 1973, p. 14.

15. Masayoshi Kanabayashi, "Honda's Accord: How a Japanese Firm Is Faring in Its Dealings with Workers in U.S.," *The Wall Street Journal,* October 2, 1981, p. 1.

16. Urban C. Lehner, "The Pros and Cons of Plain-Speaking, Japanese Style," *Wall Street Journal,* January 18, 1983, p. 30.

17. JETRO Survey, pp. 39–48.

18. For details see Chapter 4, "Innocents Abroad—The Case of Itoh (America), Inc.."

19. Tsurumi, *The Japanese Are Coming,* pp. 198–199.

20. JETRO Survey, pp. 15–20; see also Tsurumi, *The Japanese Are Coming,* p. 108.

21. Ozawa, *Multinationalism, Japanese Style,* p. 119.

22. "How the Japanese Manage in the U.S.," *Fortune,* June 15, 1981, p. 98.

23. Louis Kraar, "The Japanese Are Coming—With Their Own Style of Management," *Fortune,* March 1975, pp. 116–121, 160, 161, 164.

24. See Jack Baranson, *The Japanese Challenge to U.S. Industry* (Lexington, Mass.: Lexington Books, 1981).

25. Ibid., pp. 83–85.

26. Thomas C. Hayes, "The Japanese Way at Quasar," *The New York Times* October 16, 1981, pp. D1,9; Paul Cathey, "Japanese Managers Find Best Way to Direct U.S. Workers," *Iron Age,* May 21, 1982, pp. 73, 74; "How the Japanese Manage in the U.S.," *Fortune,* June 15, 1981, p. 102.

27. Kraar, "The Japanese Are Coming," pp. 160, 161.

28. "How the Japanese Manage in the U.S.," p. 102.

29. Ibid., p. 98.

30. The Matsushita case was constructed from the following materials: Hayes, "The Japanese Way at Quasar"; David P. Garino, "When Twain Meet: Takeover by Japanese Hasn't Hurt After All, Quasar Workers Find," *Wall Street Journal,* October 10, 1978, pp. 1, 41; Kraar, "The Japanese Are Coming," pp. 121, 160;

Frank Gibney, *Miracle by Design: The Real Reasons Behind Japan's Economic Success* (New York: Times Books, 1982), pp. 183–184.

31. See, for a more detailed discussion of the introduction processes of the quality control method at the Matsushita's Quasar, Dennis A. Ossola, "Application of Japanese Productivity and Quality Control Methods to Matsushita's Illinois Plant," in U. Krishna Shetty and Vernon M. Buehler (eds.), *Quality and Productivity Improvements: U.S. & Foreign Company Experiences* (Chicago: Manufacturing Productivity Center, 1983), pp. 172–184.

32. See L. Erik Calonius, "Factory Magic: In a Plant in Memphis, Japanese Firm Shows How to Attain Quality," *Wall Street Journal*, April 29, 1983, pp. 1, 14.

33. Confirmed by telephone conversation with Sharp's manager; also see Eduardo Lachica, "Japanese Work Ethic and Unionism Clash at Sharp of America's Memphis Factory," *The Wall Street Journal*, February 26, 1981, p. 29.

34. Urban C. Lehner, "Technology Duel: Japan Strives to Move from Fine Imitations to Its Own Inventions," *Wall Street Journal*, December 1, 1981, pp. 1, 18.

35. Tsurumi, *The Japanese Are Coming*, p. 194.

36. Ibid., p. 189.

37. The examples of the Honda's and Nissan's operations in the United States were collected from: Masayoshi Kanabayashi, "Honda's Accord: How a Japanese Firm is Faring Its Dealings with Workers in U.S.," *Wall Street Journal*, October 2, 1981, pp. 1, 25; Mike Tharp, "Honda's Move to Build $200 Million Plant in Ohio Could Spur Other Japanese Firms," *Wall Street Journal*, January 14, 1980, p. 2; John Holusha, "Honda Plant Brings a Touch of Japan to Ohio," *New York Times*, April 26, 1983, pp. 1, 45; "Nissan's Truck Plant: People and Robots Under One Roof," *Iron Age*, September 15, 1982, pp. 30, 33; Bruce Horovitz, "Japan Inc.'s Beachhead in Tennessee," *Industry Week*, May 17, 1982, pp. 45–47; William Serrin, "Nissan Brings Foreign Ways to Tennessee," *New York Times*, April 20, 1981, pp. A1, B6. Steve Lohr, "Nissan Uses Japan's Ways in Tennessee," *New York Times*, April 4, 1983, p. D11.

38. William J. Abernathy, Kim B. Clark, and Alan B. Kantzow, *Industrial Renaissance: Producing a Competitive Future for America* (New York: Basic Books, 1983), p. 40.

39. Cited in Cathey, "Japanese Managers Find Best Way to Direct U.S. Workers," p. 69.

40. Kanayabashi, "Honda's Accord," p. 25.

41. See "Nissan's Truck Plant," p. 33.

42. Kanabayashi, "Honda's Accord," p. 25; Lohr, "Nissan Uses Japan's Ways in Tennessee," p. D11.

43. Dale D. Buss, "Japanese-Owned Auto Plants in the U.S. Present a Tough Challenge for the UAW," *Wall Street Journal*, March 23, 1983, p. 33; See also "Honda of America Drops Opposition to UAW's Drive," *Wall Street Journal*, April 26, 1982, p. 5.

NINE ▰▰▰▰▰▰▰▰▰▰▰▰▰▰▰▰▰▰▰▰▰▰▰▰▰▰▰▰▰▰▰▰▰▰▰▰▰▰

Japanese Management Techniques in the United States: The Case of the American Companies

MOST AMERICAN OBSERVERS AGREE THAT JAPANESE FIRMS BY AND large have been very successful in providing quality products at competitive prices. There is also strong evidence to indicate that average worker productivity in Japan is much higher compared with that of workers in other industrialized nations of the West, including the United States. However, there is considerable disagreement as to the reasons for the Japanese success. While "bandwagon" wisdom would attribute it to the superior ways of Japanese management and the unique cultural traits of the Japanese people, there are important dissenting voices that question this reasoning, both for its accuracy and its relevance to the U.S. sociocultural environment. In this regard, the comments of William J. Weisz, vice chairman and chief operating officer of Motorola, are quite illustrative:

> The Japanese competitors do not walk on water. They did not invent creativity and innovation. They did not pioneer quality, or mass production, or marketing, or customer service.—We did!— Americans did. But they have done a good job in implementing what they continuously tell us we taught them.[1]

It should be noted that Motorola is one of the most successful companies in the semiconductor industry and has held its own against the Japanese companies not only in the United States and other overseas markets, but also in Japan. Furthermore, Motorola owned Quasar prior to its acquisition by Matsushita, which is given a large amount of credit for turning Quasar around —both technologically and financially—through the use of Japanese management techniques.

THE AMERICAN RESPONSE TO JABMAS

American corporations have generally been more cautious and selective when applying Japanese management practices to their own operations. They have the advantage of possessing a deep understanding of their sociocultural and political environment and the inherent conflict between JABMAS and that environment. However, they are often limited in their comprehension of the nuances that lie behind various Japanese management techniques. Lacking this awareness, application of these techniques by American companies often becomes difficult and their effectiveness doubtful. This caution on the part of U.S. firms is quite understandable and is based on a variety of factors.

1. American corporations have their own ethos and traditions, which conflict with the new approaches, thereby raising the level of resistance on the part of various constituencies within the organization.
2. Acceptance of new techniques also implies a recognition that current practices have not been effective. Even if this premise is accepted, there are often vested interests in the management ranks that are likely to suffer adverse financial consequences, loss of authority and status, a blow to personal pride, and loss of peer group recognition under a different organizational structure and management philosophy. They are highly motivated to offer considerable resistance to the application of JABMAS and to use their organizational status in ways that undermine the smooth application of these techniques.
3. In many business entities, labor-management relations are often quite strained. There is little mutual trust. Workers and union leaders tend to view these techniques as another management tactic to exploit the worker through work speedups, one designed to weaken trade union activity in those companies. Organized workers, therefore, may be unwilling to cooperate with any management-initiated approaches that are viewed as increasing "worker productivity" from the management's perspective but where rewards are unlikely to be shared by the workers.
4. For the most part, unions have been opposed to JABMAS-related activities because they view them as a drive toward weakening the labor movement, usurping the prerogatives of collective bargaining, and exploiting the workers by increasing output—through work speedups and automation—without giving workers a share of the gains from increased productivity. This attitude no doubt has some basis in fact, because corporations cite "cost cutting and productivity improvements" as the overwhelming reason for initiating QC and other QWL programs.[2]

There has been tremendous interest on the part of American companies in learning about JABMAS, as evidenced by the spate of books and articles and the multiplicity of seminars on theory Z during the last three or four years.[3] The prospect of applying some of the JABMAS elements to their own operations has generated a managerial revolution in the factories and offices of some American firms.[4] In many instances, it has been an indigenous response to changing conditions confronting American business firms that often predates the current JABMAS craze. In other instances, it represents an attempt to adapt the latest managerial fad, stimulated by the current interest in the Japanese economic success story.

Notwithstanding, the impetus has largely been a desire to improve American competitiveness by improving productivity. The outcome has been an increase in employee participation in the management and ownership of some American businesses and a resultant change in the relationships among workers, managers, and owners, with the expectation that it will reduce worker alienation and also improve productivity.

How widespread is this managerial revolution? The exact parameters cannot be determined precisely, but a recent study has identified more than 6,000 workplaces where managers and employees are seeking to go beyond the "we" versus "them" relationship. The list of workplaces runs the gamut from private to public sector entities and from small to large firms.[5]

A 1982 survey of 1,158 U.S. corporations conducted by the New York Stock Exchange, covering a cross section of the U.S. corporate world, provides us with some interesting findings.[6]

- Only 14 percent of all corporations with 100 or more employees have some type of worker involvement program (collected under the rubric of Quality of Work Life or QWL). However, this percentage increases with the size of the corporation and is 53 percent in the case of NYSE-listed corporations.
- Most programs are less than five years old. For example, in the case of quality circles (QCs), 74 percent of the programs are less than two years old. (No data were available from another 10 percent of the respondents.)
- A majority of the corporations (58 percent) give cost cutting as one of their reasons for initiating such programs.
- An overwhelmingly large number of programs emphasize maintaining traditional hierarchical arrangements while striving to develop better tools for management to manage the workforce in order to improve productivity. For example, 76 percent of the corporations have formal training and instruction as part of their QWL programs, followed by employee appraisal (performance evaluation) and feedback as the most popular program (72 percent of the corporations).
- Programs that reward workers for their contributions toward increased output are less frequent. For example, 25 percent of the corporations report having programs in labor-management committees and profit shar-

ing; personalized work hours (28 percent); structured plant-office space (29 percent); task forces (35 percent); and suggestion systems (38 percent).

• Although most QWL programs incorporate five or more activities, the number of employees covered by each activity is quite small, indicating a low level of penetration within the corporate ranks.

The actual application of JABMAS to date has been generally quite slow and limited mostly to the use of shop-floor quality circles (QCs). One factor that may account for this limited use of JABMAS concepts is that its application at the operating level is not very threatening to top management and requires the least amount of change in organizational structure and processes. However, use of JABMAS and its expansion beyond the shop level is likely to intensify in coming years. There is immense market pressure to develop new approaches in order to increase productivity and efficiency in U.S. companies. Furthermore, should Japanese companies achieve a significant degree of success in introducing Japanese practices into their U.S. operations, they offer a tempting opportunity for many corporate executives to take the path of least resistance and protect themselves by using management approaches that are currently in vogue.

Exhibit 9–1 shows the evolution of the issue of JABMAS, from the perspective of American business community, from the preproblem to the prevention stage. The preproblem stage ended in 1980, five years after the Japanese companies in the United States became a significant presence. This has been due primarily to two factors. First, Japanese companies entered a new and hostile environment and, in many cases, did not pay enough attention to the problems of cultural dissonance that ensued during the introduction of these techniques. The acceleration in the rate of Japanese investments in the United States during this period and their clustering in certain geographic areas (New York, New Jersey, and California) caused the problem to surface quickly and become more visible. The affected groups were able to build communication networks and combine resources to protect their interests. Second, American companies were unfamiliar with the JABMAS techniques, were not convinced of their relevance and applicability to their U.S. operations, and were therefore slow to respond.

The year 1980 marked the beginning of the problem identification stage. The issue had by then built enough momentum of its own and had become self-propelling. There was a race on the part of many U.S. companies to join the bandwagon lest they be left behind. More often than not, elements of JABMAS were introduced without adequate thought and proper groundwork. Thus, the problem identification stage is likely to be short, and American companies will most likely move into the remedy and relief stage by 1985–86.

EXHIBIT 9–1 Issue Life Cycle of the Application of JABMAS by American Companies in the United States: Stages of Conflict Evolution

Dimensions of Corporate Behavior		Preproblem Stage	Problem Identification Stage	Remedy and Relief Stage	Prevention Stage
Response Mode	Character of Response	1980	1980–85	1985–86	
Social Obligation	Do what is required by law and economic necessity. Response is defensive and proscriptive.	Type B Type C	Type A Type B	Type A Type B	Type A Type B
Social Responsibility	Mitigate negative side effects of corporate activities on society. Response is prescriptive and interactive.	Type A	Type C	Type C	Type C Type D
Social Responsiveness	Promote positive social change. Response is proactive, anticipatory, and preventive.	Type D	Type D	Type D	

Type A companies: The cosmetic approach.
Type B companies: The exploitation approach.
Type C companies: The domestication approach.
Type D companies: The indigenous approach.

205

AMERICAN STRATEGIES

Our analysis of the efforts of American companies to introduce Japanese management practices in their U.S. operations suggests that four strategies have been employed by the American companies. Please note that the discussion here is confined to those elements of JABMAS that relate to the internal aspects of management—decision-making processes or human resource management, workplace environment or the organizational culture, and the terms and conditions of employment or the extent to which the workers share in the profits generated by their increased productivity. American companies are also developing new modes of dealing with external factors in order to create a better sociopolitical environment for their U.S. operations and to develop effective competitive responses to the Japanese in the United States as well as other parts of the world. These will be discussed in the next chapter.

The strategies used by American companies in introducing elements of JABMAS in their U.S. operations are these:

- Type A companies: The cosmetic approach
- Type B companies: The exploitation approach
- Type C companies: The domestication approach
- Type D companies: The indigenous approach

The categories described here are classificatory in nature. These classes are only broadly defined and are designed to illustrate a group of practices that are symptomatic of a particular approach. Social phenomena involving human interactions are difficult to analyze in precise terms when looked upon holistically, and should not be placed within narrowly defined boundaries. Arbitrary precision, under these conditions, is just as likely to conceal valuable information as it is to elucidate it. For these reasons, U.S. practitioners of Japanese management techniques are not likely to fit neatly into a particular category at a given time. Instead, there is likely to be some overlap: A company may display most of the attributes associated with one type of classification, and yet also incorporate a few of the attributes of another type.

The Cosmetic Approach: Type A Companies

Companies applying the type A approach probably represent the majority of all U.S. companies using some elements of JABMAS. The essential characteristics of firms using the cosmetic approach are these:

- Introduction of JABMAS is invariably accompanied by a tremendous fanfare in the in-house magazines and the local media. The emphasis is on conveying an image to employees and community that the company is forward-looking in its industrial relations and willing to experiment with new modes to improve productivity and employee relations. But the principal organizational concept of top-down management remains unchanged.

- Programs are directed by the personnel or public relations departments, and there is little real top management involvement or commitment.
- There is inadequate resource allocation, and once the program is initiated, there is insufficient follow-through.
- The largest single program utilized is the Quality Circle (QC).
- The new practices are too often introduced without enough prior training for the involved workers and plant supervisors as to what is expected of them and how the QCs are supposed to function. There is greater attention to form than to substance.
- Interest groups, such as professional associations, are formed to further the cause.

The cosmetic and exploitation approaches are perhaps the most vivid examples of what is wrong with American business and why it will take an extraordinary effort to correct its collective sins of omission and commission. While there may be an emerging realization that something needs to be done, it is questionable whether there is enough commitment to do it right and a willingness to pay the price for correcting past mistakes.

Companies following the cosmetic approach are both the early adopters of new ideas and the early quitters when things don't work right. They pick the most obvious changes to make not because they are most appropriate, but because they are perceived to be the easiest. Management is obsessed with the notion of being contemporary and enlightened, with nary a thought of what it means. These companies are likely to be in the middle range of American companies in terms of size, and with product or market share niches that provide them with a respectable rate of profit and partially shelter them from intense domestic and international competition.

The most representative of this genre of companies fall into the group that is introducing QCs. It is no wonder that, according to one estimate by the International Association of Quality Circles in San Francisco, an organization formed in 1978, the number of registered QCs in the United States increased from a total of 1,000 in 1964 to 87,540 by February 1978.[7] According to the International Association of Quality Circles (Midwest City, Oklahoma), some 2,500 United States firms have QCs. The association's membership increased from a little over 1,000 to 5,000 between 1981 and 1982.[8] Another estimate places the number of registered workers at 860,000, with many more not registered with the national organization.[9]

The success stories are often anecdotal and create images of profound successes and phenomenal increases in productivity that are more reminiscent of high-pressure salesmen of resort condos than systematic studies of productivity gains that carefully identify cause-effect chains. The carnival atmosphere is complete with all the trappings of national and international conferences, where companies report their experiences and share success stories. There are grand prizes and, of course, a coterie of distinguished speakers calling believers to the fold and consultants helping converts to practice their new beliefs.[10] The whole movement is "consultant driven," with more than 150 consulting firms currently standing ready to help U.S. firms form QCs at prices ranging from $1,500 to $20,000.[11]

It is no wonder that the thousandfold explosive growth in QCs in American companies has not been accompanied by an overall increase in the competitiveness of American industry. In part, it is due to the slow rate of progress that can be expected in the early stages of the QC movement, when a great deal of time must be devoted to learning and setup costs. However, the lack of demonstrable improvement in overall productivity must be largely attributed to the overblown promotion and puffery that has accompanied the QC movement in the United States. Some observers have already noted that the movement is ". . . in danger of peaking out just as it is gaining a foothold. . . . Companies that use QC as a Band-Aid approach to productivity problems or worker unrest, without fully understanding the necessity for the right corporate climate, will eventually run into difficulty."[12]

It should be noted here that relatively few Japanese firms operating in the United States have adopted Quality Circles because of the hostility of the American working environment. Matsushita Electric, which has operated the Quasar plant in Chicago for several years, is only now introducing QCs into its Chicago operation, having spent a lengthy period preparing a firm foundation for the critical sharing of information needed for successful Quality Circle operation.[13]

U.S. corporations using the cosmetic approach adopt the social responsibility mode during the preproblem stage; they meet the societal expectations of what is desired of them. However, since their involvement is more symbolic than substantive, it soon peters out. Problems inevitably arise when the activity level of Quality Circles increases and plant managers and workers demand guidance. Management is then faced with the need to give some signal to those involved, which is not forthcoming. The management response during the problem identification stage reverts to the social obligation mode, as it exhibits extreme reluctance to follow through on its earlier demonstration of enthusiasm during the preproblem stage. Lacking sufficient commitment for the managment and allocation of adequate resources, the QCs start with a flurry of activity and then wither away for want of attention. The corporation declares the experiment a failure because of its unsuitability for the company's particular needs, lack of worker-union cooperation, or some other factors. The practice is held in disrepute and the cause of better work relations suffers a setback.

The Exploitation Approach: Type B Companies

Anything that can improve productivity—and promote lower manufacturing and labor costs—would attract the attention of companies in this group. It is not that companies in other categories do not regard increased productivity as their top priority, or that they are not concerned with lowering labor costs. The major difference between type B companies and those firms following the domestication approach, type C companies, is that whereas the latter attempt to improve productivity in collaboration and cooperation *with* the employees, the former emphasize productivity gains to be achieved *through* the employees.

Type B companies using the exploitation approach display most or all of the following characteristics:

- The management strategy toward employee relations is essentially authoritarian in character, combined with a large measure of paternalism.
- These corporations view JABMAS-related techniques as just another way of getting greater output from the workforce.
- The dominant features of JABMAS emphasized by these companies are not those of the human aspects of management, but of the machine aspects of production.
- A great deal of emphasis is placed on the measurement of individual worker productivity, and the reward system emphasizes individual production versus group output.
- The primary mode of worker motivation for participating in group activity—whether it involves quality controls or increased production—is fear. The highly paternalistic management orientation ensures that this fear is never brutally exercised or overtly manifested, but cooperation and acquiescence on the part of workers is expected and taken for granted.
- Management makes every effort to keep as large a share of the gains from productivity as possible. The workers' share is often minimal, grudgingly given, and carries a large measure of acclaimed management generosity.

Type B companies are perhaps as large in numbers as those following the cosmetic approach. Both groups are likely to be concentrated among medium-size companies. They are generally nonunionized and are likely to be located in regions that are apathetic or even hostile to trade union activity. Where a firm's workforce is unionized, relations between management and union are quite adversarial. Further, management nurtures this anti-union feeling, which is also reinforced by a sociopolitical environment that is not supportive of union activity.

Companies using the exploitation approach are not likely to publicize their efforts or label them as such. However, their presence can be inferred, at least partially, from the NYSE survey of U.S. corporations using Japanese management techniques. The companies employing between 500 and 999 workers, and the group that is likely to have a large number of both type A and B companies, reported their top four QWL activities as job design/redesign, formal training and instruction, employee appraisal and feedback, and setting employee goals.[14]

Unlike the cosmetic approach pursued by type A companies, there is a large measure of management attention to detail and a commitment to get the job done. There are, however, some major differences. The primary focus of productivity improvement relates to things that can be done on the factory floor and involve streamlining production processes, improving inventory controls, and following such other Japanese techniques as "Just in Time" and "Do It Right the First Time." The machine focus implies that manufacturing processes are not necessarily redesigned to provide a greater job challenge for the worker. Instead, the company emphasizes greater automation to reduce the number of total workers employed, and where possible job redesign to reduce the need for more skilled workers.[15] It is beside the point that simplified jobs may also be more monotonous and boring, and may in the long run create more worker dissatisfaction and alienation. Furthermore, in a throwback to the days of Taylor's scientific management, great effort is devoted to work analysis, including decomposition of individual jobs into minute components and the breakdown of worker efforts to improve work-related behavior and job performance.[16]

This approach ensures that management will always have the upper hand in dealing with workers. By reducing its dependence on workers, management also creates a fear of job losses through redundancies, thereby inducing the workers to stay in line. Through a carrot and stick approach, management provides a more positive way to ensure that workers do its bidding. The positive elements take the form of careful screening and selective hiring of employees who are in tune with the company's philosophy, and providing selective job "insecurity" for those who do not fit, thereby setting an example for others. When difficult times arrive, these companies do not hesitate to lay off employees en masse. Of course there is a corporate culture, but the corporate ethos is largely dominated by management, which insulates itself and the workforce from outside influences. These are indeed mutual obligations between management and employees. However, the pressure for fulfillment of these expectations is from the management toward the employees. Such a company can even generate employee loyalty because it selects and rewards those employees who can work in an environment of protective dependency. However, when faced with economic difficulties, management chooses the layoff route and fails to provide even a modicum of job security. The image of a harmonious family falls apart like a house of cards. Texas Instruments is a good example of a corporation that is currently going through such a transition.

The exploitation approach does not exclude QCs; rather, the scope of QCs is narrowly defined, is focused on plant-floor problems, and receives closer management direction. Worker involvement does indeed increase. However, the element of consensus building is largely missing. There is a two-way communication flow, but the communication content is quite different in each direction. Bottom-up communications consist mostly of facts, sometimes of analysis, but very rarely of suggestions. Top-down communications comprise mostly decisions, and not requests for opinions. A large portion of the communication consists of directions flowing from plant managers down to foremen, with the expectation that those directions will be carried out. While the primary objective of QC and other QWL measures, from the management's perspective, is to improve productivity and lower costs, they are sold to the workers for their intrinsic value. There is an element of hypocrisy on the part of the corporation in creating "spontaneous" participative management through the strong encouragement of senior executives.[17]

When Quality Circles succeed in generating significant savings, questions of reward inevitably arise. Management in type B companies uses recognition measures that are largely symbolic in character. In a system that is reminiscent of retiring the old man with a gold watch, a handshake, and little else, the new reward symbols may include a badge, a special citation, plaques and T shirts, or attendance at the national QC conference. It is contended that the satisfaction of making one's job easier or safer is incentive enough for the workers involved. For example, in a study of QCs in the chemical industry, Robert P. Beals of Texas A&M found that in only 30 percent of the cases did the workers receive cash for their ideas. According to Beal: "Those 30% who pay their quality circles say it's the only way to go. The 70% who don't just don't want to open up a can of worms."[18]

One factor that may contribute to the exploitation approach is the American corporation's propensity to use formal and structured top-down decision-making systems rather than an organizational environment that facilitates the optimum use of QCs. Thus, the exploitation is often less the result of deliberate intent (the American legal concept of mens rea) and more the outcome of parochial thinking. An example is the current tendency to view QCs on an engineering dimension, rather than as an aspect of human relations. Trade journals are full of proposals for the application of the QC concept that suffer from this malaise. Engineering personnel take the lead in recommending that Quality Circles be established and a work plan developed and implemented by conducting studies with a "one-second stopwatch," all under the managerial control of a supervisor designated by management. QC communication is to be handled by the weekly circulation of memos. Esprit de corps is to be generated by calculating and publishing the production results on a regular basis. The results are to be evaluated periodically by staff engineers or other upper-middle-level production management to determine whether the costs justify the benefits.[19]

Quality Circles, when implemented in this fashion, have more form than substance. They have become a production technique for the assembly line, and not a way of life that should permeate the entire organization. People continue to be treated as machines, and QC is simply a different type of lubricant that may help the machine perform faster. When it does not, drop the QC and try some other "lubricant." Thus, the whole point of the Quality Circle is misdirected, with unfortunate results for both the firm and its employees.

The management response to new techniques during the preproblem and problem identification stages is in the social obligation mode—defensive and proscriptive. The corporation does what is minimally required to get the workers involved without parting with any managerial authority and prerogatives. Despite the apparent harmonious relations between management and employees, the system suffers from a lack of mutual trust. Middle managers are opposed to participative management because they view it as coddling the workers, an infringement of their authority and prerogatives, or top management's way of finding out their real or alleged shortcomings. They also resent the time-consuming rituals that must accompany participative management as an added burden on their already heavy work schedule. Workers will not participate effectively or enthusiastically because they just do not like management; there may be a great deal of communication, but there is no dialogue.

Because of the hostile internal and external environment, the new techniques generally have a very short life span. The benefits from JABMAS accruing to the companies using the exploitation approach are likely to be small in the preproblem stage and will become successively smaller as the issue moves into the problem identification stage. Therefore, should the issue ever reach the remedy and relief stage, companies using this approach are more likely to get out of the issue arena rather than alter their response mode to that of social responsibility. However, when external conditions and the behavior of other corporations force type B companies to take some action, their responses continue to remain in the social obligation mode.

The Domestication Approach: Type C Companies

The domestication approach calls for the use of a modified form of JABMAS; the type of practice and the intensity of its use are both moderated to meet external and internal environmental conditions. This approach has been used by American companies under one or more of the following conditions:

1. Where American firms face strong competition from Japanese companies in their domestic markets and are attempting to improve their productivity and competitive strength to meet the Japanese challenge. Corporations in the automobile, steel, and semiconductor industries fall in this category.
2. Where American companies have entered into joint venture agreements with Japanese firms. The Japanese partner holds a majority interest and has an edge in production and manufacturing technology. The joint venture requires close working relations at the operational and manufacturing levels between technical and junior–middle-level line executives from the joint venture partners.
3. Where U.S. corporations are facing poor economic conditions and declining market shares and must reduce labor costs to survive. Workers and their unions are concerned about job security and protection from layoffs. The threat to corporate survival and workers' jobs is very real and, unless some action is taken, quite imminent.
4. Where U.S. corporations have had a very poor record of product quality, cost efficiency, and market competitiveness. Invariably they were the high-cost producers and not competitive generally with other U.S. producers, and certainly with overseas suppliers, notably the Japanese. When companies are in mature or declining industries, they are often saddled with large plants that are obsolete, and corporate investment in plant modernization lags grossly in comparison with foreign competitors.
5. Where there is a long history of poor management, and inefficient and often antagonistic employee relations and union-management relations. Unions have been very complacent about the need for improved productivity and corporate profitability, and much more interested in seeking a bigger share of an already shrinking pie.
6. Where the industry is facing a very high rate of growth and technological change that requires a tremendous and simultaneous infusion of large amounts of capital, creative people, and market savvy. This combination often leads to sloppy management, high employee turnover, and lack of attention to consumer needs. The condition is likely to be concealed in the short run in increased sales and revenues. At the same time, the industry faces strong competition from well-disciplined and well-financed foreign suppliers who are willing to buy into a market share to reduce their costs, and to postpone current profits for future growth in sales and earnings.

Companies using the type C approach follow a variety of paths in the application of Japanese management techniques to their operations. However, there are some commonly shared attributes:

- Most changes have been introduced within the last two years and have been in response to economic conditions and market pressures. These pressures have affected both the elements of JABMAS selected by type C companies, and the extent of their adaptation.
- A great deal of emphasis has been placed on changes at the plant level and in manufacturing processes; Quality Circles and worker participation predominate. At the same time, other techniques of improving plant efficiency and worker productivity, such as production scheduling, automation, inventory controls, quality improvement, and waste reduction, are emphasized.
- Application of JABMAS has, in most cases, been preceded by more direct measures of cost reduction: wage and work rule concessions from employees and unions, worker layoffs, price concessions from suppliers, and even government assistance.
- Companies using this approach devote considerable time and energy in the preplanning stage to ensure that all significant problems have been anticipated and satisfactorily resolved. There is strong emphasis on training of supervisors and extensive communication and discussion with employees and union leaders to secure their understanding and cooperation.
- In the initial stages, only those elements of JABMAS are introduced that can be readily adapted to the firm's needs. This is especially true for firms confronted with poor economic conditions and declining market shares.
- There is a strong and visible commitment by top management to the application of new techniques. This is in sharp contrast to the companies following the cosmetic and exploitation approaches. Top management involvement is evidenced by three factors: (a) The companies do not try for quick fixes and immediate returns; instead new management approaches are evaluated for their long-term payoff. (b) Employee involvement is not confined to shop level, but penetrates higher levels, including professional and technical staffs, and also certain levels of management. (c) Tremendous effort is expended to integrate the new techniques into overall corporate operations, and not to introduce them piecemeal. In other words, there is indeed an emphasis on changing the corporate culture.

The corporate response mode for type C companies during the preproblem stage is that of social obligation. At this stage, the company is beset by extreme financial difficulties and is struggling for survival. Therefore, the emphasis is on immediate cost reduction. There is intense pressure to undertake direct measures to reduce costs and improve cash flows. Unions and workers are asked to make wage concessions and relax work rules, and to accept layoffs, in the hope that the corporation will survive and there will be better times for all.

The response mode changes to that of social responsibility during the problem identification stage as the corporation scrambles to meet societal expectations and narrow the credibility gap between its performance and those expectations. By narrowing the gap, the corporation earns the trust of its internal and external constituencies. This helps the firm to hold its own during the remedy and relief stage, when there is intense pressure not only to demonstrate that its performance has indeed improved, but also to compensate the victims of its past wrongs. By remaining in the social responsibility mode during this stage, companies following the domestication approach gain in public trust. They contain the magnitude of publicly imposed penalities on the one hand and retain a measure of flexibility and autonomy in their internal operations on the other.

As we will demonstrate in the discussion that follows, the domestication approach has certain limitations. It does not adequately prepare corporations to cope with uncertain futures. Corporations using the domestication approach emphasize doing what is known rather than experimenting with what is unknown but may be more promising. This is not surprising, given the very low starting base of productivity and innovation applicable to most of the firms in this group. They feel quite comfortable in the social responsibility mode during the prevention stage, and let others take the lead.

One of the primary conditions necessitating the type C approach on the part of U.S. firms has been the dissatisfaction of the American public with the poor quality of products and services provided by the U.S. companies, and the willingness of the American consumer to buy "foreign" goods despite the adverse impact on the U.S. balance of trade and payments. Custumer sovereignty and freedom to choose are deeply rooted in the American culture. Anyone who advocates purchase of goods made locally, but unsatisfactorally, by pleading patriotism walks on broken crutches.

And the differences in quality can indeed be great. According to Joji Arai, manager of the Japan Productivity Center in the United States, the malfunction rate in U.S.-made TV sets is 4 percent, compared with only 0.4 percent in the case of Japanese-made TV sets. Four out of 100 U.S.-made new cars need to be repainted before delivery to the buyer; the rate for Japanese cars is one per thousand. In 1978, 74 percent of all Chrysler Omni and Horizon owners reported mechanical problems. GM, in the introductory year of 1979 for its Citation, reported 61 percent owner dissatisfaction. On a similar volume of sales, Japanese car warranty expenses are estimated to be only one-fifth that for American vehicles.[20] It is not surprising, therefore, that GM and Ford have spearheaded the drive to use JABMAS and are identified with the domestication approach.

The most dramatic examples of the domestication approach are the Pontiac Division of General Motors and Ford's Louisville assembly plant. Both companies have employed modified forms of JABMAS, and the results have been phenomenal. Japanese techniques have been confined mostly to manufacturing processes at the plant level. The efforts have been particularly significant because both GM and Ford are unionized, and the United Auto Workers is not only one of the more powerful U.S. unions, but has been a vigorous adversary in labor negotiations with GM and Ford.

GM calls its approach the Quality of Work Life (QWL). Ford calls the process Employee Involvement (EI). Hourly and salaried workers at 95 of GM's 147 plants have been learning QWL; 60 of Ford's 76 plants are involved in EI. The major characteristics are more employee participation and less dictatorial styles of management. The key to QWL or EI is decentralization of decision making and diffusion of information. Previously, information had been the exclusive property of the plant engineers and suppliers of parts and materials and was not shared with employees on the factory floor. Now plants are divided into work units that determine their production rates within plantwide limits. When work groups experience problems, they can call in not only the plant engineers, but the vendors as well. The leader of a work unit, or the coordinator, is selected by the members of the work unit. Instead of accumulating power, management has shown a willingness to share power and draw upon the experience of all company personnel.[21] More important, the assembly line worker has now become involved in planning and organizing the operational processes to be employed in building new cars. Thus, when Ford began production of its new Ranger truck at the Louisville facility, drawings, models, and mockups were sent to the factory line for worker comment. Management received 749 proposals and adapted 542. The outcome was the most defect-free vehicle built in the United States and well within the reach of the best Japanese quality. It was manufactured at a plant that only a few years before had been described as a "war zone," with the lowest quality rating of all U.S.-made Ford vehicles.[22]

Two significant advantages are present in the Louisville plant adoption of EI. Both were products of the extensive preplanning by Ford to ensure resolution of problems before the implementation of EI. At Louisville, both management and labor are committed to making EI work. A new manager who believed in human relations management took over the plant, which was a prime candidate for closing. The plant's UAW chairman, who was also new, thought there must be a better way of doing things than through adversarial relations and was willing to cooperate with management in order to save the plant. Both men benefited from the willingness of Ford and UAW at the highest echelons to devise new ways to keep Ford in the black and meet the Japanese challenge. The Japanese competitive threat and the possibility that the plant might be closed also served as an incentive to put aside labor-management differences. The outcome was the creation of a new organizational environment in Louisville that encouraged workers to work with rather than fight the EI concept. They perceived that the purpose of EI was to be for the benefit of both management and workers. The workers were willing to accept a speedup in the assembly line and changes in the work rules that would have sent them out on strike in earlier days.

The Louisville EI story indicates that the potential to achieve quality and productivity is present in American firms, even those characterized by adversarial labor-management relations, when the circumstances are right and there is a will to respond. Both management and labor officials openly committed themselves to a positive view of worker participation, and there was a willingness on the part of management to sacrifice some of its prerogatives and share the benefits with workers. It further demonstrates that quality control is not just a work unit at the end of the production line, but a state of mind that must prevail from top to bottom, from plant manager to union leader to production trainee.[23]

The advantage of the domestication approach is the flexibility it affords American business firms. It is not necessary to adapt all aspects of JABMAS, only those elements that are necessary to enhance a firm's competitive posture. For example, Black & Decker Manufacturing Company (B&D) was faced with competition from Makita Electric Works and other Japanese tool companies, which had captured 20 percent of the professional tool market, the equivalent of Black & Decker's market share. Realizing that there was no end in sight, B&D decided to meet the competition head on by matching and beating the Japanese at their own game. After carefully dissecting the products of Japanese competitors, the company decided that "their tools weren't all that different from ours." The key to the Japanese success, B&D concluded, was streamlined production operations and the development of a team spirit among the factory personnel that resulted in higher productivity and product quality.

B&D proceeded to improve its production efficiency by building robots capable of performing several factory functions and reducing the distance components had to travel through the factory. It also encouraged both intra- and interfirm competition among the workforce. Workers were divided into four teams at the Hampstead facility and assigned to one of four autonomous plants-within-a-plant. Production and quality performance was reported by team. B&D hoped to create the kind of team spirit that gave the Japanese firms their competitive edge. Although not all the workers were equally enthusiastic about the changes, general support was forthcoming as a necessary response to the Japanese competition. The financial future of the company was at stake, and the workers feared loss of their jobs if the company folded. It was easy to identify the Japanese competition as the "enemy" and to encourage workers not to permit B&D to "take a back seat to the Japanese."[24]

There are numerous other examples of improvement in productivity and phenomenal cost savings. Companies like Lockheed, Hughes Aircraft,

Harris Corporation, Cheseborough Pond, Hewlett Packard, Cincinnati Milacron, Brunswick Corporation's Mercury Marine Unit, Dover Corporation, and a host of others have reported immediate and sizable gains from the application of Japanese techniques, especially those relating to worker participation at the factory level.[25]

A large number of improvements have come from making changes that on reflection appear obvious and should have been made a long time ago. These changes are simply a reflection of better management, and have little to do with Japanese management techniques. Nevertheless, they were made possible because of the new competitive environment created by the Japanese, and a sense of urgency and mission that made acceptance of changes feasible on the part of both workers and supervisors.

The process of change is not without pain. Management is threatened by worker participation in areas formerly considered its exclusive domain, and workers are now asked to risk their job security without assurance that, as they sacrifice today, they will reap the rewards tomorrow. Companies often institute changes in a sequential fashion to spread the transition costs over time, even though there is a long-term commitment to reorganizing the firm. Thus, Itel Corporation of Santa Clara, even though it began its job simplification more than two years ago, has still only exposed 20 percent of its administrative staff to its new procedures. Further, it started with the "low hanging fruit" departments characterized by routine activities that were relatively easy to streamline and would provide rapid proof of the program's success.[26]

Type C firms tend to adopt JABMAS with caution, particularly when the change is a dramatic one for the firm and threatens existing power structures and processes. A variety of JABMAS ideas are tried in the hope that one will succeed. Groundwork is carefully laid by using the classic management ploy of calling in consultants to support a previous management decision. They, in turn, give lectures and team-building and sensitivity-training seminars to company personnel. Members of management who are intrigued with the new ideas are recruited to start the process. This was the scenario followed by Westinghouse's construction group, representing 7 percent of the Westinghouse workforce, when it decided to adopt participation management from top to bottom as a means of improving productivity.

Westinghouse soon found that building participative management teams required subtle leadership and a long training period. Sometimes the participative group's lack of experience resulted in wrong decisions, and then management was faced with the dilemma of whether to let the wrong decision stand or intervene and undermine the participative process. President Coates of the construction group "took the middle road" by reserving the right to override the consensus decision of his participative teams but exercising that right sparingly and gradually submitting more and more decisions to the consensual process as the groups gained experience. Although Westinghouse started with the realization that participative management was not a quick fix and that two years were needed before tangible results could be expected, it nevertheless covered all bets by testing a panoply of other management concepts, ranging from matrix management to robotic automation.[27]

Is the domestication approach the solution to our problems? Although the jury is still out, the authors have reservations as to its long-term prospects. At best, we consider it to be an interim solution. Despite careful planning, slow and careful nurturing, and long payoff times, many of the projects started with great fanfare have faced quick demise. Once obvious changes have been made and easily achievable successes scored, the process suffers saturation pains. Employee enthusiasm begins to wear thin because extra efforts do not seem to yield measurable results. Psychic rewards are not followed by monetary rewards, and when they are, the rewards are not considered large or equitable enough by the employees. Thus, while workers in the automotive and airline industries were forced to take wage cuts and make work rule concessions to enable their firms to survive, they were confronted with a management determined to keep costs down when those companies returned to profitability. In the effort to maintain enthusiasm, management often creates excitement by publicizing even small gains. This tactic, however, also creates heightened expectations of reward sharing that management either considers unreasonable or is unwilling to accord.

The selective application of JABMAS also creates problems of internal inconsistency. Although Honeywell, for example, emphasizes internal efficiency of manufacturing operations and employee satisfaction through participative management, it also keeps the old system of paying its bills after an average of 56 days, thereby using interest-free funds.[28] Although the automobile companies improve internal systems, their attitude toward suppliers is primarily that of exerting pressure against price increases. Management allocates the largest share of productivity gains to stockholders and to itself while the employees face an uncertain future in terms of layoffs or are made to feel happy through the psychic pleasure of having a job well done.

When the domestication approach is used in a joint venture, the Japanese partner is generally the controlling partner. The Japanese firm naturally takes the credit for the success of the venture and seeks further penetration of the operations by introducing more JABMAS techniques, some of which run counter to work and union expectations and American norms of doing business. As we saw in the previous chapter, this often leads to conflict between employer and employees. As evidence builds up, it is likely that organized workers will be less likely to cooperate "on faith" in the application of JABMAS to a joint venture. They may instead ask for contractual quid pro quos before entering into such an arrangement, thereby negating the entire spirit of willing participation and lessening of the adversarial relationships.[29]

Lacking the ingredients of the Japanese cultural and corporate ethos, where group performance is the norm and individual dissatisfaction is not even recognized, the American attempt to create a "new corporate culture" along the lines of Theory Z may be doomed to failure. To the extent that the new corporate culture removes the destructive aspects of authoritarian and counterproductive management styles, the process is successful because it harmonizes corporate culture with American societal values. Beyond a certain point, however, a totally participative and group-oriented management style runs counter to the American ethos of individualism and ceases to be beneficial. As we will show in the next chapter, this is indeed one of its greatest limitations and the one that is likely to create problems for American industry. The challenge for the future is not how to manage the present better, but how to face an increasingly uncertain and risky future. Within the American cultural context, it is the creativity and entrepreneurship of the individual and not arbitrarily created harmony, albeit well intentioned, that will provide the answer.

Moreover, as we shall demonstrate in the next chapter, Theory Z is a gross misrepresentation of the Japanese management system even within the Japanese cultural context and does not begin to grasp the nuances of American culture and value set. Therefore, a myopic advocacy of Theory Z or its counterparts can be not only counterproductive, but positively damaging to American industry and business institutions. The objective to be achieved is not in question. It is the means of reaching that end that is the crux of the problem. To the extent that the domestication approach has worked, the question is whether its success should be attributed to Japanese management techniques modified to meet American conditions or to American modifications that have saved the day for JABMAS. We contend the latter to be the case and conclude that, if a little modification is successful, even more should be even more successful. To put it differently, a truly indigenous approach must lead to an even better solution.

The Indigenous Approach: Type D Companies

A number of U.S. corporations have long followed management and employee relations practices that bear a striking resemblance to those associated with the Japanese companies. Among the most notable of these corporations are AT&T, Eastman Kodak, Hewlett-Packard, IBM, and McDonald's.[30] These companies devote tremendous effort to creating a work environment in which employees can closely identify their interests with those of their employers. There is enormous emphasis on product quality, innovation, and customer satisfaction.

Human resource management is a focal point for managerial action, and the organizational culture is supportive of this management focus. Financial rewards are not limited to top management and the stockholders, but are shared throughout the organization. Elements of this environment generally include no layoffs, a largely salaried rather than hourly based wage system, above-average wages and benefits, employee training, promotion from within, and a genuine interest in all aspects of employee welfare that permeates the entire corporate hierarchy and is an integral part of the corporate culture.

The corporate philosophy, modus operandi, management system, and employee relation practices of these and similar firms have been used by advocates of Japanese management practices, notably Ouchi in his Theory Z, to argue that JABMAS can be transplanted to the United States. Such a conclusion is unwarranted and may be misleading if other U.S. companies were to replicate the success of these companies by introducing Japanese management practices in their organizations. The analogy suffers from three serious drawbacks:

1. The indigenous approach was utilized by many American firms long before Japanese management practices penetrated the Western consciousness and became part of the lexicon of the American business community. Thus to hold these companies up as successful examples of JABMAS in the United States is post hoc rationalization and cannot be construed as proof of a theory.
2. Proponents of JABMAS use selective evidence to make their point. For example, Peters and Waterman, in their *In Search of Excellence,*[31] show a far broader list of successful American companies that share some—and, in many cases, quite different—but not all the characteristics attributed to Theory Z. Thus, not being inclusive, Theory Z does not explain anything and cannot be considered a theory at all.
3. Although these companies share some apparent similarities with the Japanese companies in terms of corporate culture, management practices, and employee relations policies, the rationale for their creation and the process by which they were developed and applied are quite different and are solidly rooted in American cultural values and sociopolitical environment. For example, Peters and Waterman identify eight attributes that, in their opinion, "characterize most nearly the distinction of the excellent, innovative companies."[32] These are a bias for action; closeness to the customer; autonomy and entrepreneurship; hands-on, value driven; stick to the knitting; simple form, lean staff; and simultaneous loose-tight properties.[33] It should be noted here that Peters and Waterman use criteria for measuring success far more rigorous and objective[34] than those used by Ouchi, who does not even clearly state his definition of what constitutes a successful company.

In other circumstances, it would be quite inappropriate to include these companies in this discussion because, by definition, the indigenous approach is not an example of the application of Japanese management techniques in the United States. However, we do so because the description completes the picture in terms of describing various approaches to management excellence and developing successful economic organizations, and because it also serves as a frame of reference. We hold that American companies must evolve indigenous strategies in order to succeed.

As we have argued, success in the future will go to those nations and institutions that can manage their resources in a highly uncertain and rapidly changing economic, technological, and sociopolitical environment. JABMAS compares poorly with successful and innovative American companies in nurturing creativity and entrepreneurship, and in managing under conditions of high risk and uncertainty. However, we agree with Peters and Waterman that one of the critical strengths of the successful companies is that they are "especially adroit at continually responding to changes of any sort in their environments." Nevertheless, we also disagree with their analysis and with their list of the attributes of excellence for successful American companies.

In Search of Excellence chooses successful companies on certain financial criteria during the period 1961 to 1980 and proceeds to identify those commonly shared characteristics that account for the success of the selected companies. This analysis, unfortunately, is flawed and detracts from an otherwise highly useful and informative book. The arbitrary selection of the time period helps to exclude certain companies that, in another time period, would have met the authors' criteria of both successful and excellently managed companies. Both Xerox and Polaroid fall into this category. For similar reasons, the authors might wish they had not included other companies that have, only one year after the publication of the book, been shown to be poor managers of change and "not excellent" at all. Data General, National Semiconductor, and Texas Instruments, among the authors' original list, belong in this group.

So we find that the authors' companies are not always successful in responding adroitly to changes in their environments. There may indeed be criteria that differ from the ones identified by Peters and Waterman that would account for the emergence of certain companies as excellently managed during particular time periods. By focusing on a specific time period, and especially financial measures of success and corporations as units of analysis, the authors miss an important opportunity to isolate the ingredients of corporate success that are more generic and longer lasting.

The authors' definition of environment may be too restrictive and somewhat artificial. Corporate success in a given environment depends not only on an understanding of economic functions, but also of sociopolitical factors. It is becoming increasingly apparent that quite often a corporation's profitability may be affected to an equal, if not a greater extent, by changes in societal expectations and in the sociopolitical and regulatory environment. By using historical data, the authors assume that the nature, complexity, and integrity of future changes will not be materially different from those in the past, and that strategies that have worked well in the past in dealing with those changes will be equally appropriate in the future. We contend that both assumptions are untenable.

By choosing companies that were successful during a specific time period and then analyzing their success, the authors have resorted to post facto rationalization. *In Search of Excellence* may be a good description of successful companies—and may even serve to explain why these companies succeeded—but it is not a good predictor of whether these or other companies will succeed in the future. In addition, the choice of companies as the unit of analysis forces Peters and Waterman to find commonly shared attributes that are often contrived. Moreover, all attributes are considered equally important. They miss the opportunity for a more careful analysis that could have yielded relative rankings of different attributes in terms of their importance in helping corporations adapt in a rapidly changing economic, technological, and sociopolitical environment. The selection of corporations as the unit of analysis also prevents Peters and Waterman from investigating other attributes that may be found in different combinations among other corporations and provide additional clues as to how companies might evolve and develop indigenous responses to a changing environment.[35]

In Chapter 11, we intend to remedy this situation by developing a set of attributes or operating characteristics that might be adapted by U.S. corporations in different combinations to cope with an uncertain external environment. Our emphasis will be on isolating and identifying certain ingredients for potential success within a framework that considers corporations as living organisms interacting with various elements of a holistic environment. A successful adaptation strategy would necessarily call for corporations' choosing responses that are uniquely suited to their own strengths and weaknesses from among a family of attributes and combining them in different proportions to meet particular needs.

Type D companies using the indigenous approach have consistently performed well by being in the social responsiveness mode during the first three stages of the issue life cycle. They have successfully anticipated societal expectations during the preproblem, problem identification, and remedy and relief stages, and are playing an active role in the formulation of those expectations. However, as we will note in the next chapter, the attributes of the indigenous approach as defined in this section are somewhat static. Although these attributes would no doubt keep type D companies in step with changing environmental conditions as we move into the prevention stage, they are unlikely to play an anticipatory and proactive role in the prevention stage unless they evolve a new set of strategies that call for a greater and more dynamic interaction between the institution and its environment.

NOTES

1. William J. Weisz, "Meeting the Japanese Challenge to American Industry," *Vital Speeches of the Day*, 48, 14, (May 1, 1982), pp. 440–443.
2. New York Stock Exchange, *People and Productivity: A Challenge to America* (New York, 1982), pp. 5–6.
3. William Ouchi, *Theory Z: How American Business Can Meet the Japanese Challenge* (Reading, Mass.: Addison-Wesley, 1981); see also Richard Tanner Pascale and Anthony G. Athos, *The Art of Japanese Management: Application for American Executives* (New York: Simon and Schuster, 1981); Ezra F. Vogel, *Japan as Number One: Lessons for America* (Cambridge, Mass.: Harvard University Press, 1979); and Richard Tanner Johnson and William G. Ouchi, "Made in America (Under Japanese Management)," *Harvard Business Review*, 52, 5 (September–October 1974), pp. 61–69.
4. Charles Burck, "Working Smarter," *Fortune*, June 15, 1981, pp. 68–73, vividly describes this factory-floor revolution applying Japanese management techniques at Pontiac's division of General Motors. An article in *Chemical Week* entitled "Quality Circles: How Chemical Companies Use a Japanese Tool," December 8, 1982, p. 36, relates the application of QC practices in the American chemical industry.
5. John Simmons and William J. Hares, "Reforming Work," *The New York Times*, October 25, 1982, p. A19.
6. New York Stock Exchange, *People and Productivity*.
7. "A Quality Concept Catches on Worldwide," *Industry Week*, April 16, 1978, p. 125.
8. "Quality Circles: How Chemical Companies Use a Japanese Tool."
9. "Quality Control Circles Pays Off Big," *Industry Week*, October 29, 1979, pp. 17–24.
10. Isolated illustrations of phenomenal success stories can be found in most trade journal articles describing QCs in their respective industries. See, for example, Perry Pascarella, "Quality Circles: Just Another Management Headache?" *Industry Week*, June 28, 1982, pp. 50–55; "Business Refocuses on the Factory Floor," *Business Week*, February 2, 1981, pp. 91–92; New York Stock Exchange, *People and Productivity;* and "Quality Control Circles Pays Off Big."
11. "Quality Circles: Just Another Management Headache?" Ibid., p. 53.
12. Statement of Dr. David Dotlich, corporate manager of human resources development, Honeywell Corporation, quoted in Perry Pascarella, "Human Management at Honeywell," *Industry Week*, July 27, 1981, p. 35.
13. Robert E. Cole, "A Japanese Management Import Comes Full Circle," *The Wall Street Journal*, February 22, 1983, p. 28.
14. New York Stock Exchange, *People and Productivity*, p. 44.
15. Jeremy Main, "How to Battle Your Own Bureaucracy," *Fortune*, June 29, 1981,

pp. 54–58; and "Westinghouse's Cultural Revolution," *Fortune,* June 15, 1981, pp. 74–93. These articles describe some of the approaches to job simplification at Intel and Westinghouse. We are not suggesting that Intel and Westinghouse follow the exploitation approach. Quite to the contrary, both companies fall into category C, the domestication approach. The difference is not what is done, but how and why it is done. Both companies exercise a large measure of consensus decision making that makes job simplification and other related measures more palatable to employees.

16. Main, "How to Battle Your Own Bureaucracy," p. 56.
17. "Westinghouse's Cultural Revolution," p. 80.
18. "Quality Circles: How Chemical Companies Use a Japanese Tool," pp. 38–39.
19. Charles D. Williams, Jr., "How You Can Optimize the QC Function in Your Firm," *Industrial Engineering,* March 1981, pp. 48–51.
20. Harry B. Ellis, "More Lessons from Japan—Case Studies Show Why U.S. Firms Lag on Productivity," *The Christian Science Monitor,* December 15, 1980, pp. 1, 13.
21. Bryan H. Berry, "Can GM Redesign the Manager-Worker Relationship?" *Iron Age,* March 10, 1982, pp. 37–42. See also Robert H. Guest, "Quality of Work Life—Learning from Terrytown," *Harvard Business Review* 57, 4 (July–August 1979), p. 76; and Charles G. Burck, "Can Detroit Catch-Up?" *Fortune,* February 8, 1982, p. 34.
22. Jeremy Main, "Ford's Drive for Quality," *Fortune,* April 18, 1983, pp. 62–70; and John Hoerr, "Commentary," *Business Week,* March 1, 1982, p. 91.
23. Norihiko Nakayama, ". . . And Some Japanese Remedies," *The New York Times,* March 30, 1980, Sec. 3.
24. Betsy Morris, "Striking Back—Black & Decker Meets Japan's Push Head-On in Power-Tool Market," *The Wall Street Journal,* February 18, 1983, pp. 1, 8.
25. See, for example, "Commentary: Smudging the Line between Boss and Worker," *Business Week,* March 1, 1982, p. 91; Pascarella, "Quality Circles: Just Another Management Headache?"; "Quality Circles Pays Off Big," *Industry Week,* October 29, 1979, p. 17; "Quality in the Making," *Money,* August 1981, p. 40; and John A. Young, "One Company's Quest for Improved Quality," *The Wall Street Journal,* July 25, 1982, p. 10.
26. Main, "How to Battle Your Own Bureaucracy," p. 54.
27. "Westinghouse's Cultural Revolution."
28. Perry Pascarella, "Humanagement at Honeywell," *Industry Week,* July 27, 1981, p. 33.
29. See, for example, John Koten, "GM-Toyota Venture Stirs Major Antitrust and Labor Problems," *The Wall Street Journal,* June 10, 1983, p. 1.
30. For some other examples of companies employing the indigenous approach, see Ouchi, *Theory Z.*
31. Thomas J. Peters and Robert J. Waterman, Jr., *In Search of Excellence* (New York: Harper & Row, 1982). Peters and Waterman identify following companies as having met all their criteria for excellent performance during the period 1961–1980: Allen-Bradely, Amdahl, Atari (Warner-Communications) Avon, Bechtel, Boeing, Bristol-Myers, Caterpillar, Cheseborough-Pond, Data General, Digital Equipment, Dana Corporation, Delta Airlines, Disney Productions, Dow Chemi-

cal, DuPont, Eastman Kodak, Emerson Electric, Flour, Frito-Lay (Pepsico), Hewlett-Packard, Hughes Aircraft, IBM, Intel, Johnson & Johnson, K-Mart, Levi-Strauss, Mars, Marriott, McDonald's, Maytag, Merck, Minnesota Mining & Manufacturing, National Semiconductor, Proctor & Gamble, Raychem, Revlon, Schlumberger, Standard Oil (Indiana)/Amoco, Texas Instruments, Tupperware (Dart U Craft), Wal-Mart, and Wang Labs.

32. Ibid., p. 13.
33. Ibid., pp. 13–16, 119–325.
34. Ibid., pp. 17–26.
35. For a very thoughtful, but quite critical, review of *In Search of Excellence,* see Daniel T. Carroll, "A Disappointing Search for Excellence," *Harvard Business Review* 61, 6 (November–December 1983), pp. 78–88.

TEN ▚▚▚

How and Where Shall the Twain Meet?

THE JAPANESE MIRACLE: AN EVALUATION

ONE OF THE MAIN OBJECTIVES OF THIS BOOK WAS TO UNDERTAKE A systematic analysis of Japanese management practices not only as a system of concepts and techniques, but more important, as the product of a unique sociopolitical context. This analysis was particularly aimed at evaluating the Japanese system in terms of its relevance for, and applicability to, the Western cultural and sociopolitical environment in general, and that of the United States in particular. We believe we have made a convincing case that the phenomenal economic success of Japan during the last thirty years or so cannot be ascribed solely to superior management techniques or employee relations practices. Nor can it be attributed mainly to "farsighted" and "enlightened" government direction of the Japanese economy and business institutions. Instead, it is based largely on an astute exploitation and adaptation of the unique factors in Japanese history and the sociocultural environment that have allowed Japan to generate enormous loyalty and productivity on the part of its people, and to direct those energies to a narrowly defined political and economic end.

We have also demonstrated the fact, and this is a point rarely made by promoters of the Japanese system, that this success has been achieved at enormous cost to the Japanese people and their environment. Despite all its success, Japanese management is not necessarily either more humane or more efficient, as some of its promoters would have us believe. Women, who make up more than one-third of the Japanese labor force, have quadrupled the part-time labor force in the last two decades. Their salaries are often necessary to maintain their family's middle-class status (70 percent of them are married). But their wages are half those of men, and they receive no fringe benefits or long-term security even though they work the same number of hours as men. They are even denied the opportunity to take entrance examinations leading to professional careers that are open only to men. According to Emiko Shibayama, "Women part-time workers are holding down the entire Japanese wage scale."[1] It would appear that use of part-time women workers is part of "Japan's international economic strategy for the 1980s."[2] Also, the less than 30 percent of workers who are part of the system are effectively denied economic mobility and have few rights of self-expression. Furthermore, the system has tolerated, until quite recently, a major abuse of its physical environment and ignored serious health hazards, and in many cases permanent physical damage, to those who have become victims of this engine of growth.

The Japanese system displays many of the elements of a command economy, albeit a flexible and more open one. And like all command economies, it can, and it has, achieved remarkable success in forcing its resources in a narrow developmental path. However, like all command economies, it can also become a captive of past success because past values become enshrined by an overvaluation of the policies and attitudes that brought success.

To the two factors already mentioned above we must now add a third one, which we believe has also played an important part in the Japanese miracle. This has to do with the manner in which the Japanese have managed to bend the rules of the game of international trade to their own benefit. What started out as an infant-industry argument by which Japan wanted to protect its industries from foreign competitors while it was rebuilding a war-devastated economy became a permanent albeit moving set of barriers whereby the Japanese protected their industries from foreign competitors while exploiting overseas market with all the quiet innocence of efficient traders competing in open markets for their fair share. It is ironic that both the United States and the Western European nations, when seeking more equitable treatment from the Japanese, have been defeated by a propaganda offensive wrapped in an atmosphere of injured innocence; it has been one small David confronting many Goliaths.

In this chapter, we put both the theory and practice of the Japanese business and management system under a microscope with a view to seeing what lies ahead for the system not only in terms of its applicability in the U.S. environment, but in terms of its impact on American corporations and the latter's ability to compete efficiently with the Japanese in domestic and overseas markets. This analysis will be done both at the macro level (business-government relations), and also at the micro level (management of the enterprise).

SOCIETAL EXPECTATIONS AND BUSINESS PERFORMANCE: THE NOTION OF A LEGITIMACY GAP

Societies and nations are living organisms, continuously changing and evolving. This is equally true for the United States and for Japan. In the United

States, change is a way of life. But although changes are easily accepted, America does not have a system of shared values strong enough to allow it to absorb the tremors that inevitably accompany changes in the social system. Japan has a largely homogeneous society and a stable set of values. However, the system is averse to change, especially change introduced from without, and therefore even small changes are very painful and create severe cultural shocks.

Social and economic institutions must also change in response to changing societal expectations. Those who anticipate changes in the environment and react to them positively survive and grow; those who do not stagnate and die. Both Japanese and American societies are changing, and American and Japanese management systems must also change. The failure of the American system has been amply demonstrated, but the success of the Japanese system in coping with a changing future is not certain either.

American corporations have failed because their short-run, pragmatic approach has led them to ignore the long-run consequences of their activities. Japanese corporations also risk failure because their secure environment has made them insensitive to changing societal expectations. The cumulative negative side effects of their activities are unlikely to be ignored or accepted in the future by the Japanese people. It is doubtful whether either of the systems can justify itself, in its present form, within its own sociocultural framework. To claim that one or the other can be transplanted, and would perform to expectations, is doubly suspect.

An evaluation of the performance of an institution, in this case JAB-MAS or ABMAS, must be to a large extent culturally based and temporally determined. A specific action is more or less socially responsible *only* within the context of time, place, and environment. Institutions survive and prosper to the extent that they meet society's expectations and thereby gain legitimacy. The larger the legitimacy gap between a society's expectations and institutional (corporate) performance, the greater the likelihood that the society will impose conditions on the institution and may even restrict its sphere of activity.

The notion of a legitimacy gap is not only rooted in the present; it also encompasses the future. It combines both facts (rational behavior) and perceptions (value orientations in causality and intent) that lend meaning to behavior. The legitimization process is not confined to an institution's activities (products and services in the case of business institutions), but extends to many other spheres: internal decision making; perception of the external environment; manipulation of that environment—physical, social, and political—to make it more receptive to the institution; and the nature of accountability to other institutions in the system.[3]

Viewed in this context, the social legitimacy or appropriateness of JABMAS can be examined within two cultural frameworks: Japan and the United States. The efficacy of JABMAS within Japan's recent past and present context has been discussed in detail earlier. What remains to be done is to see how the system might fare in Japan itself in the future. Japanese society is undergoing a gradual transformation whose pace is likely to accelerate. Change is being brought about as a consequence of internal pressures as groups seek to broaden their share of the economic pie and as people's expectations change in response to new realities. There are also external pressures as the Japanese are exposed to other cultures and value systems and are forced to examine their own within a broader perspective. Moreover, as other nations develop new strategies to respond to the Japanese challenge, the Japanese themselves must modify current responses to meet an altered international environment.

It is our contention that Japanese business is facing an environment beset with a high degree of uncertainty and risk. There is a greater measure of international competitiveness and a less protective domestic environment. The economic environment simultaneously requires a high level of techno- logical innovativeness and individual creativity. The production process must be at once cost effective and almost error free, requiring a large measure of automation and capital intensiveness. The service sector must be able to provide a high caliber of field support to the users of new high-technology products and manufacturing processes and at the same time absorb large numbers of workers rendered unemployed by the structural changes in the industrial system.

These attributes are more characteristic of the American economy in its present state than of the Japanese. What we are suggesting is that in the foreseeable future Japan is likely to face problems similar to the ones cur- rently confronting the economies of the United States and other West Euro- pean industrial societies. Can JABMAS meet this challenge? If so, then it is perhaps the answer to a great many of our problems. If not, how can it be forced to change? If these changes will alter JABMAS in some fundamental ways, it would be sheer folly for us to try and become more like the Japanese while they are trying very hard to become different from what they are. The next two sections address this question.

JABMAS IN A CHANGING JAPANESE SOCIETY

A careful review of business and economic activities in Japan in recent years shows that JABMAS has been undergoing significant change. Although the changes have not as yet attracted mass attention, they are affecting the con- cepts and practices that are at the core of JABMAS and provide it with its most distinctive, and widely appreciated, characteristics—lifetime employ- ment, a seniority-based wage system, and consensus decision making.

Three major factors account for these changes. One is the slowdown in Japan's economic growth and the resulting constraint on corporate expansion, which has exposed corporate inefficiencies in terms of an excessive labor force, a cumbersome decision-making process, and lack of innovativeness in generating new products and ideas. For example, in January 1983 the unemployment rate in Japan stood at 2.72 percent of the workforce, an all-time high since the government began keeping statistics in 1953. There were 1.65 million jobless Japanese, an increase of 300,000 from a year earlier. According to some experts, these figures would be considerably higher if the Japanese measured their unemployment figures the way other industrial nations do.[4] Moreover, given the changes that are currently under way in Japan, the unemployment problem may get worse as Japan's sluggish economy gets better. The squeeze on profits has forced many companies to abandon or modify their traditional management practices in the struggle for survival.

Two, Japan can no longer compete on the basis of production efficiencies alone; it is facing severe competition from other low-cost producers like South Korea and Taiwan. It must therefore compete in the area of high technology, which is associated with a high degree of risk and uncertainty, conditions for which JABMAS is ill-suited in its traditional form. Three, the Japanese people are themselves changing, and new generations are less apt to respond to traditional incentives and to conform rigidly to traditional social norms.

There is another irony in this situation. In their effort to cope with the new international environment, Japanese companies are modifying their traditional management practices as they relate to their employees in Japan. These changes also alter the social contract between Japanese workers and employers, between different groups of workers, and between society and business. Having unilaterally changed the terms of the social contract, Japanese business has unhinged these management practices from their social moorings, further contributing to the disequilibrium that currently prevails in Japan. The social contract that has acted as a binding agent is fraying. No one has yet come to grips with the consequences of its breaking, but the prospects are quite ominous.

Slow economic growth accompanied by increased competition from other industrializing countries, notably South Korea, has forced many Japanese companies to shift strategies and alter structures to meet the new realities. There is now greater willingness to allocate corporate resources on the basis of operating divisions in terms of contribution to revenues, cash flows, or role in the diversification and growth strategy. There is greater emphasis on international growth and expansion, including withholding the export of technologies that would strengthen the competitive position of countries like South Korea in Japan's traditional overseas markets, Western Europe and the United States. In terms of structure, some companies are introducing elements of functional management and are separating lifetime employment from the seniority-based wage system.[5]

Let's look more closely at some of the major changes currently under way in traditional Japanese management practices and the external factors that may significantly influence the direction of those changes.

Lifetime Employment

Although lifetime employment is extended to far fewer than a majority of Japanese workers, it is nevertheless one of the underpinnings of JABMAS. It creates a high degree of employee loyalty and is also congruent with Japan's value set. The success of lifetime employment in the past has depended not only on its inherent values of providing a flexible and dedicated workforce, but also on an uninterrupted high rate of economic growth.

During the postwar years, Japanese companies have resorted to a number of techniques to maintain lifetime employment during periods of normal business downturn. These include encouraging employees to take early retirement; placing permanent employees in maintenance and other routine and even trivial jobs previously performed by temporary workers, or not performed at all; transferring employees from one company to another within a group of companies; transferring employees from parent company to supplier firms; and lending workers from companies with excess capacity to those experiencing temporary shortages of labor. In a study by Sumitomo Bank, it was estimated that in 1977 manufacturing companies in Japan had a million "extra" workers who were assigned such jobs as messengers and doorkeepers.[6]

Until recently, large Japanese companies have been able to keep their lifetime employees on the payroll through these and similar practices. But their effect on individual workers and on the society has been painful. Moving regular employees to take jobs usually filled by temporary or outside workers had an effect similar to bumping in the United States, where an employee with greater seniority pushes out one with lower seniority. Workers pushed out in Japan by regular employees were those who had little protection and therefore could least afford to be without jobs. Transferring employees from the parent company to subsidiaries or suppliers does reduce the parent company's payroll. But it also forces subsidiaries and supplier firms to lay off their own employees to accommodate "imports" from the parent who may be less competent, equipped, or even interested in holding the jobs. Furthermore, employees in smaller companies—a condition typical of supplier firms—enjoy comparatively fewer lifetime guarantees and are therefore more vulnerable to external economic conditions. The situation is exacerbated when these companies are forced to absorb surplus employees from the parent company. Early retirement also forces otherwise experienced and capable workers to become "temporary" workers in order to support themselves—and without the benefits and job security of their earlier status.

In the past these hardships were tolerated and even accepted because downturns were considered short-run phenomena, and the hardships the price that must be paid by the few to maintain the overall vigor of the economic system. The selective displacement and relocation of workers was undertaken in a compassionate manner that took into account individual circumstances. Companies requested "early retirement" of those who had other means of financial support, or whose financial needs could be met from reduced income without too much hardship. Moreover, early retirement was accompanied by bonuses, albeit quite small, as an expression of the company's appreciation for loyalty and service. These bonuses were in addition to the usual retirement allowances and benefits an employee had earned for his years of service with a company.

Now, the situation has changed. Confronted with slowing economic growth and increased international competition, the Japanese see that the need to reduce the workforce is no longer temporary. Japanese companies have moved forcefully to reduce costs by upgrading plant and equipment and reducing the workforce as fast as they can. This is especially true in industries where foreign markets account for a large proportion of sales. For example, over a ten-year period Hitachi has trimmed its workforce by 15 percent or almost 76,000 workers, while tripling its sales. And the end is nowhere in sight. According to a survey by the Labor Ministry, about 29 percent of Japanese manufacturing companies believe they have excess workers, and 16 percent of them are currently considering cutbacks.[7]

These techniques of employee reduction have gained an aura of permanence, and employers' tactics have lost their gentility. Japanese companies are using coercive measures that are ripping the fabric of Japanese employer-worker relations and in the United States would be regarded as illegal. Excess capacity in such smokestack industries as steel, shipbuilding, and aluminum has forced companies to take drastic measures to reduce their payrolls. Many of the older, and slower, approaches are no longer available. Both inter- and intracompany transfers are becoming rare. For example, it was reported that in 1983 only two companies were able to make arrangements to transfer some of their employees to another company. Kawasaki Steel Corporation and Sumitomo Metal Industries, both of which had been hit by the recession, were able temporarily to transfer 80 and 40 of their employees, respectively, to a still growing minicar producer, Suzuki Motor Company.[8]

Early retirement is becoming increasingly less "voluntary." In the effort to make large cuts in payrolls, many companies have resorted to harrassing employees into voluntary and early retirement. For example, in February 1983 some petrochemical companies were pushing employees who were 45 or older to "voluntarily" retire.[9] In another case, between March and September 1979 Mitsui Heavy Industries removed 2,400 employees, 700 of whom were transferred to Toyota and other Mitsui subsidiaries. The remaining 1,700 were forced to take early or voluntary retirement.[10]

Those who retire early or "voluntarily" face significant hardships, mainly because they have little prospect of finding a job with a large corporation that pays comparable wages and carries the same prestige and social status. Even jobs at lower wages as temporary workers have become increasingly scarce in a recession economy. An even more important fact to remember is that "early" or "voluntary" retirement practices affect largely older workers. These people contributed to Japan's economic growth and corporate success in the 1960s and early 1970s by making great sacrifices and are now again being forced to suffer.

A major drawback of the lifetime employment system is the inherent rigidity in the size of the workforce. Since the oil crisis of 1973–74, many Japanese companies, in addition to cutting back the number of employees, have been making their workforces more flexible by reducing the number of lifetime employees and increasing the number of temporary workers. This category includes seasonal workers, part-time workers, and female workers who can be laid off at the companies' convenience. It would appear that the structure and composition of the workforce in large Japanese companies is beginning to skew, albeit gradually, toward more nonlifetime or temporary workers.[11] One indication of this shift can be measured in the number of university graduates who find jobs that even promise lifetime security. According to estimates by Nippon Recruitment Center, a private employment agency, in 1983 less than 28 percent of Japan's 230,000 university graduates were able to find work with the major companies that are more apt to offer "regular" or lifetime job opportunities.[12]

One aspect of the lifetime employment system is the network of interpersonal relationships that provides another of the building blocks of the Japanese management system. The system is very insular and resistant to the inclusion of outside experts. However, as more and more Japanese companies move into high-technology areas, they are finding it impossible to develop and train people in large enough numbers from within to meet their needs. They must therefore seek an infusion of outside talent, especially at the professional and managerial levels.

All these changes are having a significant impact on the traditional employer-employee relationship. Although its dimensions are not yet clear, certain observations are possible. The success of lifetime employment is based on a dual set of expectations and mutual obligations between employers and workers. The employer guarantees a lifetime job at reasonable rates commensurate with the company's own growth and profitability. The employee is expected to work diligently and dedicate himself to the success of the employer. So as more and more companies begin to lay off excess workers, those workers feel betrayed. Those who remain behind realize that it is not "their" company any more, and that they may also be discharged if the company decides it cannot keep them. When older workers are forced to take early retirement in increasingly larger numbers, a sense of abandonment adds to the feeling of betrayal. The changes adversely affect employee loyalty and morality, making the workforce less dedicated and dependable.

The Seniority-Based Promotion and Wage System

The seniority-based promotion and wage system, coupled with lifetime employment, implied that almost all regular employees would receive higher positions and responsibilities as they reached "appropriate" age levels. This is easily accomplished in a growing company and an expanding economy. But problems occur when the economy can no longer absorb the expanding cadre of middle- and upper-level managers. Japanese companies are reducing some of the excess through early retirement. When this is not possible, promotions are achieved through elevation into undefined positions and newly established ranks.[13]

The bloated middle in the organization, however, has the undesirable effect of slowing down an already cumbersome decision-making process. Some companies have even gone so far as to put excess middle-level managers who were incapable or incompetent into sideline positions without specific job responsibilities. These managers are usually called *madogiwa-zoku,* or those who sit along windows. They get paid, but they do not do any work; they sit by windows and spend their days looking through them. This is a rather clear message that the employee is not wanted.[14] *Madogiwa-zoku* are largely people between the ages of 40 and 55 who have not reached top management positions or who have little prospect of reaching top management before retirement.

The older employee suffers emotionally, financially, and socially because all aspects of his life are inextricably intertwined with his employment and place of work. The system also has a demoralizing effect on younger people who are just behind the baby boom generation and foresee little opportunity to be promoted to top management by the time they are 55. According to a study by the Tokyo Chamber of Commerce, only 10 percent of current employees are ever likely to get managerial positions in other companies, down from 62 percent in 1965.[15]

While sidelining employees may help in promoting younger, more qualified employees, it is also fraught with danger. And it is a technique not particularly suited even to the Japanese system. It creates friction between employees of the same age, thereby weakening the bonds among members of primary groups, and strains working relationships between primary and secondary groups. It also promotes favoritism, because in an ill-defined organization, where job responsibility is not specific and performance is group-oriented, measurement of individual performance is never totally objective and contains a large element of personal judgment and feeling. Large companies are developing alternative career paths that increasingly incorporate some aspect of compensation directly related to an individual's performance. This change signals a distinct departure from traditional Japanese practices.

Decision Making by Consensus

The strength of decision making by consensus lies in its deliberativeness and in the involvement of all those who will be responsible for the implementation of decisions. Japanese companies are confronting new conditions that make some of the virtues of the existing systems also their main drawbacks:

1. The rapid rate of technological growth and change introduces new risks and uncertainties, calling for different types of inputs into the decision-making process, ones that do not fit the organizational structure. In fact, the most important skills necessary to evaluate risks may not even be available within the organization.
2. The nature of markets, competition, and lead times for making decisions is becoming increasingly shorter, requiring fast reaction times.
3. The need to protect all those involved creates a bias toward risk avoidance.

These conditions are forcing Japanese companies to modify the consensus decision-making style. Companies with the greatest exposure to new technologies and new competition, such as Sony, are also the ones breaking away from the conventional systems. And this trend is accelerating. Some companies are striving to reduce the length of decision-making time by sidelining "excess" middle managers and limiting the number of people involved in the decision process. Other companies encourage senior executives to work closely with middle and lower-level managers, to inform them of the overall strategies of the firm and management's thinking, thereby providing those below with a clearer indication of the types of actions that will receive top management's approval.[16]

    Some Japanese companies have also attempted to use the matrix system to overcome the problem of incorporating new inputs into their decision-making structures. The most notable examples are Seiko, Matsushita, and Sumitomo Bank.[17] It is argued that the Japanese management system already shares some of the characteristics of the matrix system. Its lack of rigid structure and open communication system make it particularly suitable for the matrix system. However, a careful analysis of the Japanese system and the matrix form leads us to believe that this is not the case. Despite overt similarities, Japanese consensus decision making and corporate culture are inimical to the matrix type of organizational structure and decision making. The former is geared to risk avoidance by encompassing all known and potentially important elements in the decision-making process. It is insular; it avoids what it considers threatening and therefore does not want to see. The matrix system, on the other hand, has as its primary objective risk management by incorporating diverse, and hitherto unconventional, elements into the process. The two systems are geared to achieve fundamentally different objectives and flourish in very different corporate cultures.[18]

These changes in the Japanese system are not without their problems. Any shortening of the process tends to "exclude" people who were previously part of the management team. A reduction in the time span and more direct involvement by top management lead to dissatisfaction among the lower ranks, who consider their initiative and expertise not adequately appreciated by the company. Thus the system acquires more and more of the trappings of Western-style top-down decision making, which the corporate culture is not equipped to handle. The result is alienation and the erosion of employee loyalty.

The Not So Loyal Unions

One of the triads of JABMAS has been the company-based union that sees its fortunes tied to those of the company. The system has worked so far because employers have given first preference to the interests of the employees in making structural decisions. Employee loyalty was fostered through lifetime employment, a seniority-based wage system, and a generous sharing of corporate prosperity. However, the new employer tactics are causing strains in the traditional company-union relationship.

In the past, Japanese workers and unions had willingly embraced automation because it improved productivity and wealth. Now, unions are viewing the new trend toward automation with alarm. Driven by a need to cut costs rapidly, Japanese companies have quickened the shift toward automation and robotics, with the primary objective of reducing the size of the workforce. They are paring their existing payrolls and hiring fewer new workers. In 1982, for example, Nissan Motor Company hired 2,650 new blue collar workers. In 1983, it planned to hire less than half that number. Nissan's explanation for fewer new recruits was increased competition from such low-wage countries as South Korea, lower auto exports to the United

States and West European countries due to voluntary quotas, and reduced need for workers due to extensive investment in robotics and other labor saving-equipment.[19]

The worsening unemployment situation has been exacerbated by new automation. Added to these are the structural changes brought by the new manufacturing technology. Older workers are finding their skills obsolete, and are increasingly being reassigned, often repeatedly. In the past, reassignments were infrequent and confined primarily to younger, unskilled workers. Older workers are also being asked to work under the supervision of younger, more technically trained workers, thereby disrupting the traditional seniority-based relationships. Among the younger workers, there is an increasing disparity in wages. The technically trained few, the new elite on the shop floor, receive higher wages compared to the vast majority of similar-age but unskilled workers.

Even more important, the robotic-based automation has increased the trend toward greater use of part-time employment because previously skilled tasks can now be performed by relatively unskilled workers pushing buttons. Some 4.2 million of Japan's 58.3 million workers are part-timers, up 21 percent from five years ago. More than two-thirds of them are women. A large majority of part-time workers put in seven hours or more a day in some occupations. They receive between one-half to two-thirds the wages of the full-time employees and have no fringe benefits.[20]

As a consequence of all these changes, there is beginning to be a noticeable shift in the traditional union acquiescence to management needs and willingness to accept management's explanations at face value. In particular:

- The General Council of Trade Unions of Japan has launched a campaign to spread work by reducing the average work week from 5.5 days to 5 days.
- Unions have won agreements aimed at protecting the job of older workers. These include provisions for training in new skills, protection against job or wage downgrading, and sharing the productivity benefits of new technology.
- To save the jobs of older workers, unions are also demanding an increase in the current mandatory retirement age of 55 years. They have already won this concession from some major trading houses, and from steel and electric appliance makers.
- To help offset the effect of these measures on new recruits, Japan's Council of Metalworkers' Unions and other labor groups have begun a nationwide campaign to persuade employees to spread the work by taking all the paid vacation time they earn each year.
- Efforts are also under way to cut the growth of part-time jobs.

If these efforts do not succeed, they may very well force the unions to become more militant. However, to the extent that they do succeed, they will dissipate some of the savings in wage costs generated by the companies through automation. They will also adversely affect Japan's international competitive position and potentially hurt its exports and domestic employment.

The New Ferment in Japanese Society

There are also indications of social unrest in Japanese society that are likely to weaken the traditional bonds between corporations and workers. The high-technology industries—especially electronics, telecommunications, and biotechnology—are catching the disease of Silicon Valley. Three factors account for this tendency:

1. Decision making by consensus, employed by many large companies, often discourages initiative and the pursuit of imaginative ideas. The basic premise of consensus decision making is homogeneity among members, not heterogeneity.
2. Personnel policies such as seniority-based wage and promotion systems cannot better compensate highly specialized employees who are fully aware of the value of their services to the company.
3. Probably most important, many Japanese have started to question the notion of single-company loyalty and compensation based on seniority rather than performance. Most Japanese workers still acquire company-specific skills through in-house training, and are reluctant to move. This practice is reinforced by strong social norms that make it difficult for employees to find work with other employers.[21]

However, as the Japanese become more exposed to Western culture and standards, their traditional norms are weakening. Workers with high-technology skills are finding it easier to change jobs and demand skill-based wages.

For the first time, young engineers and other individuals with specialized skills are forsaking the security of large corporations and are joining smaller firms or opting to establish their own firms, in search of quick growth and bigger financial rewards.[22] The most dramatic demonstration of this phenomenon came to light in early 1980 when 80 computer technicians and salesmen walked out from lifetime jobs at Ishikawajima-Harima Industries, Japan's second-largest heavy machinery maker, and formed Cosmo-80, a computer systems design consulting firm.[23] The company is owned and operated by the employees.

Some large Japanese companies in high-tech industries and markets have become painfully aware of their inability to promote individual creativity that goes beyond more efficient application of existing technologies. Realizing that small size and an entrepreneurial environment are important for the innovative process, companies like Hitachi and Nippon Electric are experimenting with self-contained cells or satellite organizations to bring together employees who possess scarce skills and give them a free hand to pursue new product ideas.[24]

Japanese business is also giving up some of its hallowed traditions. For example, in 1982 chief executives of Japan Airlines and Mitsukoshi Department Stores refused to resign from their jobs, as is the custom, when their companies ran into problems.[25] Some companies are overtly forsaking traditional practices and operating more like the American companies in their management style and competitive practices.[26]

More subtle changes in attitudes are harbingers of more serious problems for the Japanese business system. For the first time, some Japanese executives are putting family and home life ahead of work life. Many managers are willingly changing jobs from big, prestigious companies to smaller, less well known companies so that they can avoid frequent tours of duty overseas,[27] spend more time with their families, and have greater freedom at work. Young people seeking their first jobs are openly expressing preferences for smaller companies and showing a disinclination to work longer hours at a sacrifice to their personal lives. Public opinion polls show a growing concern among the Japanese that there is too much work and too little play. Traditionalists are alarmed that these tendencies, especially among the young, will undermine the diligence that helped create the postwar economic miracle.[28]

There is also evidence that women are becoming more dissatisfied with their lot as their numbers in the workforce increase. A 1982 government white paper reported that although most women were still content with their responsibilities as keepers of the home, only 13 percent felt they were given equal status at work, and only 10 percent believed they were treated equally in terms of social perceptions and customs. According to Shigeo Saito, author of a national sex survey, there were increasing signs of warning from women about frustrations that were being ignored by men.[29]

RELEVANCE AND ADAPTABILITY OF JAPANESE MANAGEMENT TECHNIQUES IN THE UNITED STATES

The patterns of Japanese management techniques, and the mode of their utilization in the United States by both Japanese and American companies, were examined in detail in Chapters 5, 8, and 9. The next step, and the most critical one, is to ask whether the sociocultural antecedents, societal expectations, and evolving public needs in the United States can and will respond to the ministrations of the Japanese management system. Alternately, can the Japanese system adapt itself to meeting the needs of its host culture without, in the process, largely losing its own identity and essential characteristics? We contend that the answer to both questions is "no." As we will demonstrate, the gap between societal expectations and the adaptability of Japanese management practices to their new environment is unbridgeable. Furthermore, the changing needs of American society and its business institutions—in both their domestic and international competitive environment—make JABMAS of limited value to American business and society.

We will focus on the notion of the prevailing and the projected gap between societal expectations and corporate ability to respond to them, in the case of both American and Japanese-controlled companies in the United States. To facilitate our analysis, the cultural and sociopolitical attributes of American society have been grouped into two broad categories. The individual-group dimension refers to the primary focus of a society's concern —with the individual and the group, respectively, representing the core values of American and Japanese societies. Similarly, the business-government dimension is designed to convey the nature of political and governmental control over private economic institutions. Adversarial relations are characteristic of the American system, whereas cooperative-collusive relations are typical of the Japanese system. Management characteristics have also been grouped into two categories spanning two extremes in values. One dimension comprises all those elements that deal with the system of performance evaluation and rewards, and ranges from highly individualistic to largely group-based. The other has to do with decision-making style and ranges from top-down authoritarianism to consensualism.

Individual-Group Orientation

Exhibit 10–1 illustrates the gap between the intensity of societal expectations of corporate behavior to be individual- or group-oriented, and our perception of corporate performance on this dimension on the part of both American businesses and Japanese-controlled companies in the United States. One of the most important differences between United States and Japanese corporations lies in their congruence to the value sets of Japanese and Americans. As we demonstrated in Chapter 2 and 5, Japanese culture is rooted in groupism, whereas American culture is rooted in individualism. People in both societies form groups, for without cooperative group activities, social organization and progress are impossible. However, the major difference—and the one that is conveniently ignored by boosters of the Japanese system in the United States—is that in Japan a person must join particular groups that are

EXHIBIT 10–1 Gap between Societal Expectations and Corporate Behavior by American and Japanese-Controlled Businesses in the United States: Individual-Group Orientation

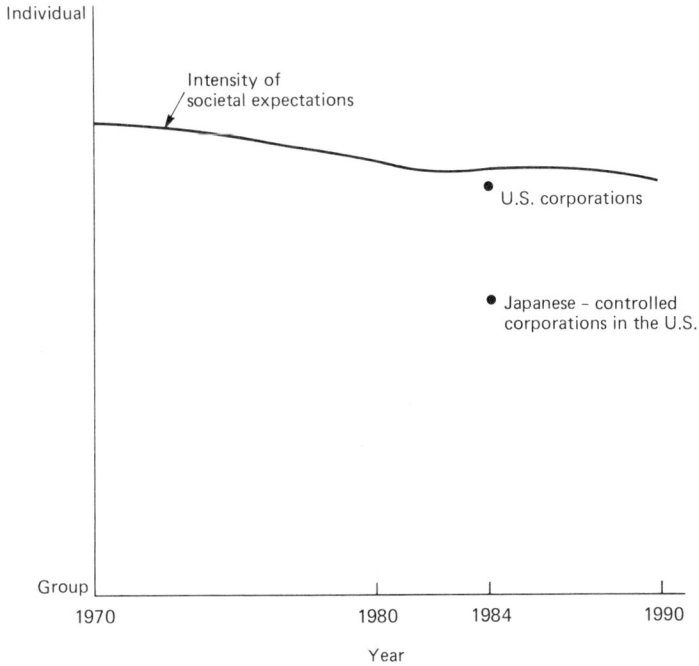

Individual

Intensity of
societal expectations

U.S. corporations

Japanese – controlled
corporations in the U.S.

Group

1970   1980   1984   1990

Year

prescribed for him or her. There is little discretion in joining and no choice of exit. There are no alternative groups from which to choose, and he or she must remain a member in good standing regardless of personal cost. The criteria for membership is not "what the group can do for me," but "what I can do for the group." The individual is indentured, body and soul, to the group. The group is a living organism whose existence is quite independent of its current membership. There is a form of egalitarianism that results in perverse inequalities by standardizing rewards that give little consideration to individual contributions or preferences.

In sharp contrast, group activity in the United States is voluntary, with multiple avenues for participation open to individuals. Membership criteria are quite the opposite from those prevailing in Japan. An individual voluntarily cooperates in the group activity based on his or her perception of the benefits to be derived from such participation. Americans engage in group activity on the basis of enlarged benefits that will accrue to them from participation, balanced against the loss of individual freedom that is surrendered to the group. Group loyalty is comparatively weak. Egalitarianism is expressed in the form of equality of opportunity, which results in different outcomes for individuals based on their individual contributions and preferences for rewards.

Many of the unique characteristics of JABMAS stem from, and receive societal support from, this collectivistic orientation. Groupism requires stability of the group and its members, lifetime employment, involvement of every member in decision making, consensual decision making or *ringisei,* and "fair" distribution of group earnings according to a seniority-based and life-style-oriented wage and bonus system. The system has survived and flourished because its underlying premise, operating conditions, and distribution of social rewards conform to cultural norms and social expectations that endow it with a strong sense of legitimacy.

Exhibit 10–1 illustrates our belief that there is a gradual, but very small, rate of decline in American society's preference for individualism, although it remains a dominant social value and is likely to continue to be so for a long time. In this we disagree with George Lodge, who in *The New American Ideology*[30] contended that American ideological values were becoming more communitarian in orientation. The current decline in individualism reflects, at best, a public concern for the often destructive aspects of excessive pursuit of self-interest at the cost of vital community interests. Public opinion polls also show that large segments of the American population want corporations to play a more active and positive role in increasing the quality of work life. In addition to jobs and income, organizations should also contribute toward making work more challenging and fulfilling. This attitude reflects public concern that the activities of large corporations do not mesh with the value of individualism.

These corporations affect every aspect of our lives; when left on their own, their pursuit of self-interest can be injurious to those who are unable to protect their interests against corporate power. Thus this group concern is more an expression of protecting one form of individualism against the excesses of other forms. There is also the realization that certain social problems cannot be solved through voluntary cooperation because the competing groups—for example, present vs. future generations—are not equally represented in the consensus-building process, and that the interests of the disenfranchised groups must be protected until they are strong enough to compete on an equal basis. The American public is also concerned that it is losing out in international competition because other societies have used collective means—state support—to subsidize their industries, so different measures are called for to compete in the international arena. What is important to note, however, is that the new emphasis on groupism does not reflect a basic change in value orientation, but only a marginal correction to meet specific social needs and remedy particular situations. There is still widespread aversion to mandatory groupism.

As Exhibit 10–1 shows, we believe there is a large gap between the expectations of Americans and the behavior of Japanese companies in the United States in terms of their orientation toward individualism. As Japanese companies establish their United States operations, they have attempted to introduce group-oriented values in those operations. These approaches have had limited success because they have been introduced at the lowest level of organization, where Japanese companies have capitalized on another American trait, a desire to have some control over one's destiny. Their success at higher levels and under more complex situations has been negligible. Fearing that forced groupism is inimical to the American mentality, Japanese managers have confined it to Japanese workers. However, as we saw in the case of Itoh (Chapter 4), this trend is fraught with danger because it creates a perverse form of discrimination that is abhorrent to most Americans, in addition to being illegal. The total integration of the American workforce into the Japanese management system is not possible both because the company cannot do it and because American workers do not want it. Japanese workers are tied into the home-office-based system of organization, compensation, and career mobility. American workers eventually want to succeed within their own sociocultural milieu. They view a paternal approach as an encroachment on their privacy and a denial of their individual rights.

Thus we conclude that a group orientation based on coercion and perceived against individual self-interest, either as a social norm or as a corporate goal, has little prospect of succeeding in the United States. If Japanese companies insist on pursuing it, the niceties of the Japanese approach will lose their appeal, and anti-Japanese feeling will intensify. Moreover, the legal and political system will not allow for individual exceptions that take into account the cultural pecularities of a foreign management system and apply to a particular set of workers. External groups will force changes on the Japanese companies by resorting to judicial processes when an apparent violation of law has taken place, thereby foreclosing any discretionary options available to the Japanese companies.

There are two other important reasons why a group orientation is not in the best interests of American society or the business community. The success of groupism in Japan is based on a set of reciprocal obligations between the group and the individual. In return for lifetime devotion and loyalty, the employee receives a lifetime guarantee of protection from the group. In the absence of such a social contract, an initially desirable shift toward a group orientation can easily lead from paternalism to despotism and totalitarianism. Lacking norms of social accountability, group leaders will consolidate their power, perpetuate themselves, and crush any opposition to their rule. Instead of more cooperative and mutually beneficial organizations, we will be saddled with repressive and highly inefficient organizations. Examples of such tendencies abound in the United States, where corporate chief executives, unfettered by effective stockholder control or independent boards, act like ruling monarchs unwilling to listen to any voices except those that are variations of their own. Although such executives may be successful in the short run, they invariably fail because, by losing their willingness to listen to and deal with dissenting opinions, they also lose their capacity to adapt to a changing external environment. One of the reasons for the failure of state-owned enterprises both in the United States and in Europe can be traced to their relative immunity to threats from the external environment.

Another important factor has to do with the changes that are currently occurring in the nature of technology and industry. We are in the throes of a second Industrial Revolution based on electronics and information management.[31] As we will demonstrate later in our discussion of business-government relations and the alleged need for an industrial policy for the United States, there is more rather than less need for individual creativity and entrepreneurship if we are to meet the challenges of the future. As we have seen, Japanese business is changing and providing for greater individual initiative in its growth industries. Groupism may be highly useful in organizing known activities with predictable outcomes where group norms can be established to motivate members to give their best efforts for the common good, where the individual is protected against group tyranny, and where collective effort is more rewarding for the individual. However, in a highly uncertain future, a group orientation is likely to retard progress because of the group's natural preference for protecting current gains and aversion toward risk taking. We will be sadly remiss in our responsibility if we give up one of our most valuable assets, individualism, for a pursuit of groupism when it is externally imposed and not voluntarily sought.

Business-Government Relations

The success of Japanese business is often attributed in part to the close cooperation between business and government. In Japan, government agencies, especially the Ministry of Trade and Industry (MITI), take a leading role in creating a national consensus for economic growth, directing industrial trends, protecting Japanese industry from external competition during periods of restructuring and development, and through administrative guidance, financial assistance, and other measures, restructuring declining industries and fostering the development of high-growth industries.[32] American business-government relations, on the other hand, have been described as largely adversarial, uncoordinated, often contradictory, and in many cases not suitable for the future.[33]

Exhibit 10–2 shows the business-government relations dimension as ranging between adversarial on the one hand and cooperative-collusive on the other. The intensity of American expectations are projected to be curvilin-

EXHIBIT 10–2 Gap between Societal Expectations and Corporate Behavior by American and Japanese-Controlled Businesses in the United States: Business-Government Relations

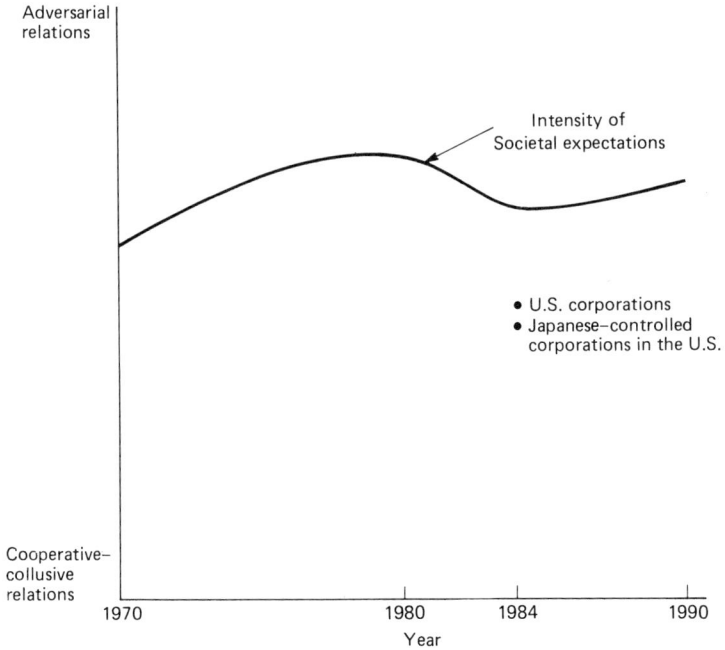

ear, although they remain overwhelmingly in favor of keeping a large distance between the two institutions. This is in conformity with the American tradition of checks and balances, and of distrust of all large institutions. At present we see an increased public desire for improved cooperation and less hostility between business institutions and the government. However, we consider it to be a temporary phenomenon, because: (1) in times of slowdown in economic activity, Americans have sought greater government intervention in the markets, including direct support of business to spur employment and economic activity; and (2) intense foreign competition, in both domestic and foreign markets, has resulted in loss of sales and market share, forcing American industry to seek government protection. Labor and other segments of the public have also been voicing support for such protection.

We feel that once the economy picks up, there will be an increase in the desire to maintain a gap between business and government. This is especially so because in the United States, excessive cooperation between business and government is not perceived to be in the public interest. Business is viewed as manipulating government agencies to achieve its ends, and through campaign contributions and lobbying trying to influence behavior of elected officials in directions inimical to consumer and public interests. Even the present recognition of the need for less destructive and confrontational type of business-government relations has not changed the original perception. For example, opinion polls show that people, by and large, recognize that government regulation is often cumbersome, inefficient, and leads to higher prices. Nevertheless, the large majority of the American public prefer to maintain current levels of government regulation of business, and even increase it, in areas dealing with health, worker safety, and pollution.

It was shown earlier that in the case of the other three dimensions, the behavior of Japanese and U.S. corporations differed markedly from each other in terms of meeting societal expectations of the American public. However, in the case of business-government relations dimension, there is a striking agreement among U.S. and Japanese firms that there should be a more cooperative relationship between business and government. This is despite the fact that the American public is unlikely to share this view.

In the case of the Japanese companies, this attitude is understandable. As was shown in Chapter 2, Japanese business and government have had a long tradition of close cooperation where business closely identified with the policy goals of the Japanese government, and where the government provides a variety of direct and indirect support to help business succeed within the framework of Japan's overall policy objectives. The relationship is highly symbiotic and incestuous. Business not only thrives under the benevolent protection of the government, but through an intricate web of cultural, economic and sociopolitical relations, plays an important role in the determination of national agenda itself, thereby minimizing the scope of future conflict during the implementation phase.

The Drive Toward an Industrial Policy for the United States

The growing desire for similar cooperation in the United States is in strong contrast to the American business philosophy of free markets and minimum government intervention. It also runs counter to American cultural norms and values. Thus, in a special report analyzing America's current economic malaise, *Business Week* blames it on a failure by labor and management to end their adversary relationship, contradictory government regulation and policies, and the decline of the infrastructure and the educational system. Furthermore, it argues that decades of recessions, bouts of roaring inflation, near-depression levels of unemployment, the deteriorating competitiveness of basic industries, sliding productivity, the painful adjustment to dependence on high-priced foreign oil, and a stagnating standard of living have shaken America's confidence in its ability to prosper and remain the world's leading industrial power.[34] These concerns have led to a concerted effort by a number of powerful groups, including some large industries and organized labor, to promote a national planning system in which business, labor, and government would cooperate to develop a more rational program for the "reindustrialization" of America.

In the past, there have been many occasions when the United States considered some form of national economic planning. The idea was invariably scrapped because it was considered ideologically flawed and practically unworkable.[35] The current drive for national economic planning is being presented under the rubric of "industrial policy," which is perceived as somewhat narrower and more pragmatic in scope.[36] In many ways, it is more ingenious and highly ambitious. Unlike the old idea of national planning, which was aimed at developing a national design while leaving the lower-level decisions to the private sector, the new approach asserts that it can make those decisions better by predicting the winning and losing industries in the world competitive game, and selecting particular industries and corporations in the winning industries for special government attention and help.[37] The program is being advocated in one form or another by all the Democratic presidential candidates. According to Senator Kennedy: "Historically, the unifying issue for the Democratic party has been the economic issue. We need the restoration of our economy. The basis for the restoration is the development of an industrial policy."[38] The Reagan administration, worried about the Democrats gaining an edge, has created a National Commission on Industrial Competitiveness headed by J. A. Young, president and chief executive officer of Hewlett-Packard.[39]

The supporters of the new industrial policy offer a number of reasons for advocating such a program.[40]

1. The United States has been de-industrializing, as shown by the sharp decline in national output and employment devoted to manufacturing products. There is an absolute decline in the nation's heavy and basic industries, and the edge in high-technology industry is either gone or is going.[41]
2. U.S. management and labor may not be able to make the necessary structural transition from older, declining heavy industries to newer, high-technology industries. A reduction in structural unemployment would entail retraining costs that cannot be borne either by the declining industries or the unemployed workers.
3. The United States is losing its competitive edge in world export markets. The loss of competitive edge may mean the loss of world leadership.
4. Other countries have been successful with industrial policies. Government agencies have played critical roles in selecting winners in the technological race, moving capital away from ailing industries and easing the transition pains of workers through subsidies and training assistance. Again, Japan is cited as a perfect example for the United States to emulate.[42]
5. U.S. industrial policy needs more cohesiveness and greater coordination. Thus, even the staunchly free market Reagan administration has proposed the establishment of a Department of Trade and Industry (DITI), to be patterned after Japan's MITI. It is further argued that the United States already has an industrial policy in that it intervenes quite significantly in many aspects of industry and trade, but that implementation of these policies is scattered among different government departments that often pursue contradictory policies.[43]

The new concept of an industrial policy covers a large number of ideas as to definition, process, and desired outcomes. There is no unanimity as to what such a policy might entail, making it difficult to evaluate the arguments made by its advocates. Nevertheless, certain common threads can be perceived.

1. The plan will have some type of mechanism for coordinating labor, business, and government efforts.[44] For example, Owen Bleber of the United Auto Workers would create a National Strategic Planning Board with members from labor, business, government, and public interest groups; a bureau to help rehabilitate waning industries and their workers; various industry strategy committees; and a national technology commission. Others would set up a Federal Industrial Coordination Board with members from banking, industry, labor, government, and the public to set national,

regional, and sectoral industrial goals, and an Economic Cooperation Council to map long-term economic strategy.
2. There would be a centralized bureaucracy staffed by dedicated civil servants who would collect data, create coalitions, develop strategies, coordinate diverse interests, and implement policies. It is recognized that this would create an entrenched bureaucracy with tremendous power to make and influence national economic policy. But Ezra Vogel argues that although transplanting the Japanese experience would not be easy, the United States has no choice but to establish a cadre of senior-level bureaucrats who are paid competitive salaries and allowed a great deal of freedom to manage programs in their respective areas.[45]
3. One of the most important elements of the policy would be the selection of winners and losers, and spurring the winners with capital and other measures to expedite their progress while helping the losers to adjust to their reduced size.[46]

These proposals for an industrial policy have evoked strong criticism and opposition from a great number of distinguished economists of every orientation. They have also been criticized by political scientists, sociologists, and other opinion leaders. Herbert Stein, chairman of the Council of Economic Advisors under President Nixon, calls the industrial policy proposals a mechanism for creating a "corporate-union welfare state."[47] Charles Schultze, president-elect of the American Economic Association (1983–84), states: ". . . one of the measures this nation does not need is an industrial policy under which the Federal Government, through loans, subsidies, and other devices, tries to play an important role in allocating investment among individual firms."[48] We concur with these observations and contend that the case for an industrial policy is based on faulty data. The successes of MITI and an industrial policy in Japan are grossly exaggerated, while their failures are glossed over. Moreover, as we will demonstrate, the premise on which the need for an industrial policy is based is inaccurately stated. It attempts to solve problems that will not respond to its ministrations. It would only create more problems in the process.

To begin with, proponents have oversold the role of an industrial policy in Japan's success and the efficiency with which it has worked in that country. The Japanese miracle, as we have tried to demonstrate, has been the product of a complex set of interdependent factors, none of which alone, or in combination with other factors, can produce similar results in an alien environment. Nor is it certain that it will produce similar results even in its own environment in the future, given a change in that internal environment and the influence of new international trends. The success of MITI in the period immediately following World War II was made possible by the obvious nature of what needed to be done to rebuild Japan, and by cultural and sociopolitical factors that facilitated a coalescing of various interests and a centralized direction of effort.[49] As Charles Schultze points out, "Japanese save and invest 30 to 35 percent of their Gross National Product, compared to 17 to 19 percent in the United States. . . . If you invest 30 percent of your income, you can do many things that you simply cannot do with only 18 percent."[50] He argues that it is this feature, coupled with cooperative labor-management relations, that explains Japan's success, and not an industrial policy. A high rate of directed investment has enabled Japan to have a modern and efficient plant in a variety of export-oriented industries and thereby dominate world markets.

Even with the supportive environment, however, the record is not unblemished. MITI has not always done well in picking winners, and the outlook is even more cloudy. MITI tried to keep Honda out of its restructuring of the automobile industry. Honda succeeded even in the face of MITI's discouragement and without any government help. Japan's modern steel industry is suffering from excess capacity, and shipbuilding is hemorrhaging from heavy losses. Moreover, MITI's chances of picking winners in the high-tech race are not guaranteed when both the nature and the degree of risk are not easily ascertained. As Dr. Arno N. Penzias, a Nobel Laureate in physics, points out: "The magnificent cooperation of the Japanese in cultivating their inherent homogeneity, diligence and hard work will not necessarily guarantee future success. . . . thinking alike is better suited to running smooth production lines than to exploring and innovating."[51] A case in point, according to Penzias, is artificial intelligence, or inventing machines that seem to think, where the Japanese are avowedly making a strong and concerted push to overtake the Americans. The field is highly complex and full of surprises; breakthroughs cannot be guaranteed in the developmental stages simply by preselecting the most promising lines of inquiry.

But even if the idea of an industrial policy has some theoretical merit, its successful implementation in the United States is highly questionable. The ultimate test of an industrial policy must rest on two factors: (1) whether it can develop a method that will permit the nation to choose the winners and discard the losers, and (2) whether such a process can indeed predict who will be the winners and who must be the losers. The proponents of an industrial policy recognize these problems and suggest giving responsibility to some type of regulatory body composed of representatives of competing interests, or a bureaucracy with great discretion to make decisions independent of political intervention. A coalition of business and other interest groups would not create new industries; it would protect existing industries. Professor Herbert Stein, former CEA chairman, argues that labor would certainly not want to contribute to the contraction of an industry in which high wage rates are a major part of the problem. For that matter, industry leaders would not deliberately seek to write off large chunks of investment.

Instead, there would be greater emphasis on "protecting" industries and "preserving" jobs. There is ample historical evidence to prove this. Furthermore, it is unrealistic to expect congressional representatives to give up their authority in areas that vitally affect the economies of their localities and therefore their constituents.[52] MITIzation is incompatible with the way America works. . . . To put it succinctly, there is probably not a major industrial country from which the U.S. can copy *less* than from Japan," asserts political scientist Amitai Etzioni.[53]

The concept of an industrial policy will be hard to apply because it raises serious constitutional, legal, political, and social questions. Under the American political system, it is impossible for the U.S. government to discriminate between individuals, institutions, and regions. The entire orientation of the system is toward creating checks and balances, and developing elaborate rules and procedures to ensure fairness even at the cost of efficiency. It accepts organized chaos instead of a smoothly run tyranny, and lets the market choose winners and losers rather than a group of "wise men."

Finally, there are serious administrative difficulties in implementing such a policy. The political system is not designed to develop a cohesive policy.[54] Nor can it accomplish this objective by abdicating its role to an independent body of interest group representatives. In the last analysis, any decision must depend on the quality of the available information and the capability and the integrity of the decision makers. Nothing in the arguments presented by the supporters of an industrial policy shows that the new decision makers would somehow have qualitatively different information than is currently available to managers in the private sector or that they will somehow be better qualified to evaluate that information and produce superior decisions.

Employee Compensation

The mode and nature of employee compensation, both in absolute and relative terms, strongly influences the character of employee-employer relations, organization structure and productivity, and employee morale, satisfaction, and notion of self-worth. In a broader sense, it also affects social harmony because a very large part of an industrial nation's workforce is comprised of wage earners. Employee compensation is determined by three sets of factors: external equity or market price; internal equity, a wage structure that treats equally all employees with similar skills and contributions; and the financial ability and willingness of a firm to meet workers' demands and expectations. These three factors do not always work in tandem.

External equity is important if an employer is to attract workers with scarce skills, if worker mobility is commonplace, and if an employer competes for scarce talent with other companies. And yet a significant measure of disparity among the wages of different workers that is not perceived by large segments of a corporation's workforce to be based on differential skills invariably leads to discontent and alienation. It can also cause low morale and may drive workers toward unionization and loss of management control over labor costs. An organization's willingness and ability to pay a given wage reflects not only a recognition of market and internal equity factors, but also management's judgment as to labor's share of a company's revenue stream.

Exhibit 10–3 illustrates the employee compensation dimension from

EXHIBIT 10–3 Gap between Societal Expectations and Corporate Behavior by American and Japanese-Controlled Businesses in the United States: Employee Compensation

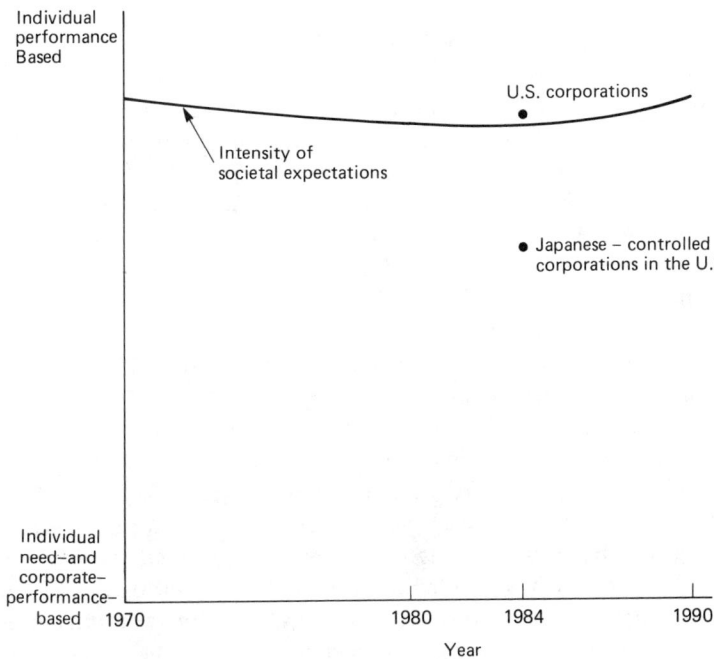

a system based on individual performance to a system based on individual need and corporate performance, or ability to pay. At one end of the spectrum the relationship is best described as "give and take"; an individual seeks the most he or she can get based on the individual's perception of his or her value to the organization, and the organization seeks to pay the least it can based on its perception of the worth of the employee and what it would have to pay to secure that employee's services. It is a highly rational approach that treats labor as simply another resource. At the other end of the spectrum is the "community" approach; an employee provides labor and the employer rewards him or her based on group performance and the employee's needs. The corporation is seen as a community that takes care of its members' welfare and shares benefits with all members, principally its employees and, to a lesser extent, its shareholders. The individual performance-based compensation system is more typical of the American approach to employee compensation, whereas the community approach is used by the Japanese, and especially by large Japanese corporations. But in neither case do businesses operate at the extreme end of the spectrum, or use one or the other method exclusively.

A comparison between Exhibits 10–1 and 10–3 shows that American society places even greater emphasis on an individual-based reward system than on an individual orientation in ordering societal priorities. At present there is some tendency toward a bit more emphasis on individual needs and corporate performance. This is in line with an increased shift toward a group orientation (Exhibit 10–1). However, we feel strongly that a trend toward a "community" approach to employee compensation in the United States will be very limited in scope, and that Americans will continue to seek rewards based on individual performance. The current trend toward individual and corporate need-based compensation systems reflects both a set of social changes that have been occurring in American society and a new economic and competitive environment.

In examining this dimension, it is necessary to begin with the realization that an important thrust in American society, particularly during the past two decades, has been toward ensuring greater equality among individuals. In the beginning, the approach was largely negative and directed toward removing any barriers that might frustrate an individual's or a minority group's drive toward self-fulfillment or deny them opportunities to compete in the marketplace for noneconomic reasons. There was no guarantee that an individual would achieve a given objective, only that he or she would not be denied the "opportunity" to try. But as minority groups experienced difficulties in moving into the mainstream of American society—because of their inability to overcome past historical discriminatory patterns, among other things—the focus changed to equality of outcome. The societal approach was now positive affirmative action—and designed to help these groups "catch up" with the rest of society by providing a minimal guarantee that they would achieve some of their objectives.

Since work occupies a major portion of an individual's life and is the economic means by which he or she enjoys the material benefits of society, the nation's attention has been focused on employment practices in the fight against social discrimination. Expectations in this regard were codified into law with the passage of the Civil Rights Act in 1964. To ensure that discriminatory values were no longer a factor in employment decisions, it was necessary to eliminate the concept of "person" from the employment equation and focus instead on the concept of "job." Factors such as loyalty, attitude, and the ability to "get along" are personal in nature. Judgments about them are subjective and might hide a discriminatory decision. The societal objective was to establish more value-neutral criteria that would eliminate discrimination based on considerations of age, race, color, sex, and so on. This could be best accomplished by focusing on the work outcome that was desired, particularly since objective criteria could be developed to measure job performance. The employee thus became a position rather than a person, and the term "job-related" became part of the legal and managerial lexicon and the benchmark by which all employment decisions were measured. It was the triumph of individual rationalism over group humanism in employment matters, cast in concrete through legislation and court decisions.

While the social legislation of the sixties imposed certain constraints on an employer's right to hire and compensate employees, the legal basis of employee-employer relations remained intact. Without a contractual obligation, an employer may fire a worker for a good reason, a bad reason, or no reason at all.[55] The system is supposed to work because market forces and the enlightened self-interest of employers and workers should produce mutually satisfactory transactions. It does not always work well because of the unequal bargaining power of corporation and workers. It may also frustrate important elements of public policy. So more recently, courts have been curtailing the "at will" rights of employers to fire workers in bad faith, or in cases where a worker's constitutional right of free speech has been violated.[56]

Current economic conditions have also brought some changes in traditional employee compensation methods in the United States. Deregulation and intense foreign competition have brought many U.S. companies to the brink of bankruptcy. There have been massive layoffs. As a consequence, more and more firms are demanding, and workers—both unionized and nonunionized—are making, concessions. They are giving back wage and benefit gains previously won in return for keeping more workers employed. There is also a new spirit of cooperation in which workers and management are getting together to solve common problems. There is greater disclosure of financial information by management to workers' representatives and a greater willingness on the part of management to involve worker representatives in top-level corporate decision making.

One should, however, be very careful in reading too much into this trend. Social legislation has not removed or even seriously curtailed the performance-based compensation system; it has made it more rational by removing the nonrational and capricious elements from the process. Similarly, the state has an obligation to intervene in private contracts when an overriding public interest is at stake. This is indeed the situation if, for example, an employer chooses to dismiss an employee for the latter's refusal to lobby for the passage of a law supported by the employer, or in the case where the employee has performed his duties to the satisfaction of the employer for a long time and has thereby acquired an equity in the job. Such an employee, because of age and company-unique skills and experience, often finds it very difficult to secure comparable employment in the event of being fired.

Recent "givebacks" and "cooperation" have taken place in an era of mutual suspicion and pressures, and except in a few cases, left a large residue of bitterness among all parties. Having won some initial concessions, a number of corporations have used the threat of closing individual plants, played workers from different communities against each other, and extracted further wage concessions. Workers have accused corporations of bad faith, have denied further demands for concessions, and in many cases have insisted on regaining lost benefits as the firm's financial situation has improved, regardless of the effect such "gainbacks" may have on the long-term profitability or international competitiveness of the firm.

Nor have the workers always presented a picture of solidarity. When confronted with demands for "givebacks," many unions have opted for a two-tier wage system in which current members retain or even increase their wages and benefits in return for allowing the company to hire new workers at much lower wages. Ironically, although this system creates distortions between wages and performance, it also brings the wages of new workers more in line with their value to the employer, thereby restoring the principle of a performance-based compensation system.

How does the current behavior of American and Japanese companies compare with the expectations of the American people? We believe there is a somewhat greater emphasis among the U.S. corporations on individual performance-based compensation, reflecting their concern for prevailing high wages, that makes their products uncompetitive. The society, on the other hand, may be showing increased concern for the plight of the unemployed and the potential for abuse of coercive power on the part of employers. Even so, the gap between the two is so small as to be insignificant. It may simply reflect an increased level of self-serving rhetoric by all concerned.

Given the dominant characteristics of the Japanese compensation system, it is not surprising that a large gap exists between it and the norms and expectations of Americans. To narrow this gap, Japanese-controlled companies in the United States combine the two approaches in rewarding their employees. As in Japan, many Japanese affiliates appraise their employees' performance slowly and offer compensation packages that are comparable in total wages to those of American companies. They are, however, structured differently to take into account individual needs; for example, incorporation of seniority, and no layoffs based on the company's convenience. But compared to the compensation system in Japan, that of Japanese affiliates in the United States is more oriented toward the individual performance-based system. This is partly because Japanese managers believe American employees can be better motivated by such a system. They seldom offer Japanese-style seniority-based wages, large profit- or revenue-based bonuses, or generous fringe benefits, such as subsidized housing and entertainment, and mountain lodges for vacations.

We do not foresee the gap between American and Japanese practices narrowing to any significant degree in the foreseeable future. The acceptability of the Japanese system in the United States, unless that system is drastically modified, is questionable. There are a number of reasons for this contention.

1. Many Japanese companies adopt a two-tier system of compensation in the United States. It is patently illegal, and it is also perceived as discriminatory by American workers who do not adequately appreciate the social contract under which the Japanese workers operate, and which in any case is not open to the American workers.[57] Those who have little desire for upward mobility may take advantage of such a system because *their* benefits may well exceed the costs. On the other hand, those who do want to rise may not prefer it because they perceive the costs as exceeding the benefits.[58]

The magnitude of the gap may be somewhat narrowed in the future as Japanese-controlled corporations acquire additional knowledge and skills and incorporate more American-style rewards into their compensation systems. However, current success in improving productivity at the shop floor level may encourage many Japanese companies to continue their present strategies. They may be further encouraged by the movement to adopt Japanese techniques in American companies. Moreover, many Japanese corporations, knowing that maintenance or enhancement of their "image" as a good place to work is important for attracting certain employees, may behave in a cohesive way. Still another aspect of the problem relates to the fact that Japanese corporations learn and change slowly. As mentioned earlier, many expatriate managers stay for a short period of time in the United States and are discouraged from learning the foreign culture and its ways of doing business. Those who are "contaminated" by foreign customs are likely to be pushed out of the mainstream of Japanese corporate life. The high level of homogeneity in Japanese companies may even discriminate against those with "different" ideas.

2. Another reason for this gap stems from the often discriminatory promotion practices toward American citizens employed in Japanese-controlled companies. Japanese companies have the most difficulty integrating "foreigners" into their decision-making system, which requires a common sharing of cultural norms, a knowledge of the political workings of the organization, and an intuitive feeling about the corporate culture. Therefore, as long as the Japanese parent company does not substantially change its internal workings comparatively larger numbers of Japanese expatriate managers will be needed for the communication and watchdog functions.

3. Even where the Japanese system may have applicability, Japanese companies are unwilling to extend its benefits to local employees. In part this is due to the feeling of many Japanese companies that their system is culture-unique and cannot work in other countries. It is also influenced by an extreme ethnocentricity on the part of the Japanese. Japanese management practices, rather than being viewed as humanistic, have come under extensive criticism for their insensitivity to local conditions and to local workers' needs and aspirations.

In his book *The Japanese Are Coming*,[59] Yoshi Tsurumi narrates a number of instances in which he met Japanese union leaders visiting overseas plant locations of Japanese companies. They were primarily concerned with the welfare of the Japanese expatriates and ignored the problems of Japanese companies' local workers. A 1981 study conducted under the auspices of The Center for Southeast Asian Studies, Kyoto University, identified a similar gap between expectations and performance for Japanese firms operating in Southeast Asia.[60] Four aspects of the Japanese-style management system were examined: lifetime employment, wages, labor unions, and *ringisei*. Of the Japanese firms surveyed, 57.6 percent reported that lifetime employment was not adaptable to local conditions or had to be drastically modified, since non-Japanese were not interested in working for only one firm for an entire lifetime. More revealing was the inability of Japanese managers to use the wage system of JABMAS; 12.1 percent did not even attempt to adapt JAB-MAS compensation practices to the local scene, and 79.1 percent had to modify it to some degree to make it workable. Only 3.4 percent of the Japanese firms surveyed were able to use the JABMAS wage approach without revision.

Two observations emerged from the findings of this study that are pertinent to our examination of the gap between societal expectations and the behavior of Japanese firms doing business in the United States. First, the authors noted that it was the larger and more tradition-bound firms that experienced the greatest difficulty in adapting their management style to new environmental conditions. Not only did their managers have a vested interest in protecting the system, but they were victims of the same bureaucratic inertia that has hampered some American firms in responding to new conditions in the United States. It is not surprising, therefore, that the two Japanese firms sued for employment discrimination under U.S. laws, Itoh and Sumitomo, were major Japanese trading companies known for their conservatism.

Second, lack of managerial flexibility in responding to new conditions was linked primarily to lack of overseas experience, aggravated by managerial parochialism in functioning in a non-Japanese working environment. The result was "feelings of insecurity" for Japanese managers taken away from their cultural "hothouse" and forced to operate in an unfamiliar and often more unfriendly environment. One Japanese manager frankly admitted that Japanese managers did not know any other system and had no choice but to go along with JABMAS, despite its faults. The insularity of Japanese culture may be an asset in Japan, but it is rapidly becoming a liability in the rest of the world because other societies do not place the same value on groupism and loyalty. To suggest that JABMAS can or should be exported into the United States not only ignores the reality of the American sociopolitical environment, but the unsuccessful experience of Japanese firms attempting to use JABMAS in other sociopolitical settings.

Top-Down versus Consensus Decision Making

An organization designs its decision processes to achieve its goals and objectives efficiently. Those goals and objectives reflect the power structure, internal and external influences and coalitions, and the culture of the organization. American corporate organizations are essentially authoritarian in character. This is true regardless of whether their structure is functional or divisional, and whether the top executive is an entrepreneurial leader or a professional manager. In either case the bureaucracy is relatively tightly controlled, reflects the decision style of the chief executive, and operates to meet the strategic goals set by top management, usually comprised of a small group of executives.[61]

The essential features of American business organizations were discussed in Chapter 6 and need not be elaborated here. Suffice it to say that decision making in American organizations is largely characterized as top-down. Downward communications consist primarily of orders for implementation, and upward communications consist of reports on performance and accomplishment. All elements of the institution operate in a contractual capacity. In one sense, even the top managers are hired hands because they report to the board of directors. However, this distinction is more illusory than real, because the chief executive officer is invariably the chairman of the board and exercises a strong influence over its structure and composition. In addition, management effectively restrains the board's oversight role through its control of information flow and of proxy and election machinery, and by a sizable management representation among the board membership.

The essential elements of the Japanese corporate organization and decision-making system were described in detail in Chapter 3. They include collective decision making or bottom-up, consensus-type decision making; verbal and nonverbal communication or behind-the-scene maneuvers; and information transmittal by implicit understanding. It is a largely closed system with minimal external influence. The organization is dominated by an active bureaucracy with a long tradition and strong internal coalitions. The decision process is formal and incremental; leadership is circumspect. Top management's preferences for particular strategies are informally and indirectly filtered down. Strategy implementation, just like strategy development, is done through a painstaking process of consensus building and a formal and rigid process of consultation that begins at the bottom rather than at the top.

More recent research indicates that Japanese companies use a top-down rather than a bottom-up consultative process. Top management uses the process largely to reduce ambiguity and uncertainty and to a much lesser extent to seek employee consent. There is a great deal of lateral communication that is intended to build familarity with a decision rather than negotiate its parameters.[62]

Exhibit 10–4 presents our view of changing societal expectations with regard to decision-making style in economic organizations.Unlike the graphs of individual versus group orientation and the compensation systems, this graph shows a precipitous decline in people's willingness to accept the traditional authoritative style of top-down corporate decision making. It is interesting to note that in the case of U.S. corporations, the gap between people's expectations and their perception of corporate behavior is increasing. The consensual approach used by Japanese corporations thus may have a distinct advantage in coming closer to meeting societal expectations. The reasons for this gap are not hard to find, and unless U.S. corporations take measures to narrow it, the situation does not augur well for American business.

There is an emerging trend in the United States toward encouraging and, in some instances, demanding greater opportunities for individuals to participate in the affairs of the institutions of which they are members. This has been particularly true, both historically and currently, in the public sector, and it is emerging as a dominant trend in the private sector. This thrust toward greater individual involvement in group matters and the move away from institutional autocracy is in keeping with past and current American cultural and sociopolitical values. It seems only fair and proper, within the American context, that an individual should have some say in matters that

EXHIBIT 10–4 Gap between Societal Expectations and Corporate Behavior by American and Japanese-Controlled Businesses in the United States: Top-Down versus Consensus Decision Making

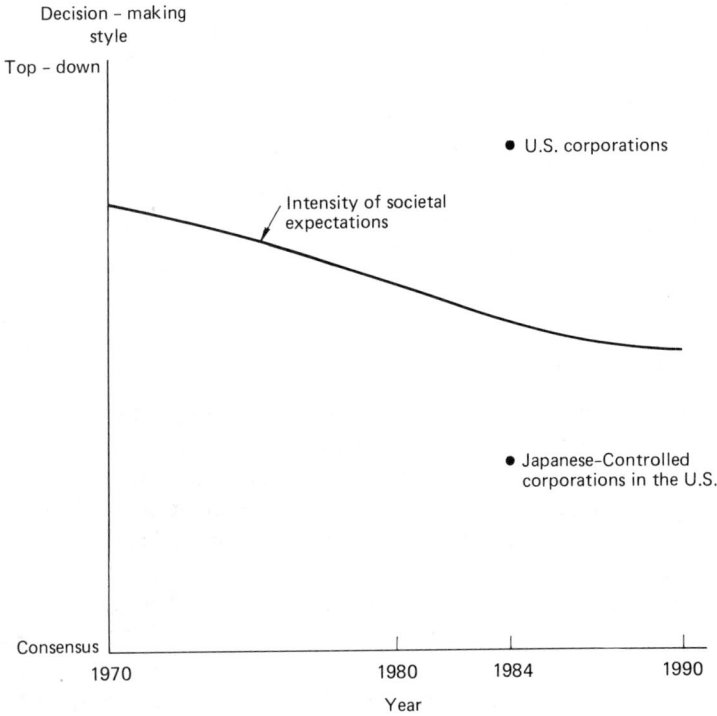

personally affect him or her. It also explains the current trend in American politics toward greater use of referendums and initiatives to decide crucial political issues. These devices permit voters to bypass the legislative process and vote directly on proposed legislation.

It is not a gigantic step to transfer this political concept to the work environment. To grant a person political equality at the ballot box and then deny it in the workplace is a contradiction in cultural values. To permit an autocrat to rule the workplace is still another contradiction. Worker democracy or worker participation in the decision-making processes of institutions is only one aspect of a long-term movement in American society toward associational participation. It is against this backdrop that we will compare the gap between societal expectations and the JABMAS and ABMAS approaches to decision making.

Historically, American workers have achieved a degree of control over their environment through collective bargaining; professional white collar employees have achieved similar results through codes and standards developed by professional societies. However, in all these cases the approach has been that of the contract: Management concedes certain rights in return for certain benefits. An elaborate legal structure ensures that all parties negotiate in good faith and that the rules of the game are strictly adhered to. Still, the relationship is adversarial in nature, and the parties do not yield any more than they have to. Over the years, managements have clearly specified areas considered their perogative and therefore not negotiable. This is true even in corporations in which the workforce is not unionized and a closer and more cooperative relationship exists between management and labor.

In the United States, the firm has been viewed by management as a functional organization of individuals contractually hired as specialists to fill a specific job in the company. Their involvement is a rational one. Since jobs are clearly defined by contract, employees are reluctant to perform any tasks not specifically assigned by job description. Management is equally unwilling to have them expand their activities into areas not outlined in the job description, particularly if the expansion is into management areas. American firms tend to favor a pyramid organization, with authority flowing down. They separate the manager or professional in order to establish the hierarchy within the organization and discourage familiarity on the part of the staff. American executives tend to isolate themselves from the company's laboring personnel with executive dining rooms and designated parking places. So sharp is the difference between employer and employee in American business that organizational personnel are viewed in terms of "white collar" and "blue collar" workers, and blue collar workers are perceived as second-class citizens in their own organizations.

American management has prided itself on its professionalism and on the phenomenal success and growth of American business at home and abroad. However, as the performance of American corporations has faltered in competition with the Japanese, this claim is being increasingly challenged. American executives have a host of reasons for this poor showing: high labor costs, expensive and heavyhanded government regulation, and subsidization of foreign businesses by their governments. However, American management must also share blame for being short-term-oriented and complacent, and for neglecting fundamental business principles such as modernizing plant and equipment, maintaining a happy workforce, and keeping a satisfied customer base. When American management asks workers to "give back" some of their hard-won wages and benefits, workers are demanding a greater say in management to ensure that all groups make sacrifices and that the corporation manages itself in a manner that protects the interests of the workers.

In the past, American corporations have sought worker participation, but without much success. The failure was due to two reasons. Participation was encouraged only in narrowly defined areas that were often viewed by the workers as nonsubstantive. The business community also believed that the lack of strong empirical evidence for a causal relationship between job satisfaction and job performance meant that productivity gains could be better achieved through financial incentives and a work environment carefully controlled and defined by management. This situation, however, is changing. Years of employee alienation are reflected in lack of employee sympathy for the corporate plight. There is a feeling that management is interested in employees' concerns only when it needs their cooperation. Workers' rights have also been strengthened through various laws regulating conditions in the workplace. An even more fundamental change has been in the character of the workplace itself. The high-technology industries, and automation of older, more mature industries, require an educated and skilled workforce that is unlikely to follow orders blindly. Moreover, their relative scarcity creates opportunities for job mobility, leading these workers to demand a greater say in structuring their work life and to seek greater involvement in corporate decisions. It is not surprising that worker involvement in corporate decision making is probably the greatest in high-technology industries.

It is apparent that economic, social, and political pressures for more employee involvement in corporate decisions at all levels will continue to increase in the future. Unfortunately, there is little evidence that corporate America is willing to respond. To a large extent, managements are constrained by financial and legal restrictions, stockholders, and financial markets from giving employees a real voice in corporate management. A no less important factor is the reluctance and resistance of the present generation of managers to subjecting their decisions to scrutiny by employees. Compared to their predecessors, who were trained in the school of hard knocks, these managers are the products of business schools, professionally trained in all the scientific methods of management, and are at home with discounted cash flows, asset diversification and management, and market share strategies. Their confidence has been severely shaken by the poor showing of American business in international competition against Japanese managers who rarely are business school graduates and who manage their businesses in a more humanistic and "unscientific" manner. Unless these managers change, or are replaced by those who will, American business is unlikely to improve its competitive position.

In Japan, corporations, and especially large corporations, use *ringisei* or consensus-type decision making in their Japanese operations. In their U.S. operations, Japanese affiliates have used either the top-down decision-making style or a hybrid system combining elements of both the American and the Japanese styles. Unlike the compensation system, which Japanese companies can offer unilaterally, decision-making style involves a significant element of two-way communications that must be understood and accepted by all parties in order to be effective.

At present, the gap between the performance of Japanese companies and societal expectations on the decision-making dimension appears to be smaller than that for the American corporations, and might become even narrower in the foreseeable future. However, it is unlikely that this gap will ever be closed. The gap may stem not from the unwillingness of Americans to be integrated into a Japanese organization, but from confusion and distrust of the system practiced by Japanese-controlled corporations in the United States. It is probably impossible for the Japanese companies to expect American employees to commit themselves to a single organization without a supportive social context. There is also tremendous reluctance on the part of Japanese companies to broaden the scope of consensus-style decision making. Consultation is practiced largely at lower levels of the organization and involves shop floor or other routine decisions. At middle and upper management levels, the scope of consensus-style decision making involving American managers is quite narrow, and often practiced in form rather than substance.

The important role played by groups is inimical to the successful integration of non-Japanese who do not, and are unlikely ever to be able to, become part of the groups in the home office in Japan. American executives thus become frustrated and dissatisfied when they find their recommendations ignored or rejected without apparent reason or rational justification. A consensus-style decision-making process confined to the U.S. subsidiary and its operations will also prove unsatisfactory because Japanese subsidiaries are more integrated and closely controlled by their parents in Japan. Perhaps the most serious problem in instituting consensus-style decision making lies in the sharing of responsibility, which is directly or indirectly tied into the reward system. An American executive who is responsible for the improvement or success of an operation expects immediate recognition and rewards that directly reflect his contribution to the enterprise. However, an individual performance-based reward system is in direct conflict with a consensus-style decision-making system. The Japanese executive is rewarded on the basis of shared responsibility and group-oriented compensation, and the success of an entire organization. A two-tier decision-making system will be incompatible because the decisions cannot be neatly separated. Nor can the success of a local subsidiary be evaluated separately from the contribution and support of the parent company.

THEORY Z: A MODEL FOR INTRODUCING JABMAS IN THE UNITED STATES

Having described and compared the cultures and management systems of the United States and Japan, and having argued forcefully that JABMAS will not lead Americans to the promised land, it behooves us to address the claims made by proponents of the Japanese management system for how it can be employed successfully in the United States. The most ardent advocate of this approach is William Ouchi.[63] In his *Theory Z,* Ouchi asserts that the problem of low productivity in the United States will not be solved with monetary and fiscal policies or through more investment in research and development. Productivity, according to Ouchi, is a problem of social organization. Instead of the hierarchical rules symptomatic of bureaucratic organizations in the American corporate world, we need a corporate culture that engenders employee loyalty and cultivates trust and cooperation, greater worker involvement, and motivation to excel, and thus greater productivity. Ouchi asserts that Theory Z is universal in its orientation and can be applied to all industrial nations.

The essence of Theory Z lies in a set of assumptions. Strong cultural norms and values influence individual behavior and organizational goals. Managers are impelled to create a system of incentives, such as a lifetime employment, seniority-based wage system that binds employees to the organization and creates intense loyalty. The secret of successful organizational effort is to be found in intimate working relationships that inhibit interpersonal competition and rivalry, and breed trust and cooperation. These positive relationships transform the organization into a "tribe" or "clan" with its own ethos and culture. They yield for the employee a sense of community, security, and autonomy; contribute to job satisfaction; and thereby lead to greater productivity (Exhibit 10–5).

The success of Japanese business is asserted to be based on its following the principles of Theory Z. Ouchi also suggests that some maverick American corporations have succeeded in maintaining a technological lead and high worker productivity even in the face of overall declining American competitiveness. The most attractive aspect of Ouchi's theory is that its lessons can be taught, transplanted successfully, and work equally well for the American corporation. Theory Z, however, suffers from a number of serious flaws. It is not a theory, it does not fit known facts, it is not based on humanism, and it does not apply to the United States.

Theory Z Is Not a Theory

The test of a theory is its ability to identify and define variables and constructs in a manner that fits known facts and offers logical explanations for a given

EXHIBIT 10–5 Ouchi's Theory Z

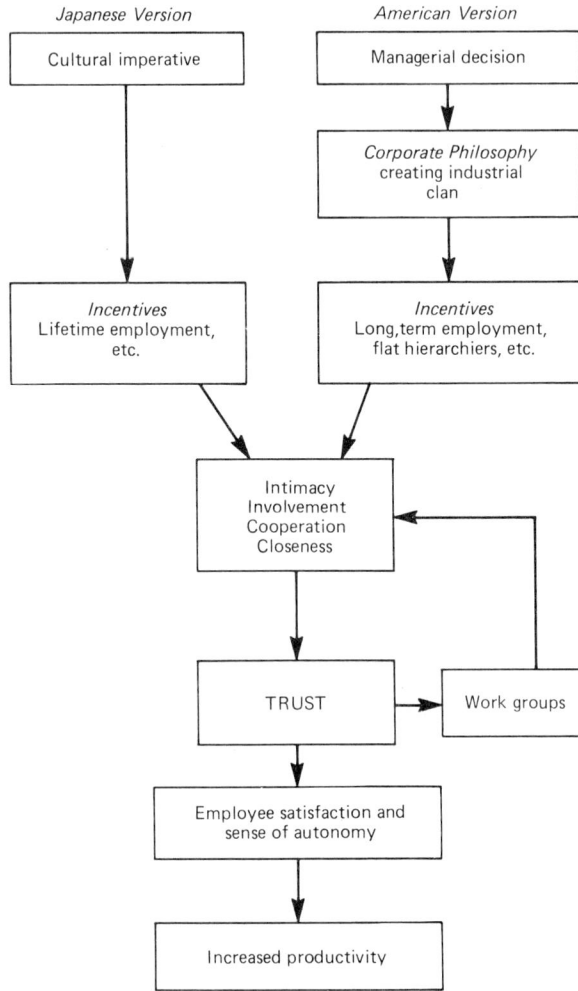

SOURCE: Reproduced from Jeremiah J. Sullivan, "A Critique of Theory Z,"
Academy of Management Review, 8, 1 (January 1983), p. 133.

phenomenon. Theory Z describes certain aspects of the behavior of a group
of companies called Type Z companies. But Type Z is just a label and does
not have any particular meaning.

The findings are not based on sufficient empirical data. Despite the
author's statement that intensive interviews were conducted with a large

number of chief executives of American and Japanese companies, both in Japan and the United States, it subsequently becomes clear that only a handful of interviews were conducted; that all of them were not conducted by the author; and that of those interviews, only three were in Japan and none in the United States. Thus the claim of extensive research would appear to be exaggerated.[64]

Theory Z Does Not Fit the Known Facts

Ouchi derives support for his thesis from the Japanese model, which he claims resembles Theory Z organizations in the United States. There are indeed certain similarities between the two types of organizations. Both have somewhat similar management practices, such as lifetime vs. longer-term employment, extensive on-the-job training, implicit control mechanisms, and slow evaluation and promotion. On the surface, both display an intimate and harmonious working atmosphere that stresses employee involvement and cooperation. However, despite the superficial similarities, some critically important differences in working relationships, control mechanisms, and motivation distinguish the Japanese management system from the Theory Z organization.

Ouchi's description of the links between cultural imperatives and management practices and their relation to increased productivity as they apply to Japanese corporations, and as they can be practiced in the United States, is presented in Exhibit 10–5. The controlling and motivating mechanisms in Japanese organizations are not humanism and egalitarianism, but hierarchy, authority, power, and domination. As we demonstrated earlier, egalitarianism as a cultural trait does not exist in Japan. The hierarchical relations are enforced through strong social sanctions; direct orders are not required. Hierarchical authority relationships are not confined to the corporation, but extend to all aspects of Japanese society: The old over the young, the senior over the junior, "the husband over the wife, the sons over the daughters . . . the well born over the base."[65]

> Everyone knows his place in the system, so it is unnecessary to kick people or shout at them. Of course, "discipline" and "hierarchy" are Western terms; the Japanese talk of "expected behavior" and "harmonious relations." Once we understand that the Japanese do what their superiors expect of them, everything falls into place. This is why industrial workers make suggestions, permit labor-saving devices, and strive for zero defects. . . . Under such a system, decision-making by consensus is easy—no one would hold out against the group, and certainly not against the boss.[66]

The source of pressure lies in the hierarchical structure of Japanese society. It should be noted that a sense of "class" or "caste" as such does not exist for most Japanese. And yet, as we demonstrated in Chapters 2 and 3, a ruthless and rigorous form of class distinction is practiced in Japan: "The upper class does, like any healthy oligarchy, admit a few nouveaux, but most of the mass stays in its assigned place."[67] If the system is so culturally congruent and voluntarily followed, why does it bestow its benefits on less than one-third of the population, and why is it that a large majority of the people are willing to forego its munificence, which is considered culturally desirable and socially attainable?

Ouchi's explanation of the linkages between cultural imperatives and a humanistic and people-oriented management leading to increased worker productivity conveniently ignores an abundance of evidence to the contrary. Sullivan[68] cites a number of research studies that point to a different direction. In a study by Pucik, it was found that career path in a number of Japanese companies is greatly influenced by managers' functional specialization.[69] Lifetime employment is a culturally sanctioned ideal rather than an industrial reality for most Japanese.[70] There is strong employee resentment of the company's "moral levers" and a kind of helplessness in the face of a superior's autocracy and authoritarianism.[71] As Bruce-Briggs observes, "The heralded openness of Japanese executives to their subordinates does not reflect 'feminine' intimacy but masculine dominance."[72]

One of the most important control mechanisms in large Japanese corporations is fear of loss of prestigious lifetime employment and of "face," which is reinforced by severe social sanctions against those who fail to meet corporate expectations. If an employee is fired from a large corporation, he and his family face tremendous difficulties, both financial and social. His prospects of finding another job at another large-scale company are almost nonexistent. Even a smaller company may hesitate to employ him for fear of retaliation from his former employer. Note that most large firms belong to a *keiretsu* (industrial group). The fired employee has no chance of employment with other member companies in the group; even those of another group would not employ him as a matter of policy. As we noted earlier, many Japanese companies, faced with slow economic growth and a higher level of competition, have been pushing out their "poorer" performers. During earlier periods of high rates of economic growth, an employee with lower than expected performance was usually transferred "honorably" to a related company in order to save his face. This is becoming increasingly difficult.

Therefore, the lifetime employment privilege, coupled with other personnel policies, such as the seniority-based wage and promotion system, work as a "stick and carrot" in managing employees. These policies are carefully designed to put constant pressure on employees to work hard. Compulsory retirement for those who do not climb the corporate ladder to upper middle management by age 55 to 58 is a tremendous pressure on the employees because of the financial hardship that confronts them after retirement.

Language also acts as a strong social instrument for maintaining control and order. The values promoted from above may be those of *on* (obligation) and *giri* (duty), but the most pertinent value subscribed to from below is *gaman* —patience, endurance, putting up with it.[73] Top managers can afford to be polite and intimate with their juniors, confident that their "requests" will be carried out diligently because the price of failure is so high. In other words, it is not trust that drives employees to work hard, but fear of punishment. We contend that Exhibit 10–6 provides a more accurate explanation of Japanese worker productivity than the one advanced by Ouchi.

EXHIBIT 10–6 An Anti-Theory Z Explanation of Japanese Productivity

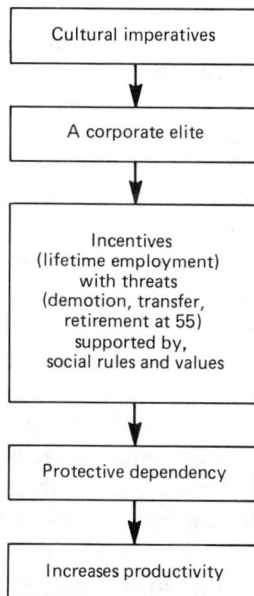

```
┌─────────────────────────┐
│  Cultural imperatives   │
└─────────────────────────┘
            │
            ▼
┌─────────────────────────┐
│   A corporate elite     │
└─────────────────────────┘
            │
            ▼
┌─────────────────────────┐
│       Incentives        │
│  (lifetime employment)  │
│       with threats      │
│   (demotion, transfer,  │
│     retirement at 55)   │
│       supported by,     │
│  social rules and values│
└─────────────────────────┘
            │
            ▼
┌─────────────────────────┐
│  Protective dependency  │
└─────────────────────────┘
            │
            ▼
┌─────────────────────────┐
│  Increases productivity │
└─────────────────────────┘
```

Theory Z Is Not Based on Humanism

The basis of Theory Z is allegedly humanistic. The organization is geared toward satisfying individual needs, and this creates trust and a desire for excellence. However, Theory Z is institutional in its orientation rather than individual. The organizational ethos is geared to making individuals conform to corporate values rather than having corporate values meet workers' needs. Everything is set up to make it difficult if not impossible for the individual not to belong. Under these conditions, it is easy for managers to appear participative. As Robbins points out: "It would be inconsistent with the goal of those in power to use their discretion over how the organization is designed to create a structure that would lessen their control." The attractiveness of Theory Z lies not in the fact that "it will democratize the workplace," but in the fact that it provides a mechanism for enhancing managerial control.[74]

Theory Z Is Unworkable in the United States

The alleged successes of Theory Z in the United States are based on poor and weak data. Companies identified by Ouchi as being Type Z had developed their systems long before Japanese management techniques became fashionable. Although they may share some outward characteristics with JABMAS, their means of acquiring those characteristics have been quite different. A better picture emerges when we examine more recent attempts by American companies to introduce JABMAS. As we showed in Chapter 9, these have been largely cosmetic and exploitative, confined to employee participation at the lower level, and discarded when pressures mounted for management to follow through. Unlike in Japan, managers in the United States cannot entirely decide for themselves how the benefits accruing from improved productivity will be shared; other groups in society are not so pliant as in Japan.

Theory Z organizations have the potential for gaining too much power over their members. According to Ouchi, Theory Z induces employees to identify their interests closely with those of the firm. The employees share the same values and needs as the firm and commit themselves to achieve common goals by working together. The goals, however, are not common. By law and by custom, management puts the interests of stockholders above those of its employees. Those are the assets of the firm, and not necessarily of the individuals. Thus individual freedom may be sacrificed in the name of benefit to the firm. The justification for such institutional power is that the organization becomes a focal point of employees' lives, in place of family or other social institutions. Ouchi argues that in an industrial mass society, all social institutions become weak and no longer offer strong guidance for individual behavior and a stable, satisfying psychological and emotional environment. In such a society, Theory Z institutions can promulgate rules or values for their members that will foster social order and stability.

This myopic view of American society's ideology and value set, and of the role of corporate leadership, is certainly odd. We are not sure that even corporate leaders would want to set the moral tone for America. We are certain the American people would not accept it. Theory Z will not work in the United States because it is inconsistent with American cultural norms and values. Moreover, without the social support available in Japan, management in the United States cannot impose it on the workers. America is a pluralistic society. Corporate America and political America do not share an identity of purpose or uniformity of goals. In Japan, political and economic elites are linked through many common bonds and thus can pursue their goals to the exclusion of goals held by others. This cannot be the case in the United States, where individual rights and voluntary cooperation, based on self-interest among an informed people, is the basis of institutional governance.

NOTES

1. "Women: A Separate Sphere," *Time,* August 1, 1983, p. 69.
2. Ibid.
3. The notion of legitimacy gap as a concept for evaluating corporate behavior in terms of its societal appropriateness has only recently begun to be explored in scholarly research and writings on issues dealing with business and public policy. See, for example, S. Prakash Sethi, "An Analytical Framework for Making Cross-Cultural Comparisons of Business Responses to Social Pressures," in Lee E. Preston (ed.) *Research in Corporate Social Performance and Policy,* vol. 1 (Greenwich, Conn.: Jai Press, 1978), pp. 27–54. See also Edwin M. Epstein, *The Corporation in American Politics* (Englewood Cliffs, N.J.: Prentice-Hall, 1969), pp. 254–255; Kenneth E. Boulding, "The Legitimacy of the Business Institution," in Edwin M. Epstein and Dow Votaw, *Legitimacy, Rationality, Responsibility: Search for New Directions in Business and Society* (Santa Monica, Calif.: Goodyear, 1978), pp. 88–89; John Dowling and Jeffrey Pfeffer, "Organizational Legitimacy: Social Values and Organizational Behavior," *Pacific Sociological Review,* 18, 1, (January 1975), p. 131; Richard J. Ryberg, "Defining the Social Issue Concept," *1981 Proceedings* (Southwest Division, Academy of Management), pp. 231–232; James Post, *Corporate Behavior and Social Change* (Reston, Va.: Reston Publishing, 1978), p. 284; and Peter L. Berger, "New Attack on the Legitimacy of Business," *Harvard Business Review,* 59, 5 (September–October 1981), pp. 82–89.
4. Masayoshi Kanabayashi, "Japan Frets over Rising Joblessness," *Wall Street Journal,* April 13, 1983, p. 31.
5. Yasuo Okamoto, "Nihon Kigyō no Grand Strategy" [The Grand Strategy of Japanese Business], *Chūō Kōron Keiei Mondai,* trans. Mamoru Ishikawa, *Japanese Economic Studies* (Summer 1982), pp. 3–47.

6. Masayoshi Kanabayashi, "Economic Woes Spur Firms in Japan to Alter Lifetime Job Security," *Wall Street Journal,* December 21, 1977, p. 1.

7. Kanabayashi, "Japan Frets over Rising Joblessness."

8. Masayoshi Kanabayashi, "Japan's Recession-Hit Companies Make Complex Arrangements to Avoid Layoffs," *Wall Street Journal,* February 17, 1983, p. 32.

9. Ibid.

10. Edward Boyer, "How Japan Manages Declining Industries," *Fortune,* January 10, 1983, p. 60.

11. Takafusa Nakamura, *The Postwar Japanese Economy: Its Development and Structure,* trans. Jacqueline Kaminski. (Tokyo: University of Tokyo Press, 1981), pp. 248–252.

12. "Lifetime Employment May Be on Its Last Legs," *Business Week,* September 5, 1983, p. 98.

13. "The Outlook: Japan Worries about a 'Gray' Future," *Wall Street Journal,* June 1, 1981, p. 1.

14. For some examples of these phenomena, see Nihon Keizai Shimbun, *Salary-Man: Document #2* (Tokyo: Nihon Keizai Shimbun, Inc., 1981); in Japanese.

15. Kanabayashi, "Economic Woes Spur Firms in Japan to Alter Lifetime Job Security," p. 25.

16. Naomi Yamaki, *Japanese Management [Nihon no Management]* (Tokyo: Nihon Noritsu Kyokai, 1980), pp. 174–179; Ichiro Hattori, "A Proposition on Efficient Decision-Making in the Japanese Corporation," *Columbia Journal of World Business* 13, 2 (Summer 1978), pp. 14.

17. Hattori, "A Proposition on Efficient Decision-Making in the Japanese Corporation," p. 12; Richard T. Pascale and Anthony G. Athos, *The Art Of Japanese Management: Applications for American Executives* (New York: Simon and Schuster, 1981), p. 33; and Akihiro Okumura, *Nihon no Top Management [Japanese Top Management]* (Tokyo: Diamond Publishing Company, 1982), pp. 100–102.

18. S. Prakash Sethi and Nobuaki Namiki, "Japanese Style Consensus Decision-Making in Matrix Management: Problems and Prospects," in David I. Cleland (ed.), *Matrix Management Systems Handbook* (New York: Von Nostrand Reinhold, 1984), in press.

19. Ichiro Saga, "Japan's Robots Produce Problems for Workers," *Wall Street Journal,* February 28, 1983, p. 21.

20. "A Spark of Militancy in the Land of Loyalty," *Business Week,* September 5, 1983, p. 96.

21. Steve Lohr, "Japan's New Nonconformists," *New York Times,* March 8, 1983, pp. 25–27.

22. Robert C. Christopher, "Changing Face of Japan," *New York Times Magazine,* March 27, 1983, pp. 87–90.

23. "The Exodus That Shook the Establishment," *Business Week,* December 14, 1981, p. 118; see also Christopher, "Changing Face of Japan," p. 90.

24. Lohr, "Japan's New Nonconformists," p. 27.

25. Urban C. Lehner, "Heads of Japan Air Lines and Mitsukoshi Department Store Bucking a Venerable Japanese Tradition," *Wall Street Journal,* September 22, 1982, p. 35.

26. Masayoshi Kanabayashi, "Japanese Retail Chain Grows Rapidly, Aided by Un-Japanese Ways," *Wall Street Journal,* August 21, 1981, p. 1.

27. Masayoshi Kanabayashi, "Some Japanese Balk at Overseas Jobs," *Wall Street Journal,* July 9, 1982, p. 21.

28. Clyde Haberman, "All Work and Now a Little Play Make Japan Fret," *New York Times,* September 9, 1983, p. A-2.

29. "Women: A Separate Sphere," *Time,* August 1, 1983, p. 68.

30. George C. Lodge, *The New American Ideology* (New York: Knopf, 1976).

31. James Botkin, James Dimancescu, and Ray Stata, *Global Stakes: The Future of High Technology in America* (Cambridge, Mass.: Ballinger, 1982); Charles Tavel, *The Third Industrial Stage: Strategy for Business Survival* (Oxford, Eng.: Pergamon Press, 1980).

32. For a description both favorable and critical of Japanese business-government relations, see Chalmers Johnson, "MITI and the Japanese International Economic Policy," in Robert A. Scalapino, (ed.), *The Foreign Policy of Modern Japan* (Berkeley: University of California Press, 1977), pp. 227–280; Chalmers Johnson, *MITI and the Japanese Miracle: The Growth of Industrial Policy, 1925–75* (Stanford, Calif.: Stanford University Press, 1982); and Naoto Sasaki, *Management and Industrial Structure in Japan* (Oxford, Eng.: Pergamon Press, 1981).

33. See, for example, Robert Reich, *The Next American Frontier* (New York: Random House, 1983); Robert B. Reich and Ira Magaziner, *Minding America's Business* (New York: Harcourt Brace Jovanovich, 1982); Ezra Vogel, *Japan As No. 1: Lessons for America* (Cambridge, Mass.: Harvard University Press, 1979). Lester Thurow, *The Zero-Sum Society* (New York: Basic Books, 1981).

34. "Industrial Policy: Is It the Answer?" *Business Week,* July 4, 1983, pp. 54–62; George Gilder, "A Supply-Side Economics of the Left," *The Public Interest* (Summer 1983), pp. 29–43.

35. A. Lawrence Chickering (ed.), *The Politics of Planning: A Review and Critique of Centralized Economic Planning* (San Francisco: Institute of Contemporary Studies, 1976); Herbert Stein, "Don't Fall for Industrial Policy," *Fortune,* November 14, 1983, pp. 64–78; Karen Arenson, "Debate Grows over Adoption of National Industrial Policy," *New York Times,* June 15, 1983, sec 1, pp. 1, 14.

36. Michael L. Wachter and Susan M. Wachter, *Toward A New Industrial Policy?* (Philadelphia: University of Pennsylvania Press, 1981); Jack Baranson, *The Japanese Challenge to U.S. Industry* (Lexington, Mass.: D.C. Heath, 1983).

37. Stein, "Don't Fall for Industrial Policy," p. 65.

38. Cited in Bruce Bartlett, "Industrial Policy: Crisis for Liberal Economists," *Fortune,* November 14, 1983, pp. 83–90.

39. "The Point Man for 'Industrial Policy,'" *Business Week,* July 25, 1983, pp. 23–24.

40. Charles Schultze, "Industrial Policy: A Solution in Search of a Problem," *California Management Review* 25, 4 (Summer 1983), pp. 5–16; Robert Reich, "Why the U.S. Needs an Industrial Policy," *Harvard Business Review,* 60, 1 (January–February 1982), pp. 74–81; William J. Abernathy, Kim B. Clark, and Alan M. Kantrow, "The New Industrial Competition," *Harvard Business Review* 59, 4 (September–October 1981), pp. 68–81; Bruce R. Scott, "Can Industry Survive the Welfare State," *Harvard Business Review,* 60, 5 (September–October 1982), pp.

70–84; G. C. Lodge and W. R. Glass, "U.S. Trade Policy Needs One Voice," *Harvard Business Review*, 61, 3 (May–June 1983), pp. 75–83; Stein, "Don't Fall for Industrial Policy"; Laura Tyson and John Zysman, "American Industry in International Competition: Government Policies and Corporate Strategies," *California Management Review*, 25, 3 (Spring 1983), pp. 27–52.

41. Reich, *The Next American Frontier;* see also an article by the same title, in *The Atlantic Monthly;* pp. 43–58; see also Baranson, *The Japanese Challenge to U.S. Industry.*

42. Ezra Vogel, "Guided Free Enterprise in Japan," *Harvard Business Review*, 56, 3 (May–June 1978), pp. 161–170; Eleanor M. Hadley, "The Secret of Japan's Success," *Challenge*, 26, 2 (May–June 1983), pp. 4–10.

43. Amitai Etzioni, "The MITIzation of America?" *The Public Interest* (Summer 1983), pp. 44–51.

44. Arenson, "Debate Grows over Adoption of National Industrial Policy," p. 14.

45. Vogel, *Japan As No. 1: Lessons for America.*

46. The best-known advocate of this approach is Robert Reich, *Minding America's Business* and *The Next American Frontier.* See also Lester Thurow, *The Zero-Sum Society.*

47. Stein, "Don't Fall for Industrial Policy," p. 65; see also Bartlett, "Industrial Policy: Crisis for Liberal Economists," and Gilder, "A Supply-Side Economic Policy of the Left."

48. Schultze, "Industrial Policy: A Solution in Search of a Problem," p. 15.

49. Johnson, *MITI and the Japanese Miracle.*

50. Schultze, "Industrial Policy: A Solution in Search of a Problem," pp. 12–13.

51. Arno A. Penzias, "Let's Not Outsmart Ourselves in Thinking-Computer Rush," *Wall Street Journal*, September 13, 1983, p. 34.

52. Stein, "Don't Fall for Industrial Policy."

53. Etzioni, "MITIzation of America," p. 47, emphasis in the original. See also Amitai Etzioni, *An Immodest Agenda: Rebuilding America Before the 21st Century* (New York: McGraw Hill, 1983).

54. J. L. Badaracco, Jr., and D. B. Yoffie, "Industrial Policy: It Can't Happen Here," *Harvard Business Review*, 83, 6 (November–December 1983), pp. 96–105.

55. "Protecting 'at will' Employees against Wrongful Discharge: The Duty to Terminate Only in Good Faith," *Harvard Law Review* (1980) 93, 8, pp. 1816–1844; Charles G. Bakaly, Jr., and Joel M. Grossman, *Modern Law of Employment Contracts* (New York: Law & Business/Harcourt, Brace Jovanovich, 1984).

56. Ibid.; see also Karen Blumenthal, "Fighting Back: Discharged Employees Take Firms into Court," *Dallas Morning News*, February 10, 1983, sec. D, pp. 1–2. The article discusses a California lawsuit, *Lawrence M. Clearly V. American Airlines,* where the court ordered American Airlines to rehire an employee who was fired, without good cause, after having worked with the company for over twenty years; "Legal Challenges Force Firms Revamp Ways They Dismiss Workers," *Wall Street Journal*, September 13, 1983, p. 10; Charles G. Bakaly, Jr., and Joel M. Grossman, "Does First Amendment Let Employees Thwart the Boss?" *Wall Street Journal*, December 8, 1983, p. 30.

57. This position is being contested by the Japanese companies in lawsuits currently before the United States Supreme Court. For relevant legal citations, see Chapter 4 of this book.

58. Frank Gibney, *Miracle by Design,* (New York: Times Books, 1982). pp. 181–196.
59. Yoshi Tsurumi, *The Japanese Are Coming,* (Cambridge, Mass.: Ballinger Publishing Co., 1976). p. 299.
60. Shin'ichi Ichimara, "Japanese Firms in Asia," *Japanese Economic Studies* (Fall 1981), pp. 33–52.
61. For a discussion of power structure in organizations, see Dan E. Schendel and Charles W. Hofer (eds.), *Strategic Management: A New View of Business Policy Planning* (Boston: Little, Brown, 1979), editors' note in chap. 2, pp. 53–63; Henry Mintzberg, "Organizational Power and Goals: A Skeletal Theory," in Schendel and Hoffer (eds.), pp. 64–79.
62. N. Hatvany and C. V. Pucik, "Japanese Management Practices and Productivity," *Organizational Dynamics* 9, 4 (1981), pp. 5–21; cited in Jeremiah J. Sullivan, "A Critique of Theory Z," *Academy of Management Review,* 8, 1 (January 1983), pp. 132–142.
63. William G. Ouchi, *Theory Z* (1981).
64. William Bowen, "Lessons from Behind the Kimono," *Fortune,* June 15, 1981, pp. 247–250.
65. B. Bruce-Briggs, "The Dangerous Folly Called Theory Z," *Fortune,* May 17, 1982, p. 44.
66. Ibid., p. 44.
67. Ibid.
68. Sullivan, "A Critique of Theory Z," pp. 136–138.
69. V. Pucik, "Promotion and Intraorganizational Status Differentiation Among Japanese Managers," *Academy of Management Proceedings,* 1981.
70. R. C. Clark, *The Japanese Company* (New Haven, Conn.: Yale University Press, 1979).
71. Ibid., pp. 187–188.
72. Bruce-Briggs, "The Dangerous Folly Called Theory Z," p. 44.
73. Ibid.
74. Stephen P. Robbins, "The Theory Z Organization from a Power-Control Perspective," *California Management Review,* 25, 2 (January 1983), pp. 73–74.

ELEVEN ▚▚▚▚▚▚▚▚▚▚▚▚▚▚▚▚▚▚▚▚▚▚▚▚▚▚▚▚▚▚▚▚

Rejuvenating America's Business: The Challenge

MOST AMERICANS HAVE COME TO BELIEVE, AND CRITICS NEVER TIRE OF reminding us, that America has lost its competitive edge in world markets. Our basic industries are declining, and before too long, we may even lose our lead in high-technology industries. Furthermore, if drastic measures are not taken to reverse this trend, it will have grave consequences for our economic well-being and our national security.

Credit for Japan's spectacular performance is accorded to its superior management, diligent workforce, cooperative labor-management relations, and an active government that coordinates the nation's industrial policies and business activities with a view to gaining world leadership. Governments of foreign nations are also accused of creating unfair competition for America's industries through keeping American business out of their home markets and subsidizing their industries in export markets. Conversely, blame for America's poor performance is placed, in part, on myopic management, adversary labor-management relations, and an overpaid, indifferent, poorly trained, and lazy workforce. The U.S. government is also blamed for its avowed adherence to policies of laissez faire, while in practice it pursues regulation of the economy in a manner that is haphazard, uncoordinated, and contradictory.

American business and management has claimed a large measure of credit, and rightly so, for the past phenomenal growth in America's economy and the American standard of living. It must now also bear a large part of the blame for the current malaise. While many other government measures and external factors—economic and social—may have played a contributory role, they are unlikely to have been the determining factors. Moreover, in the last analysis, it is management that must ultimately create the mechanisms

276

that will improve the performance of economic institutions in the new technological society.[1]

Governments in democratic societies must respond to societal concerns when private institutions have failed to meet people's needs. American government, more so than most other governments, has been quite reticent in its regulation of business except where there is strong expressed public preference for such intervention—for example, environmental pollution, worker health and safety, and efficient working of the markets. Furthermore, other nations, notably Japan, have also had to contend with economic upheavals like the increase in oil prices. And unlike America, they have fewer domestic resources or large home markets to cushion the shock. Nor is American business a powerless giant, passively reacting to external conditions. Instead, it is a dynamic organism, actively interacting with the environment, affecting it and molding it, while at the same time involved in the process of creative adaptation.

Moreover, the primary source of the problems does not lie in the macro area (government policies), but in the micro area (corporate activities and management decisions). It is true that Japan has been enormously successful in the period since World War II, whereas the United States has been in a comparative state of relative decline. However, the decline is not as steep or widespread as is commonly alleged. Instead, it is found in specific sectors and industries such as basic metals and automobiles, where we may have lost largely because of changing comparative advantages, poor management decisions, or overall trends in the U.S. and world economies. For example, during the 1970s, before the current recession began, United States industrial performance was equal or superior to that of most other industrial nations by almost all measures. During these ten years, total employment in the United States increased by 26 percent, compared to 8 percent in Japan. Moreover, the United States was doing equally well in terms of its share of manufacturing in gross national product, investment in R&D, international trade, and sectoral shifts in investment.[2]

Nor can we blame a decline in America's work ethic—defined to mean working hard and effectively for the sake of the work itself[3]—as the source of our problems. Conventional wisdom has it, and public opinion surveys confirm it, that American workers' work behavior has deteriorated and that there has been a secular and significant decline in American workmanship during the last five or ten years. This is attributed to a weakening of the moral fiber and work-supportive values of American society. For example, in one Lou Harris study, 79 percent of the respondents believed that, compared to ten years ago, people had less pride in their work, while another 73 percent believed that motivation to work had declined in the same period.[4] In another study by Yankelovich, it was found that 87 percent of the nation's government and business leaders blamed a decline in motivation to work on deteriorating work ethic norms.[5]

A recent national public opinion study by the Public Agenda Foundation, however, found that the American work ethic remains quite strong and may be growing stronger. A majority of the workers professed "to having an inner need to do the very best job that they can, regardless of pay"; nearly two-thirds preferred "a boss who is demanding in the name of high quality"; and only 27 percent rejected the notion of the work ethic in preference to other reasons for work, such as purely financial transactions.[6] The study concludes that real cause for the commitment gap, a worker's desire to work compared with actual work performance, lies in a striking failure of managers to support and reinforce the work ethic.[7]

Therefore, our solutions must originate with corporate management and be rooted in the multitude of decisions taken by individual managers as they perceive new opportunities and take risks to exploit them. Even more important, the success of future ventures must depend not on the bureaucratic skills of preservation and protection on the part of government, but on the entrepreneurship, the process of creative destruction, and above all, on the organizing and motivating skills of individual managers in effectively mobilizing and utilizing physical and human resources.

In Chapter 10, we examined the problems and prospects of adapting Japanese business and management practices in the United States. We believe we have made a convincing case that while our problems are real, they are unlikely to be solved by emulating the Japanese. We have demonstrated that such a course would be counterproductive and unworkable. We now turn our attention to some of the corrective measures we must take to become more productive and competitive in domestic and world markets.

Our recommended avenues for change cover three areas: American business and management practices, business and government relations, and international terms of trade and competition. These measures are built on the strengths inherent in our cultural norms, individual and community traits, political system, factor endowments, and organizational structures. Moreover, they are designed to exploit our strengths rather than protect our weaknesses. And in dealing with our competitors, they are aimed at making them abide by the rules of the game in international trade rather than changing our behavior to play the game according to their rules.

THE MANAGEMENT CHALLENGE

In terms of traditional management activities, five areas determine the success or failure of an enterprise: financial, manufacturing or production-related activities, human resource management, marketing, and strategic management. To this must be added a sixth: the management of external relations—that is, business-government relations and dealing with other external constituencies. For in a hostile external environment, sociopolitical factors often have as much, if not more, impact on a firm's performance as the economic and market factors.

The fundamental failure of important segments of American business lies in a disregard for basic management principles: concern for the quality of product, workforce, consumers, and long-term perspective. Therefore, our strategies for change must address these vital concerns. In discussing these changes we will not only analyze the sources of the problems, but also examine some of the indigenous approaches developed by American corporations to cope successfully with the issues of maintaining a loyal and productive workforce, a flexible and responsive management structure, efficient manufacturing operations, a satisfied consumer base, and a highly profitable enterprise. Finally, we will examine the terms of international trade between Japan and other industrial countries and the negotiating strategies the United States might adopt to engineer a more equitable arrangement without further delay.

The Decline of Basic Industries

The largest and the most pronounced declines in productivity and international competitiveness in American industry have been recorded in sectors like mining, steel and automobiles, and consumer appliances, sectors that have been the traditional mainstay of America's economic growth. These industries are also characterized by:

1. Entrenched unionized labor which has successfully bargained for restrictive work practices and wage rates not compensated by productivity gains.
2. An oligopolistic industry structure in which price competition has become less important in determining market share.
3. A significant slowdown in product innovation and product differentiation symbolized by cosmetic and superficial changes.
4. A large protected domestic market that enabled managers to postpone plant innovation and modernization. The increased costs arising out of expensive labor and outmoded plants could be passed on to consumers.
5. Inefficient managements willing to accept increased labor costs and postpone modernization, in an effort to maintain production and current profits at the expense of future declines in competitiveness and the resultant loss of markets.
6. Sacrifice of product quality and disregard of consumer interests. Rather than being considered the best, "Made in America" came to be identified

in the minds of many Americans with shoddy workmanship, indifferent service, and uncompetitive prices.

There has been a decline in emphasis on manufacturing in American industry, as if there is nothing more that can be learned in this area. An increasing number of chief executives of large corporations have been lawyers or financial experts and accountants, people with little expertise or interest in manufacturing operations. In the process, the marketing emphasis has shifted from sustenance and growth of a satisfied customer base to management of the sales force to maximize the short-run sales generated by each dollar of selling expenses.

To these specific factors, we must add two general factors that permeate American industries. The first has to do with misguided attitudes about the basic purpose of business. American businesspeople never seem to tire of saying that they are in the business of making money. Businesses are treated as so many assets that should be juggled for their return on equity. The quarterly earning reports and stock price fluctuations receive more focus and attention and influence business decisions to a greater extent than long-run strategic considerations. Since short-run stock prices are affected not only by the underlying earnings potential of a firm, but also by current market fads, American firms appear to demonstrate herdlike behavior: becoming conglomerates, creating "synergistic" diversification, or gaining a foothold in high-tech industries. The glamour acquisitions of one period become the albatrosses of the next. Solid businesses are starved of new funds necessary to keep up with new technology, and are instead milked for cash needed to fuel management's new ventures. Quite often it is the same management that took credit for bold diversifying moves in the go-go 1960s, and now claims credit for making the "painful" decisions by writing off large chunks of assets, sharply cutting the workforce, and preparing their companies to meet the "changed" economic circumstances.

In the process, American business has lost sight of one of the most important facts of life. In a free and open market, it may be in the business of making money. But the consumer doesn't owe it a living. Therefore, unless the consuming public is satisfied with the product or service, it will not support a business through repeat purchases. Profit is the reward for having a satisfied clientele. The clientele must necessarily come first, otherwise there won't be any profits for the firm to enjoy.

Even firms like Chrysler seem not to have yet fully learned this lesson. The competition from Japan has forced the American auto industry to the wall. Yet, when voluntary import quotas created a shortage for certain types of cars, American industry responded by raising the prices directly and also indirectly through loading cars with expensive optional equipment. An un-named Chrysler official was reported to have said to a *Wall Street Journal* reporter that the company was in the business of making money and that this was its opportunity to do so.

The second factor pertains to a secular decline of public trust in all large social institutions in general, and in America's big business in particular. The decline in public trust in America's business leadership manifests itself in greater government regulation of business activity. It also constrains management's discretionary decision-making power by not allowing it enough latitude to experiment with new approaches. Various corporate constituencies constantly battle to predetermine their shares of the pie, thereby robbing managements of most of their flexibility in dealing with new circumstances.

The Changing Nature of Competition

The late seventies brought home to American businesses a new type of competition. Not only were foreign companies taking away large shares of America's traditional international markets, but they were also invading their traditional home markets. The new international competition had two distinct characteristics: (1) There was tremendous emphasis on quality, and compared with American firms, the foreign competitors delivered a higher quality/price ratio. (2) Foreign products also offered greater innovation and product variety.

American industries were buffeted at the high and the low end of the consumer products markets and also in many of the smokestack basic industries. American businesses that suffered the most were those that were saddled with outmoded plants, comparatively high wage costs, inefficient management, and a hostile consumer base. The affected industries have blamed subsidized foreign businesses, their own high labor costs, and expensive environmental regulation for their problems. They have also sought increased government protection from foreign competition. However, these factors offer only partial explanation. Studies show that environmental regulations have at best added no more than 5 to 6 percent of the total cost of plant and equipment, that the gap in wage rates between the United States and other countries is narrowing, and that in any event, consumers are willing to pay higher prices for foreign goods in affected industries because they perceive them to be better value in relation to price. Other measures taken by American business have included giving up the lower end of the market or trying to gain economies of scale by enlarging plants or production runs. Both strategies have been less than successful. By giving up the low end of the markets, they have provided a large consumer base to the foreign competition from which it can assault the more lucrative higher end of the market. Moreover, the new competition of the eighties is not in mass-produced, highly standardized products, but in more specialized goods available at reasonable prices to highly segmented markets. The result has been a secular decline in the U.S. comparative advantage in standardized products manufactured in highly capital intensive plants and using relatively unskilled labor.

Consider, for example, the plight of the U.S. auto industry. During the last fifteen years, the auto markets have become truly international. There is a large number of financially strong competitors. As one keen analyst of the industry observes: "These new international players, moreover, have quite a different approach from that of the U.S. Big Three: their plans consist of radically new strategies, modes of operation, and production experience . . . the novel competitive challenge they present cannot be overcome by the familiar responses U.S. companies have long used against each other. Strategically, the Big Three are well prepared to fight not this new war, but the last one."[8]

The new manufacturing technologies have radically changed the economics of manufacturing, where economies of scale, based on large production runs of standardized products and using low-skilled labor, no longer deliver lower product costs measured in terms of consumer-driven product attributes. Although the present system creates production economies through lower unit manufacturing costs, it also leads to greater specialization, longer production runs, and a certain rigidity in the types of products manufactured.

The emerging computer-integrated manufacturing technology, on the other hand, creates greater flexibility, makes possible shorter production runs, facilitates the creation of more customized products, offers faster responses to changes in market demand, provides for greater control and accuracy of processes, and reduces manufacturing in-process time. The new technology radically alters the terms of tradeoff between changeover and inventory costs in favor of the former, with profound implications for corporate strategy. It requires greater emphasis on manufacturing engineering rather than operations management.[9] By providing greater flexibility in creating product differentiation and shorter response times, it creates tremendous new marketing opportunities for the corporation. Two observers of this process, Professors Goldhar and Jelinek, suggest that American industry must shift its focus from economies of scale to economies of scope. The latter involves creating efficiencies that are brought by variety and not volume. This is made possible through the use of manufacturing technology that makes feasible the application of leading edge processing techniques to smaller production runs.[10]

One of the major strengths of the Japanese companies has been their emphasis on integrated manufacturing processes. They have exploited this advantage by building greater options—added value—into their production, thereby increasing product variety. When combined with better quality controls, the Japanese have been able to compete both at the lower and the higher ends of markets.

Ironically, the so-called modern practices of American management may have also contributed to their decline.[11] As Hayes and Abernathy point out: "These new principles, despite their sophistication and widespread usefulness, encourage a preference for (1) analytic detachment, rather than the insight that comes from 'hands on' experience and (2) short-term cost reduction rather than long-term development and technological competitiveness. It is this new management gospel, we feel, that has played a major role in undermining the vigor of American industry."[12]

Research also shows that American management's overdependence on rational financial models, such as discounted cash flow and present value analysis, may have contributed to its bias toward shorter-term investment and risk-aversion strategies.[13] When combined with a system of compensation that emphasizes both short-run and stock-market-based performance, it caters to exploitation of current assets, forgoing of plant updating, and a preference for investments with shorter payback periods. The result is an inevitable loss of emphasis on innovation, R&D, and long-term investments.

The Need for Increased Competition

To survive, grow, excel, and compete effectively in domestic and international markets, American industry needs *more* and not less competition. The entire industrial process is undergoing rapid technological change that makes the current notions of basic and mature industries obsolete, if not irrelevant. The new technological revolution not only offers opportunities for a vast array of new products and product improvements, but also has the effect of radically changing the production processes.[14] The technological revolution has lowered the traditional entry barriers (large capital investment in fixed assets) by which established large-scale smokestack industries used to keep out new entrants. At the same time, it has raised exit barriers; existing industries cannot easily extricate themselves from their markets without losing enormous amounts of assets and often endangering their net worth. To adapt to these changes, American business must go through the process of "creative destruction."[15]

Given the nature of the American political system, it is unrealistic to assume that such a process of creative destruction and sectoral shift can be accomplished by greater government intervention in the marketplace. Our entire history argues against it, and contemporary events confirm it. The most ardent supporters of protection in the guise of industrial policy are invariably those industries that are burdened by high production costs and faced with more efficient and aggressive competitors.[16] While these industries have cried for greater protection, they have not always used the protective umbrella and resultant increase in revenues to invest in plant modernization, but instead have opted for diversification away from their core businesses, thereby having consumers and not shareholders bear the brunt of their diversification moves.[17]

When import quotas have provided shelter for domestic industries, the companies involved have often used the opportunity to fatten their bottom lines rather than lower prices and expand their market shares.[18] Import quotas that start out to be voluntary and short run have a tendency to become mandatory and long term because the beneficiaries find the advantages too great to give up and therefore create a political constituency to maintain them.

Although a good case can be made for protecting domestic industries from unfair foreign competition, the preferred remedy should be import tariffs rather than quotas. Both approaches have their objective in protecting domestic producers from subsidized foreign competition, but tariffs pass the windfall profits to the government, rather than giving them to local producers. They also do not restrict consumer choice to the same extent as quotas, thereby keeping pressure on domestic producers to compete in the marketplace for consumer patronage by offering products and services at competitive prices. Studies by Robert Lawrence of the Brookings Institution show that sectoral shifts in new investments in American industry without government intervention have been occurring as rapidly as those in Japan and more rapidly than in countries like West Germany, France, and the United Kingdom.[19] Moreover, where deregulation of domestic industries has taken place, there have been dramatic improvements in productivity, growth, and consumer welfare, notwithstanding certain painful dislocations caused by redistribution of income from protected factors of production that are forced to give up their monopoly rents.[20] The same is true for international markets. It is highly unlikely that labor and management in the auto industry would have made the necessary adjustments in costs and improvements had they not faced competition from foreign imports. Basic industries like pulp and paper that were willing to take a longer perspective and invest in plant modernization have been successful in maintaining their global competitive position; more protected industries like textiles have not fared as well.

Improvements in Manufacturing Processes and Investment in New R&D

There must be greater emphasis on improving manufacturing processes in a manner that is not merely cost effective; manufacturing should be integrated into a total production process designed to incorporate the new technologies. Dispassionate and well-informed observers of Japanese production methods have concluded that the Japanese strength in consistently producing high-quality products with very low defect rates at competitive prices does not lie in superior technology or automation alone. "The Japanese factory is not, as many believe, a prototype of the factory of the future. If it were, it might be, curiously, far less of a threat. The Japanese have achieved their current level of manufacturing excellence by doing simple things very well, and slowly improving them all the time."[21]

The important lesson to be learned from Japan is not *how* they do it, but *what* can be accomplished by doing it right. The Japanese method is a complex network of manufacturing practices, worker organization, managerial attitudes, and a corporate culture peculiar to Japan. The American method cannot be similar, but it can be no less painstaking. There has to be greater focus on execution and detail. Moreover, there is evidence that product quality and manufacturing process integration—on a level that compares favorably with the Japanese—has already been achieved in the United States where management has the will and the foresight to invest in plant modernization and cares about product quality and consumer satisfaction.[22] American companies like Cincinnati Milacron have been leaders in the robotics and automation—the tools of flexible manufacturing processes—that have contributed so significantly to the superiority of Japanese products and the success of Japanese enterprises. Unfortunately, while America still leads in developing the new technology, "Japan leads in applying what America invents."[23] The fault must lie with management. Except for a handful of companies like John Deere, the manufacturer of farm machinery, American manufacturers are far behind their Japanese counterparts. The explanations offered for this gap are plausible ones and short-term-oriented—namely, expense, risks, start-up problems with unfamiliar technology, and current surplus capacity. Nevertheless, there is a new emphasis on production and process engineering. Most of it is being forced on American companies by foreign competition and some companies, notably the automobile manufacturers, are taking up the challenge.[24]

Integrating new manufacturing technologies into production processes will go a long way toward meeting the Japanese challenge. However, it will not overcome it. We will be competing in those areas where the Japanese have the edge—namely, plant-floor manufacturing processes involving constant improvements in essentially existing technologies and products. We must also concentrate on areas where the Japanese and other foreign nations lag behind. These have to do with product innovations that change the character of the industry itself and often create new product uses and thereby new markets. It can be shown that American companies seem to be able to compete with Japanese companies where product life cycles are very short, and where each new generation of products is radically different from the previous ones. While large American corporations may have become more risk-averse, the entrepreneurial attitude still pervades and can be found all the way from the Silicon Valley whiz kids to the Texas wildcatters.

The new basic research is, however, quite expensive, and translating it into products even more so. American industry has a vital stake in supporting more basic research in American universities, where it has been lagging because of financial constraints. There is increasing evidence that American business has recognized this need and that efforts are being made to alleviate the situation.[25] U.S. industry must also develop cooperative arrangements to undertake joint R&D in areas where new technology involves high risk and large commitment of resources that are beyond the reach of all but the very large companies.

This is a far better approach than the Japanese model, and more in keeping with the American legal and political system. In general, the antitrust laws constitute a formidable barrier to this kind of team effort because of suspicions that such activities are a subterfuge for different types of collusive activities that are in restraint of trade. Fortunately, the U.S. government appears to be taking a more enlightened and flexible approach to industry efforts in this direction. Three recent initiatives toward cooperative research have been taken by companies in the semiconductor and computer industries through the establishment of R&D coops such as the Microelectronics and Computer Technology Corporation (MCTC) and the Semiconductor Research Corporation (SRC). This collaboration is being promoted by the Commerce Department, with the blessing of the Defense Department, as America's answer to the Japanese challenge. In the third case, the Justice Department granted immunity to a joint venture being formed by eight small companies that plan to pool their resources to compete for research and development and production contracts in electronics, lasers, and other high-technology lines.

MCTC was formed in 1982 by ten high-tech companies under the leadership of William C. Norris, chairman and CEO of the Minneapolis-based Control Data Corporation. Norris was concerned about the challenge of the Japanese computer industry in areas such as semiconductors and computers, especially the next generation of supercomputers incorporating elements of artificial intelligence. Major competitors, such as Honeywell, Control Data, and Sperry, were persuaded to work together on industry research of mutual interest and to pool their knowledge and financial resources. The Justice Department agreed not to oppose the formation of the venture.

MCTC will serve as a coordinating firm monitoring four areas of mutual research interest: advanced computer design, computer software technology, integrated circuit packaging, and CAD-CAM (computer-assisted design, computer-assisted manufacture). MCTC has its own R&D group, which will operate on a budget of $75 million in 1984 with about 250 researchers borrowed from member companies. MCTC will hold the patents but will license products resulting from its R&D effort. It will not market products on its own, leaving this task to the sponsoring companies. STC is a more sparsely staffed operation that will largely coordinate microchip technology in the nation's universities. It has already committed about $8.25 million to support 40 research initiatives in 30 universities. Current plans now contemplate moving from research to development by establishing a pilot plant whose operational technology could then be given to member firms.[26]

Renewed Emphasis on Internal Growth

When confronted with foreign competition, U.S. corporations in basic industries are increasingly opting for diversification as a means of improving market performance and profitability. In one sense, this is not a new approach. American business history is replete with merger waves, the most recent being the one in the sixties that gave birth to many of today's conglomerates.

The track record of companies that have grown through acquisitions and mergers is not an inspiring one. The mergers of the 1890–1920 period created large corporations within specific industries that provided them with both economies of scale and reduced competition, and may have benefited those companies' stockholders and managers without necessarily being in the public interest. Various research studies show that the more recent merger wave of the sixties has not served well either the corporations involved or their stockholders. Diversification into new industries generally did not increase the profitability of these corporations, and may have actually hurt their performance. There is conflicting evidence as to the effect of conglomerate mergers even during the go-go years of 1960s. Studies show that while certain mergers were beneficial, the overall effect of mergers on the efficiency and ROI of the combined ventures was not above average. The argument presented here is confined to the issue of efficiency of resource usage and not bigness or concentration per se—that is, issues dealing with the antitrust aspects of mergers and acquisitions. Evidence in those areas is inconclusive, and a strong case cannot be made for bigness and concentration or for corporate size and reduced competitiveness.[27]

Operating in mature industries does not necessarily mean poor growth or declining profitability. In fact, available research shows that some of the most profitable companies during the 1970s were to be found in such mature industries as steel, tire and rubber, heavy-duty trucks, construction equipment, and major appliances. Companies in these slow-growth industries that kept plants modernized and operating efficiently earned returns on equity and capital consistently far higher than the equity returns for technology leaders in high-growth markets.[28]

Corporate executives who have not been associated with efficient and competitive operations in their own industries are unlikely to find the solutions to their problems in mergers and acquisitions that propel them into high-tech, high-growth industries. As Professors Hayes and Garvin observe: "Bitten, perhaps, by the merger bug and unwilling to adjust their inflation hurdle rates, many American managers have found reinvestment in existing businesses less than desirable. Under siege in a changing world, they recall the economic Camelot of the 1960s and believe that it still exists somewhere, waiting to be found outside their corporate bunker. Had they placed less faith in the misleading objectivity of their discounting techniques, they might be spending their time and resources reinforcing their own bunker walls."[29]

There are a variety of reasons why diversification through acquisition may not necessarily be the strategy for firms in mature industries that are currently facing intense foreign competition and declining markets. Decisions to acquire high-growth companies in high-tech glamour industries are often based on a "follow the leader" mentality. The large number of suitors makes the fewer available companies prohibitively expensive to buy. Companies in high-growth industries are often owned by entrepreneurs who are reluctant to sell. When acquired, these entrepreneurs often find the corporate world not to their liking and may leave soon thereafter, thereby depriving the new owners of a critical asset. And finally, new companies may have research interests and a product mix that may be superficially appealing, but may provide a poor fit or support to the acquiring company's existing businesses.[30]

No industry is permanently basic or is likely to remain mature and declining forever. There are indeed different growth industries at different times, but the new industries also carry a high failure rate for individual companies, and the successful ones carry a high acquisition price. On the other hand, mature industries offer tremendous opportunities for new innovations and entrepreneurship to break through the declining curve and start a new growth trend. The entire history of industrial development bears witness to this trend. Even in today's depressed steel industry, smaller steel mills are thriving against both domestic and foreign competition. American executives would do well to give serious consideration to reinvestment and modernization in industries they know well rather than going after potential gushers that may turn out to be dry wells.

As Peter Drucker aptly points out: "Mindless diversification does not work. There is no easy business. Also, in most no growth institutions, the main earnings stream, for many years ahead, will have to come from the existing mundane business. And if this business is neglected in the excitement of 'diversification' into 'growth businesses' or into 'cash cows,' everything will go down the drain—including the red-hot acquisition." He goes on to suggest that if the only thing the acquiring company has to contribute to the new acquisition is money, the result will predictably be catastrophe.[31]

The New Realities of Technology and the Perils of Planning

We are witnessing a new industrial revolution where the nature of technological change is not evolutionary but revolutionary, not continuous but discrete, not gradual but drastic. Moreover, these changes are not restricted to certain high-technology industries, but permeate every industrial sector. In health care and pharmaceuticals, it is biotechnology and generic engineering.[32] In machine tools, it is robotics. In consumer industries, it is the microcomputer. In basic metals, it is the plastics, carbon fibers, and other substitute materials. In most industries, it is the information explosion and our ability to process and assimilate information that is wreaking havoc with traditional notions of planning horizon, risk assessment, and asset management.

The corporate executive is increasingly confronted with the need to make decisions when faced with truly innovative product alternatives. This situation offers greater freedom to choose, but also increases the risks. The quantity of available information is invariably insufficient and its quality uncertain. Lead times for making decisions are becoming longer, requiring heavy investment commitments, and the risk of betting on the wrong product is measured in major losses of net worth, if not extinction of the company. The decisions require not so much current knowledge as a sense of vision, not narrow specialization but breadth of understanding about how seemingly unrelated ideas and processes might create new products and spawn whole new industries.[33] Under these conditions, what are needed are not the financial tools of measuring discounted current value of some future flow of earnings, but schemes for assessing the risk itself. To use the conventional argument, that all risks are equal when the future is unmeasurable, is really begging the question.

And yet this is precisely the quality that has been downgraded in American management teaching and practice in the last three decades. We are suffering from a tyranny of large numbers. Our emphasis on scientific management has produced very narrowly trained managers who analyze their external environment through the tinted glasses of their specializations. At the corporate level, managers have become more interested in asset preservation and risk diversification than in "real" asset creation, which often carries with it greater risks.

The new industrial revolution also brings with it the need for managing a new kind of employee—the scientist, the thinker, the idea man; the person who at the same time is an expert in one field but also has the vision to draw together seemingly unrelated elements from different fields into meaningful wholes; who is not afraid of the unconventional or the unusual, and who is willing to listen to the unorthodox and not be restricted by the prevailing scientific dogma.[34] This employee needs a looser work environment in which he or she can explore new ideas. It is not surprising that such an employee will be a highly qualified expert in his or her area. What is more important is that this employee is quite likely to be eclectic, individualistic, and entrepreneurial. Above all, he or she does not ordinarily fit the traditional corporate mode. Moreover, since new lines of inquiry or idea development are yet untested, there are no clear-cut criteria as to how one might evaluate this employee's productivity or reward him or her accordingly.

The success and growth of high-tech industries in the United States rests primarily with these individuals and the corporations that can keep them. Even in old-line industries, the companies that have grown and flourished are those whose corporate culture nurtures people who care to be different and who question the conventional wisdom and the status quo.

What is so different about the future is that the need for creating organizations that can keep innovating employees and sustain the innovative process will become the rule rather than the exception. The challenge for future managers, whether they be American or Japanese, is not to protect what they have, but to adapt the process of creative destruction that is taking place at an increasingly accelerated pace.

To meet this new challenge, we must make a renewed commitment to long-range planning and strategy development. Planning, however, should not be viewed as a series of sequential steps within a predetermined time schedule. Instead, there should be greater emphasis on forecasting of alternative futures based on the state of the society and the economy, the competitive environment, new information generation, consumer preferences, product innovation, and the development of new and potentially radical technologies. Planning horizons should be holistic and therefore deliberately imprecise to accommodate the imperatives of not only intended strategies, but also strategies that emerge despite planned intentions.[35]

Given our assumptions of increasingly larger time horizon strategy implementation, uncertainty of the quality of data, and higher risks, it is important that plans be flexible enough to take advantage of unanticipated opportunities. Strategic process should not be confused with budget formulation; instead it should be viewed as a continuing stream of overlapping decisions with relaxed requirements for specificity as decisions move away from the present and into the future.

Integration of Public Affairs with Business Strategy and Operations

American business must treat the public policy aspects of its activities as an integral part of its overall strategic planning and operations and not merely as an appendage to its business, to be managed as business-government relations, community affairs, or charitable contributions.

At the macro level, concern for public attitudes and societal expectations should pertain not only to the second-order effects of corporate activities, but also to general societal concerns. The notion of corporate social responsibility does not revolve around the charitable activities of a corporation, but pertains to a more important question. To wit: What role should the large corporations and their executives play in the determination of the national agenda?

In Chapter 9 we discussed the notion of the legitimacy gap and a secular decline in public trust. In a pluralistic society, public choices are determined by those institutions that advocate a public purpose and are able to make persuasive arguments so that people accept their choices.[36] By advocating a corporate purpose that makes corporate self-interest paramount and public interest a side effect, American corporations have undermined some of the values of capitalism itself,[37] and have increasingly abrogated their right to choose how social priorities will be determined and public choices defined to other social institutions. They have been forced largely to react and defend. Of late, however, there has been an increasing inclination on the part of corporate executives to become more actively involved in the sociopolitical arena, as can be seen in the establishment of many nontraditional business groups, such as the Business Roundtable. To a significant extent, this trend has been forced on the corporations because of increasing governmental regulation of corporate activities and public concern about corporate power and how it is exercised by corporate leaders. Surveys show that chief executives of some of the largest U.S. corporations spend almost half of their time dealing with external constituencies, notably government agencies, legislative bodies, the news media, religious organizations, and other public interest groups.

Unfortunately, a large part of these activities still revolve around defending the status quo and corporate prerogatives. The corporation is reacting to external factors rather than being an active agent of social change. Corporate political involvement, under these conditions, risks further public alienation and an erosion of public trust in business that is likely to result in increased governmental intervention in corporate affairs.[38] Unless the corporation can define its social role in a way that clearly embodies a notion of public interest and employs language in stating a public position that is perceived by the public as embodying such a notion, it will be forced to accept the role defined by its critics[39]—a role that will not serve corporate interests and may not necessarily be in the interest of the larger society either.

Ironically, Japanese corporations, and to a lesser extent European corporations, are not confronted with this schism between public interest and corporate purpose. In a homogeneous Japanese society, where all institutions share a common value set and where government and business have a long tradition of a close working relationship, this posture does not create unacceptable conflicts between business and other social institutions. Indeed, when conflicts do arise they are easily suppressed, and their effect on corporate behavior is minimized. Moreover, Japanese corporations assiduously practice a rhetoric of corporate social responsiveness that contributes to conflict avoidance even when underlying issues are substantive and not easily resolved.[40]

In today's American society, the impact of sociopolitical factors on a corporation's performance is as great, and in many cases far greater, than that of the economic and market factors. For the former not only intervene directly in corporate activities, but also indirectly as they affect the economic climate through the nation's fiscal and monetary policies. Therefore, corporations must develop organizational structures and decision-making processes that make external affairs and public concerns an integral part of their long-range planning and investment decisions. This approach should help the corporation develop relevant and effective responses to external societal pressures and problems. Such responses must be proactive rather than reactive and designed to present the corporate position in a manner that embodies the notion of the public interest.[41]

The Role of Corporate Culture

Business literature, both popular and scholarly, is replete with references to the need for a corporate culture, the glue that holds the organization together. One of the reasons for the superiority of Japanese business organizations is attributed to the existence of a corporate culture that avoids the cult of individualism, builds group loyalty and a mutual support system, and provides an environment that encourages individual employees to excel and give their best to the organization. Proponents of introduction of the Japanese system in the United States strongly advocate the creation of a corporate culture that duplicates most, or all, of the qualities of the Japanese corporate culture.[42]

Culture is indeed an important ingredient for the survival and continuity of all institutions, not only business organizations. In fact, no organization is lacking in some type of culture. The unanswered questions, however, are these: How much and what type of corporate culture do we need in order to meet the future?[43]

Corporate culture is not without its problems. While it provides bonds of community, it also creates insularity. Corporations, like older more traditional societies and nations, can be so steeped in their cultures that they become rigid and inflexible. Unable to evolve and adapt, they fracture and collapse when the external environment becomes hostile and the internal values appear less important to the new generation of employees. It is not surprising that many corporate "turnarounds" are effected after the new management sweeps out the old guard and makes an irreparable break with the past.

Japanese corporate culture is institution-oriented and independent of the value set of the individual employees, although it harnesses the social norms of its workforce to the institution's benefit. As we noted in earlier chapters, the organization uses both selective recruitment and coercive enforcement to ensure worker allegiance to corporate values. The fact that strong social penalties also exist against nonconformity provides further inducement.

The proponents of corporate culture in America project it as primarily constituency-driven. The role of profits includes the importance of building a loyal workforce and a market base of satisfied customers. Inculcation of the corporate culture becomes a management function; it becomes a manipulative tool that must be managed as a part of the corporate strategy to achieve management goals. Corporate culture so defined becomes too narrow. It runs the danger of filtering out both new values and new employees that do not fit a preconceived mold. In the process, it may end up protecting those individuals who support the institutionalized structure and uphold the symbols of the corporate culture while undermining its substantive aspects. Like the priests in a pagan temple, they uphold the ritualistic forms of cultural observation, while at the same time hastening that culture's demise through deeds that undermine its core values and show them as poor role models for others to follow. Thus when external environment forces unintended strategic options on the corporation, they are viewed as crises rather than unrealized opportunities. Such an organization is poorly equipped to adapt to a changing external environment. Many successful companies, such as Texas Instruments and Eastman Kodak, that are noted for their strong corporate cultures have had a difficult time coping with the new competitive environment and the changing values of the new generation of employees.

The essence of a successful corporate culture does not lie in a unique set of shared values that converts its people into a tribe separate from the environment surrounding them. This approach is akin to controlling or managing the external environment and is quite typical of the dominant strategic posture of American business in all its operations. We view the corporate culture in a more holistic mold—one that internalizes the values of the external environment rather than insulating the organization from it. Here again we do not argue for the creation of "tribes" that would foster group harmony and worker loyalty, and thereby bring greater products.[44] Instead, we propose a corporate culture that nurtures the American values of individualism, initiative, and enlightened self-interest. The critical element here is management. Therefore, we should restructure the managerial reward system to encourage long-term perspectives, technological innovation, risk-taking, and consumer satisfaction. A large part of the decline of American industry can be "attributed to the attitudes, preoccupations and practices of American managers. By their preference for serving existing markets rather than creating new ones and by their devotion to short-term returns and 'management by numbers,' many of them have effectively foresworn long-term technological superiority as a competitive weapon. In consequence, they have abdicated their strategic responsibilities."[45]

The primary characteristics of this concept of corporate culture are these:

1. The culture contains a set of ethical standards that define a corporation's identity and its public and private integrity.[46] These ethical standards, or core values, are institution-oriented and transcend the interests of various constituencies. At times of stress they provide the test against which the corporation measures its behavior as a socially relevant institution. Unlike the operational norms, which must change with changing times, core values are more stable and provide the yardstick for evaluating the appropriateness of changes in corporate behavior modes.

2. The core values of corporate culture do not create conflicts for an employee between adherence to desired corporate behavior and personal ethics that have greater congruity to socially accepted norms of ethical behavior. Corporate ethics in such a corporate culture become a positive force and not a constraint. They encourage an employee to do his or her best not only because it is in the corporate interest, or his or her financial well-being, but because it is the right thing to do and is in the interest of the society of which this corporation is an integral part.

3. This corporate culture would enhance individualism rather than suppress it. There would be a greater drive for individual expression, a sense of accomplishment, and the demonstration of excellence.[47]

IMPROVING MANAGEMENT PRODUCTIVITY AND PERFORMANCE

One of the critical needs of the American corporation is to improve the productivity and performance of its managers. We have already discussed four dimensions of this problem: coping with the new technologies and plant modernization; planning and strategy development under conditions of increasingly higher risks and uncertain information; nurturing the creativity of a new type of expert-scientist who is both individualistic and eclectic, but who is critical to the success of the firm; and managing external affairs. To this we must add two additional factors. The first pertains to the restructuring of the management reward system so that it provides greater incentives for managing the long-term interest of the firm, improving its technological edge, and maintaining its long-term competitive position.

Another factor has to do with the management of the entire work-force, whose character is also changing. This would require restructuring the firm's organization and decision-making processes, and also redesigning the employee compensation system so that it is better attuned to achieving improved employee performance and contributions to total corporate welfare.

Restructuring the Management Reward System

There has been a dramatic shift in the road to the top in large corporations away from those with technical and marketing skills to those with financial and legal backgrounds.[48] The fact that tenure at the top of large American corporations is very short—lasting, in most cases, less than five years—does not help the situation.[49] Moreover, the compensation system for top management is biased toward rewarding short-term financial performance and turn-around specialists, with emphasis on cash and asset portfolio management. For example, a recent study by Booz-Allen & Hamilton showed that during the period 1971–1981, total senior management compensation in Standard & Poor's 400 corporations increased by 10 percent in real terms, while stockholder value (stock price change plus dividends) decreased by 2 percent. The study concluded: "Executive compensation programs in too many U.S. corporations have rewarded handsomely for performance that has not benefited shareholders equally."[50] To this we must add the more bizarre and self-serving devices of a reward system that provide senior executives with "safe harbor" and "golden parachutes" in the event of hostile takeover attempts that may have been induced by the management's lackluster performance in the first place. Even when there has been a shift in executive compensation from short-term to long-term, the results have not been appreciably different for the corporations or their stockholders.[51]

A variety of reasons account for this phenomenon:

1. There is heavy reliance on accounting measures of performance, which may not be related to true economic performance. For example, management can increase bookkeeping profits through a faster deterioration of its capital base by postponing plant modernization and investing the funds in other ventures with a shorter payback period. As Professor Rappaport of Northwestern University's School of Management points out: "Earnings growth can be achieved not only when management is investing at a rate of return above that demanded by the market, but also when it is investing below the market rate and thereby decreasing the value of the common shares. This is the case because the earnings figure does not reflect changes in risk or changes in expectation about inflation."[52] This approach also ignores the effects of incremental working capital and fixed investment needed to make the business grow. All these factors are critical in measuring the economic value of the enterprise. For example: "Many companies during the

1970s showed impressive double-digit annual earnings per share growth rates . . . while providing their shareholders minimal or negative rates of return from dividends plus share price changes. In sum, the problem associated with performance measurement is not only the undue emphasis on the short-term, but also the most fundamental problem of measurements based on an appropriate bottom line."[53]

2. There is the phenomenon of increased pay for increased size, where growth is rewarded for its own sake. Studies show a high correlation between firm size and executive compensation.[54]

3. When long-term performance is considered, fewer than one-third of the managers participating in annual bonus plans are included in the long-term performance incentive plans. Furthermore, annual bonuses invariably constitute a greater percentage of total incentive plans for senior management.[55]

4. Market performance may occur because of a variety of external factors beyond the control of corporate managers, who may thus be rewarded or penalized for considerations unrelated to their contribution to the profitability of the enterprise. Thus Professor James March comments:

> Executives in American industries make reputations by managing accounts rather than managing technology, service, or products. The statement is overdrawn. There are some important constraints. But there is a very real risk that our incentive schemes encourage too much attention to the management of accounts and too little attention to the management of the fundamental concerns of business.[56]

Economic Value-Based Management Reward System. The major issue, therefore, is "not pay-for-performance, but rather pay for *what* performance."[57] We must develop a reward system that provides incentives to managers for creating real long-term values for the enterprise. Furthermore, to be effective, the system should be based on factors that are largely controllable by the management, and on criteria that are objective, verifiable, and rationally acceptable to those whose performance is to be measured.[58]

To accomplish this objective, two elements should be added to the performance measurement of top management: (1) innovation rate and product life cycle, and (2) variable manufacturing costs.

Innovation Rate and Product Life Cycle. In calculating overall revenues of the company, consideration should be given to the rate of technological change in end-use products in a particular industry. The more rapid the rate of technological change, the greater should be the emphasis on new products in a company's product mix. Thus, if the average product life span in a given industry is five years and approximately 20 percent of industry sales consist of new products, the company's product mix in a given year must have at least 20 percent of revenues contributed by new products in that year, and the total product mix should not have any products five years or older. Of course, the greater the contribution of newer products to the firm's total revenues, the better would be the management's performance. A premium is thus placed on new products that ensures the long-term profitability of the company. This process also avoids the problems of short-term versus long-term by internalizing long-term valuations in short-term measurement criteria.

For comparison purposes, an industry should not be biased against innovation through acquisition at the fully developed end of the product life cycle. This would encourage both in-house research and development and also discourage the tendency toward "dressing up the numbers" through acquisitions.

Variable Manufacturing Costs. The second element in evaluating managerial performance relates to the manufacturing end of a firm's operations. Since plant automation and modernization invariably result in lowering variable costs, any performance criteria should include a firm's variable unit costs of production or manufacturing when compared with industry averages or the least-cost producer in the industry.

These two measures can be used not only at the overall corporate level, but also at the division and subsidiary level, making it possible to include a large number of managers in such an incentive system. Moreover, it would force managers, especially in mature industries, to strive for a growth-and-renewal strategy instead of a maintenance strategy.

Management of the Workforce

To date, American corporations, when faced with lower-priced and better-quality foreign imports, or domestic competitors with lower cost structures, have fought back primarily through savings in labor costs. These savings have been achieved primarily through a reduction in existing wages and a relaxation in work rules. These approaches yield immediate results and allow the corporation to survive. They do not, however, necessarily improve physical or qualitatively better output per man-hour but instead reduce cost per man-hour. And they will not offer a long-term solution to a company's problems. Workers resent them because they see them as a one-way street, enriching the stockholders at the expense of the workers. The wage factor will increasingly lose its relevance once wages in affected industries fall in line with prevailing U.S. wage trends and the gap between wages in the United States and other countries is further narrowed, as indicated by current trends. Moreover, in the last analysis American industry must work smarter, not merely harder, if it is to become more competitive in the international arena.

Studies show that while there is strong work ethic among American workers, it is not being channeled at the workplace. People's commitment to their jobs has been declining in the United States. According to a study by the Public Agenda Foundation, over 75 percent of the people interviewed stated that they could be significantly more effective on their jobs than they were. Nearly half of all jobholders (44 percent) stated they did not put much effort into their jobs over and above what was required to hold on to a job.[59]

Traditionally, automation of the manufacturing process has been used for two purposes: (1) To accelerate production processes and improve product quality, and (2) to simplify jobs so that they can be performed by unskilled workers. The management objective has been to reduce direct labor costs and give it greater control of overall costs. The new technological revolution makes the old Taylorization approach of scientific management ineffective. Rather than increasing managerial control, the new technologies have had the perverse effect of actually increasing employee discretion over how the job is to be performed. Although the new technologies reduce direct labor input per unit of output, the new technology also requires a kind of worker who is more educated, is in greater demand and is more mobile, and seeks greater control over his or her work environment. Even the blue collar workers, although declining in numbers, have greater discretion on the job in newer plants.

A Yankelovich survey shows, for example, that a large number of current jobholders feel they have a "great deal of discretion" over the quality of their work (63 percent); discretion over effort (45 percent), and "freedom to decide how to do my work" (43 percent). Yankelovich calls it the "discretionary effort," defined as "the maximum amount of effort and care an individual could bring to his or her job, and the minimum amount of effort required to avoid being fired or penalized; in short the portion of one's effort over which a jobholder has the greatest control."[60] The higher the level of worker discretion over his effort, the lower will be the ability of management to control on-the-job work performance. Workers' productivity and performance under these conditions will be greatly influenced by their commitment to the job, their willingness to work over and above the controllable minimum. Under these conditions, traditional management tools of rewards and punishments become less effective.

What is required, therefore, is a new approach to organizational structure, decision-making processes, and incentives for superior work performance. Managing such an employee requires not an autocratic style with the trappings of power, but a more collegial style where informed consent of the governed becomes increasingly important. It will not do to have communications that flow downward as orders and upward as performance reports; there must be intelligent dialogue. It is not enough for management to demand performance and sacrifices while considering itself immune to such measures or questioning on the part of employees. Nor would managers be able to unilaterally decide, without a contract, how a corporation's profits are to be shared. To do so would alienate employees who can largely influence the outcome of profits and therefore may choose not to perform.

These conditions, however, will not be met by resorting to the old standbys of unilaterally designed job enrichment and/or job satisfaction programs. Studies show no direct relation between job satisfaction and job performance. Moreover, attributes of job satisfaction may even run counter to conditions required for improved job performance. And in the final analysis, an overwhelming majority of workers seek in their jobs conditions that relate more to improved job performance than workplace happiness.[61]

Nor will management be able to seek greater work commitment on the part of American workers along the lines of Theory Z and the Japanese system, where by emphasizing the notion of group and by increasingly divorcing individual performance from individual rewards, workers are supposed to work together for the common good. American managements will have to *convince* employees that they are competent to ask what they ask, that what they ask is reasonable, and that the employee stands to benefit from increased effort.

In the following two sections we will discuss two separate aspects of management performance, those pertaining to organization structure and decision-making processes, and the system of job-related incentives and disincentives.

Organization Structure and Decision-Making Processes

Large American corporations are, first and foremost, bureaucratic in structure, with a vertical-hierarchical decision-making process. These organizations cannot exist without some form of centralized control and coordination which ensures that top management exercises a large measure of control over the activities of its far-flung units. And yet such a system also thwarts individual initiative and innovation. Large bureaucratic organizations accomplish these conflicting objectives through a system of rules and procedures that prescribe solutions to a variety of operational decisions, thereby standardizing corporate responses in similar situations or activities. Needs for discretion and independent action are satisfied by decentralizing decision making through a system of "profit centers." Responsibility for individual action is matched with commensurate rewards for selecting the "right" responses and penalties for selecting "wrong" responses from a preselected menu of choices.

The system works fairly well under stable conditions, where technology, markets, and sociopolitical environments are highly predictable and largely controllable. It fails badly when the conditions of stability do not hold, making for conflicts between the personal goals of the individual and those of the organization.

The values of a bureaucratic system are highly inimical to individual initiative and performance. The system creates an ambiguous and irrational reward system. The star symbol of such an organization is the CEO, and all credit for good performance accrues to him. He then distributes this credit within the organization based on his personal assessment and on the recommendations of those immediately below him. This distribution of credit is not based strictly on performance; it includes many personal factors.

Bureaucratic decision making is also group-oriented. This is done to ensure an individual's identification with corporate successes and also to diffuse responsibility for failures. The interlocking system of a hierarchical structure necessitates a strong measure of loyalty to one's superior, even at the expense of corporate welfare, because the superior plays a critical role both in giving credit for good performance and in pinning blame for bad performance.

These tendencies are further aggravated in mature industries, where companies typically have managerial systems that require successive reviews before an action can be taken. This is made possible because in a low-growth situation, the pressures are presumed to be "cost" and not "market" driven.

Decentralized-Centralization. One way to overcome these problems would be through an organization structure that uses a "decentralized-centralization" approach. This approach is based on a system of values (corporate culture) that is in harmony with both its external environment and the value set of the individual employees, who as a group are constantly changing. The best analogy is that of the cell system in a biological organism, where cells are constantly dividing, multiplying, and re-creating themselves to satisfy the needs of the organism as it responds to a changing environment. Each cell "learns" to function in a new manner without changing its basic structure or primary purpose. All the instructions are automatically encoded in the new cells, and no new training and orientation is called for. And yet there is very little conflict or unnecessary overlap between the operations of various cells.

An excellent example of the cell-system type of decentralized centralization can be found in the history of the British Empire. It is a marvel how the British were able to run their far-flung empire in a period with no telephones and extremely slow communication and transportation systems. They were able to conquer and administer countries and populations many times larger than their own, using local people to run those countries with very few expatriates. The British were able to accomplish this by so thoroughly imbuing their administrators—both British and locals—with their cultural norms and value set that they were almost clones, as far as these norms and values were concerned. Given a particular situation, it was reasonably certain that the administrator involved would behave in a predictable manner, one that would be quite similar to the behavior of any other administrator who might have been placed in similar circumstances. This approach minimized the dual need for constant communication to seek guidance and approval on the one hand, and monitor performance on the other. And yet, a consistently high rate of positive behavior was elicited from different cells.

Under the decentralized-centralization system, the focus of authority does not have to rest at the top; instead, authority and responsibility are assumed by individual cells and cell members or leaders in proportion to their needs. The organization is not identified by its chief executive, but by its accomplishments. These are accredited to the institution and identified with different people sharing the limelight at different times.

This allows the system to be managed by fewer administrators who are engaged in the supervision and coordination of the activities of other managers, thereby flattening the organizational pyramid and making for shorter communication links. Since individual jobs have greater flexibility as to how they can be performed, they become "high discretion" jobs. In the process they become more attractive to the new kind of employee who seeks greater control over the work environment and wants to be evaluated for output rather than process. The increased challenge and the opportunities for growth minimize the need for constant upward movement as the only manifestation of success. The top executive's role is also modified; he leads not by authority, but by demonstration. He does not assume his power, but earns it. He is more of a facilitator than a dictator. This approach provides all the advantages of a matrix system of organization, with none of the disadvantages of multiple reporting channels and a top-heavy need for coordination.

The Four Principles of Cell Organization. In the cell organization, management and communication are determined by four factors:[62]

1. *Principle of Community of Interest.* People are clustered together in cells where they share common interests and informational needs. The focus of the cell is people, not specific activities. Therefore, although cells may have some overt similarities to strategic business units (SBUs), they are

not alike. In the latter case, the rationalizing criterion is the cohesiveness of the people, which determines the character of the cell. A cell-type organizational design based on the principle of community of interest allows for fermentation of new ideas without the bureaucratic and debilitating questions of turf and political infighting in large organizations that stifle many promising projects in their infancy.

A cell organized on the basis of community of interest may either be identical to one particular SBU or may contain a number of SBUs— which may be for bookkeeping purposes. The cell's boundaries are quite well defined, displaying the characteristics of large within-cell cohesiveness and between-cell variance.

Each cell has a formal administrative structure designed primarily to facilitate the work of the cell. However, the administrator is not the focal authority in the cell; authority instead rests in the persons with the "knowledge" and "skills" that form the core values of the cell. The administrator in a cell is more akin to an office manager rather than the executive in charge of a particular activity or functional area.

2. *Principle of Concentric Circles of Influence.* This principle determines the power structure of the cell. It divides the people in a group in terms of their relevance and importance to the cell's core values or purpose. From that core, influence spreads in waves through a ripple effect. Cell leadership is based not on what a member does, but how his or her actions influence the activities of other members in the group. The leadership of the group is not structured and carries few coercive elements of authority. Instead, it is constantly revolving among members, depending on the nature of the cell's activities at a particular time and its importance to the overall goals of the larger organization.

3. *Principle of Rough Terrain.* Notwithstanding the principle of community of interest, interaction between cells does not always take place at the cell boundaries. Instead there is an intentional overlap between various cells which is accomplished by having at least some cell members with membership in more than one cell, and by keeping the cell boundaries amorphous and ragged. The principle of rough terrain thus allows for the existence of interstices or holes that can occupy the idea space left by existing cell activities. This approach encourages the fermentation of new ideas by allowing them maneuvering space, enables the cells to subdivide and multiply, and facilitates development of more flexible and adaptive responses on the part of the organization to a changing external environment.

4. *Principle of Redundancy in Communication Channels.* Large bureaucratic organizations are typified by communication flows that are primarily vertical in character and efficient in execution. Downward communications consist largely of orders; upward communications are mainly comprised of im-

plementation and performance reports. At the same time, communication messages are made very precise and kept to a minimum to avoid overburdening the communication channels and causing misinterpretation of the messages.

This system works fairly well when both the needs of the system and the character of the personae are relatively stable. However, its predictability and stability are also its major weaknesses. The narrowness of the communication channels and control mechanisms filter out most alien noises as static—and yet these noises might be the early warning signals that the organization should heed, but instead is tuning out.

The communication breakdown is particularly likely to take place in times of crisis, when rapid adjustments are called for in response to fast-changing external environments. In a bureaucratic organization, a drive for self-protection and a fear of the unknown cause the people to smother information that is unfamiliar and unpleasant. The normal channels of communication between hierarchical ranks become hopelessly "jammed," and it becomes virtually impossible for those at the top to find out what is really happening.

The ability of an organization to respond speedily and effectively to a changing external environment depends, to a large extent, on the existence of certain redundancy and wastefulness in the communication system in normal times that allow for informal, lateral, and even extraneous communications to seep through the system. They give an organization survival value in times of crisis, for they develop and keep open spare channels of communication and reserves of energy that can be drawn upon for serious purposes in times of crisis. The great threat to survival can easily be efficiency based parsimony and rigidity in organization structure and communication channels.

Employee Compensation and Performance Evaluation

Industrial relations in the United States have been going through a period of traumatic change, and there is no end in sight. For example:

1. A long list of companies in industries as diverse as airlines, automobile manufacturing, meat packing, steel, and trucking have been cajoling workers and unions to make concessions in wages and work rules called "givebacks" in order to lower labor costs and make industries and companies more productive and competitive. When persuasion has not worked, managements have used more drastic means, such as bankruptcy or strikes, to force concessions from the workers. Companies like Continental Airlines and Greyhound Corporation are illustrative of this trend.

2. An increasing number of companies have become more determined not to yield to unions and resist any moves that would loosen their control over labor costs.

3. To make the concessions palatable to workers and their unions, companies have offered inducements: equity participation (Eastern Airlines); two-tier wage scales where current wage levels are protected and even increased for existing employees, while a far lower wage level is agreed upon for newer employees (American Airlines, Boeing); greater job security (Ford, General Motors); workers through their union representatives becoming more involved in top-level corporate decision-making (Chrysler, Eastern Airlines); and workers actually acquiring the entire company through ESOP or other plans (GM's Hyatt Roller Bearing Plant in Clark, N.J.).

4. A large number of companies have started highly touted programs in quality of work life and worker participation in decision making as evidenced in quality circles. These changes have led many corporate executives and other interested persons to suggest that a new era of more cooperative and productive labor-management relations has begun in the United States. It is also suggested that the new labor-management relations—which largely mimic the employee relations practices of the Japanese management system —will transform the typically adversarial relationship between American management and workers to a largely cooperative one where everybody works together for the common good.

We disagree with this assessment both because prevailing evidence does not support it, and also because it is based on erroneous and untenable assumptions. All evidence points to the fact that employees have been extremely unwilling to make concessions on wages and work rules. They believe the problems were brought about largely by management incompetence and corporate greed and that they were being asked to make proportionately greater sacrifices than the management or the stockholders. In some cases, the foreign competitive advantage is very large and unfairly achieved by the exporting companies with foreign government assistance. Therefore, solutions must be developed at the governmental level. Under these circumstances, nothing will save the business and any concessions will provide temporary breathing space which the management will use to increase its options at the expense of workers. Consequently, workers are increasingly rejecting management demands for givebacks; where concessions have been made, they have been a "marriage of convenience," to be broken the moment there is an improvement in the company's financial situation.

Corporate managements have been extremely reluctant to share true decision making with workers. Companies are using the hard economic times, and also the new modes of worker participation, as a means of either weakening or breaking the existing unions, or alternately keeping unions out. Many of the job security plans negotiated by unions during the 1980–81 recession have turned out to be full of loopholes, leaving the workers distrustful of both their union leaders and the companies.[63]

Although there is as yet no conclusive evidence, studies indicate that, with some notable exceptions, a very large number of worker participation programs are nothing more than public relations efforts. They lack management commitment, and are designed to gain greater output for workers rather than to share management control.[64] Even Westinghouse, which has adopted the quality circle movement with a missionary zeal, does not claim to have done so to give workers greater voice in management. William A. Coates, head of Westinghouse's construction group and one of the corporation's strongest advocates of quality of work life programs, states that these programs are perceived by management not as "giving up controls but rather [as] gaining a ton and a half of help."[65]

It is therefore highly unlikely that the current situation will bring about a significant change for the better in labor-management relations in the United States. Neither the management nor organized labor has shown any willingness to give up on their preferred positions because they do not as yet trust each other enough to expect "fair exchange" in such participative approaches. Moreover, given the American sociocultural norms, the political realities, and the legal and economic aspects of corporate structure, the prospects for extensive cooperation between labor and management, along the lines of the Japanese model, are indeed limited because of the differing interests and priorities of the two groups.

And yet changes must take place, because the survival and prosperity of American business and the continued employment and welfare of American workers depend on it. The solutions, however, must be found within the context of American society, where both responsibility for work and reward for performance are based on individual effort and its contribution to corporate welfare.

It was mentioned earlier that the new technologies have created a workforce that has greater discretion in defining both the scope of the job and how it must be done. This is true not only at the upper end of the workforce, among professional and technical workers, but also among assembly-line blue collar and clerical workers. This creates two problems. One, it makes difficult the traditional American practice of developing precise job specifications and then measuring performance against those specifications. Thus performance evaluation includes increasing elements of subjectiveness. Two, since employees have increasingly greater discretion as to how a job can best be performed, management has proportionately less control over the amount and quality of work that can be extracted from an employee under fear of job loss or other penalties. Therefore, employees *must* be persuaded and convinced that it is in their interest to do a better job and give their best effort to work performance.

To accomplish this:

1. Management will genuinely have to share significant decision making with employees. Workers will have to have a voice not merely in developing solutions, but in defining the problem itself. Some management prerogatives will have to be sacrificed in the process, and management will have to share financial and operating information with workers so that discussions take place with a common data base.
2. The new system will put severe demands on management to demonstrate its competence. This is likely to be an impossible task if the corporation is managed along the traditional hierarchical lines. However, if the corporation adopts the new management style outlined in the previous section, the demonstration of competence will be a natural outcome of the process because this must be the preferred technique.
3. There must be a sense of equitable treatment and equality of sacrifice. It does not behoove management to grant itself hefty salary increases and bonuses while asking workers for givebacks. The cases of GM and TWA are recent examples. In both cases, the management had to cancel the increases before it could convince workers to accept demands for givebacks. What employees think of the top management has a powerful influence on their attitudes toward the company, their work behavior, and the quality of their work, and these opinions eventually determine productivity and corporate profits.[66]
4. It is counterproductive to develop compensation strategies where the main objective, if not the sole objective, is to weaken unions or even keep them out. There is some evidence that current pressure on the part of employers for givebacks has had the effect of unifying different unions against a common employer(s), as is currently happening in the airline industry, or throwing out union leaders who were considered less militant. In the new high-discretion jobs, the employee is likely to resent and successfully resist management's anti-union actions, regardless of his or her preference for union representation.
5. Employees must have a stake and share in the overall prosperity of the corporation. Equity participation and profit sharing are two approaches that have shown remarkable success in eliciting greater employee effort. A study by the New York Stock Exchange showed that companies with equity and profit-sharing plans were at the forefront of all American companies in involving workers in participative decision making and in scoring the greatest productivity gains.[67]

Evidence also shows that new high-technology industries, such as computers, electronics, and biotechnology, have been very successful in attracting top scientist-entrepreneurs who thrive in the new competitive environment. For example, in the emerging biotechnology industry, drawn by generous stock ownership plans, the new breed of scientist-entrepreneurs have turned fledgling companies into winners, and in the last few years have swamped the U.S. Patent and Trademark Office with nearly 1000 patent applications. It is not surprising that Genentech, which was founded in 1976 and is now one of the leading companies in the field, has 90 percent of its employees as shareholders.[68] The situation is not different in more mature industries, where despite some major failures, employee-owned companies have also shown remarkable resilience, survival, and growth under extremely adverse conditions.

While having a stake and sharing in the overall prosperity of the company are important, by themselves they are not enough. Workers must have a compensation system that rewards them directly for differential and superior performance and for their contributions to improved productivity and corporate performance. The most obvious form of such a system is the piece-rate system, which with some modifications to prevent worker exploitation, has been used quite successfully by Lincoln Electric to improve both quality and quantity of worker productivity to such an extent that it is in a class by itself.[69]

Piece-rate systems, however, are anathema to unions, which view them as manipulative and exploitative and designed to create discord among workers. Moreover, since most new jobs are acquiring the character of white collar jobs, new systems must be developed that create differential reward systems based on employee performance.

Such a system should also provide for compensation that can be an effective substitute for blanket job security and other fringe benefits. Experience has shown that the needs for job security of various classes of workers are quite different from the needs of management to retain certain types of workers. Management can offer a "layoff" premium where an employee can trade off part of his job security for higher current wages. More experienced and skilled workers are likely to opt for layoff premiums, assuming correctly that the company needs their scarce skills and that they are unlikely to be affected by layoffs. Younger employees, on the other hand, may be willing to accept lower current wages in return for a lower layoff exposure. The arrangement would thus meet the needs of both the workers and the employers.

A similar approach can be used for fringe benefits. A cafeteria approach—defined contributions instead of defined benefits—allows employees to choose specific fringe benefits more appropriate to their needs. When combined with a system whereby the employee shares in the savings

accrued through efficient utilization of the services, it simultaneously serves
the interests of employees and employers.

The Role of Trade Unions

The new technology-based workforce also creates a unique set of problems
and challenges for trade unions. Traditional union activity and worker solidarity is based on the twin notions of protecting employees from the arbitrary
and capricious behavior of employers, and gaining equitable rewards for
workers doing similar work. American unions have emphasized differential
wage scales based on job complexity, so that workers are paid equally in
different job classifications. Income differentials are created through the
creation of more job classifications and seniority levels. Where job classification cannot be easily done in terms of objective output and management has
a large measure of discretion in evaluating performance, as in white collar
jobs, unions have striven to create a combination of skill and experience
levels through training and certification to create the justification for differential wages for their members. However, in both cases the jobs are almost
always fragmented to make them into "low-discretion" work, and all workers
receive similar wages within a given classification.

The new "high-discretion" employee does not find either of these
conditions to his liking. Because of his control over his work, his need for
union protection against arbitrary management behavior is greatly reduced.
He is a professional, quite skilled and very proud of his knowledge and
competence. He also understands the penalties for poor performance both
for the corporation and the economy. Therefore, he is unlikely to tolerate
incompetence and slovenly work among his colleagues or accept rewards
based on the lowest common denominator. American unions, therefore, will
have to modify their thinking and approach to industrial relations if they wish
to remain viable social institutions and continue to effectively represent the
new "high-discretion" worker.

INTERNATIONAL TERMS OF TRADE AND COMPETITION

A significant part of the Japanese success in international trade must be
attributed to Japan's adroitness in exploiting the liberal trade policies of the
Western nations, notably the United States, while at the same time sheltering
its domestic markets from foreign competition both for industries where
Japan has an inherent comparative disadvantage (agricultural products) and
for industries where Japan intends to develop an international competitive
edge and therefore uses domestic markets to secure time and generate resources for strengthening Japanese manufacturers. While Japanese business

and labor deserve tremendous credit for building a highly productive economic machine, a no less significant measure of the success of this endeavor is due to deliberate government policies that are highly nationalistic, protectionist, and patently unfair toward foreign imports and international competition in their home markets.

For a long time, Japan insisted on protecting its domestic industries under the guise of a need to rebuild its war-torn economy and give its industry a transitional period to gear up to meet foreign competition on an equal footing. However, when continuing massive trade surpluses made a mockery of such an argument, Japan was forced to move gradually toward a freer trade.[70]

Regrettably, in this case, Japan's rhetoric has far exceeded its actions —and this appears to be a deliberate policy. For it serves Japanese interests admirably so long as the United States and other industrialized nations continue to acquiesce to the Japanese onslaught, employ negotiating strategies that are self-defeating, and do not fashion more realistic responses to the Japanese challenge.

The Japanese strategy in maintaining an international trade hegemony includes, among others, the following elements:

1. Continuing to proclaim the need for greater international trade liberalization and insisting that Japan is playing its part in it. The rhetoric becomes especially loud when there is increased pressure on the Japanese to correct the trade imbalances.
2. Starting the negotiating process with an extremely untenable position that has a large divergence between what Japan seeks and what it may eventually agree to do. Thus every concession made appears large—and in retrospect turns out to be largely symbolic and often minuscule.
3. When confronted with demands for trade liberalization, responding by appointing a commission to study the problem, having joint negotiating sessions, expressing an identity of interest with the other side, and making a public announcement of "policy agreement" with tremendous fanfare. The implementation details are invariably left to be worked out later—and are often scrubbed by bureaucrats or adopted in a manner that frustrates the purpose of the earlier accords.
4. Delaying the process of liberalization as long as possible, or at least until such time as the domestic industry has gained an edge and liberalization is unlikely to yield foreign companies any significant advantage.
5. Blaming the lack of imports on Japan's cultural traits, which make the Japanese averse to buying imported products; Japan's traditional marketing and distribution channels, which are hard for foreign companies to penetrate; and the unwillingness of foreign companies to exercise enough patience in cultivating the Japanese market, and to devote enough resources to develop products suited to Japanese tastes. As examples of the

rewards that are bestowed on the virtuous and the industrious, a few successful foreign companies, like Coca-Cola, are trotted out for all to see and emulate.

The reality, however, is quite different from what the Japanese themselves perceive, what they would like Americans to believe, and what is manifested in facts. Japan's monetary and fiscal policies consistently provide tax advantages to exporters, while its cheap yen gives an added competitive price advantage to Japanese exports. Despite years of negotiations—and successive liberalizations—Japan still allows only paltry amounts of beef, oranges, and other food imports from the United States. Through other nontariff barriers, like product certification and process controls, Japan has successfully denied market entry, or made it prohibitively expensive, for foreign products to compete in such diverse areas as pharmaceuticals, health care, and cosmetics. The U.S. government allows import of Japanese products after making field visits to Japan to ensure that the Japanese factories are meeting U.S. requirements. Japanese organizations can certify that an exported product meets U.S. certification requirements. Japanese, on the other hand, do not send inspectors to visit U.S. plants. They also do not accept product certification by foreign agencies. Consequently, Japanese customs officials inspect imports in lots, thereby causing interminable delays and expense. Foreign manufacturers are expected to conform to strict Japanese specifications. The Japanese government rejects all or a large part of foreign data, and insists on local testing, thereby negating the advantage of performance that the foreign manufacturer might have over the locally made products. Japan's government-owned monopolies, notably tobacco and telecommunications, have consistently prevented foreign products from competing in Japan against their own products or those manufactured by their Japanese suppliers.

Japan's protectionist policies are more evident than ever in the current conflict over importing computer gear, such as value-added networks and other computer software, and in the purchase of telecommunication equipment by Japan's telephone monopoly, NTT. In the former case, the Japanese government is developing legislation that restricts foreign ownership to 20 percent in the high-technology field of value-added networks, which permit different computers to communicate over public or leased lines; mandates the licensing to Japanese companies of all computer software that is deemed to be in the public interest, and also determines "reasonable" royalty rates and licensing fees. The "public interest" in this case is to be determined by the appropriate government ministry. The legislation grants copyright protection for computer software for only 15 years compared to 75 years in the United States. According to Clyde V. Prestowitz, a U.S. Commerce Department official, "There are areas in which American companies have a clear competitive advantage. The Japanese say that their protectionist days are long past. But where they are behind, you see moves like this to protect their markets."[71] Of the proposed legislation, another American computer official noted: "A cynic might conclude that the Japanese are trying to legalize software pirating."[72]

In the case of the three-year-old U.S. agreement with Japan whereby Nippon Telephone and Telegraph (NTT) was supposed to give greater access to U.S. suppliers in its purchasing program, the consensus is that the program has had so little real impact that Japanese have gained a great deal more through reciprocity, which allowed the Japanese to bid for U.S. government purchases.[73] For example, in response to the U.S.–Japan agreement that envisaged larger purchases of U.S. products by NTT, the then president Akigusa Tokuji remarked that "the only thing NTT would buy from the United States is mops and buckets."[74]

Moreover, it is not only the United States, with its lazy workers and short-term-oriented managers against which Japan enjoys a merchandise trade surplus. This condition exists for most of the world including Taiwan and South Korea, which are considered to have traits of frugality and industriousness similar to the Japanese, and which have succeeded in competing with the Japanese in other countries all over the world but have failed to penetrate the Japanese market. Professor Chalmers Johnson, the distinguished scholar on Japan and a student of Japanese government bureaucracy, maintains that the lack of "internationalization" of the Japanese economy cannot be attributed to national character or cultural traits," to any degree greater than in other open capitalist countries . . . Japan's problem of internationalization concerns government policy."[75]

The United States therefore must develop a twofold strategy for dealing with the Japanese. The first element of this strategy has to do with creating a new reality concerning the deliberate trade imbalance and its associated pains not as the Japanese like to believe it, but as the Americans and other foreign nations see it. The second element of this strategy has to do with a new negotiating stance that forces the Japanese to play the game not according to their rules, but according to the rules followed by other players. Since we are dealing with a government policy, traditional negotiations that have not worked before are unlikely to work in the future. The new negotiating strategy would call not for bilateral agreements, but international agreements with both international and bilateral retaliatory measures that are automatically reactivated in case one or the other party does not implement the terms expeditiously and diligently.

Creating a New Reality

Both the Japanese government and the Japanese people have come to believe in their own propaganda as to the inherent superiority of Japanese industry. To correct this situation, we should take measures that would bring home to the Japanese the pain inflicted on other nations by its protectionist policies. Some of the measures that can be used to accomplish this are as follows:

1. We should establish a commission comprising government, business, and labor leaders to make an estimate of the potential loss of exports to Japan as a consequence of its protective policies. These estimates can be used as a starting point for retaliating against Japanese imports. If it is estimated that in a particular year the United States is likely to be deprived of $10 billion in exports to Japan, U.S. policies should be so structured as to reduce Japanese imports by $10 billion.
2. The imports should be restricted not through quotas, but through import tariffs that would have the added advantage of keeping open consumer choices, generating additional revenues for the U.S. government, and undercutting the Japanese government's tax subsidies for exported products.
3. Where the Japanese government has used particularly onerous measures to discourage foreign imports, the U.S. government should adopt similar measures to raise the level of conflict and increase its visibility. For example, the Japanese government insists that all American cigarettes should be sold through the state tobacco monopoly and restricts advertising in Japan of imported tobacco to English-language media. The U.S. government, as a highly dramatic gesture, may decree that Japanese automobiles henceforth could be advertised in the United States only in Japanese-language media.[76] Similarly, the United States may also consider withdrawing foreign certification of products from all countries that do not accord similar privileges to U.S. products. This measure would affect the Japanese most adversely and should bring home to them the need for comparable treatment.
4. Of critical importance is the need for the United States to communicate directly to the Japanese people its reasons for taking such actions. This cannot be accomplished by depending on the Japanese press. Instead, the U.S. government and U.S. industry should undertake an active communication program—advocacy advertising—in the Japanese press so that we can convey this message in our own words and in a manner that is most effective from the American perspective.

Negotiating Strategy

In negotiating with the Japanese, Americans have followed a strategy of rational expectations that has been both ineffective and self-defeating. The essence of a successful negotiating strategy is to create a lasting equilibrium among the demands made by opposing parties. This equilibrium would be such that any movement away from it would be counterproductive for both parties. The equilibrium point, however, is influenced by a number of important factors, both substantive and process-oriented. They include:

- The starting point on the bargaining continuum for the opposing parties.
- Expected reaction and response by one party to the demands made by the other party.
- The real and perceived gap between one's starting or bargaining position and movement toward the equilibrium point.
- The pressure of time and urgency in achieving an agreement on the part of the different parties.
- The degree of specificity in different parties' terms of agreement.
- The measure of authority exercised by the representatives of the negotiating parties to commit their principals.

In their negotiations with the Japanese, Americans have invariably been at the other end of the spectrum from the Japanese on all these dimensions, thereby consistently yielding both the procedural and the substantive advantage. The Japanese have entered all negotiations believing that any outcome will entail a loss of their competitive advantage and giving up part of what they already have. They therefore immediately project the image of negotiating from strength. Americans, on the other hand, have been made to feel, and seem to have convinced themselves, that what they are seeking are "concessions" they must persuade the other side to make voluntarily. Americans are therefore negotiating from weakness.

In their negotiating strategy, Japanese have used tactics that are best described as brinkmanship. They include making outrageous demands as starting points for negotiations. Moreover, these demands for retaining the status quo are advanced in an emotional way: Any departure from the status quo is treated as an affront to the Japanese people and a denial of their rights. Such a posture immediately puts the other party on the defensive, thereby forcing it to accept even minor and symbolic movement on the Japanese position as a significant victory. The Japanese, on the other hand, garner a tremendous psychological and propaganda victory by appearing to be magnanimous and statesmanlike. In this, they are helped by the Americans.

In contrast to the Japanese, American negotiators have followed a strategy of realistic demands. They put their most reasonable expectations on the table as the starting point. At the same time, given the openness of American society, the Japanese can easily ascertain the Americans' bargaining posture. Thus the Japanese have the dual advantage of making small concessions in real terms appear large because of the differences in the starting points of the two. They also appear to be more flexible than the

Americans because of the latter's narrow margin of maneuverability, having started negotiations from a position much closer to the Americans' desired equilibrium point.

The Japanese gain another advantage through their negotiating techniques. They make grand gestures in making agreements on broad principles that can be watered down in the implementation phase. They are always in no hurry, while Americans appear to be pressed for time; they are always hedging their bets by indicating that the negotiators lack authority to make definitive commitments and that all commitments must be ratified and possibly modified by political leaders. The resultant large measure of specificity on the part of the Americans both on the initial bargaining position and the agreed-upon final terms forces them to observe the terms of any agreement rigidly. The Japanese can postpone implementation and dilute the terms simply by resorting to the built-in leakages in the agreements and the negotiating procedures. And finally, American negotiators suffer a further handicap because they are trying to keep Japan as a strong political ally while at the same time confronting it economically

American negotiators need to adopt a new two-pronged strategy in order to gain better control over the negotiating procedures and also reach a more stable and favorable equilibrium point. The first step in this direction will be for the Americans to change their negotiating posture from one of weakness (what can we persuade the Japanese to give us) to one of strength (what the Japanese must have from us). Once we have decided how the Japanese have been treating U.S. business and industry inequitably, we should take unilateral action to impose new conditions—to create a new reality the Japanese would want to alter. Moreover, to ensure that the Japanese take such an approach seriously, we should endow it with a large measure of emotionalism and a sense of moral indignation. This should create a situation of "saving face" if the Japanese insist on reverting to the previous position before negotiations can start. It will also generate support for such a policy among the American people, who would see the two positions in sharper relief and with greater clarity.

The second step has to do with negotiating posture. Rather than advancing the most reasonable demands as a starting point, the American bargainers should employ all the tactics of the Orient. These include making vague demands that may appear outlandish, but at the same time expressing uneasiness at making them. Our negotiators should appear at once empathetic to the Japanese concerns, but at the same time helpless in yielding too much because of past Japanese actions and our domestic political situation. Above all, having unilaterally imposed the conditions we want to accomplish —just like the Japanese—we must exercise extreme patience and be very deliberate in our negotiations to ensure that when an agreement is reached, it is equitable and mutually satisfactory.

NOTES

1. Theodore Levitt, "Management and the Post-Industrial Society," *The Public Interest,* 44 (Summer 1976), pp. 69–103.
2. Charles Shultze, "Industrial Policy: A Solution in Search of a Problem," *California Management Review,* 25, 4 (Summer 1983), p. 7; Robert Z. Lawrence, "Changes in U.S. Industrial Structure: The Role of Global Forces, Secular Trends and Transitory Cycles." Unpublished Paper (Washington, D.C.: The Brookings Institution, 1983); and Robert Z. Lawrence, "Is Trade Deindustrializing America? A Medium-Term Perspective," *Brookings Papers on Economic Activity,* 1 (1983), pp. 129–171.
3. Daniel Yankelovich and John Immerwahr, *Putting the Work Ethic to Work* (New York: The Public Agenda Foundation, 1983), p. 4.
4. Louis Harris Associates/Amitai Etzioni, *Perspectives on Productivity: A Global View* (Sentry Insurance, 1981), p. 81. Cited in Yankelovich and Immerwahr, *Putting the Work Ethic to Work,* p. 19.
5. Cited in Yankelovich and Immerwahr, *Putting the Work Ethic to Work,* p. 4.
6. Ibid., pp. 19–24. This publication also cites numerous other public opinion studies that confirm the prevalence of strong work-ethic-related values among the American people.
7. Ibid., p. 5.
8. William J. Abernathy, Kim B. Clark, and Alan M. Kantrow, "The New Industrial Competition," *Harvard Business Review,* 65, 5 (September–October, 1981), p. 71.
9. J. D. Goldhar and Mariann Jelinek, "Plan for Economies of Scope," *Harvard Business Review,* 61, 6 (November–December, 1983), pp. 141–148. See also Donald F. Barnett and Louis Schorsch, *Steel: Upheaval in a Basic Industry* (Cambridge, Mass.: Ballinger, 1983).
10. "Plan for Economies of Scope," p. 142.
11. For some examples of this line of thought, see J. Sterling Livingston, "Myth of the Well-Educated Manager," *Harvard Business Review,* 49, 1 (January–February 1971), pp. 77–89; John A. Wagner III, "The Organizational Double Bind: Toward Understanding of Rationality and its Complement," *Academy of Management Review,* 3, 4 (October 1978), pp. 786–795; Thomas I. Isaack, "Intuition: An Ignored Dimension of Management," *Academy of Management Review,* 3, 4 (October 1978), pp. 917–921; Harold J. Leavitt, "Beyond the Analytic Manager," *California Management Review* (Spring 1975), pp. 5–12; and Harold J. Leavitt, "Beyond the Analytic Manager: Part II," *California Management Review* (Summer 1975), pp. 11–21.
12. Robert H. Hayes and William J. Abernathy, "Managing Our Way to Economic Decline," *Harvard Business Review,* 58, 4 (July–August, 1981) p. 68. The emphasis on "hands-on" experience was also recognized as one of the traits of successful American companies by Thomas J. Peters and Robert H. Waterman, *In Search of Excellence* (New York: Harper & Row, 1982), pp. 279–291. For additional discussion of the nature of changing technology and its impact on production processes and marketing strategies, see Robert Reich and Magaziner, *Minding America's Business* (1982); and "Marketing: The New Priority," *Business Week,* November 21, 1983, pp. 96–106.

13. Robert H. Hayes and David A. Garvin, "Managing as if Tomorrow Mattered," *Harvard Business Review,* 60, 3 (May–June, 1983), pp. 70–79.

14. Abernathy et al., "The New Industrial Competition," p. 77.

15. Herbert Stein, "Don't Fall for Industrial Policy," *Fortune,* November 14, 1983, p. 70.

16. Steel and auto industries, and their labor unions, are in the forefront of such moves. Other industries that have successfully sought similar protection include textiles and apparel makers.

17. Examples abound of such diversification moves. One of the most prominent of these has been U.S. Steel's acquisition of Marathon Oil Corporation.

18. Robert L. Simison and John Koten, "Auto Makers' Earnings Are Increasing Sharply Despite Mediocre Sales," *Wall Street Journal,* December 19, 1983, pp. 1, 19.

19. Lawrence, "Changes in U.S. Industrial Structure," and "Is Trade Deindustrializing America?"

20. "Deregulating America," *Business Week,* November 28, 1983, pp. 80–96.

21. Robert H. Hayes, "Why Japanese Factories Work," *Harvard Business Review,* 59, 4 (July–August, 1981), p. 57. See also Goldhar and Jelinek, "Plan for Economies of Scope."

22. Steven C. Wheelwright, "Japan—Where Operations Are Really Strategic," *Harvard Business Review,* 59, 4 (July–August, 1981), pp. 67–74; Peters and Waterman, *In Search of Excellence.* The success of minimills in the steel industry is all U.S. steel shipments and the share is likely to rise to 35 percent by 2000. "The Steel Workers Dig In Against a Cleveland Mill," *Business Week,* January 23, 1984, p. 37. For a discussion of the electronics industry's responses to the Japanese challenge, see William H. Davidson, *The Amazing Race: Winning the Technorivalry with Japan* (New York: Wiley, 1984).

23. John Holusa, "The New Allure of Manufacturing," *New York Times,* December 18, 1983, sec. 3, p. 1F.

24. Ibid.

25. S. Prakash Sethi, "A Strategic Framework for Dealing with Schism between Business and Academe," *Public Affairs Review* (1983), pp. 44–59; Charles J. Ping, "Bigger Stake for Business in Higher Education," *Harvard Business Review,* 59, 5 (September–October, 1981), pp. 122–129.

26. Robert D. Hershey, Jr., "Inman's 2nd Career: Tackling Japanese Technology," *New York Times,* March 8, 1983, sec. Y, p. 10; and "High-Technology Companies Team Up in the R&D Race," *Business Week,* August 15, 1983, pp. 94–95; "Joint Venture Is Approved," *New York Times,* September 21, 1983, p. A13. Francis X. Clines, "Reagan Seeks Joint Research," *New York Times,* September 13, 1983, p. A13; Eleanor M. Fox, "From Antitrust to a Trust in Business," *Across the Board* (November 1981), pp. 59–67; "New Weapons against Japan: R&D Partnerships," *Business Week,* August 8, 1983; William C. Norris, "How to Expand R&D Cooperation," *Business Week,* April 11, 1983, p. 21; "Suddenly U.S. Companies Are Teaming Up," *Business Week,* July 11, 1983, pp. 71–74; Willie Shatz, "Antitrust Pendulum Swings," *Datamation,* 28, 2 (February 1982), pp. 102B–102F.

27. Kenneth M. David, "Looking at the Strategic Impact of Mergers," *Journal of*

Business Strategy, 2, 1 (Summer 1981), pp. 13–22; R. H. Mason and M. B. Gonzwaard, "Performance in Conglomerate Firms: A Portfolio Approach," *Journal of Finance,* 31, 1 (March 1976), pp. 39–48; Michael A. Gort, *Diversification and Integration in American Industry: A Study by the National Bureau of Economic Research* (Princeton, N.J.: Princeton University Press, 1962); Richard P. Rumelt, *Strategy, Structure and Economic Performance* (Boston: Graduate School of Business, Harvard University, 1974); and Roger W. Hearne, "Fighting Industrial Senility: A System for Growth in Mature Industries," *Journal of Business Strategy,* 3, 2 (Fall 1982), pp. 3–20. For contrary evidence and arguments, see Yale Brozen, *Concentration, Mergers, and Public Policy* (New York: Macmillan, 1982); U.S. Congress– Senate, *Mergers and Economic Concentration,* parts I and II, *Hearings,* Subcommittee on Antitrust, Monopoly and Business Rights of the Committee on the Judiciary, 96th Cong., 1st Sess., March–April 1979.

28. William K. Hall, "Survival Strategies in a Hostile Environment," *Harvard Business Review,* 58, 5 (September–October, 1980), pp. 75–85.

29. Hayes and Garvin, "Managing as if Tomorrow Mattered," p. 77.

30. Hearne, "Fighting Industrial Senility," p. 3.

31. Peter F. Drucker, "Making Room in No-Growth Firms," *Wall Street Journal,* December 30, 1983, p. 8. See also Peters and Waterman, *In Search of Excellence,* chap. 10.

32. For an example of radical changes currently taking place in the pharmaceutical-health care industries and their potentially enormous impact on the fortunes of companies, see Jerry Bishop, "New Technique to Produce Proteins May Alter Biotechnology Industry," *Wall Street Journal,* November 8, 1983, p. 31 For a good discussion of the explosive growth in the commercial development of biotechnology, see "Biotech Comes of Age," cover story, *Business Week,* January 23, 1984, pp. 84–94.

33. For some examples of successful companies, see Peters and Waterman, *In Search of Excellence.* We do not agree with the authors' checklist of various measures to success—see our discussion in Chapter 9 of type D companies using the indigenous approach. However, two elements of the list are quite important: the ability of a corporation to manage ambiguity and paradox, and to foster autonomy and entrepreneurship.

34. An interesting example of the type of visionary described here can be found in Roger Lowenstein, "Astronomer Believes Oil and Gas Deposits Are Old as the Earth: Thomas Gold's Idea Suggests Vast But Deep Reserves; Dinosaur Theory Extinct?" *Wall Street Journal,* December 13, 1983, p. 1.

35. Henry Mintzberg, "Patterns in Strategy Formation," *Management Science,* 24, 9 (May 1978), pp. 934–948.

36. There is a large and growing body of literature on the subject of corporate social responsibility and corporate social involvement. Examples of some selected readings are: Dow Votaw and S. Prakash Sethi (eds.), *The Corporate Dilemma: Traditional Values versus Contemporary Problems* (Englewood Cliffs, N.J.: Prentice-Hall, 1973); S. Prakash Sethi (ed.), *The Unstable Ground: Corporate Social Policy in a Dynamic Society* (New York: Wiley, 1974); Lee E. Preston (ed.), *Research in Corporate Social Performance and Policy,* Vols. I–IV (Greenwich, Conn.: Jai Press, 1978–1982); Francis W. Steckmest, *Corporate Performance: The Key to Public Trust*

(New York: McGraw-Hill, 1982); S. Prakash Sethi and Carl L. Swanson (eds.), *Private Enterprise and Public Purpose* (New York: Wiley, 1981); Seymour Martin Lipset and William Schneider, *The Confidence Gap: Business, Labor and Government in the Public Mind* (New York: Macmillan, 1983). Readers are also encouraged to peruse various scholarly and professional journals, such as *Business and Society Review, California Management Review, Harvard Business Review, Journal of Business Ethics,* and *The Public Interest.*

37. Irving Kristol, "When Virtue Loses All Her Loveliness—Some Reflections on Capitalism and 'The Free Society,' " *The Public Interest,* 21 (Fall 1970), pp. 3–15.

38. S. Prakash Sethi and Nobuaki Namiki, *Public Perception of and Attitude Toward Political Action Committees (PACs)—An Empirical Analysis of Nationwide Data—Some Strategic Implications for the Corporate Community,* SR 82-12, Center for Research in Business and Social Policy, The University of Texas at Dallas, 1982; S. Prakash Sethi, "Corporate Political Activism," *Public Relations Journal,* November 1980, pp. 14–18; and Steven Markowitz, "Can Business Survive a Pro-Business Environment?" Remarks delivered to the American Assembly of Collegiate Schools of Business (AACSB) Conference on Business Environment/Public Policy and Business Schools of the 1980s. University of California, Berkeley, July 28, 1981.

39. Paul Weaver, "Corporations Are Defending Themselves with the Wrong Weapon," *Fortune,* June 1977, pp. 186–196.

40. S. Prakash Sethi, *Japanese Business and Social Conflict: A Comparative Analysis of Response Patterns with American Business* (Cambridge, Mass.: Ballinger, 1975).

41. I am indebted to Steven Markowitz, General Manager of Government Relations, Continental Group, Inc., for his thoughtful comments as to how public affairs could be integrated into the corporate function (S. Prakash Sethi). See also Archie B. Carroll and Frank Hoy, "Integrating Corporate Social Policy into Strategic Management," *Journal of Business Strategy,* 4, 3 (Winter 1984), pp. 48–57.

42. William G. Ouchi, *Theory Z: How American Business Can Meet the Japanese Challenge* (Reading, Mass.: Addison-Wesley, 1981); Ezra Vogel, *Japan As Number One: Lessons for America* (Cambridge, Mass.: Harvard University Press, 1979).

43. In describing the attributes of successful American corporations, Peters and Waterman in their book *In Search of Excellence* find the existence of a strong corporate culture a necessary precondition for a drive toward excellence. "Without exception, the dominance and coherence of culture proved to be an essential quality of the excellent companies. Moreover, the stronger the culture and the more it was driven toward the marketplace, the less need was there for policy manuals, organization charts, or detailed procedures and rules." (p. 75). Excellent companies, according to Peters and Waterman, do not make a distinction between the interests of the employees and those of the organization; these companies make a sustained effort to provide meaning to every employee's work derived through commonly shared values; and one of the primary functions of the top management was the shaping of a corporate culture.

44. Bro Uttal, "The Corporate Culture Vultures: Can They Help Your Company," *Fortune,* October 17, 1983, pp. 66–73.

45. Hayes and Abernathy, "Managing Our Way to Economic Decline," p. 70.

46. Bowen H. McCoy, "The Parable of the Sadhu," *Harvard Business Review*, 61, 5 (September–October, 1983), pp. 103–108.

47. David Ewing, "Due Process: Will Business Default?" *Harvard Business Review* 60, 6 (November–December 1982), pp. 114–122.

48. Data from Golightly & Co. International (1978), cited in Hayes and Abernathy, "Managing Our Way to Decline," p. 75.

49. "Turnover at the Top," *Business Week,* December 19, 1983, pp. 104–110.

50. Louis J. Brindisi, Jr., "Why Executive Compensation Programs Go Wrong," *Wall Street Journal,* June 18, 1952, p. 26.

51. Carol J. Loomis, "The Madness of Executive Compensation," *Fortune,* July 12, 1982, pp. 42–46; "How America's Top Moneymakers Fared in the Recession," *Business Week,* May 9, 1983, p. 84; and Ann M. Morrison, "Those Executive Bailout Deals," *Fortune,* December 13, 1982, pp. 82–87; "Executive Compensation: Looking To the Long Term Again," *Business Week,* May 9, 1983, p. 80.

52. Alfred Rappaport, "How to Design Value-Contributing Executive Incentives," *Journal of Business Strategy,* 4, 2 (Fall 1983), p. 50.

53. Ibid., p. 50.

54. David H. Ciscel and Thomas M. Carroll, "The Determinants of Executive Salaries: An Economic Survey," *Review of Economics and Statistics,* 62, 1 (February 1980), p. 7. Cited in Rappaport, p. 50.

55. Alvin O. Ballak and Robert C. Ochsner, "Sixth Annual Hay Report on Executive Compensation," *The Wharton Magazine* (Fall 1982), pp. 54–57.

56. James G. March, "Executive Decision Making: Some Implications for Executive Compensation," in David J. McLaughlin (ed.), *Executive Compensation in the 1980s* (San Francisco: Pentacle Press, 1980), p. 133.

57. Rappaport, "How to Design Value-Contributing Executive Incentives," p. 49.

58. Ibid., pp. 51–52.

59. Yankelovich and Immerwahr, *Putting the Work Ethic to Work,* pp. 2–3.

60. Ibid., pp. 1, 17.

61. Ibid., p. 6.

62. These ideas have been in the incubation stage with one of the authors. They have been presented, in part, in some earlier publications, and are being elaborated here. See, for example, Sethi, "A Strategic Framework for Dealing with Schism between Business and Academe."

63. Dale E. Buss, "Lifetime Job Guarantees in Auto Contracts Arouse Second Thoughts among Workers," *New York Times,* April 18, 1983, p. 27.

64. Chapter 9 cites a number of studies showing the very few instances where worker participation programs have been working with any degree of success. For some additional citations, see James O'Toole, "Thank God It's Monday," *The Wilson Quarterly* (Winter 1980); and S. A. Levitan and C. M. Johnson, "Labor and Management: The Illusion of Cooperation," *Harvard Business Review* 61, 5 (September–October 1983), pp. 8–16.

65. Cited in Levitan and Johnson, "Labor and Management: The Illusion of Cooperation," p. 10. See also "Westinghouse's Cultural Revolution," *Fortune,* June 15, 1981, pp. 74–93.

66. Richard S. Ruch and Ronald Goodman, *Image at the Top* (New York: Free Press, 1984).

67. New York Stock Exchange, *People and Productivity: A Challenge to America* (New York, 1982). See also Samuel J. Davy, "Employee Ownership: One Road to Productivity Improvement," *Journal of Business Strategy* (Summer 1983), pp. 12–21.

68. "Biotech Comes of Age," pp. 86–87.

69. Maryann Mrowca, "Ohio Firm Relies on Incentive-Pay System to Motivate Workers and Maintain Profits," *Wall Street Journal*, August 12, 1983, p. 17; and William Serrin, "The Way That Works at Lincoln," *New York Times*, January 15, 1984, p. 4F.

70. It would not serve any useful purpose to describe specific instances of Japanese actions delaying and protracting trade negotiations in response to Western complaints, because this has been a continuing process. Readers can easily find material through a perusal of standard economic and business journals and even leading national newspapers. For a brief discussion of the latest round of frustrating dialogue between Japanese and American negotiators, see Urban C. Lehner, "U.S.–Japan Phone Gear Pact Totters," *Wall Street Journal*, July 27, 1983, p. 28; Henry Scott Stokes, "Peeling Away Japan's Trade Barriers," *New York Times*, April 17, 1983, pp. F1, 33; "A U.S. Computer Standard Is Stalled in Japan," *Business Week*, July 4, 1983, p. 35; Urban C. Lehner, "Japan Showing Interest in Trade Talks," *Wall Street Journal*, April 21, 1983, p. 33; Masayoshi Kanabayashi, "Japan's Farmers Renew Fight Against Relaxing of Curbs on U.S. Food Imports," *Wall Street Journal*, August 22, 1983, p. 18; John Kotten, "How Toyota Stands to Gain from the GM Deal," *Wall Street Journal*, February 14, 1984, p. 16; "Japan and the U.S. Are Back on a Collision Course," *Business Week*, July 18, 1983, p. 64; and Urban C. Lehner, "Japan's Bureaucrats Stalling on Rules to Ease Imports, U.S. Officials Contend," *Wall Street Journal*, August 10, 1983, p. 34.

71. Steve Lohr, "Japan Trade Bars Worry U.S." *New York Times*, January 18, 1984, p. D22.

72. Ibid.

73. Lehner, "U.S.–Japan Phone Gear Pact Totters," p. 28.

74. Cited in Chalmers Johnson, "The 'Internationalization' of the Japanese Economy," *California Management Review*, 25, 3 (Spring 1983), p. 22.

75. Ibid., p. 10.

76. Ibid., p. 22.

BIBLIOGRAPHY ▰▰▰▰▰▰▰▰▰▰▰▰▰▰▰

Abernathy, William J., Kim B. Clark, and Alan M. Kantrow. *Industrial Renaissance: Producing a Competitive Future for America* (New York: Basic Books, 1983).

——, ——, and ——. "The New Industrial Competition," *Harvard Business Review*, 59, 1 (September–October 1981): 68–81.

Ackerman, Bruce A. *Private Property and the Constitution* (New Haven, Conn.: Yale University Press, 1977).

Aharoni, Yair. *The No Risk Society*, (Chatham, N.J.: Chatham House, 1981).

Akio, Morita. "Japanese Viewpoints: "Do Companies Need Lawyers? Sony's Experiences in the United States," *Japan Quarterly*, 30, 1 (January–March, 1983).

Albemarle Paper Company v. *Moody*, 422 U.S. 403, 95 S. Ct. 2362 (1975).

American Jewish Congress v. *Carter*, 190 N.Y. Supp. 2nd Series 218 (1959).

Amsden, D. M., and R. T. Amsden (eds.). *QC Circles: Applications, Tools and Theory* (Milwaukee: American Society for Quality Control, 1976).

Armentano, Dominick T. *Antitrust and Monopoly: Anatomy of a Policy Failure* (New York: Wiley, 1982).

Avigliano, et. al. v. *Sumitomo Shoji America, Inc.,* 638 F 2nd 552 (1981).

Baake, E. W., Clark Kerr, and Charles Anrod (eds.). *Unions, Management and Public* (New York: Harcourt Brace Jovanovich, 1967).

Badaracco, J. L., Jr., and D. B. Yoffie. "Industrial Policy: It Can't Happen Here," *Harvard Business Review*, 83, 6 (November–December 1983): 96–105.

Bainton, Roland H. *The Reformation of the Sixteenth Century* (Boston: Beacon Press, 1952).

Bakaly, Charles G., Jr., and Joel M. Grossman. *Modern Law of Employment Contracts* (New York: Business and Law/Harcourt Brace Jovanovich, 1984).

Ballak, Alvin O., and Robert C. Ochsner. "Sixth Annual Hay Report on Executive Compensation," *The Wharton Magazine* (fall 1982): 54–57.

Baranson, Jack. *The Japanese Challenge to U.S. Industry* (Lexington, Mass.: Lexington Books, 1981).

Barnett, Donald F., and Louis Schorsch, *Steel: Upheaval in a Basic Industry* (Lexington, Mass: Ballinger, 1983).

Bartlett, Bruce R. "Industrial Policy: Crisis for Liberal Economists," *Fortune,* November 14, 1983, pp. 83–90.

Benedict, Ruth. *The Chrysanthemum and the Sword* (Boston: Houghton Mifflin, 1946).

Bennett, John W., and Iwao Ishino. *Paternalism in the Japanese Economy: Anthropological Studies of Oyabun-Kobun Patterns* (Westport, Conn.: Greenwood Press, 1963).

————, and Solomon B. Levine. "Industrialization and Social Deprivation: Welfare, Environment, and the Postindustrial Society in Japan." In Hugh Patrick (ed.), *Japanese Industrialization and Its Social Consequences* (Berkeley: University of California Press, 1976), pp. 456–465.

Benson, George C. S. *Business Ethics in America* (Lexington, Mass.: Lexington Books, 1982).

Berger, Peter L. "New Attack on the Legitimacy of Business," *Harvard Business Review* 59, 5 (September–October 1981): 82–89.

Berry, Jeffrey M. *Lobbying for the People: The Political Behavior of Public Interest Groups* (Princeton, N.J.: Princeton University Press, 1977).

Bethell, Thom. *Television Evening News Covers Inflation, 1978–79* (Washington, D.C.: The Media Institute, 1980).

Blaker, Michael K. *Japan at the Polls: The House of Councillors Election of 1974* (Washington, D.C.: American Enterprise Institute, 1976).

Bolling, R., and J. Bowles. *America's Competitive Edge: How to Get Our Country Moving Again* (New York: McGraw-Hill, 1982).

Botkin, James, James Dimancescu, and Ray Stata. *Future Stakes: The Future of High Technology in America* (Cambridge, Mass.: Ballinger, 1982).

Boulding, Kenneth. "The Legitimacy of the Business Institution." In Edwin M. Epstein and Dow Votaw (eds.), *Legitimacy, Rationality, Responsibility* (Santa Monica, Calif.: Goodyear, 1978), pp. 83–98.

Bowen, William. "Lessons from Behind the Kimono," Books and Ideas, *Fortune,* June 15, 1981, pp. 247–250.

Bowman, G. "What Helps or Harms Promotability," *Harvard Business Review,* 42, 3 (May–June 1964), pp. 184–196.

Boyer, Edward. "How Japan Manages Declining Industries," *Fortune,* January 10, 1983, pp. 58–63.

Brenner, Steven N., and Earl A. Molander. "Is the Ethics of Business Changing?" *Harvard Business Review,* 55 (January–February, 1977): 57–71.

Browne, H. Monroe. Preface to Arnold J. Melstner (ed.), *Politics and the Oval Office* (San Francisco: Institute for Contemporary Studies, 1981).

Brozen, Yale. *Concentration, Mergers, and Public Policy* (New York, Macmillan, 1982).

Bruce-Briggs, B. "Prospect of a Planned America." In Lawrence A. Chickering (ed.), *The Politics of Planning: A Review and Critique of Centralized Economic Planning* (San Francisco: Institute for Contemporary Studies, 1976).

————. "The Dangerous Folly Called Theory Z," *Fortune,* May 17, 1982, pp. 41–44.

Burck, Charles G. "Working Smarter," *Fortune,* June 15, 1981, pp. 68–73.

————. "Can Detroit Catch Up?" *Fortune,* February 8, 1982, pp. 34–39.

Campbell, John C. *Contemporary Japanese Budget Politics* (Berkeley: University of California Press, 1977).

Carroll, Archie B., and Frank Hoy. "Integrating Corporate Social Policy into Strategic Management," *Journal of Business Strategy,* 4, 3 (Winter 1984): 48–57.

Carroll, Daniel T. "A Disappointing Search for Excellence," *Harvard Business Review,* 61, 6 (November–December, 1983): 78–88.

Cartwright, D., and A. F. Zander (eds.), *Group Dynamics,* 2nd ed. (Evanston, Ill.: Row, Peterson, 1960).

Cathey, Paul. "Japanese Managers Find Best Way to Direct U.S. Workers," *Iron Age,* May 21, 1982.

Caves, Richard E. "Industrial Organization." In Hugh Patrick and Henry Rosovsky (eds.), *Asia's New Giant: How the Japanese Economy Works* (Washington, D.C.: The Brookings Institution, 1976).

Chamberlain, Neil W., *Business and Environment: The Firm in Time and Place* (New York: McGraw-Hill, 1968).

————. *Remaking American Values—Challenge to a Business Society* (New York: Basic Books, 1977).

Chandler, Alfred D., Jr., *The Visible Hand: The Managerial Revolution in American Business* (Cambridge, Mass.: The Belknap Press, 1977).

Chatov, Robert. "The Role of Ideology in the American Corporation." In Dow Votaw and S. Prakash Sethi, *The Corporate Dilemma: Traditional Values Versus Contemporary Problems* (Englewood Cliffs, N.J.: Prentice-Hall, 1973).

Chickering, Lawrence A. (ed.). *The Politics of Planning: A Review and Critique of Centralized Planning* (San Francisco: Institute for Contemporary Studies, 1976).

Ciscel, David H., and Thomas M. Carroll. "The Determinants of Executive Salaries: An Economic Survey," *Review of Economics and Statistics,* 62, 1 (February 1980): 7–13.

Clark, R. C. *The Japanese Company* (New Haven, Conn.: Yale University Press, 1979).

Cleland, David I. (ed.). *Matrix Management Systems Handbook* (New York: Van Nostrand, 1984).

Cole, Robert E. "Learning from the Japanese: Prospects and Pitfalls," *Management Review* (September 1980): 22–28, 39–42.

————. *Japanese Blue Collar: The Changing Tradition* (Berkeley: University of California Press, 1971).

Conference Board. *Corporate Directorship Practices: The Public Policy Committee,* Research Report No. 774 (New York, 1980).

——. *Corporate Directorship Practices: The Planning Committee,* Research Report No. 810 (New York, 1981).

——. *Extra Pay for Service Abroad,* Report No. 665 (New York, 1975).

——. *Compensating Key Personnel Overseas,* Report No. 574 (New York, 1972).

Connelly, William E. *The Bias of Pluralism* (New York: Norton, 1978).

Conputopia. *IBM Spy Jiken no Zenbu* [All about the IBM Spy Incident] (Tokyo: Computa-Eigi, 1982).

Craig, Albert M. "Functional and Dysfunctional Aspects of Government Bureaucracy." In Ezra F. Vogel (ed.), *Modern Japanese Organization and Decision Making* (Berkeley: University of California Press, 1975), pp. 11–15.

Cummings, L. L., and D. Schwartz. *Performance in Organizations: Determinants and Appraisals* (Glenview, Ill.: Scott, Foresman, 1973).

Curtis, Gerald. "Big Business and Political Influence." In Ezra F. Vogel (ed.), *Modern Japanese Organization and Decision Making* (Berkeley: University of California Press, 1975).

Cyert, R. M., and J. G. March. *A Behavioral Theory of the Firm* (Englewood Cliffs, N.J.: Prentice-Hall, 1963).

Dachler, H. P., and B. Wilpert. "Conceptual Dimensions and Boundaries of Participation in Organizations: A Critical Evaluation," *Administrative Science Quarterly,* 23 (1978): 1–39.

Dahl, Robert A. *Pluralistic Democracy in the United States* (Chicago: Rand McNally, 1967).

Dalton, James G. "Political Action Committees: Reshaping the U.S. Electoral/Legislative Scene," *Professional Engineer* (September 1980): 11–14.

David, Kenneth M. "Looking at the Strategic Impact of Mergers," *Journal of Business Strategy,* 2, 1 (Summer 1981): 13–22.

Davidson, William H. *The Amazing Race: Winning the Technorivalry with Japan* (New York: Wiley, 1984).

Davis, Paul A. *Administrative Guidance in Japan—Legal Considerations,* Bulletin No. 41 (Tokyo: Sophia University Socio-Economic Institute, 1972).

Davy, Samuel J. "Employee Ownership: One Road to Productivity Improvement," *The Journal of Business Strategy,* 4, 1 (Summer 1983): 12–21.

Deal, Terence E., and Allan A. Kennedy. *Corporate Cultures* (Reading, Mass.: Addison-Wesley, 1982).

Dehner, W. Joseph, Jr. "Multinational Enterprise and Racial Non-discrimination: United States Enforcement of an International Human Rights Policy," *Harvard International Law Journal,* 15 (1974): 71–125.

DeVos, George A. "Apprenticeship and Paternalism." In Ezra F. Vogel (ed.), *Modern Japanese Organization and Decision Making* (Berkeley: University of California Press, 1975), pp. 210–227.

Diebold, William. *Industrial Policy as an International Issue* (New York: McGraw-Hill, 1980).

Dillenberger, John, and Claude Welch. *Protestant Christianity* (New York: Scribner's, 1954).

Doi, Takeo. *The Anatomy of Dependence* (Tokyo: Kodansha International, 1973).

———. "Giri-Ninjo: An Interpretation." In R. P. Dore (ed.), *Aspects of Social Change in Japan* (Princeton, N.J.: Princeton University Press, 1967).

Dore, Ronald P. *British Factory–Japanese Factory: The Origins of National Diversity in Industrial Relations* (Berkeley: University of California Press, 1973).

———. "Introduction." In Satoshi Kamata, *Japan in a Passing Lane* (New York: Pantheon, 1982).

Dowling, John, and Jeffrey Pfeffer. "Organizational Legitimacy: Social Values and Organizational Behavior," *Pacific Sociological Review,* 18, 1 (January 1975), pp. 122–136.

Drucker, Peter F. "What We Can Learn from Japanese Business," *Harvard Business Review,* 49, 2 (March–April 1971): 110–122.

———. "Behind Japan's Success," 59, 1 *Harvard Business Review* (January–February, 1981): 83–90.

———. "What Is 'Business Ethics'?" *The Public Interest,* 63 (spring 1981): 18–36.

Dumaine, Brian. "Intergraph: A Good Old Boy Scores Big," *Fortune,* July 11, 1983, pp. 126–131.

Dyer, L., D. D. Schwartz, and R. D. Therault. "Managerial Perceptions Regarding Salary Increase Criteria," *Personnel Psychology,* 190 (1976): 233–242.

Eells, Richard, and Clarence Walton. *Conceptual Foundations of Business* (Homewood, Ill.: Irwin, 1974).

Eisenberg, Melvin Aron. The Structure of the Corporation—A Legal Analysis (Boston: Little, Brown, 1976).

Epstein, Edwin M. *The Corporation in American Politics* (Englewood Cliffs, N.J.: Prentice Hall, 1969).

———, and Dow Votaw. *Legitimacy, Rationality, Responsibility* (Santa Monica, Calif.: Goodyear, 1978).

Etzioni, Amitai. "The MITIzation of America?" *The Public Interest,* 72 (Summer 1983): 44–51.

———. *An Immodest Agenda: Rebuilding America Before the 21st Century* (New York: McGraw-Hill, 1983).

Ewing, David W. "Due Process: Will Business Default," *Harvard Business Review,* 60, 6 (November–December 1982): 114–122.

———. Freedom Inside The Organization (New York: Dutton, 1977).

————. *Do It My Way or You're Fired: Employee Rights and the Changing Role of Management* (New York: Wiley, 1983).

First National Bank of Boston v. *Bellotti,* 435 U.S. 765, 98 S.Ct. 1407 (1978).

Flippo, Edwin B., and Gary M. Munsinger. *Management,* 5th ed. (Boston: Allyn and Bacon, 1982).

Foulkes, Fred K., "How Top Nonunion Companies Manage Employees," *Harvard Business Review* 59, 5 (September–October 1981): 90–96.

Foy, N., and H. Gadon. "Worker Participation: Contrasts in Three Countries," *Harvard Business Review,* 54 (May–June 1976): 71–83.

Fox, Eleanor M. "From Antitrust to a Trust—in Business," *Across the Board* (November 1981): 59–67.

Fox, William M. "Japanese Management: Tradition under Strain," *Business Horizons* (August 1977): 76–85.

French, J. R. P., and B. Raven. "The Bases of Social Power." In D. Cartwright and A. F. Zander, (eds.), *Group Dynamics,* 2nd ed. (Evanston, Ill.: Row, Peterson, 1960).

Fritschler, A. Lee, and Bernard H. Ross. *Business Regulation and Government Decision-Making* (Cambridge, Mass.: Winthrop 1980).

Fujita, Yasuhiro. "Does Japan's Restriction on Foreign Capital Entries Violate Her Treaties?" *Law in Japan,* 3 (1969): 172–179.

Galbraith, John Kenneth. *The New Industrial State* (Boston: Houghton Mifflin, 1978).

Gibney, Frank. *Miracle by Design: The Real Reasons behind Japan's Economic Success* (New York: Times Books, 1982).

Giddens, Anthony. *Capitalism and Modern Social Theory: An Analysis of the Writings of Marx, Durkheim and Max Weber* (Cambridge, Eng.: Cambridge University Press, 1971).

Gilder, George. "A Supply-Side Economics of the Left," *The Public Interest,* 72 (Summer 1983): 19–43.

Gluck, Frederick, Stephen Kaufman, and A. Steven Walleck. "The Four Phases of Strategic Management," *The Journal of Business Strategy,* 2, 3, (Winter 1982): 9–21.

Goldhar, J. D., and Mariann Jelinek. "Plan for Economies of *Scope,*" *Harvard Business Review,* 61, 6 (November–December 1983): 141–148.

Goldwin, Robert A. *Political Parties in the Eighties* (Washington D.C.: American Enterprise Institute for Public Policy Research, 1980).

Gompers, Samuel. "The Philosophy of Trade Unions." In E. W. Baake, Clark Kerr, and Charles Anrod (eds.), *Unions, Management and the Public* (New York: Harcourt Brace Jovanovich, 1967).

Goodman, P. S. *Assessing Organizational Change: The Rushton Quality of Work Experiment* (New York: Wiley, 1979).

Gort, Michael A. *Diversification and Integration in American Industry: A Study by the National Bureau of Economic Research* (Princeton, N.J.: Princeton University Press, 1962).

Greasser, Julian, Kochiro Fujikura, and Akio Morishima. *Environmental Law in Japan* (Cambridge, Mass.: MIT Press, 1981).

Green, Mark J., and Norman Waitzman. *Business War on the Law* (Washington, D.C.: The Corporate Accountability Research Group, 1981).

———— (ed.). *The Monopoly Makers: Ralph Nader's Study Group Report on Regulation and Competition* (New York: Grossman, 1973).

Griggs v. *Duke Power Company,* 401 U.S., 91 S.Ct. 849 (1971).

Guest, Robert H. "Quality of Worklife: Learning from Terrytrown," *Harvard Business Review,* 57 4 (July–August 1979): 76–87.

Hadley, Eleanor M. "The Secret of Japan's Success," *Challenge,* 26, 2 (May–June 1983): 4–10.

Hall, John Whitney, and Richard K. Beardsley. *Twelve Doors to Japan* (New York: McGraw-Hill, 1965).

Hall, William K. "Survival Strategies in a Hostile Environment," *Harvard Business Review,* 58, 5 (September–October 1980): 75–85.

Hanami, Tadashi. *Labor Relations in Japan Today* (Tokyo: Kodansha International, 1979).

Hasegawa, N. "Environment Problems and Management," *Management Japan,* 6, 2, (Autumn 1972): 14–16.

Hattori, Ichiro. "A Proposition on Efficient Decision-Making in the Japanese Corporation," *Columbia Journal of World Business,* 3, 2 (Summer 1978): 7–15.

Hatvany, N., and C. V. Pucik. "Japanese Management Practices and Productivity," *Organizational Dynamics,* 9, 4 (1981): 5–21.

Hayes, Robert H., and David A. Garvin. "Managing as if Tomorrow Mattered," *Harvard Business Review* 60, 3 (May–June 1982): 70–79.

————. "Why Japanese Factories Work," *Harvard Business Review,* 59, 4 (July–August 1981): 56–66.

————, and William J. Abernathy. "Managing Our Way to Economic Decline," *Harvard Business Review,* 58, 4 (July–August 1980): 67–77.

Hearne, Roger W. "Fighting Industrial Senility: A System for Growth in Mature Industries," *Journal of Business Strategy,* 3, 2 (Fall 1982): 3–20.

Helmich, D. L., and W. B. Brown. "Successor Type and Organizational Change in the Corporate Enterprise," *Administrative Science Quarterly,* 17, 3 (1972): 371–388.

Helvoort, Ernest Van. *The Japanese Working Man: What Choice? What Reward?* (Vancouver: University of British Columbia Press, 1979).

Henderson, Bruce D. *Henderson on Corporate Strategy* (Cambridge, Mass.: Abt Books, 1979).

Henderson, Dan F. *Foreign Enterprise in Japan* (Chapel Hill: University of North Carolina Press, 1973).

Hiroshi, Ushikubo. *Shin Kachyo Gaku* [New Studies on Section Chief] (Tokyo: Sangyo Noritsu Daigaku Shuppanbu, 1981).

Holcomb John L. "Citizen Groups in Business." In S. Prakash Sethi and Carl Swanson (eds.), *Private Enterprise and Public Purpose,* (New York: Wiley, 1981).

Holland, Susan S. "Exchange of People among International Companies: Problems and Benefits," *Annals,* 424 (March 1976): 52–66.

Horovitz, Bruce. "Japan Inc's Beachhead in Tennessee," *Industry Week,* May 17, 1982, pp. 45–47.

Horowitz, Donald L. *The Courts and Social Policy* (Washington, D.C.: The Brookings Institution, 1977).

Howard, Ann, and James A. Wilson. "Leadership in a Declining Work Ethic," *California Management Review,* 24, 4 (Summer 1982): 33–46.

Huddle, Norie, Michael Reich, and Nahum Stiskin. *Island of Dreams: Environmental Crisis in Japan* (New York: Autumn Press, 1975).

Huse, E. *Organization Development and Change,* 2nd ed. (St. Paul, Minn.: West, 1975).

Immigration and Naturalization Service v. *Jagdish Rai Chadha,* et al. *U.S. Law Week,* 51, 41, extra ed. No. 2 (1983).

Interfaith Center on Corporate Responsibility. *Church Proxy Resolutions* (New York, January 1983).

Isaac, Thomas I. "Intuition: An Ignored Dimension of Management," *Academy of Management Review,* 3, 4 (October 1978): 917–921.

Ishida, Hideo. "Human Resources Management in Overseas Japanese Firms," trans. William Testa, *Japanese Economic Studies,* 9, 1 (Fall 1981): 53–81.

Ishida, Takeshi. *Japanese Society* (New York: Random House, 1971).

Ishimura, Shin'ichi. "Japanese Firms in Asia," *Japanese Economic Studies,* 9, 1 (Fall 1981): 33–52.

Jackall, Robert. "Moral Mazes: Bureaucracy and Managerial Work," *Harvard Business Review,* 61, 5 (September–October 1983): 118–130.

Janis, I. L. *Victims of Groupthink* (Boston: Houghton Mifflin, 1972).

Japan External Trade Organization. *Zaibei Nikkei Shinshutsu Kigyo no Keiei no Zettai* [Japanese Manufacturing Operations in the United States] (Tokyo, September 1981).

"Japanese Managers Talk about How Their System Works," *Fortune,* November 1977, pp. 131–132.

Japan Society. *The Economic Impact of the Japanese Business Community in New York, 1978* (New York: The Japan Society, Inc., with the cooperation of

Conservation of Human Resources, Columbia University, April 1978), pp. 18–19.

Jenkins, David. *Job Power, Blue and White Collar Democracy* (New York: Penguin, 1973).

Johnson, Chalmers. "MITI and the Japanese International Economic Policy." In Robert A. Scalapino (ed.), *The Foreign Policy of Modern Japan* (Berkeley: University of California Press, 1977), pp. 227–279.

———. *MITI and the Japanese Miracle: The Growth of Industrial Policy, 1925–1975* (Stanford, Calif.: Stanford University Press, 1982).

———. "The 'Internationalization' of the Japanese Economy," *California Management Review,* 25, 3 (Spring 1983): 5–26.

Johnson, Richard Tanner, and William Ouchi. "Made in America (Under Japanese Management)," *Harvard Business Review,* 52, 5 (September–October 1974): 61–69.

Kamata, Satoshi. *Japan in a Passing Lane: An Insider's Account of Life in a Japanese Auto Factory* (New York: Pantheon, 1982).

Kikuchi, Seiichi. *Nigai America: Shinshutsu Nihon Kigyo No Zittai to Taio* [Bitter America: Realities and Countermeasures of Japanese Companies in the United States] (Tokyo: Nihon Noritsu Kyokai, 1982).

Kintner, Earl W. *An Antitrust Primer: A Guide to Antitrust and Trade Regulation Laws for Businessmen,* 2nd ed. (New York: Macmillan, 1973).

Kobayashi, S. "Change to Other People Oriented Management" [Tanin-kankei Keiei e Tenkanseyo], *Chuo Koron* (Spring 1974): 103–112.

Kono, Toyohiro. "Japanese Management Philosophy: Can It Be Exported?" *Long Range Planning,* 15, 3 (June 1982): 90–102.

Korn/Ferry International. *Board of Directors Annual Study* (New York, 1978).

———. *Board of Directors Annual Study* (New York, 1980).

Kotter, John P. "What Do Effective General Managers Really Do?" *Harvard Business Review,* 60, 6 (November–December 1982): 156–167.

Kraar, Louis. "The Japanese Are Coming—With Their Own Style of Management," *Fortune,* March 1975, pp. 116–121, 160–161, 164.

Kristol, Irving. "When Virtue Loses All Her Loveliness—Some Reflections on Capitalism and 'the Free Society'," *The Public Interest,* 21, (Fall 1970): 3–15.

Lasch, Christopher. *The Culture of Narcissism* (New York: Norton, 1978).

Lawrence, Robert Z. "Is Trade Deindustrializing America? A Medium-Term Perspective," *Brookings Papers on Economic Activity,* 1 (1983): 129–171.

Lee, Sang M., and Gary Schwendiman. *Management by Japanese Systems* (New York: Praeger, 1982).

Levitan, Sar A., and Clifford M. Johnson. "Labor and Management: The

Illusion of Cooperation," *Harvard Business Review*, 61, 5 (September–October 1983): 8–16.

Leavitt, Harold J. "Beyond the Analytic Manager," *California Management Review*, 37, 3 (Spring 1975): 5–12.

———. "Beyond the Analytic Manager: Part II," *California Management Review*, 37, 4 (Summer 1975): 11–21.

Levitt, Theodore. "Management and the 'Post-Industrial' Society," *The Public Interest*, 44 (Summer 1976): 69–103.

Levy, Harold. "Civil Rights in Employment and the Multinational Corporations," *Cornell International Law Journal*, 10, 1 (December, 1976): 1–56.

Lewis, John Fulton. *Who Are Those Guys? A Monograph for Business on the News Media Today* (Washington, D.C.: The Media Institute, 1981).

Lipset, Seymour Martin. *Emerging Coalitions in American Politics* (San Francisco: Institute for Contemporary Studies, 1978).

———, and William Schneider. *The Confidence Gap: Business, Labor, and Government in Public Mind* (New York: Macmillan, 1983).

Livingston, J. Sterling. "Myth of the Well-Educated Manager," *Harvard Business Review*, 49, 1 (January–February 1971): 77–89.

Lodge, George. *The New American Ideology* (New York: Knopf, 1976).

———, and W. R. Glass. "U.S. Trade Policy Needs One Voice," *Harvard Business Review*, 61, 3 (May–June 1983): 75–83.

Loomis, Carol J. "The Madness of Executive Compensation," *Fortune*, July 12, 1982, pp. 42–46.

Lutz, Raymond (ed.). *Finance, Economics, and Accounting: Handbook for Managers and Engineers* (New York: Wiley, 1984).

Maanen, J. Van. "Breaking In: Socialization to Work." In R. Dubin, (ed.), *Handbook of Work, Organization and Society* (Chicago: Rand McNally, 1976)

Maccoby, M. *The Gamesman* (New York: Bantam, 1976).

MacIver, R. M. "Bases and Types of Association." In Clarence Walton and Richard Eells (eds.), *The Business System* (New York: Macmillan 1967).

MacKnight, Susan. *Japan's Expanding Manufacturing Profile* (Washington, D.C.: Japan Economic Institutes of America, 1982).

Macy, B. A., G. E. Ledford, and E. E. Lawler III. *Bolivar Quality of Work Experiment 1972–78* (New York: Wiley Interscience, in press).

Magaziner, Ira, and Robert R. Reich. *Minding America's Business: The Decline and Rise of the American Economy* (New York: Harcourt Brace Jovanovich, 1982).

Magnet, Myron. "Managing by Mystique at Tandem Computers," *Fortune*, June 28, 1982, pp. 84–89.

Main, Jeremy. "How to Battle Your Own Bureaucracy," *Fortune*, June 29, 1981, pp. 54–58.

March, J. G., and H. A. Simon. *Organizations* (New York: Wiley, 1958).

————. "Bounded Rationality, Ambiguity, and the Engineering of Choice," *The Bell Journal of Economics,* 1 (1978): 587–608.

Markowitz, S. "Can Business Survive a Pro Business Environment?" Remarks delivered to the American Assembly of Collegiate Schools of Business (AACSB) at a conference on Business Environment/Public Policy and Business Schools of the 1980s, University of California, Berkeley, July 28, 1981.

Marty, Martin E. *A Short History of Christianity* (Cleveland: William Collins and World, 1975).

Mason, R. H., and M. B. Gonzwaard. "Performance in Conglomerate Firms: A Portfolio Approach," *Journal of Finance,* 31, 1 (March 1976): 39–48.

McCoy, Bowen H. "The Parable of the Sadhu," *Harvard Business Review,* 61, 5 (September–October 1983): 103–108.

McGregor, Douglas. *The Human Side of Enterprise* (New York: McGraw-Hill, 1960).

McKean, Margaret A. *Environmental Protest and Citizen Politics in Japan* (Berkeley: University of California Press, 1981).

McLaughlin, David J. *Executive Compensation in the 1980s* (San Francisco: Pentacle Press, 1980).

Meadows, Edward. "Japan Runs into America, Inc.," *Fortune,* March 22, 1982, pp. 56–61.

Melohn, Thomas H. "How to Build Employee Trust and Productivity," *Harvard Business Review,* 61, 1 (January–February 1983): 56–60.

Merton, R. *Social Theory and Social Structure* (New York: Free Press, 1968).

Miller, J. "Decision-Making and Organizational Effectiveness: Participation and Perceptions," *Sociology of Work and Occupations,* 7 (1980): 55–79.

Millstein, Ira M., and Salem M. Katsh. *The Limits of Corporate Power* (New York: Macmillan, 1981).

Ministry of International Trade and Industry. *Tsusho Sangyo-Sho Niju-nen Shi* [Twenty-Year History of MITI] (Tokyo, 1969).

Mintzberg, Henry. *The Nature of Managerial Work* (New York: Harper & Row, 1973).

————. "Patterns in Strategy Formation," *Management Science,* 24, 9 (May 1978): 934–948.

————. "Why America Needs, But Cannot Have, Corporate Democracy," *Organizational Dynamics* (spring 1983): 5–20.

————. "Organizational Power and Goals: A Skeletal Theory." In Dan E. Schendel and Charles W. Hoffer (eds.), *Strategic Management* (Boston: Little, Brown, 1979).

Moore, Dan S. "New Expatriate Policies Announced by Exxon," *Innovations in International Compensation,* 4, 1 (New York: Organization Resources Counselors, March 1978): 3–8.

Moore, Thomas. "Industrial Espionage of the Harvard B-School," *Fortune,* September 6, 1982, pp. 70–76.

Morita, Akio. "Japanese Viewpoints: Do Companies Need Lawyers? Sony's Experiences in the United States," *Japan Quarterly,* 30, 1 (January–March 1983): 2–8.

Morrison, Ann M. "Those Executive Bailout Deals," *Fortune,* December 13, 1982, pp. 82–87.

Nader, Ralph, and Mark J. Green (eds.). *Corporate Power in America* (New York: Grossman, 1973).

———, Peter Petkas, and Kate Blackwell. *Whistle Blowing* (New York: Grossman, 1972).

Nakamura, Takafusa. *The Postwar Japanese Economy: Its Development and Structure.* Trans. Jacquiline Kaminski (Tokyo: University of Tokyo Press, 1981).

Nakane, Chie. "An Interpretation of Group Cohesiveness in Japanese Society." Paper presented at the regional seminar, Center for Japanese and Korean Studies, Berkeley, University of California, March 1, 1974.

———. *Japanese Society* (Berkeley: University of California Press, 1972).

———. *Human Relations in Japan* (Tokyo: Director General of the Public Information Bureau, Ministry of Foreign Affairs, 1972).

Nash, Laura L. "Ethics without the Sermon," *Harvard Business Review,* 59, 6 (November–December 1981): 78–90.

Negandhi, A. R. "Profile of the American Overseas Executive," *California Management Review,* 9, 2 (Winter 1966): 57–64.

Newcomer, M. *Nippon Express U.S.A., Inc.* v. *Esperdy,* 261 F. Supp. 561 (S.D.N.Y. 1966).

New York Stock Exchange. *People and Productivity: A Challenge to Corporate America* (New York, 1982).

Nihon Keizai Shinbun. *Salary Man* Doc. No. 2 [in Japanese] (Tokyo: Nihon Keizai Shinbun, Inc., 1981).

Nisbet, Robert A. *The Quest for Community* (New York: Oxford University Press, 1953), as reproduced in Clarence Walton and Richard Eells (eds.), *The Business System,* vol. II (New York: Macmillan, 1967).

Norris, William C. "How to Expand R & D Cooperation," *Business Week,* April 11, 1983, p. 21.

Nothstein, Gary Z., and Jeffrey P. Ayres. "The Multinational Corporation and the Extraterritorial Application of the Labor Management Relations Act," *Cornell International Law Journal,* 10, 1 (December 1976): 1–58.

Novak, Michael. "Mediating Institutions: The Communitarian Individual in America," *The Public Interest* 68 (Summer 1982): 3–20.

Nozick, Robert. *Anarchy, State, and Utopia* (New York: Basic Books, 1974).

OECD. *The Development of Industrial Relations Systems: Some Implications of Japanese Experience* (Paris, 1977), pp. 19, 25–26.

Ohmae, Kanichi. *The Mind of the Strategist: The Art of Japanese Business,* (New York: McGraw-Hill, 1982).

Ohno, Taiichi. *Toyota Seisan Hoshiki* [The Toyota Production System] (Tokyo: Diamond Publishing, 1978); chap. 1, "How the Toyota Production System Was Created," [Needs Kara No Shuppatsu], trans. J. T. Gallagher, *Japan Economic Studies* (Summer 1982): 83–101.

Okamoto, Yasuo. "Nihon Kigyo no Grand Strategy" [The Grand Strategy of Japanese Business], *Chuo Koron Kikan Keiei Mondai,* trans. Mamoru Ishikawa, *Japanese Economic Studies* (Summer 1982): 3–47.

Okumura, Akihiro. *Nihon no Top Management* [Japanese Top Management] (Tokyo: Diamond Publishing, 1982).

Ossola, Dennis A. "Application of Japanese Productivity and Quality Control Methods to Matsushita's Illinois Plant." In U. Krishna Shetty and Vernon M. Buehler (eds.), *Quality and Productivity Improvements: U.S. and Foreign Company Experiences* (Chicago: Manufacturing Productivity Center, 1983), pp. 172–184.

Ouchi, William G. *Theory Z: How American Business Can Meet the Japanese Challenge* (Reading, Mass.: Addison-Wesley, 1981).

———, and A. Jaeger. "Type Z Organization: Stability in the Midst of Immobility," *Academy of Management Review,* 3, 2 (April 1978): 305–314.

Ozawa, Terutomo. *Multinationalism, Japanese Style: The Political Economy of Outward Dependency* (Princeton, N.J.: Princeton University Press, 1979).

Pascale, Richard Tanner. "Zen and the Art of Management," *Harvard Business Review,* 56, 2 (March–April 1978): 153–162.

———, and Anthony G. Athos. *The Art of Japanese Management: Applications for American Executives* (New York: Simon and Schuster, 1981).

Patrick, Hugh, and Henry Rosovsky (eds.). *Asia's New Giant: How the Japanese Economy Works* (Washington, D.C.: The Brookings Institution, 1976).

Perrow, C. *Complex Organizations: A Critical Essay,* 2nd ed. (Dallas: Scott, Foresman, 1979).

Peters, Thomas J., and Robert H. Waterman, Jr. *In Search of Excellence: Lessons from America's Best Run Companies* (New York: Harper & Row, 1982).

Ping, Charles J. "Bigger Stake for Business in Higher Education," *Harvard Business Review,* 59, 5 (September–October 1981): 122–129.

Pomper, Gerald M. "The Decline of the Party in American Elections," *Political Science Quarterly,* 92, 1 (Spring 1977): 21–41.

Post, James. *Corporate Behavior and Social Change* (Reston, Va.: Reston, 1978).

Presthus, R. V. *The Organizational Society* (New York: Vintage, 1965).

Preston, Lee E. (ed.). *Research in Corporate Social Performance and Policy,* vols. I–IV (Greenwich, Conn.: Jai Press, 1978–1982).

"Protecting 'at Will' Employees against Wrongful Discharge: The Duty to Terminate only in Good Faith," *Harvard Law Review,* 93, 8 (1980): 1816–1844.

Pucik, V. "Promotion and Intraorganizational Status Differentiation among Japanese Managers," *Academy of Management Proceedings,* 1981.

Punch, Counterpunch: 60 Minutes vs. Illinois Power Company (Washington, D.C.: The Media Institute, 1981).

Quinn, J. B. *Strategies for Change: Logical Incrementalism* (Homewood, Ill.: Irwin, 1980).

Rappaport, Alfred. "How to Design Value-Contributing Executive Incentives," *Journal of Business Strategy,* 4, 2 (Fall 1983): 49–59.

Rawls, John. *A Theory of Justice* (Cambridge, Mass.: The Belknap Press, 1971).

Regents of the University of California v. Bakke, 438 U.S. 265, 98 S.Ct. 2733 (1978).

Reich, Charles A. "The New Property," *Yale Law Journal,* 73 (April 1964): 733–787.

Reich, Robert, and Ira Magaziner. *Minding America's Business* (New York: Harcourt Brace Jovanovich, 1981).

———. "Why the U.S. Needs an Industrial Policy," *Harvard Business Review,* 60, 1 (January–February 1982): 74–81.

———. "The Next American Frontier," *The Atlantic Monthly,* March 1983, pp. 43–58.

———. *The Next American Frontier* (New York: Random House, 1983).

Richardson, Bradley M., and Taizo Ueda (eds.). *Business and Society in Japan: Fundamentals for Businessmen* (New York: Praeger, 1981).

Robbins, Stephen P. *Management Organizational Conflict: A Non-traditional Approach* (Englewood Cliffs, N.J.: Prentice-Hall, 1974).

———. "The Theory of Organization from a Power Perspective," *California Management Review,* 2, 5 (January 1983): 67–75.

Rohlen, Thomas P. "The Company Work Group." In Ezra F. Vogel (ed.), *Modern Japanese Organization and Decision-Making* (Berkeley: University of California Press, 1975).

———. *For Harmony and Strength: Japanese White Collar Organization in Anthropological Perspective* (Berkeley: University of California Press, 1974).

Rowan, Roy. "How Harvard's Women MBAs Are Managing," *Fortune,* July 11, 1983, pp. 58–79.

————, and Thomas Moore. "Behind the Lines in the Bendix War," *Fortune,* October 18, 1983, pp. 156–168.

Ruch, Richard S., and Ronald Goodman. *Image at the Top* (New York: Free Press, 1984).

Rumelt, Richard P. *Strategy, Structure and Economic Performance* (Boston: Graduate School of Business, Harvard University Press, 1974)

Ryberg, Richard J. "Defining the Social Issue Concept," *1981 Proceedings* (Southwest Division, Academy of Management), pp. 231–236.

Sasaki, Noato. *Management and Industrial Structure in Japan* (New York: Pergamon, 1981).

Scalapino, Robert A. (ed.). *The Foreign Policy of Modern Japan* (Berkeley: University of California Press, 1977).

Schein, Edgar H. *Process Consultation: Its Role in Organization Development* (Reading, Mass.: Addison-Wesley, 1969).

Schendel, Dan E., and Charles W. Hoffer (eds.). *Strategic Management: A New View of Business Policy Planning* (Boston: Little Brown, 1979).

Schien, E. G. *Career Dynamics* (Reading, Mass: Addison-Wesley, 1978).

Schultze, Charles. "Industrial Policy: A Solution in Search of a Problem," *California Management Review,* 25, 4 (Summer 1983): 5–15.

Schumpeter, Joseph A. *The Theory of Economic Development: An Inquiry into Profits, Capital, Credit, Interest and the Business Cycle* (Cambridge, Mass.: Harvard University Press, 1968).

Scobel, Donald N. "Business and Labor—from Adversaries to Allies," *Harvard Business Review* (November–December 1982): 114–122.

Scott, Bruce R. "Can Industry Survive the Welfare State," *Harvard Business Review,* 60, 5 (September–October 1982): 70–84.

Seligman, Daniel. "The Politics and Economics of 'Public Interest' Lobbying," *Fortune,* November 5, 1979, pp. 74–75.

Selznick, Phillip. *TVA and the Grass Roots* (Berkeley: University of California Press, 1949).

Sethi, S. Prakash. *Business Corporations and the Black Man* (New York: Harper & Row, 1970).

————. "Drawbacks of Japanese Management," *Business Week,* November 24, 1973.

————. *Japanese Business and Social Conflict: A Comparative Analysis of Response Patterns with American Business* (Cambridge, Mass.: Ballinger, 1975).

————. *Advocacy Advertising and Large Corporations* (Lexington, Mass.: D. C. Heath, 1977).

————. *Testimony before the Commerce, Consumer, and Monetary Affairs Subcommittee of the Government Operations Committee, House of Representatives.* Ninety-fifth Cong., 2nd Sess., July 18, 1978.

————. "An Analytical Framework for Making Cross-Cultural Comparisons of Business Responses to Social Pressures." In Lee E. Preston (ed.), *Research in Corporate Social Performance and Policy,* Vol. 1 (Greenwich, Conn.: JAI Press, 1978), pp. 27–54.

————. "Problems for Foreign Companies: Compliance with U.S. Discrimination Laws," *Management Review* (June 1979): 32–33.

————. "Hiring Alien Executives in Compliance with U.S. Civil Rights Laws," *Journal of International Business Studies* (Fall 1979): 37–50.

————. "A Conceptual Framework for Environmental Analysis of Social Issues and Evaluation of Business Response Patterns," *Academy of Management Review,* 4, 1 (January 1979): 63–74.

————. *Corporate Governance: Composition and Committee Structure of Corporate Boards—Volumes I & II,* Special Report No. 80-02 (1980).

————. "Interfaith Council on Corporate Responsibility." In S. Prakash Sethi, *Up Against the Corporate Wall,* 4th ed. (Englewood Cliffs, N.J.: Prentice-Hall, 1982).

————. "A Strategic Framework for Dealing with the Schism between Business and Academe," *Public Affairs Review* (1983): 44–59.

———— (ed.). *The Unstable Ground: Corporate Social Policy in a Dynamic Society* (New York: Wiley, 1974).

————. "Corporate Political Activism," *Public Relations Journal* (November 1980): 14–18.

————, Bernard J. Cunningham, and Patricia M. Miller. *Corporate Governance: Public Policy—Social Responsibility Committee of Corporate Board: Growth and Accomplishment,* Special Report No. 79-01 (1979).

————, and Nobuaki Namiki. "Japanese Style Consensus Decision Making in Matrix Management: Problems and Prospects of Adaptation." In David I. Cleland (ed.), *Matrix Management Systems Handbook* (New York: Van Nostrand, 1984), pp. 431–456.

————, and ————. *Public Perception of and Attitudes Toward Political Action Committees (PACs)—An Empirical Analysis of Nationwide Data—Some Strategic Implications for the Corporate Community,* Special Report No. 82-12, (Dallas: Center for Research in Business and Social Policy, The University of Texas at Dallas, 1982).

————, and Carl L. Swanson. "Are Foreign Multinationals Violating U.S. Civil Rights Laws," *Employee Relations Law Journal,* 4, 4 (Spring 1979): 485–524.

————, and ————. *American Subsidiaries of Foreign Multinationals and U.S. Civil Rights Laws: Can Alien Executives Be Treated Differently Than American Executives?* Working Paper No. W-79-02 (Dallas: Center for Research in Business and Social Policy, The University of Texas at Dallas, 1979).

————, and ———— (eds.). *Private Enterprise and Public Purpose* (New York: Wiley, 1981).

————, ————, and Kathryn Rudie Harrigan. *Women Directors on Corporate Boards,* Special Report No. WP-81-01 (Dallas: The Center for Research in Business and Social Policy, The University of Texas at Dallas, 1981).

————, ————, and Nobuaki Namiki. "Transfer and Adaptation of Cultur- ally Unique Management Practices to Other Socio-Cultural Environments: The Case of Japanese Management Practices in the U.S.." Paper presented at the Japanese Management Techniques Conference, sponsored by the University of Lethbridge, Alberta, Canada, March 18, 1983.

Shatz, Willie. "Antitrust Pendulum Swings," *Datamation,* 28, 2 (February 1982): 102B–102F.

Shetty, U. Krishna, and Vernon M. Buehler (eds.). *Quality and Productivity Improvements: U.S. and Foreign Company Experiences,* (Chicago: Manufactur- ing Productivity Center, 1983).

Sloane, Arthur A., and Fred Whitney. *Labor Relations,* 2nd ed. (Englewood Cliffs, N.J.: Prentice-Hall, 1972).

Smith, Adam. *Inquiry into the Nature and Causes of the Wealth of Nations* (New York: The Modern Library, 1937).

Smith, Nelson, and Leonard Theberge (eds.). *Energy Coverage—Media Panic* (New York: Longmans, 1983).

Spencer, William I. "Recognizing Individual Rights Is Good Business," an address delivered at the Third National Seminar on Individual Rights in the Corporation, Washington, D.C., June 12, 1980.

Spiess, Michael E., Jack K. Hardy and Benjamin F. Rountree v. *C. Itoh & Co. America,* Civil Action 75-h-267, First Amended Complaint filed February 21, 1975, United States District Court, Southern District of Texas, Hous- ton Division.

Starbuck, W. H. "Organizations As Action Generators," *American Sociological Review,* 48 (1983): 91–102.

Stau, B. M., and L. L. Cummings. *Research in Organizations,* vol. 4. (Green- wich, Conn.: Jai Press, 1983).

Steckmest, Francis W. *Corporate Performance: The Key to Public Trust* (New York: McGraw-Hill, 1982).

Stein, Herbert. "Economic Planning and the Improvement of Economic Policy." In Lawrence A. Chickering (ed.), *The Politics of Planning: A Review and Critique of Centralized Economic Planning* (San Francisco: Institute for Contemporary Studies, 1976).

————. "Don't Fall for Industrial Policy," *Fortune,* November 14, 1983, pp. 64–82.

Stone, Christopher D. *Where the Law Ends: The Social Control of Corporate Behavior* (New York: Harper & Row, 1975).

Strauss, G. "Workers Participation in Management: An International Per- spective." In B. M. Stau and L. L. Cummings, *Research in Organizations,* Vol. 4 (Greenwich, Conn.: Jai Press, 1983).

Sullivan, Jeremiah. "A Critique of Theory Z," *Academy of Management Review*, 8, 1 (January 1983): 132–142.

Swanson, Carl L. "The Federal Regulatory Process—Public Sector Intervention in Private Sector Affairs." In Raymond Lutz, (ed.), *Finance, Economics, and Accounting: Handbook for Managers and Engineers* (New York: Wiley, 1984).

———. "Corporations and Electoral Activities: The Legal, Political and Managerial Implications of PAC's." In S. Prakash Sethi and Carl L. Swanson (eds.), *Private Enterprise and Public Purpose* (New York: Wiley, 1981).

Symonds, William. "Washington in the Grip of the Green Giant," *Fortune*, October 4, 1982, pp. 136–142.

Taira, Koji. *Economic Development and the Labor Market in Japan* (New York: Columbia University Press, 1970).

Tannenbaum, A. S., B. Kavicic, M. Rosner, M. Vianello, and J. S. Weiser. *Hierarchy in Organizations: An International Comparison* (San Francisco: Jossey-Bass, 1974).

Tannenbaum, Frank. "The Balance of Power in Society," *Political Science Quarterly*, 61, 4 (December 1946): 481–504.

Tavel, Charles. *The Third Industrial State: Strategy for Business Survival* (Oxford, Eng.: Pergamon Press, 1980).

Taylor, Frederick W. *Scientific Management* (New York: Harper & Row, 1947).

Theberge, Leonard (ed.). *Crooks, Conmen, and Clowns: Business in TV Entertainment* (Washington, D.C.: The Media Institute, 1981).

Thurow, Lester. *The Zero-Sum Society* (New York: Basic Books, 1981).

Tocqueville, Alexis de. *Democracy in America,* trans. Henry Reeve (New York: Knopf, 1946).

Tokyo Sansei v. *Esperdy,* 198 F. Supp. 945 (S.D.N.Y. 1969).

Toyota No Genba Kanri [Shop Floor Management] (Tokyo: Nihon Noritsu Kyokai, 1970).

Tsuda, Masumi. "Lifetime Employment and Seniority-Based Wage System," paper presented at International Symposium on the Japanese Way of Management and International Business, Tokyo, November 27–28, 1973. Sponsored by Japan Management Conference Board, Tokyo.

Tsurumi, Yoshi. *The Japanese Are Coming: A Multinational Interaction of Firms and Politics* (Cambridge, Mass.: Ballinger, 1976).

———. "Japanese Competition Can Be Healthy," *Pacific Basin Quarterly*, 9 (winter–spring 1983).

Tsuzu, S. "KOGAI—Environmental Disruption in Japan—The Story of Three Cities," *Unesco Courier* (July, 1971): 6–13.

Tyson, Laura, and John Zysman. "American Industry in International Competition: Government Policies and Corporate Strategies," *California Management Review*, 25, 3 (Spring 1983): 27–52.

Ueno, I. "The Situation of Management Education in Japan," *Management Education*, (Paris: OECD, 1972).
Ui, Jun. "The Singularities of Japanese Pollution," *Japan Quarterly* (July–September 1972).
United States v. *United Mine Workers of America*, 30 U.S. 258 67 S.Ct. 677 (1947).
U.S. Congress–Senate. *Mergers and Economic Concentration*, parts I and II, *Hearings*, Subcommittee on Antitrust, Monopoly and Business Rights of the Committee on the Judiciary, 96th Cong, 1st Sess, March–April 1979.
United States Steel Workers of America v. *Weber and Kaiser Aluminum Corporation*, 443 U.S. 193, 99 S.Ct. 2721 (1979).
Uttal, Bro. "Here Comes Computer Inc.," *Fortune*, October 4, 1982, pp. 82–90.
———. "The New Corporate Culture Vultures," *Fortune*, October 17, 1983, pp. 66–73.

Veblen, Thorstein. *The Theory of the Leisure Class: An Economic Study of Institutions*, (New York: Macmillan, 1912).
Virginia State Board of Pharmacy v. *Virginia Citizens Council*, 425 U.S. 748, 96 S. Ct. 1817 (1976).
Vogel, Ezra F. *Japan As Number One: Lessons for America* (Cambridge, Mass.: Harvard University Press, 1979).
———. "Guided Free Enterprise in Japan," *Harvard Business Review*, 56, 3 (May–June 1978): 161–170.
Votaw, Dow. "The New Entitlements and the Response of Business." In S. Prakash Sethi and Carl L. Swanson (eds.), *Private Enterprise and Public Purpose* (New York: Wiley, 1981).
———, and S. Prakash Sethi (eds.). *The Corporate Dilemma: Traditional Values versus Contemporary Problems* (Englewood Cliffs, N.J.: Prentice-Hall, 1973).

Wachter, Michael, and Susan M. Wachter (eds.). *Toward a New Industrial Policy?* (Philadelphia: University of Pennsylvania Press, 1981).
Wagner, John A. III. "The Organizational Double-Bind: Toward an Understanding of Rationality and Its Complement," *Academy of Management Review*, 3, 4 (October 1978): 786–795.
Wallich, Henry C., and Mabel I. Wallich. "Banking and Finance." In Hugh Patrick and Henry Rosovsky (eds.), *Asia's New Giant: How the Japanese Economy Works* (Washington, D.C.: The Brookings Institution, 1976).

Warner, W. L., and J. C. Abeggen. *Occupational Mobility in American Business and Industry* (St. Paul: University of Minnesota Press, 1955).

Weaver, Paul. "Corporations Are Defending Themselves with the Wrong Weapon," *Fortune,* June 1977, pp. 186–196.

———. "Regulation, Social Policy and Class Conflict," *The Public Interest,* 50 (Winter 1978): 45–63.

Weber, Max. *The Protestant Ethic and the Spirit of Capitalism* (New York: Scribner's, 1958).

Weil, Frank A. "U.S. Industrial Policy: A Process in Need of a Federal Industrial Coordination Board," *Law and Policy in International Business,* 14, 4 (1983): 981–1040.

———. "An Industry Plea for the Freedom to Compete, *Business Week,* June 6, 1983, pp. 59–60.

Weisz, William J. "Meeting the Japanese Challenge to American Industry," *Vital Speeches of the Day,* 48, 14 (May 1, 1982): 440–443.

"Westinghouse's Cultural Revolution," *Fortune,* June 15, 1981, pp. 74–93.

Wheelwright, Steven C. "Japan—Where Operations Really Are Strategic," *Harvard Business Review,* 59, 4 (July–August 1981): 67–74.

Whitehill, Arthur M., and Shin'ichi Takezawa. "Workplace Harmony: Another Japanese 'Miracle'?" *Columbia Journal of World Business* (Fall 1978): 25–39.

Willetts, Peter (ed.). *Pressure Groups in the Global System* (New York: St. Martin's, 1982).

Williams, Oscar F. "Business Ethics: A Trojan Horse?" *California Management Review,* 24, 4, (Summer 1982): 14–24.

Yamada, Mitsuhiko. "Japanese-Style Management in America: Merits and Difficulties," trans. Dennis M. Spackman, *Japanese Economic Studies,* 9, 1 (fall 1981): 1–30.

Yamaki, Naomi. *Japanese Management* [Nihon no Management] (Tokyo: Nihon Noritsu Kyokai, 1980).

Yanaga, Chitoshi. *Japanese People and Politics* (New York: Wiley, 1965).

Yankelovich, Daniel, and John Immerwahr, *Putting the Work Ethic to Work* (New York: The Public Agenda Foundation, 1983).

Yoshino, Michael. *Japan's Managerial System: Tradition and Innovation* (Cambridge, Mass.: MIT Press, 1968).

Zeigler, Harmon. *Interest Groups in American Society* (Englewood Cliffs, N.J.: Prentice-Hall, 1964).

Zwerdling, D. *Workplace Democracy: A Guide to Workplace Ownership, Participation, and Self Management Experiments in the United States and Europe* (New York: Harper & Row, 1980).

Author Index

Subject Index